THREE DOLLAR DREAMS

Lynne Bowen

The Coal Tyee Society
presents

THREE DOLLAR DREAMS

LYNNE BOWEN

OOLICHAN BOOKS

Lantzville, British Columbia

1987

Canadian Cataloguing in Publication Data

Bowen, Lynne, 1940-
    Three dollar dreams

    A project of the Coal Tyee Society.
    Includes index.
    Bibliography: p.
    ISBN 0-88982-065-1

    1. Coal mines and mining — British Columbia —
Vancouver Island — History. 2. Coal-miners —
British Columbia — Vancouver Island — History.
I. Coal Tyee Society.   II. Title.
HD9554.C23B75 1987   338.2'724'0971134   C87-091473-1

Publication of this book has been financially assisted by the Canada Council.

Published by
OOLICHAN BOOKS
P.O. Box 10
Lantzville, British Columbia, Canada V0R 2H0

Printed and bound in Canada by
MORRISS PRINTING COMPANY LTD.
Victoria, British Columbia

To the Memory of

John (Jock) Gilmour
and
Desmond Ivan Crossley

The author would like to acknowledge the following organizations for
their financial assistance:

Canada Council Non-Fiction Writing Programme
Coal Tyee Society

The Coal Tyee Society would like to acknowledge the following
organizations for their financial assistance:

Boag Foundation
Malaspina College
Provincial Archives of British Columbia Sound and Moving Images
Division

CONTENTS

Illustrations follow page 96

MAPS

by Gary L. Crocker

Preface

This is a book about a time when a young boy could start in the mine as the lowest of workers and could become, through a lot of hard work and a little luck, a boss or even a millionaire. This is also a book about a time when many, no matter how hard-working, did not achieve their dream and settled for a lot less.

Three Dollar Dreams fulfills a promise I made to myself and the Coal Tyee Society when I said that I would tell the beginning of the story which ends in *Boss Whistle*. That book let the miners tell their own story; this one tries to let them do the same.

But there are no miners alive who lived in 1848 or 1864 or even 1885 so I looked for their words in diaries, letters, court transcripts, inquests, newspapers, and Royal Commissions. An impulsive diary entry, a heartfelt letter, an eye-witness testimony or a solemnly sworn statement can tell what it was like to be an ordinary person in a time before the living can remember. Newspapers, for all their inaccuracies, give a sense of day by day life and reveal the harum-scarum quality of events as they occur. All these sources were used in *Three Dollar Dreams*.

This book is dedicated to two men — one a friend and the other a dear parent and friend. I knew Jock Gilmour for the last six years of his long life. I will miss his insights and his wit. My father Des Crossley was a powerful influence in my life. One of our last projects together was part of the research for this book. He deciphered the handwriting of various minute takers and letter writers as only a person with undecipherable handwriting himself could do.

In the Coal Tyee Society I have many more friends. We have met every month for seven years and have socialized often. President Ruth Tickle is a tireless woman whose good judgment I value highly. Ruth and the rest of the executive, Nelson Dean, Kate McNeill, and Clarence Karr, will be allowed to step down only now that the book is finished. The Board of Directors includes people like Bill Cottle, a courtly gentleman with a finely tuned wit and an encyclopedic memory, and Tom Bentley, an energetic man with a keen interest in

9

history. To this core of stalwarts we have added several new members whose fresh input has enriched our meetings and this project.

Boss Whistle introduced me to many new acquaintances and useful contacts. It was through people like Peter Gordon, Dorothy Maxwell Graham, Myra and Wallace Baikie, Terri Hunter, William and Malcolm McGregor, Marely McRae, Barbara Stannard, and Seiriol Williams that I met the Kilpatricks, the Walkers, Sam Cliffe, Andrew Hunter, the McGregors, Thomas Russell, the Freemans and Martells, and William Griffiths respectively. I wish to thank them for sharing their forefathers with me.

Barbara Stannard and Seiriol Williams gave me more than an introduction to their families. Both dedicated historians, they were generous in sharing their knowledge of the Island. Seiriol died last year, having led an accomplished and full life and having enriched everyone who met him with his sense of adventure and history. History is also the avocation of Edward Bell, Mel Boe, Pauline Hemming, and Gordon Holtby, and they too contributed unselfishly to the project.

I am also indebted to the following professionals in history and archives: the staffs of the Campbell River Museum, the Cumberland Museum, the Nanaimo and District Centennial Museum, the Provincial Archives of British Columbia, the Public Archives in Ottawa, the University of British Columbia Special Collections, the United Church Archives at the University of Toronto, and the Vancouver City Archives.

Certain professionals stand out as being especially obliging: Dr. Dan Gallacher, museum curator; Sharon Keen, freelance archaeologist; Danny Moore, archivist; Dr. Patricia Roy, associate professor; Allan Specht, sound and film archivist; and Laura Sundberg, freelance researcher.

Without a computer, I would still be sitting buried in a pile of index cards trying to sort my research. Without Dann Cox and Ken Irvine, I would still be staring at my computer screen uncomprehendingly. In addition, Dann gave up an entire weekend trying to find a chapter which had been swallowed up by this most demanding of servants.

Judy Baker transcribed the taped interviews; George Edwards and Joe White showed me the sites of the Wellington mines; Brian Marshal shared the treasures of the Old Slope site; Jim Peirson and Jocelyn Currie expedited the reproduction of several historical photographs; and Diana Priestley introduced me to Martin's Mining Cases.

10

Jack Atkinson, Theresa Bennett, Jim Boutelier, Brian Bradbury, Don Campbell, Harold Cliffe, Sally Forde, John Gorosh, Jr., Dr. Peter Li, Pat Murphy, Daphne Paterson, Doug Pelly, Bud and Marjorie Sandland, Dr. Franc Scurino, Wilbur Scurr, the Zaccarelli family, and Kay Zboyovsky loaned me their archival treasures or gave me insights and encouragement.

A book is only as good as the people who change it from a manuscript to a finished product. The mapping skills of Gary Crocker, the editing skills of Rhonda Bailey and Ron Smith at Oolichan, and the care taken by the staff at Morriss Printers are essential to a successful transformation.

The writing of a book tends to take on a disproportionate importance in the mind of its creator. For being tolerant of that loss of proportion I thank my husband, Dick; my mother, Isobel; and my children, Mike, Andrew, and Elizabeth.

Foreword

Since 1978 the Coal Tyee Society has been dedicated to the presentation and publication of the coal mining history of Vancouver Island by combining the enthusiasm of dedicated amateurs with the talents of professionals. Having sponsored the award-winning *Boss Whistle* in 1982 the Society now presents *Three Dollar Dreams*. Our new book portrays the period of coal mining from 1848 to 1900, again from the perspective of the coal miners and their families.

It is not only as subjects of our books that the coal miners are important. With the help of other interested individuals, they have constituted the central core of the Coal Tyee Society since its inception, supplying technical expertise, enthusiasm, and an aura of authenticity. In return they have been able to place a new focus and perspective on their own lives, which have been rendered more meaningful both to them and to those who read our histories.

For the many involved with the Society as members or as interviewees and for those now deceased, their lives and their contribution to Canadian society will continue to live in the pages of *Three Dollar Dreams*. We are proud to present this history to the reading public.

Clarence Karr

Prologue

The men are young and hungry: hungry for change, hungry for a chance. They are as strong as a spare diet will allow and brave as only young men can be brave. They come from the Black Country of England and the lowlands of Scotland, from industrial Italy and rural China. They travel light. They travel alone and they travel in company. Some leave nothing behind, others promise to return.

A sailing ship beats to windward, lies becalmed, runs before the trades, fights the tide. A dugout canoe knifes through north Pacific waters, the dip, dip of long bladed paddles driven by Indian muscle, the high prow a match for the oncoming waves. A side-wheel steamer flaunts its agility, nudges a wharf, disgorges human cargo. An iron-horse, all funnel, cowcatcher, and wheel, takes on dusty plain, log trestle, and mountain pass and reaches the coast.

The island is remote and sea surrounded. No one comes here by accident. The eye moves from sea to rock to forest to mountain. Nothing breaks the view. The sun shines on the rain-washed green. The grey clouds cover even the hills. All is Scotch mist, shiny water, pebble beach — then the black outcrop in a jagged shoreline.

The outcrop tantalizes, promises fulfillment, beckons inland. The men scrape, drill, dig, and blast. The coal is everywhere and hidden, black, gassy, and dirty; clean, hard, and beautiful. In coal there is money and danger; there is hope and death.

The dream is all that matters; the young and the hungry see only the possibilities. The coal will make the dream come true. In the beginning, the dream is hard edged and distinct. There will be no compromises. Hard work and a clear vision of the future will succeed. Reality clouds the dream; compromise tarnishes it; drink eases the pain. Old men settle for what they can get. And they remember.

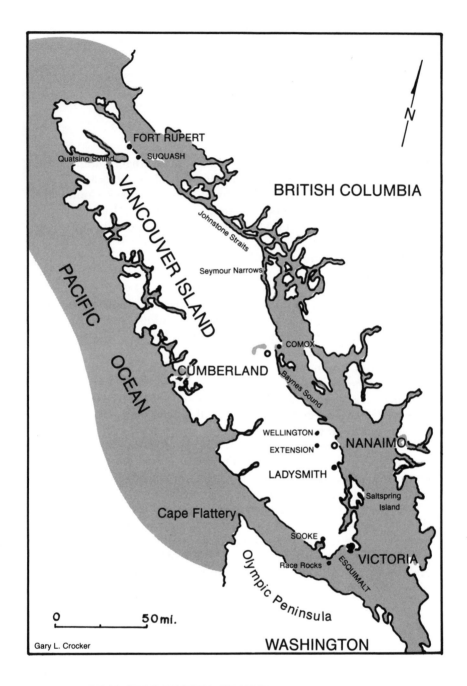

COAL COMMUNITIES OF NINETEENTH CENTURY
VANCOUVER ISLAND

CHAPTER I

CERTAIN REBELLIOUS PERSONS

... now we were on Vancouver's Island and we are put to the sinking of a Pit to look for coal a thing we never agreed for as we came out here to work coal not to look for it.

Andrew Muir, miner

From the habits of that class of men there is no possibility of getting anything like a fair day's work from them on stated wages alone...

David Landale, mine manager

Andrew Muir and John McGregor, independent colliers, lay in a bastion in irons. Their crime was refusing to dig a drain; their sentence was to remain in irons and on bread and water for two years; their judge was an irascible ship's captain named William Henry McNeill.

It was May 1850 and Muir and McGregor were far from home. A six month voyage around Cape Horn separated them from the Ayrshire coalfields where they had been born and where they had learned their trade. They had been on the northern end of Vancouver's Island for eight months, and they were disillusioned and fighting mad.

Andrew Muir's father happened to be in Manchester in 1848 when he read a newspaper advertisement in which the Hudson's Bay Company (HBC) asked for coal miners to work on Vancouver's Island. That the Company was looking for coal miners was in itself unusual. The famous British firm traded furs, not coal, but the governor of Rupert's Land, Sir George Simpson, wished to diversify the Company's activities. Rupert's Land encompassed all of what would later become Canada west of the Canadian Shield. If the diminutive governor of that vast tract of prairie, mountain and forest said coal mining was worth trying, there was no one likely to stand in his way.

For those members of the British public who were interested, the HBC lands in North America were cold, rugged, forbidding and a long way from home. By the 1840's, the influence of the Company had extended to the Pacific ocean, which was very far away indeed. It is unlikely then that the existence of coal deposits on this coast, which were reported as early as 1835, caused any stir at all at home. Indeed it caused very little stir among the HBC men who were sprinkled sparsely in forts along the coast and inland up the rivers to the interior.

William Fraser Tolmie was typical of the type of man attracted to the HBC at this time. A medical student who never took his degree, he had instead decided to devote his youth and considerable enthusiasm for life to a career as a fur trader. It was he who first reported coal on Vancouver's Island to his superiors in the Company. He was relaying what visiting Indians had told a blacksmith at Fort McLoughlin on Millbank Sound, of coal deposits at the north end of the large island off the coast. The next year in 1836, the HBC steamer *Beaver* stopped briefly to investigate the surface outcroppings.

The existence of coal on land controlled by the Company provoked only mild interest until the 1840's, when the Royal Navy began to convert from sail to steam. If Britannia was to rule the waves in steamers, there would have to be coaling stations all over the world to supply the fuel.

Tolmie and other HBC officials were taken to see the outcrops at what had now been named Beaver Harbour, and they reported to Chief Factor Dr. John McLoughlin, who in turn told the Admiralty. In 1846 a small paddle-wheeled steamer, the H.M.S. *Cormorant*, left Fort Victoria in mid-September.[1] Because she was steam-powered, she was able to manoeuvre through the narrow and turbulent Johnstone Strait which, while on the protected side of the Island, was not the route of choice for sailing vessels to the north end. They preferred the route up the west coast of Vancouver Island, although it was fog shrouded and stormy, with relentless swells waiting to pound a disabled vessel to pieces on the jagged rocky shore. Even after lighthouses were built to aid navigation, hundreds of sailors drowned as one ship after another lost its way in the fog and ran aground on the rocks. But this route was preferable to the one on the eastern side of the Island, where the narrow channels and strong currents made

---

[1] The *Cormorant* was one of two navy steam vessels ordered to the Pacific during the 1846 Oregon crisis. It was also a sailing vessel. The navy was in no hurry to convert to steam and only kept the two vessels to tow warships in confined waters.

progress impossible for a sailing vessel and just barely possible for the *Cormorant* as she struggled to reach Beaver Harbour.

The Indians proved to be more than mere tale bearers. The naval men were able to locate the formation and to trade blankets and tobacco for sixty tons of coal. It was obvious to the Indians that the white man had a use for this black rock which lay undisturbed on their beaches. Since theirs was a society whose economy was based on the potlatch, the possibility of a new source of trade goods was very attractive to them. They had become fur traders to get the white man's goods, and they would now become coal miners to get more of the same.

But two more years passed with no activity. Finally Samuel Cunard, the Scottish shipping magnate, was able to convince the British Admiralty it was necessary to protect the Vancouver Island coal deposits from the Americans, who were fresh from having successfully fought the Oregon Border dispute and were thought to be looking covetously at territory further north.

In response to this pressure from the south, the gunboats H.M.S. *Constance* and H.M.S. *Pandora* were instructed to undertake an extended visit to Vancouver's Island and in particular to the Beaver Harbour coal deposits. Captain Courtenay of the *Constance* instructed HBC officers to erect a log shed with a thatched roof to store coal and to post a notice declaring that "the Lands adjacent together with the Coal and other minerals were taken possession of for Her Majesty." The ownership of the coal having now been so efficiently determined, in the spring of 1849 the Admiralty further ordered Company men to commence the building of a proper fort. This fort would also serve secondarily as a fur trading establishment.

Thus these two arms of British overseas power took steps to promote the development of coal seams that had not been so much as observed by anyone who knew anything about coal mining. As if to enhance the unproven economic venture by giving it a distinguished name, the establishment was called Fort Rupert in honour of Prince Rupert of the Rhine, that dashing soldier and renaissance man who became the first Governor of the HBC when his cousin King Charles II granted the Company's charter in 1670.

Meanwhile, in London, the press had reported positively on tests performed by the *Cormorant* on the coal bought from the Indians. The ship's captain, Commander G. T. Gordon, was very pleased with the quality of the coal and the cheapness of the labour. As a naval officer, his expertise in judging either should have been suspect; however, his opinions captured the interest of a businessman in New York City.[2]

William Henry Aspinwall, owner of the major mercantile house, Howland and Aspinwall, had won the United States Pacific mail contract and had constructed three one thousand ton side paddle wheel steamers to carry mail between the Isthmus of Panama and the Columbia River. Aspinwall needed cheap coal available as close to his operation as possible, and Rupert coal sounded like exactly what he needed.

Sir George Simpson was the man on the front lines, and despite his eagerness to diversify the Company activities, he hedged. Notwithstanding what Commander Gordon had said to the English press, Simpson could not supply Aspinwall with any definite information regarding the quality of the coal, and he knew for certain he could not supply it as cheaply as Gordon had suggested. The coal had been purchased at a low price from the Indians, but Simpson realized that only experienced miners could dig sufficient volume to supply a commercial market. He had to convince the Board of Management of the HBC, who saw nothing wrong with using Indian labour. With their primitive tools and lack of expertise the Indians could only obtain surface coal, and it was already known from the reports of other steamers that surface coal was too soft and full of slate for ships' boilers to use effectively.

Without too much trouble, Simpson convinced the board to use experienced miners. In fact, the Company had agreed to the building of the fort partly in anticipation of the problems that might arise when the Indians found they were excluded from the coal trading process. But white miners would have to be obtained from Britain and that would take time. Despite this and despite the lack of knowledge regarding the quality of the coal, the HBC signed a contract with the Pacific Mail Steamship Company to deliver one thousand tons of coal between May 1849 and May 1850 at fifty shillings per ton.

Simpson was wise to insist on British miners, but he knew nothing of the type of expertise required. What he needed were miners whose specialty was the development of new shafts; what he asked for were men accustomed to working in established mines, or as he put it "a miner possessing both scientific and practical knowledge with six labourers accustomed to coal mining."

---

[2] Although Gordon was not an expert in judging the characteristics of steaming coal, his opinion was backed up by the engineers of the *Beaver*, who in 1836 had also said the coal was of good quality.

BRITISH COLUMBIA

QUEEN CHARLOTTE STRAIT

Malcolm Island

SUQUASH

Beaver Harbour

Hardy Bay

MUIR SHAFT

FORT RUPERT

Hope Island (Newittee)

Bull Harbour

Willes Island

SHUSHARTIE

VANCOUVER   ISLAND

Quatsino Sound

PACIFIC OCEAN

10 mi.

0

N

Gary L. Crocker

FORT RUPERT AND SURROUNDINGS

When Andrew Muir's father, John, read the HBC advertisement, he knew he was the man they wanted. He was a practical and skilled miner, and he had four sons and two nephews who were certainly "accustomed to coal mining." He was also from Ayrshire and that is where David Landale, a mine manager commissioned by the Company to hire the miners, had determined that he would find the best class of colliers for this particular job. The miners in Ayrshire had a reputation for producing more coal in a day and being less militant than those from other Scottish shires. And Scots was the nationality of choice. The Company had always preferred employees of that race.

Landale was working blind when he was asked to determine levels and methods of pay and the other terms of the contract. Mining conditions on Vancouver's Island were totally unknown to him and so he used the Ayrshire coalfield as a basis. But Ayrshire wages were determined by the standard day's output. Because it was impossible to know what this would be in the new coalfields, he suggested a fixed per annum wage and a bonus system for extra production because "[f]rom the habits of that class of men there is no possibility of getting anything like a fair day's work from them on stated wages alone. . . ."

The other stipulations were close to those contained in the standard HBC contract by which employees of the Company had been indentured for set periods of time since the Company began. The annual wage of fifty pounds was high for the times and felt to be necessary to lure men away from Britain; the oversman was to be paid at the same level as a clerk-surgeon; there was money designated for a food allowance for the miner but not for his family; miners were to build their own homes of wood with Company materials and the assistance of Company employees, although the Company was already informed that they would not know how to do this; wages were forfeit in case of absence; free passage home was to be provided at the end of the contract unless the miner was dismissed for cause. That the Company had no mining experience showed in the contract, particularly in the job designation of "working collier or labourer," which were not mining terms and did not define the miners' responsibilities in a manner that they could understand.

John Muir was a miner of several years' experience, as were his sons and nephews. When they were presented with their contracts to sign, they could see that although the wages offered were good, they were committing themselves to a set of conditions unlike any they had heretofore experienced. Being men able to read and write, they were surely able to understand the obligation they had made, and as they were still in Scotland when they signed the contracts, they had not yet placed themselves in an irreversible situation. And yet they agreed to go.

They left towns where their families had lived for generations to travel half way around the world to dig coal. They were either very brave, very foolish, or very uninformed. Or perhaps they had a dream, a dream so powerful that they could trustingly place themselves in the hands of God and the HBC.

Andrew Muir was a literate man who kept a lively diary of the family's voyage to Vancouver's Island, but nowhere does he examine, in words at least, his motivation. Whatever prompted their decision, they made it quickly, and by November 1848, just a few weeks after first reading of the jobs, they were in the Ayrshire town of Irvine on the Firth of Clyde waiting to be summoned to London. They were John Muir and his wife Anne, both in their mid-forties; their daughter Marion and her two children; their sons Andrew, John, Jr., Robert and Michael, a lad of ten; their nephews Archibald Muir and John McGregor, with McGregor's wife Mary, his sister, and his three children. The party also included John and Marion Smith and their family, who were not related to the Muirs.

When the summons came they boarded a train for a brief trip down the coast to Troon, where the Royal Consort Steamer waited to transport them to Fleetwood, a port at the mouth of the Wyre River in Lancashire. The voyage was noteworthy only in that everyone was sick for the entire sixteen hours.

To get from Fleetwood to Manchester, where they had lodgings, it was necessary to board the Preston and Ware railway, the fifty-mile distance being covered in three hours. Next day they exchanged bank notes for gold and then continued by railway across the English countryside to London. Two cabs transported eleven adults and at least six children directly to the West India docks, which were closed when they arrived, so they found lodging nearby in Mr. Montague's Jamaica Tavern.

The expenses for this trip and the one to follow were paid as part of the contract that had been signed before they left Scotland. On the morning after their arrival in London they first laid their eyes on the *Harpooner* and declared it a fine vessel. John and Andrew Muir then proceeded to the HBC office to be warmly received by Mr. Archibald Barclay, the official who had been instrumental in their recruitment. Whether this friendly reception was an indication of the social standing of the Muir family or simply a recognition of the significance

21

of the occasion, Andrew does not say, but so far the atmosphere around this expedition was warm and optimistic and did not presage the bitter ending of the Company's first encounter with proud coal miners.

As his later actions would show, Andrew Muir was certainly among the most proud of men, and he would rebel against even his own parents when his rights were abused. But it was a measure of the man that during the six months' voyage from the West India docks, through the slow passage down the English Channel alternating days of sailing with nights at anchor, through "fearful squalls" and "perfect Hurricanes," through bad beef and drunken crew, Andrew remained cheerful and philosophical. He characterized the ship as "not at all the worst of places" and joked about the difficulties of sharing a bunk with Archibald Muir when the movement of the ship made them roll on top of each other continuously.

When the first squall of the voyage tested their mettle, "My Man Archy," as Andrew called his cousin, gave way to superstitious incantations which involved wishing he had a hold of his Mother's cat's tail. Andrew himself was "frighted . . . out of his wits" and the women stayed in bed sipping a little wine each day "for nourishment." Once the squall ended, My Man Archy signaled the return of his health by eating two scones, much to the relief of his erstwhile roommate.

Each passenger took a turn cooking, but Andrew obviously did more than his share and viewed another male passenger with disdain when that man said he was above such domestic chores. "I must confess it is too good a job for him or any one of his stamp. . . ." Besides being willing to pitch in, Andrew was also open to new experiences; he relished experimenting with shark ("it did taste very well although some of our company could not get over the idea of eating the devourer of human beings") and turtle soup, prickly pears, American beans and wild fowls caught on an uninhabited island. Off the coast of South America just opposite Valparaiso they spent "a rapturous day ashore" on Crusoe's Island. They returned to the ship loaded with peaches, quinces, pigeons, fresh fish and, best of all, fresh water.

But the ebullient Andrew showed quickly that he was not a man to be trifled with when he learned after only three weeks out that they were being begrudged the fresh meat. "I gave them to understand I was not a tool in their hands to be used as they thought proper. . . ." In a later argument with the ship's doctor and the captain over the allotment of provisions, Andrew expressed the wish that "one day I shall be able to see justice done to its full extent and that the transgressor may be punished...."[3]

The captain was a religious man who held two church services on Sunday and gave a Bible and a prayer book to each of the sailors. Christian gifts did not make a holy crew. They surreptitiously ate an entire cask of the good beef brought on board by the miners and then refused to reef the sails during a storm until the Captain opened a second cask. Until the crew resolved their grievances it was necessary for the passengers to divide into two watches to work the boat into Valparaiso. Passengers who were willing to help were rewarded with a glass of grog, which Andrew declared to be "very acceptable."

By the end of May they were nearing their destination. In a flowery passage Andrew Muir considers

the swelling of emotions of the captive when the happy time of his capitivity under which he has been groaning is coming to an end and the glorious son [sic] of liberty is about to dawn, through those dismal walls within which he is enthralled, such are the emotions arising in our breast as we behold drawing to a close the period of our long confinement...

To this man who regarded a ship's voyage as a period of confinement, his subsequent incarceration in the bastion must have been bitter indeed.

As they entered the Straits of Juan de Fuca at Cape Flattery the ship became becalmed. While in that state it was visited by a large number of Indians who came on board and would not leave until they were pushed off. Andrew recorded breathlessly:

Some of them on reaching their canoes made an oration in their own tongue which we could not understand we thought it was nothing good with about forty canoes round the vessel and making such an unearthy noise and being forced off the deck we flew to our Arms ready for action the Indians had all bows and arrows, fortunately a breeze struck up which took us away out of their reach...

As soon as the first Vancouver Island coal miners disembarked at Fort Victoria on June 1, 1849, they all, with the exception of their leader, went to discuss rations with the Chief Factor, James Douglas. They had intended to ask for a shilling a day in lieu of rations until they found out how much the food cost on the Island, most of it being brought in from elsewhere. Douglas agreed to give them fourteen

---

[3] Another Doctor, Alfred Benson, later expressed the opinion that the Scottish miners could not adapt to the taste of salt beef because they were so used to oatmeal!

pounds of flour, ten and a half pounds of beef or venison or "as much Salmon fresh as could be equivalent," one pound of sugar, four ounces of tea, three gills of rum per week, "which he said was as much as any man could destroy."[4]

As the miners left Fort Victoria with their families almost three months later aboard the Company vessel *Mary Dare*, they had already had their first disagreement with the Company in their interpretation of their duties. For the entire time they were in Fort Victoria they had been put to work blasting rock for the dockyard, a task that had to be completed before they left for Fort Rupert. The Company did not understand that they had hired proud men with specialized talents, not common labourers. In a letter written shortly after the miners left, Company official Eden Colvile reported to the London office that the miners left Victoria very well satisfied, having worked very well while there. Chief Factor James Douglas had a much different assessment of that summer when he reported having had the utmost difficulty getting the Muirs off to Fort Rupert. The proud Scottish miners had not taken their treatment lightly. Their unhappiness would grow as the months progressed.

The pride and skill of the Scottish collier was born in serfdom. Legislation in the seventeenth century to ensure a supply of labour for the mines in Scotland had meant that by the beginning of the eighteenth century miners were bound like serfs to the coal they worked. A collier could also be bound to a coalmaster for life by accepting "arles" or bounty money. Security for these loans was his childrens' future labour, thus enslaving another generation. So inevitable was the practice that it became a routine part of the ritual in the baptism of colliery children.

The Emancipation Act of 1775 ended serfdom in Scottish coalfields, but the Act was full of provisions to prevent the sudden exodus of colliers and so it took several years and some petitioning for an individual to gain his freedom. Even then, the mining community remained homogeneous and set apart. There were two main reasons for this. Because marriage to a collier meant working in the mines, it was usually necessary for a Scottish miner to marry within the coal fraternity since only colliers' daughters were willing to do such work. In addition, a Scottish antipathy to working underground resulted in a continual scarcity of labour with the result that miners became increasingly aware of their value and their bargaining power.

[4] A gill is a liquid measure equal to a quarter pint.

By the early nineteenth century, this awareness of their value and pride in their skills made the by now independent colliers realize they had the right to control their own workplace. Industry was booming in the west of Scotland and the growing number of iron smelters lured colliers from one pit to another with the prospect of better wages. Living conditions improved so much that miners began to indulge in conspicuous consumption. The purchase of clocks and furniture for their houses, silver watches and shoes for themselves, silk stockings and Kirk seats for Sunday, sugar and soap, tobacco and education demonstrated to their fellow citizens that they no longer could be considered inferior.

When a series of sharp drops in the economy of the coalfields after 1817 threatened this higher standard of living, colliers indulged in a certain amount of union activity. However, the strength of these unions was challenged by the hiring of thousands of unskilled Irishmen as strikebreakers and, indeed, by the independent collier himself, for it was understood that since a miner required skill to do his job, he was entitled to control his own workplace and bow to no man or union.

By the 1840's the percentage of skilled colliers had decreased but those who remained were able to do almost any work that was necessary to keep a pit functioning. Working at his own pace underground with little supervision, able to stop to eat when he pleased and go about the business of hewing coal in the way he judged best, the independent collier worked with the strength of a labourer and the skill of an artisan; he required good judgment and expertise, a knowledge of practical geology, and the use of various tools. Around the age of eighteen a Scottish coal miner, having served his apprenticeship, attained the status of "a full man," which was celebrated in a secret ceremony called "brothering" during which an oath based on the Bible was administered and toasted with strong drink.

This pride and independence made Scottish colliers ambivalent about unions. The piecework system under which they chose to labour set one man against another. However, they did realize that if they controlled their production they could control the market, and so they set a maximum level of output. No man was to earn above a certain amount per day. This was set as his "darg" or day's work. Working rules were adopted to encourage adherence to the darg, and factors that increased or decreased output, such as location of the working place and quality of the coal, were carefully considered. The size of the darg was also adjusted for men with families or with sons working with them. Such was the background of the small group of expatriate Scots, six men and one boy, who sailed into Beaver Harbour aboard the *Mary Dare* on September 24, 1849.

At the north end of Vancouver's Island, the land lies low, covered with trees which almost meet the ocean save for a thin margin of grey rock. The clouds often lie low there too, brushing tree tops and rocky cliffs. The trees are dark green, the sea is grey. The harbour does not enfold. It is open to the north and lets in the northwest winds. The islands in the harbour are steep sided. The water is deep, and the coastline shelves away so gradually no large boat can approach the shore.

The crew of the *Mary Dare* lowered a tender and ferried her passengers in shifts to the south shore where a four sided stockade of roughhewn logs intruded on the natural setting. Two bastions and four nine-pounders gave it a warlike demeanor designed to impress the Kwakiutl Indians, who had been there first and were not impressed by the guns at all. Tradition has it that the first time the cannon was fired, the Indians pursued the ball and brought it back, offering to trade it so it could be fired again.

Thirty-five Canadians, Kanakas, and Englishmen lived at Fort Rupert that summer, surrounded by hundreds of Indians.[5] A pre-fort Indian population of two hundred at the most had mushroomed with the advent of the HBC. The lure was the trade goods, like blankets and tobacco, which could be earned by digging coal or supplying the whites with fish, fresh meat, furs, and firewood.

The HBC men were used to Indian customs, but the fresh recruits from Scotland were not. On the day after their arrival, the Muirs awoke to see sixteen war canoes in the harbour. On the beach, sixteen poles had been erected, each with an Indian's head impaled on it. The Indians' intent was not to frighten the new whites but rather to honour Anne Muir as the first white woman to arrive. They showed their respect by offering her a choice of any two of the heads.

A state of guarded peace and mutual exploitation existed between the hundreds of Indians and the handful of whites. Each group could be useful to the other but so could each do the other harm. The very existence of the stockade revealed the Europeans' lack of trust for the people on whose land they were trespassing. Just inside the gates of the fort were two houses, one on either side, which formed an alley

---

[5] At this time, years before Confederation, the term "Canadians" referred to French-Canadians. Kanakas were from the Sandwich Islands (Hawaii) where the HBC had recruited extensively.

into the inner fort. These houses were used for trading and marked the beginning of the inner yard into which no Indian was allowed.

Clustered around the outside, the Indian village was a rabbit warren of narrow dirty footpaths between small huts. The village was dirty to the white man's eyes and so were the people, but they were "by no means repulsive" with their dark, robust good looks and vermilion painted faces. The men tied their hair in a bunch on top of their heads. Both sexes wore only blankets and hats made of cedar root platted together to provide shelter from the rain. The children were nude or half-naked.

It was in the misinterpretation of Indian customs that the white population of the fort perceived a threat. Despite a problem with thievery and periodic tribal wars between visiting or marauding tribes, it soon became apparent to the whites that the Indians were open and intelligent, if untamed. They looked after their own needs well and had a system of laws in which offenses were punished, fines levied, and murder of a member of one's own tribe decried. Murder of the members of some other tribe was another thing entirely and much to be congratulated.

These people accepted the arrival of the Europeans with equanimity. They were curious to see how they could benefit from these newcomers who brought blankets and tobacco with them to trade. If the HBC men wanted to pay them for digging coal, that worked well for everyone. However, as always, when Europeans entered a primitive culture, they imposed their system of justice and land ownership on their unsuspecting hosts. When this happened at Fort Rupert, the results were violent and very nearly ended coal mining before it started.

The local Indians had been digging surface coal at Suquash (Saaquash), six miles to the south, for about ten years. Despite their primitive methods using adzes or axes, hammers or crowbars or whatever implement came to hand, they had been able to acquire considerable trade goods by selling coal to passing ships. They were understandably upset, therefore, when they saw the white miners begin a shaft about half a mile from the fort. Only four days after work was begun the Indians surrounded the shaft and threatened to kill the miners unless compensated for the land.

If the Indians were unhappy with the beginning of HBC mining, so were the miners. Already dismayed by their treatment in Fort Victoria, they had been disappointed when they surveyed the coast by canoe to find an inhospitable beach unsuitable for loading coal and the presence of whin, a hard rock which was very difficult to drill through. By late October it was a disgruntled group indeed who began to work on the first pit by digging a drain to take away the surface water. Andrew Muir muttered "... now we were on Vancouver's Island and we are put to sinking of a Pit to look for coal a thing we never agreed for as we came out here to work coal not to look for it."

The contract signed before they left Scotland had been based on the current practices in that country and had nothing to do with the conditions they found when they arrived in the New World. A conflict arose over building their own houses. Although the contract required them to do this, they had no skills for carpentry. Consequently, aside from building the chimneys and digging the wells, they could only look on while Company employees grudgingly did the building. It is not surprising then that when the miners required protection from the Indians, the Company men refused to oblige them.

The fort operated under ship's discipline, a necessary measure for all HBC forts to control employees in the isolated trading posts. Certain hours of work were expected of the Company men and these varied considerably from what the miners expected. They were used to the darg and would take time off when it suited them. They were used to underground workings and here there were none. They did not know how to sink a shaft and yet were expected to do just that. There were no proper mining tools available; nor were there long enough drilling rods; nor was there a pump to remove the water. John Muir was given control over the miners, but with only a relative as a supervisor they became an increasingly unruly group. They resisted as well the attempts of the fort managers to impose Company discipline upon them.

The situation was further exacerbated by the lack of success in finding a proper seam of coal. Their contract had provided for an annual wage of fifty pounds with a bonus paid for coal dug over thirty tons. However, until coal was found it was impossible for the miners to dig for any coal, let alone bonus coal. After some negotiations, James Douglas reluctantly agreed to pay them an extra payment of two shillings sixpence per day in place of the bonus system.

There seemed to be no redeeming features to life at Fort Rupert. In the miners' eyes everything needed improvement. The houses provided shelter from the weather it was true, except for when it rained — then the water came in the hole in the roof that served as a chimney. The floors were bare earth covered with broken clamshells and there was only one bake oven, in the centre of the inner courtyard of the fort, for the use of everyone. Because agriculture had been neglected in the Pacific Northwest foodstuffs had to be imported, which made them expensive. The miners were not able to adjust to the alternative, which was a spare diet that the Company men accepted with little complaint.

When Indians appeared around the diggings four days after mining commenced in late October, threatening to kill unless compensated for their land rights, no help or protection was forthcoming from the Company men. The miners stopped working until pickets were erected around the pit. Then, despite their unhappiness, they returned to work, having decided to continue for the sake of their manager and themselves.

Fall dragged into winter. The few tools provided were poor and the work frustratingly slow. When clay was needed, work was stopped while the miners searched the beaches for it. Whenever a ship appeared to take on coal, Indians and miners had to work together to dig it from the surface pits at Suquash and transport it five miles up the coast to where the ships waited in the shelter of Beaver Harbour. The laborious process of loading the vessels with baskets of coal brought out in canoes and dumped into a large tub lowered from the foreyard took about one month per ship.[6]

All through the dark and wet winter months the shaft went deeper and deeper. Having made the commitment to work for their own sakes and, in fact, having no other alternative, the miners bided their time. The pit gradually grew in depth day after day until it had reached seventy feet without striking coal. Company officials seemed to be unaware of the undercurrent of discontent. Douglas reported in February that the miners appeared satisfied, and John Work, another Company official, described them in March as being in high spirits.

As winter gave way to the spring of 1850, a ship dropped anchor at Esquimalt near Fort Victoria at the other end of the Island. The Company ship *Norman Morison* had come to the end of a troubled voyage from England. During the five months at sea twenty people on board had been stricken with smallpox, and despite the best efforts of John Helmcken, the young doctor on board, one person had died. This, coupled with an unusually rough rounding of Cape Horn

[6] This process was shortened somewhat in the summer of 1851 when the captain of the U.S.S. *Massachusetts* discovered at Suquash a lane of seaweed which acted as a breakwater and allowed the ships to anchor off the surface diggings, thus avoiding the five mile canoe trip.

during which the passengers and crew had subsisted on pea soup and porridge, resulted in a disgruntled ship's company when they at last sighted Cape Flattery. Then they were subjected to day after day of calms. Whenever the wind did come up, they were able to make progress down the straits only to drift helplessly back out to sea when the wind dropped again.

When they eventually rounded Race Rocks and fired the two gun signal of HBC ships, four members of the crew were particularly unhappy. And when the pilot came on board bringing news that gold had been discovered in California, the four deserted. They were just the first of many sailors to leave their ships lured by easy money in the gold fields, but the four deserters from the *Norman Morison* did not get far. They were quickly apprehended and confined until they could be taken home in irons on the ship *England*. That ship would first go to Fort Rupert where the prisoners' destiny became entangled with that of the coal miners.

Dr. John Helmcken, who had hardly had time to recover from the arduous voyage from England, was immediately posted to Fort Rupert. He left Fort Victoria on the continuation of the voyage of the *Norman Morison*. His shipmates also included a contingent of English labourers who had come from England in the Company service to augment the Fort Rupert labour force. These Englishmen had at first refused to eat the food provided on the ship and had thrown it overboard. Their indignation had lasted only until their bellies were empty and then they had begged to have their rations restored. Even so, the experience had not taught them any long-lasting lessons for they continued to make demands which would only add to the turmoil at Beaver Harbour.

Meanwhile, the discontented miners at Fort Rupert had found a champion. Richard Blanshard was a man with a job but with nothing to do. He had been appointed the first Governor of the Colony of Vancouver Island and had arrived to find that his job was being done for all intents and purposes by James Douglas. He was expected to introduce the Island to government, but he had no headquarters, no army, no police, not even a jail. With time on his hands he decided to make a vice-regal visit to the only other settlement in the colony.

Blanshard arrived at Fort Rupert at the end of March, 1850. During the course of his stay, he spent two hours at the Muirs' house. This visit was duly reported by the Chief Trader, Captain McNeill, to his superior, James Douglas. In McNeill's opinion Blanshard was too sympathetic to the miners' complaints and increased their discontent by listening to them and by behaving in a manner that McNeill judged to be unbecoming to a person of his rank.

Although Blanshard had had no experience in colonial government, he was an intelligent man and trained as a barrister. His sympathetic hearing of the miners' grievances and subsequent report to the colonial office that they were "unprovided with proper implements, discontented with their employers, and can scarcely be induced to work" seems merely to be an accurate observation of the situation. However, it provided ammunition for those in the colony who viewed his presence as an unnecessary intrusion and helped hasten his ultimate departure.

Captain William Henry McNeill, the Chief Trader at Fort Rupert and the man in charge, was a native Bostonian turned British citizen. His temper was legendary. He had been hired by the HBC to regulate its maritime operations, a task he performed from the deck of the *Beaver*, whose single black funnel and side-wheels were a familiar sight to the Indians, and whose manoeuvrability in the days when steam boats were rare made her an ideal headquarters for McNeill's activities. When he came to Fort Rupert his reputation as a stern ship captain blended well with the Royal Navy style administration practiced by the Company.

To be second-in-command to such a man cannot have been easy. It was especially difficult for George Blenkinsop because McNeill happened also to be his father-in-law. A good-natured and courageous Cornishman, Blenkinsop was twenty-eight years old when he was left in charge of the fort during one of McNeill's frequent absences. His assistant was Charles Beardmore, a tall, wiry man with red curly hair, a good-natured approach to life, and an unquestioning loyalty to the Company. That loyalty inclined him toward bending the truth when he thought it was in the Company's interest. These two young men were left to deal with the disparate collection of discontented English labourers, disgruntled miners, and rambunctious Indians who lived at Fort Rupert in April of 1850.

It was the rambunctious Indians who seemed to start the trouble that spring. The winter had been a frustrating one for the miners, but they held their tempers and continued to work under the hostile eyes of the Indians. When after five months the pit had still yielded no coal, the miners, and Andrew Muir in particular, could take it no longer.

How could we be thought to stand and work our work without them their annoyances by day and their thieving depridations [sic] by night...men that people sees with their own eyes go out and in five minutes return with

31

two of their neighbours heads in their hands it certainly teaches this lesson not to be trusted.

Andrew had become the miners' spokesman. His talk was of revolution, of the Company's day having gone by, and of men beginning to hold up their heads. More specifically Muir demanded two shillings sixpence a day over their regular pay. It all made Blenkinsop very nervous. He sent dispatches by canoe to Fort Victoria asking for advice and support.

By April 21st the miners were working at almost anything but mining. Some were sinking a well, some blasting rock for a chimney, and some digging drainage ditches. Andrew Muir and John McGregor said that if they were to be labourers then Blenkinsop must give them a piece of paper saying they were labourers and then they would do labouring work for the rest of their contract. Blenkinsop ordered them into the hall and said they had broken their agreement as soon as they landed on the Island, referring presumably either to their agreeing to do the rock work at Esquimalt or to their complaints in Fort Victoria about the rations. He also threatened to take a pistol and "shoot them like a crow," just as McNeill had once threatened to do.

In response to this bit of bravado, Andrew Muir said he wanted no trouble and would work as a labourer until word came by ship what was to be done. The other miners agreed and returned to work on the drainage ditches for several days. All was quiet until John McGregor and Andrew were told to dig a drain which would lead out of the Fort below a Kanaka's house. Describing the house as "a place with the smell hardly fit for a pig to go in," the two men refused to work, complaining also that they were not acquainted with removing roots and therefore could not proceed.

Blenkinsop announced that since they were doing only half their work and sitting idle for the rest of the day they were breaching their contract and should be charged a penalty of fifty pounds. Even in the harsh disciplinary climate of a HBC fort, a fine of a full year's salary was extraordinarily stiff and reflected Blenkinsop's desperation more than the severity of the crime. When he also charged Muir with being "a rebellious person" who kept the men off their duty, Muir chose to regard that as defamation of character and "so that we could not please with our work we stop for the present until matters are settled." It was April 26, 1850. The first Vancouver Island coal miners' strike had begun.

The first week of the strike went by in a pastoral calm as the miners, free of their frustrating tasks, paddled canoes around the small islands, lay on the beach, and traded for venison and other articles with the Indians. So calm was the atmosphere even Mrs. McNeill and her daughter, Mrs. Blenkinsop, had a picnic outside the fort.

The calm was only superficial, however, and behind the scenes harsh words were exchanged between Blenkinsop and several of the miners. My Man Archy became involved twice in altercations with the acting chief trader. John Muir Sr. was at a loss what to do and after witnessing a verbal duel between Andrew and Blenkinsop complained that he never got respect from his sons. The senior Muir was not a party to the strike and made it plain that he was not to be considered a troublemaker; indeed he continued his fruitless quest for coal, speaking confidently whenever asked about its elusive presence.

On May 3rd Captain McNeill returned to Fort Rupert. He called a meeting in the hall, where he "commenced swearing like a madman," threatening the assembled miners and ordering them to return to work. When the miners replied that they would not return to work until tried fairly by English law, McNeill ordered Andrew Muir and John McGregor put in irons in one of the bastions.

[D]uring the time they were putting the Iron on McGregor and I we were treated in the most shocking manner possible called everything we could be called and threatened to be shot like dogs and dared not open our Mouth so we remained silent the time they were putting on the Irons the last words he said on us two going out was we should remain in Irons and on bread and water for two years, the others were to finish the well and then take the same fate.

There must have been employers since who have envied the HBC its power to end a strike by imprisoning the strikers. In fact, in the next seventy years the legal and military arms of government would intervene in several Vancouver Island coal miners' strikes, but none was able to match the power of the HBC in its ability to swiftly intervene in disputes with its employees.

Andrew was placed in the upper bastion and McGregor in the lower, which had no roof. On the second day McGregor was brought to where Muir lay. There being no beds and no blankets, the two men huddled together at night to keep each other warm. A cold rendered Muir partially deaf, but he was refused medical attention for five days. On the third night they asked to have the irons taken off, and that was granted for the time between 8:00 p.m. and 6:00 a.m. Some days they were allowed to walk on the gallery, some days not. The bread and water regimen was only broken twice when they were given soup for dinner.

On May 7th, John Smith and Robert, John Jr., and Archibald Muir were also imprisoned. Two days later all of the miners were ordered down to the hall where McNeill, Blenkinsop, Beardmore, Captain Dodd of the *Beaver*, Doctor Helmcken, and John Muir Sr. were assembled. Captain McNeill had changed tactics. Whereas before the miners "had durst not open our mouth," now they were urged to state their minds freely. Whereas before they had been sworn at and ordered to work, now they were implored to go to work or do anything until the steamer should return, at which time they would be tried properly.

The change in tactics was a direct result of the May 1850 deadline for supplying coal to the Pacific Mail Steamship Company. The HBC was desperate to provide at least a token amount of coal and needed the miners to transport surface coal if not to find it underground. But they refused to cooperate. They had been imprisoned falsely and would do no more work until their case had been tried and settled. McNeill told them to go outside and consult with each other. When they returned they were as determined as ever. They were told to go away again and talk about it until after dinner.

At 5:00 p.m. McNeill sent for the miners and was told that they had not changed their minds. They were sent back to the bastion but under much less stringent conditions. There were to be no irons, wives could cook their rations, and they could have beds. Beardmore was ordered to bring an ear syringe from the doctor for Muir, who commented that "this is rather pleasanter but still in Prison." They stayed there for two more days when they were allowed to go home on the condition that they neither speak to any man nor attempt to go outside. They were to receive neither rum nor powder.

While in confinement Andrew Muir wrote to Richard Blanshard saying he would bring action for false imprisonment. Blanshard's response was to appoint Dr. Helmcken magistrate, but given the time necessary to transport letters to and from Fort Victoria, Helmcken did not know of his appointment until June 22nd, more than a month after Muir's letter was written.

The restrictions on the miners were but the official side of a more pervasive persecution which now manifested itself against all the members of the mining families. Unable to get food from the Company store and unable to hunt for themselves without powder, the miners were dependent on the largess of the Indians, but when young Michael Muir attempted to come through the gate with three salmon he was stopped, while a French-Canadian was allowed through carrying the same booty. When Michael was stopped again, this time with fresh meat, his father confronted Blenkinsop, who was once again in command.

Blenkinsop said he would not allow anyone to purchase or trade anything with the Indians, but when the Indians refused to bring their goods to him he was forced to allow the miners to trade or be responsible for them starving. His methods remained tyrannical, however. When Anne Muir, Mary McGregor, and Marion Smith were given two deer which they skinned and butchered, the baskets in which they were carrying the meat were ripped from them at the Fort gate by Blenkinsop and Beardmore. They were told that the Company would trade for it and send it to them and whatever the Company had to pay for it would be charged to their husbands. Andrew recorded his mother's reaction.

[S]he would rather suffer anything than breed a disturbance but they had trodden too much on good nature . . . she boldly said she was a free woman and had no meat from the Coy. therefore she would buy her meat from the best and cheapest market . . . after a little more altercations the Baskets with the women carrying them came over to the house triumphant over the cowardly rascals who should attack a woman two to one . . .

The Indians seemed to favour the miners. In contrast to the English labourers, who were having trouble convincing the Indians to sell them fresh meat, the miners could get it whenever they wanted it. Indian cooperation was fortunate, for although Douglas had agreed to provide fresh meat and, in fact, the Company was providing John Muir Sr. with mutton, Andrew had not received any fresh meat from the Company since his arrival.

The general situation at Fort Rupert began to deteriorate further. French-Canadians and Kanakas drank rum in large quantities and went unpunished, even though the miners were allowed no rum at all. The drunken Company men began to fight and shoot their guns, forcing a Kanaka to seek refuge in Smith's house. Andrew allowed his indignation to run free.

[M]ark the craft of the officers in giving them rum, they put this injunction on them 'Not to tell the Englishmen it is like telling a man to thrust his hand in the fire and not burn himself, a person might as well live in the worst place of common fame in Glasgow as live here where vice of every kind is permitted here and is allowed to pass unheeded and yet this is in the Service of the H.B. Coy.

Into this sad and angry community came another complication on May 24th. The barque *England*, under her master Captain Brown, sailed into Beaver Harbour and dropped anchor. She had come from Fort Victoria via the west side of the Island and around the northern end to take on a cargo of coal before returning to Britain. She would stop in California on her way back down the coast. In her hold were the four deserters from the *Norman Morison*.

Visitors to the fort were always made welcome. Their presence provided a diversion and their observations enlivened conversation grown stale from too close contact with too few people. While Captain Brown was feted with bear steak washed down with copious amounts of wine and liquor, the second mate and boatswain took tea with the miners.

It would not have taken the visitors long to realize that all was not normal at Fort Rupert. The crew had only to observe Charles Beardmore running around with the Indians in search of enough surface coal to load the *England* while the miners refused to help. The same miners hired sixteen Indians to cut wood for Captain Brown, who in turn would sell it in San Francisco. After several days work the Indians practiced a little labour negotiation themselves by demanding an increase in pay from seven sticks of tobacco per day to nine.

Given the miners' work stoppage and the scarcity of coal, the normally laborious process of loading took even longer than usual. While the crew waited out the delay they entertained the inhabitants of the fort with stories of "the riches of California and the gold fields." Why, they wondered, would anyone stay in this isolated fort to be exploited by the Company when they could make easy money in California and partake of "life, beer, lovely women and reckless pleasure?"

Suddenly there was an alternative to staying in the employ of the Company. Suddenly the miners felt they had options. There was no need to stay here in Fort Rupert when they could become rich in California. The Company had not kept its part of the bargain so why should they abide by their three year contracts?

Gold fever was the catalyst in the spread of the strike to include eleven of the English labourers and eleven Canadians. Described by Helmcken as "such a miserable set of devils I firmly believe never before congregated," they were under contract to the HBC for an annual wage of twenty-five pounds, half what the miners were to receive. Following the miners' example they struck for "double pay and many other allowances inconsistent with the rules of the service." Such outrageous demands cannot have been meant seriously, nor were they regarded seriously.

As the time for the departure of the *England* drew nearer and nearer, the already tenuous discipline of the fort deteriorated more and more. Employees were insubordinate; drunken orgies fueled by liquor from the ship erupted again and again; desertion was threatened openly. If they were not allowed to leave in the *England* they would leave by canoe. This last threat particularly worried the officers, who felt that an exodus of whites would leave the fort defenseless to the Indians, who also had liquor. The fact that whites had always been hopelessly outnumbered by Indians and yet had not been harmed, seemed not to occur to the distraught Company officers. The Indian chiefs, however, were asked to promise they would neither sell anyone canoes nor allow their people to transport anyone away.

The miners had no intention of sneaking away. Their delegation, headed by Andrew Muir, approached Blenkinsop again to tell him that they had applied to Captain Brown for transportation to Fort Victoria and would leave in ten days if they did not get the extra pay they had requested in April. It was their wish to go to Fort Victoria and speak to James Douglas and then to sever their connections with the Company.

The acting chief trader ignored both the threat and the request and asked Captain Brown not to give anyone passage without a written note from Blenkinsop.[7] The Company by now had become heartily sick of the miners, who had to be coaxed and petted to stay in the service. Both sides looked forward to the next arrival of the *Beaver* on its regular run so that the dispute could be heard and settled.

Matters did not improve with the arrival of the Company ship. In fact, they became very much worse on June 27th when the *Beaver* set its hook in the harbour. The four deserters who had jumped ship at Fort Victoria assumed that the *Beaver* had come for them. Being by now accustomed to running away from difficult situations, they again slipped over the side and disappeared.

The *Beaver* carried a proclamation warning all against disturbing the peace and asking for special constables to support Dr. Helmcken, who had just been informed five days before that he was the magistrate of Fort Rupert. The ship also brought correspondence relating to the miners' grievances but offering them no satisfactory solution.

---

[7] Captain Brown's word may not have been too reliable. When asked not to sell liquor, he denied having given liquor to anyone, but the new supply could only have come from his ship.

Poor John Helmcken was in over his head, but he agreed to serve as magistrate, reasoning that if anything happened he would be blamed for refusing. He was twenty-six at the time and green as grass. When, supported by Blenkinsop and Captain Dodd, he called a meeting on the evening of June 27th to read the proclamation, he was surprised and alarmed to find that no one, not even the men he had known on the voyage of the *Norman Morison*, would volunteer as a special constable. His inexperience with the law and the lack of books to instruct him left the young doctor without the slightest idea of how to proceed. It cannot have made him feel reassured when the *Beaver* left to continue its regular run up the coast.

The long awaited inquiry, promised for June 29th before this inexperienced and timorous magistrate, was preceeded by a barrage of complaints by the miners, the labourers, and even a group of Kanakas who wanted to take their discharge from the Company in California instead of the Sandwich Islands as their contracts required. The beleaguered Helmcken then cancelled the inquiry, feeling that he could not proceed without the moral support of the ever-absent McNeill and the newly-absent Beardmore, who had been sent to Fort Victoria to report to Douglas. This postponement angered the miners further. They forgot their previous reasonable stance and demanded to leave at once.

Helmcken poured out his woes to his only confidant. He wrote in his diary

Every man had a grievance, for the most manufactured to suit his purpose; nearly the whole had the same story, breach of agreement and not the right kind of provender and beer. Indeed to judge from their tale the agent of the HBC in England had induced them to believe they would emigrate to a land flowing with wine, milk, honey and beer, where they would be nabobs and live like princes. The truth is they all wanted to get to the gold fields of California.

On the evening of July 2nd, six miners, six English labourers, and a blacksmith named Walker left Fort Rupert by canoe. The miners had threatened to leave in ten days and so they did.[8] Andrew Muir described their destination as "some Christian place." Such places were few and far between in this part of the world, and it was a

---

[8] Eden Colvile, whose letters to the Board of Management often seem to miss the point, expressed the opinion that the miners deserted chiefly because of the constant rations of salt provisions. He seemed to be echoing Dr. Benson in his assessment of Scottish miners and things pickled.

measure of their desperation that they set out in a canoe without knowing where they could go and without their wives and families.

That is not to say that they had not provided for their wives and families in their plans. The women first asked Dr. Helmcken for permission to leave on the *England,* but he wished to keep them in the fort as a lure for their husbands' return, so he offered to send them on the *Beaver* when it returned. The return of the *Beaver* had never meant good news for the mining families, so it is not surprising that they refused to wait for it this time. Two days later, on July 6th, they boarded the *England* without Helmcken's permission.

The desertion of the miners meant little to the procuring of coal — the Indians had been the only ones digging coal for several weeks anyway — but no one could replace the blacksmith, whose skill at sharpening tools was sorely missed. The miners' desertion did affect the fort in that it increased the insubordination of the other malcontents. Eleven English labourers and eleven Canadians struck for double pay and other allowances. Eight others left for Fort Victoria.

In the pursuit of "some Christian place," the errant miners had encountered some measure of trouble. Andrew described it as "knocking about in our canoe" and said that by the time they were rescued by some Indians they were very badly off. It was from the Indians, however, that they heard that three or four white men had been murdered.

The murdered men were the sailors who had jumped ship at Fort Victoria and had gone over the side again at Fort Rupert. Since then they had been living on an island outside Beaver Harbour, their presence having been reported by the Indians to Blenkinsop, who supposed them to be the miners.

Blenkinsop sent Old Whale, "a good Quochold Chief well acquainted and friendly with the miners," to retrieve them, promising a reward of blankets for each one returned. The offer of blankets was made through a Canadian interpreter who spoke in French using the expression *per tete* (per head) for "each one." In later years, this sentence was reported to have been "so much per head, dead or alive" and was used as evidence to prove that Blenkinsop had in mind a drastic solution to the problem of the deserting miners.

The Muir family must have looked back on those events often in the years that followed and in an effort to explain things to their own satisfaction may have clung to this interpretation of Blenkinsop's words as evidence of his rancor towards them. Almost thirty years later, Michael Muir would give this interpretation to an historian.

39

Andrew's version of the events was similar, but since he was not actually present when Blenkinsop said the words and since he entered the events in his diary under a date before they happened, one must assume that he wrote in his diary somewhat after the fact and that he and his family had chosen to believe this interpretation.[9]

Old Whale returned to Blenkinsop to say that the men had already left the island, and he was given a present for his trouble. The actual murders seem to have had nothing to do with Blenkinsop's orders, and the fact that they happened when the miners were hiding on one of the islands with the Indians was merely coincidental.

Having been informed that there may have been a murder of three or four white men, Blenkinsop sent an Indian named Jim to investigate. He returned saying the rumour was incorrect, but the rumour persisted.

By then, July 7th, the *England* was loaded and ready to leave, but northwesterly winds and a strong tidal current were making it difficult for the barque to make any headway. In order to proceed north to the tip of Vancouver's Island, the sailing vessel had to tack back and forth as its destination lay in exactly the direction from which the wind was coming. Sailing vessels then did not sail nearly as close to the wind as most modern ones do, with the result that the *England* spent day after day tacking back and forth outside the harbour unable to advance any further north. Each night she would anchor and each morning she would try again.

With the ship unable to proceed, Helmcken decided to paddle a canoe out to it and give the captain a letter to be mailed in San Francisco to Blanshard in Victoria, but he was unable to get near the ship in the choppy sea and strong winds. Taking shelter in a bay, he found a deserter from the fort, and it was there, too, that shortly afterward an Indian interpreter named Linecous found Helmcken. Linecous had been sent by Blenkinsop to tell Helmcken of the murder rumours. Aware that the miners were somewhere in the neighbourhood hiding out, Helmcken gave Linecous a letter to give to any white man that he found, telling them to return to the fort for protection from the murderers. When he paddled into Beaver Harbour with his

[9] Andrew's version under his June 16th entry was:

> Blinkinsop [sic] offered Indians 10 blankets for each of their heads should they bring them back only their heads, was ever such a barbarity heard off [sic], giving these bloodhounds 10 blankets for one white mans head than you should do of taking a meal of Meat, surely these things will not pass without punishment.

prisoner he found the fort in a state of excitement over the arrival of Indians from the north.

The Newittee (Newitty, Nahwitti) were a small group of Kwakiutl Indians resident twenty-five miles to the north at Bull Harbour on what is now called Hope Island. Although civil to whites, they had previously had no connection with Fort Rupert, and it was therefore strange that on July 9th, the Newittee chief, Nancy, happened to be on board the *England* as she rested at anchor from her fight against the oncoming winds and tides. When several of his tribe arrived to say his wife was sick, the chief left the ship.

In the meantime, Linecous had been to the Newittee camp and had seen Andrew Muir, who said all the miners were safe and camping at Shushartie, a location across Goletas Channel and to the south of the Newittee camp. In a note to Helmcken, Andrew said that the Indians were treating them kindly and they would not return to the fort.

One calm morning Helmcken was finally able to deliver letters to the *England* to be mailed in San Francisco for Blanshard and Douglas, informing them of events. In conversation with the Captain, he learned of Nancy's visit and of the Captain's suspicion that the Newittee had brought their chief news of the murders of the sailors, not of his sick wife.

The atmosphere at the fort had, if possible, become more fevered. "[H]ell and earth seemed mingled." There was mutiny within and thousands of excited Indians without. The *England* thrashed back and forth beyond the harbour. The two young men in charge, Blenkinsop and Helmcken, kept watch night and day. Occasionally an Indian appeared at sunset or sunrise and stood for a few minutes on top of the pickets, but the Indians' presence proved a positive one. Keeping "faithful and true to their friendship," they seemed to cow the mutineers and reason gradually returned, not coincidentally about the same time as the *England* finally disappeared.

On its way north the ship picked up the miners and other deserters and continued on its voyage to San Francisco. By July 16th Vancouver Island's first coal miners were gone, taking with them the shame of having broken a contract, the memory of rough and unjust treatment, and the frustration of having found no coal.

With the disappearance of their chief source of liquor, the mutineers left behind in the fort were now sober but still refused to work. Someone in the fort had also sent a letter to Blanshard saying that the men had been murdered because of the reward offered to Old Whale.

John Helmcken had lost his nerve completely and begged to be relieved of his position as Justice of the Peace:

As far as I could, it has been my endeavor to check or remedy complaints; these now grow beyond remedy and probably abandoning the fort shortly will be the cure. I was sent here on account of the miners. They have disappeared; so please allow me to do the same in the *Mary Dare*.

Later in life, Helmcken would call himself a "panicky greenhorn" and say that he should have had more confidence in the Indians. Because his resignation could not take effect until a Company ship arrived and this took two months, he was already a seasoned HBC officer and a much wiser man before he left the fort. The fort, too, had calmed down and life had returned to its dull routine.

It did not take the *England* long to reach San Francisco once it had cleared the Island. On July 20, 1850, Andrew Muir, his brothers, cousins, their wives and families, and the Smiths had reached San Francisco. Captain Brown escorted the party through a town grown dramatically in the two years since he had last seen it. There were one thousand ships in the harbour and people from all over the world. If a steamer could float it was used to get people up the river to Sacramento and the gold fields beyond.

Within three days the miners' party was on its way to Sacramento too, along with all of the *England*'s sailors. The steamboat on which they were travelling sold coal to other boats along the way, and the miners' wives and sisters washed clothes for other passengers. At the end of the run the party hired horses for the remainder of the trip. Bringing up the rear as they headed for the hills was the McGregor family, John and Mary mounted on horses, the three children distributed between and clinging to their parents, old world artisans now itinerant adventurers.

John Muir remained behind at Fort Rupert with the rump of his family and the establishment in turmoil. He was an oversman without men to oversee, a coal miner without coal; the labourers were still in a state of mutiny and the murders were still unsolved.

The Kwakiutls at the fort begged to be allowed to make war on the Newittee, but the offer was refused. British not Indian justice was to prevail. Charles Beardmore had just returned from Fort Victoria and was now sent out to investigate the murders and offer rewards. When Beardmore arrived at the Newittee camp, they denied any part in the murders. Strangely though, they were able to describe the murder site and Beardmore found it four miles from Shushartie.

Upon returning to the fort, Beardmore reported to Helmcken. He described finding two bodies, one shot through the heart and one hidden upright in a hollow tree, both naked. He described how he lay them on the ground and covered them with brush and how the murderers must have been marauding Indians from the north. Helmcken found the bodies as described and had them brought to the fort, where they were buried on July 16, 1850.

Because the letters taken by the *England* to be posted in San Francisco would not reach Fort Victoria for a long time, Blenkinsop sent Beardmore back there by canoe on July 18th carrying copies of the letters, dispatches from Helmcken, the latter's resignation, and Beardmore's account of the murders. Finding that Chief Factor Douglas was at Fort Langley on the mainland, he reported to him there and gave him the correspondence for Governor Blanshard, who was at Fort Victoria. Douglas then sent Beardmore back to Fort Rupert accompanied by Hamilton Moffat, a clerk, and "twelve volunteers and others" to restore peace to Fort Rupert by treating the "mutineers" as prisoners at large and feeding them bread and water until they returned to duty. Moffat also brought new men with him, replacements for those whose contracts had expired.[10]

July became August and August progressed toward September. One day, a distraught Charles Beardmore made a startling confession to Helmcken. The report he had given Helmcken one month before regarding the murders had been false, and he now wished to tell the correct version. His trip to investigate the murders had been a harrowing one it was true, but contrary to what he had told Helmcken, the Newittee had confessed to the killings. When Beardmore had returned to the *England* to request help in identifying the bodies he had been threatened by the brother of one of the dead men who promised to "sail about for twenty years to be revenged." Intimidated by these threats he had decided to tell Helmcken that the sailors had been murdered by Indians living farther north. His motive in lying, he said, had been his desire to tell the correct story first to Douglas or Blanshard in Victoria.

But Governor Blanshard had already acted on the previous false reports he had received from Helmcken. He determined that the sailors had been murdered in response to Blenkinsop's offer of a reward and that British justice must prevail. Recognizing that "though 'the Queen's name is a tower of strength' it is only so when

---

[10] Moffat stayed at Fort Rupert and soon became another McNeill son-in-law.

43

backed by the Queen's bayonets," Blanshard proposed to delay his arrival at Fort Rupert until he could come in a warship.

But all was quiet at Fort Rupert. During that turbulent summer the eight hundred Indians had actually produced seventeen hundred tons of coal. Removing trees and overlaying earth until they hit coal two to five feet below ground, they laboured furiously for one shirt per ton of coal or a two and a half point blanket or the equivalent amount of grey cotton for two tons. John Muir described their industry and perseverance as "truly wonderful and astonishing." Their success had obviously reinforced Muir's optimism, for he told Douglas that the Island had lots of coal. It was unfortunate, however, that it was deep and would be very expensive to dig.

The contract for supplying coal to Mr. Aspinwall had fizzled out. Although the HBC had offered what coal was available at a lower price, the mail company had not found the coal good enough for its needs and had never completed the contract.

The fort remained quiet. The striking miners were gone; the Indians were friendly, cooperative and industrious; and the HBC mutineers had tired of their bread and water diet and had returned to work. There was no need for a warship, but H.M.S. *Daedalus* was on its way. British justice must be done for the murders of the sailors.

The Newittee Indians had identified the three among their tribe who had killed the sailors, and they had explained the extenuating circumstances. While returning from hunting on July 7th, the three had seen three white men in a canoe and had hailed them, thinking they wished to join the miners who were camped at Shushartie. People familiar with the Newittees knew they were always civil to whites, but the three white men in the canoe knew nothing of this. They fled to an Island (possibly Willes Island) with the Indians in pursuit. One of them waved an axe threateningly and another threw a large rock at the Indians' canoe. In reprisal the Indians had killed them all, shooting, stabbing, and then stripping the bodies, sinking one in the ocean and attempting to hide another in a hollow tree.

The Newittee chief offered to pay for the lives of the sailors in blankets or furs as was their custom, but the British navy was there to enforce British justice and demanded the three culprits be handed over. When armed boats full of marines appeared at the village they found it empty. A round of gunnery practice destroyed part of it and then they left. It was late October and not a time to linger in those waters. Dr. Helmcken, too, was anxious to be away and left in December for Fort Victoria where Governor Blanshard needed his

44

medical ministrations.[11] The Indians would have to wait until the following summer to find out what the Royal Navy had in store for them.

With no subterranean coal to be found and no one to dig it even if it was found, there was no reason for John Muir to stay at Fort Rupert. His skills for finding coal, such as they were, could be used elsewhere. First he accompanied an expedition across the Island to Quatsino Sound to investigate Indian reports of coal there, then he moved his wife and son to Victoria and accompanied an expedition to the Fraser River and Burrard Inlet. When Douglas asked him to check southern Vancouver Island for coal he recommended that boring rods then on their way to Fort Rupert be sent instead to Sooke. Douglas was beginning to wonder just how much Mr. Muir knew about geology, noting that "Muir has always appeared to me over sanguine in his statements."

Douglas had not given up on Fort Rupert. During the summer just past, on July 4th to be exact, James Douglas wrote from Fort Victoria to the HBC Board of Management in London asking for replacement miners and an oversman. Given the slowness of communication between Fort Rupert and Fort Victoria, he cannot have known about the miners' desertion just the day before. His request for replacements was based on their ceasing to work rather than their leaving the fort. From a management point of view, it was logical to find new labour to replace men who refused to work; from the miners' point of view, the boss was hiring strikebreakers.

The average British citizen in the 1850's was not particularly interested in the colonies. It would take another thirty or forty years before the glory of the British Empire found a place in the hearts of ordinary people. Notices in papers cannot have excited too much interest if indeed the men qualified for the job even read the papers. But there were factors at work in Scotland that may have helped the recruiter in his task. The coal trade was in a slump, wages had been reduced, and there had been miners' strikes that summer in Scotland, too.

David Landale was again assigned to do the job and was instructed to find men whose occupations included "anything whatever in connection with mining." The Company did not care to become

---

[11] Blanshard had just resigned, having become discouraged at his lack of effectiveness and in disgrace over his handling of the Fort Rupert affair. His resignation did not take effect for another nine months.

embroiled in another argument over job designation. But Landale still considered Scots to be the best choice. He said they were a better class of people and accustomed to doing a longer day's work.

By November, 1850, Landale had found four miners in Kilmarnock, Ayrshire, but his search for an oversman with practical skill and a knowledge of geology had been fruitless. Then on November 27th he had found Boyd Gilmour, "a very good man," a man with a wife and family but not too large a family. The Board of Management wanted men with families of just the right size.

Boyd Gilmour was thirty-five years old that fall. He had married Jean Dunsmore in Ricarton, Ayrshire in 1835. On the birth registration of his second son born in 1838, he was listed as a spirit dealer, but by 1850 he was regarded as a skilled and knowledgeable mine foreman. Archibald Barclay described him as "a respectable and calm man," but the description scarcely described Gilmour at all. Respectable he probably was, calm he was not. James Douglas, who would work with him more closely and for a longer time than Barclay had, would grow as weary of Gilmour as he did of John Muir and as dubious of his knowledge of geology.

One week after his own recruitment, Gilmour wrote to Landale in great distress. Someone had received a letter from Vancouver's Island which said that "Muir's party are all left the Island and two seamen shot by orders of a Mr. Blackendish who has since been hanged." The news had greatly disturbed the miners already recruited and "they think it would be much better to ly [sic] in jail in Scotland than ly in irons in Vancouver." Gilmour demanded of Landale that he inform him if he had had knowledge of the terrible news when he recruited them.

Landale, who had just sent a boatload of machinery and tools to Rupert on the H.M.S. *Tory*, was ignorant of the situation, calling it "a monstrous absurdity." He demanded that he be told the names of Gilmour's informants. Landale was certainly justified in his indignation, for if what Gilmour said was true, then certainly the HBC Board of Management in London knew what had happened and should have informed him.

From his headquarters in Edinburgh, Landale could offer Gilmour no guarantee, but since the party was expected to leave for the New World in just six days there was no time to check with London. Landale told Gilmour he could offer nothing "farther than the agreement which will be signed by the Secretary of the most respectable Company in the Kingdom." Dismissing the rumours he told

Gilmour that if the "silly stories" still haunted the miners' imaginations, they had better deliver the ten pounds they had each been given in advance and "have done with it."

Boyd Gilmour had had his bluff called. Whether he really believed what he had read or was only reporting the fears of the miners, he wrote back to Landale the very next day saying they were "fully determined to go through the undertaking or die in the atemp [sic] however disheartening it may be." Gilmour would demonstrate this flair for the dramatic again but there was a note of desperation in the statement too. For reasons unknown, Gilmour's quick decision to emigrate was a firm one.

As a result of the rumours from Vancouver's Island two of the original recruits withdrew, but two days later, on December 9th, Gilmour could report that he had replaced them with Arthur Queegly, Archibald French, and Robert Dunsmuir. So tight was the schedule for departure that these men had to leave for London immediately, their luggage shipped in the small parcel department instead of being sent on ahead. They had to trust that there would be time before the ship sailed to purchase their supplies in London. As they made their way to Carlisle, just below the Scottish-English border, they were accompanied by David Landale. In his letters to the "secretary of the most respectable company in the Kingdom," he was still asking for confirmation of the rumours regarding the Muirs.

One man in this small group, so unceremoniously whisked away from Scotland, would become fabulously wealthy and famous. Robert Dunsmuir, a man of singular ability and determination, would parlay those traits into a fortune in coal mines, railroads, ships, iron works, and real estate. It is remarkable, then, to realize that he was a last minute addition to the party. The time between his decision to go and his departure was about one week.

He would have been aware that the Company was looking for miners because Boyd Gilmour was his uncle. But Gilmour himself was only recruited in late November, so both men had made very sudden decisions. That they each had wives and young children who accompanied them makes the precipitate decisions even more amazing.

In later years, any account of the Dunsmuir fortune would always begin with the same tight little story about him being the son of coalmasters and having been born in Hurlford and educated in Kilmarnock. The story was always the same and had a ring to it of having been carefully composed and put out for public consumption, the sort of story a famous man tells to explain his origins when he feels it is no business of anyone but himself.

Only one book-length biography of Robert Dunsmuir has been written and that by his great-grandson, James Audain. One would assume that a member of the family would have knowledge of the facts of the man's origins, but even Audain had to rely on the official version. For detail about the family's life in early Fort Rupert and Nanaimo, the great-grandson relied on newspaper and archival sources just like everyone else.[12]

The true story of Robert Dunsmuir's origins has yet to be discovered, but many tantalizing clues and pieces of information have been unearthed. Using the skills of genealogical researchers and the records that still exist in Ayrshire, a somewhat contradictory background for this fascinating historical figure emerges.

The name Dunsmuir seems to be interchangeable with the name "Dunsmore." This was a common occurrence in those times and was probably a result of the two names sounding similar to the clerk who recorded baptisms and marriages and who may have been the only person in a small community able to write.[13] There were several people named Dunsmore in the Kilmarnock area in the mid-nineteenth century including more than one named Robert.

Robert Dunsmuir's death certificate listed Burleith as his birthplace. Burleith was a mine in Riccarton, a town that in the 1850's was more important than Kilmarnock, although today the postions are reversed. Riccarton was on the main stagecoach route. Hurlford, often quoted as the official birthplace, was a small village with a mine nearby, situated one and a quarter miles east of Kilmarnock. All these mines and towns are close together and are useful here only to try to differentiate individuals.

By analyzing the names of Robert's children, genealogists have theorized that his parents' names were James and Elizabeth Hamilton Dunsmore, both of whom died in their late twenties within five days of one another in 1832 in Burleith. They had two daughters born in 1829

---

[12] This book *From Coalmine to Castle* by James Audain was the subject of litigation and has since been removed from public access.

[13] That the practice of using the two names interchangeably was common is illustrated in a report written by Reverend Thomas Crosby, a Methodist missionary who stopped in Departure Bay long enough to baptise the daughter of the local mine owner, James "Dunsmore" (Robert's eldest son).

and 1832 who also died in the same year as their parents. There is no record of a son having been born. Dunsmuir's official birth year was 1825, which would have made him seven years old in 1832. At least one researcher says he was orphaned at that age.

There is a birth certificate in existence for a Robert Dunsmore, born January 20, 1828. The parents are listed as Allan and Agnes Grant Dunsmore from Riccarton and Kilmarnock respectively. It seems likely, however, that these two people were Dunsmuir's aunt and uncle, which would make the younger Robert his cousin. Speculation on the relationship of the two families runs from Dunsmuir's having been born illegitimate (therefore not being registered as James and Elizabeth's son) to his having lived with his aunt and uncle.

It is a fact that Boyd Gilmour was also Robert Dunsmuir's uncle. Gilmour's wife was Jean Dunsmore, who was probably the daughter of Robert and Jean Kirkland Dunsmore, the parents of the James who married Elizabeth Hamilton. Gilmour was Dunsmuir's guardian when the latter became apprenticed to the former in 1841, so it is possible that after the death of his mother, Dunsmuir was raised by the Gilmours.

The most important missing information is of course Robert's birth certificate. It alone can settle the matter forever. Without the birth certificate, we can only speculate as to why it has not been found. That speculation is enhanced by the desire of many to understand both what motivated Robert Dunsmuir to leave Scotland and the origin of his determination and skill. If he was the son of James and Elizabeth Hamilton Dunsmore (and these are in fact the names of his eldest son and daughter) then he also was the son and grandson of coalmasters as his official biography always stated.

Coalmasters were mine managers who worked for the owner of the coal fields, usually an aristocrat upon whose lands the coal had been discovered. Such a position of authority, while not lofty in the scheme of things in nineteenth century Britain, should certainly have guaranteed Dunsmuir security if he had stayed in Scotland. This only serves to make his reasons for leaving so precipitously even more tantalizing.

The young woman who was his wife and upon whose iron will much of his success depended was baptised Joanna Oliver White, the first child of Alexander and Agnes Crooks White of Kilmarnock. She had married Robert in 1847 when she was nineteen and by the time they left Scotland had already borne him two little girls, Elizabeth Hamilton and Agnes Crooks Dunsmuir. By that time she had chosen to call herself Joan Olive Dunsmuir. When the ship *Pekin* left England

49

with the hurriedly assembled group of Scottish miners, Joan was pregnant with her third child.

Also enroute to Vancouver's Island, having left somewhat earlier, was H.M.S. *Tory*, bringing twenty-five "practical men" to Fort Rupert. The designation "practical miner" was a term applied to experienced mine men, but whether these passengers were in fact miners is not known. The ship bound for Fort Rupert was carrying mining equipment valued at one thousand pounds, including drilling rods and a steam engine. To make sure the engine was well tended, engineer Andrew Hunter had been recruited in July of 1850 at the request of John Muir, who had worked with him and knew him to be a "hard working industrious mechanick."

Hunter brought with him his wife and five children, rather more than the Company usually cared to bring. In fact, Hunter's main concern during the recruiting process had been his children and who would pay for their fare and meals. It speaks well for his skills that the Company was prepared to allow him more travelling money and somewhat grudgingly agreed to employ his eldest son. However, the Company refused to be committed regarding the son's wages; that was left for the officials at Fort Rupert to decide.

While most of the civilized world looked to England and its wonderful Great Exhibition in May of 1851, the Hunter party arrived at Fort Rupert on the other side of the world to find no coal mining activity and indeed no coal miners. Hunter was put to work clearing Muir's pit in preparation for Gilmour's arrival and determining a location for the engine. With the assistance of "eight steady Orkney men," he began boring in the shaft using the rods brought over on the *Tory*. Whatever spare time he had was taken up with blacksmithing, for which he received extra pay. The steam engine sat idle.

Fort Rupert had continued to receive its usual complement of employees as old contracts expired and new ones began. Edward Walker had arrived there in late 1850, having joined the Company fresh from four years in the British navy. His six-month voyage on the *Pelican*, described as "not the swiftest nor by any means the safest boat in the world," had ended abruptly at the Columbia River; from there another boat had to take him to Fort Rupert. He was twenty-five and a jack-of-all-trades who added coal mining to his list of accomplishments soon after his arrival. He was there to greet the Gilmour party when they arrived in August of 1851.

The Gilmours and the Dunsmuirs had encountered problems at the Columbia River as well. The *Pekin* had run aground on the sandbars at the mouth of this mighty river where it reaches the sea in the Oregon Territory. Although miner Arthur Queegly, blacksmith William Preston, and the *Pekin* crew all deserted, the ship's cargo was removed to the *Mary Dare* by local Indians and the HBC factor Peter Skeen Ogden, and the travellers were able to continue on up the Columbia to Fort Vancouver. Here in June of 1851, Jean Gilmour gave birth to a son, Allan Columbia, and in July her niece by marriage, Joan Dunsmuir, bore her first son, James.[14] The miners' party stayed at Fort Vancouver until September when the *Mary Dare* took them directly to Fort Rupert.

It had not been an entirely uneventful summer while Fort Rupert waited for the new miners. In response to a request by Governor Blanshard for further action against the Newittees, Rear-Admiral Hornby sent Rear-Admiral Fairfax Moresby to investigate on the H.M.S. *Daphne*, Captain Fanshawe in command. In July of 1851, the *Daphne* anchored in Beaver Harbour and sent boats on up the coast to seize the murderers. When gunfire from the shore wounded some sailors, sixty British marines attacked the Newittee village. The Indians disappeared into the woods. At day's end a burned village, twenty destroyed canoes, and several dead men, both British and Indian, gave mute testimony to the determination of both sides, but it was not until the *Daphne* left that the Newittee decided that the murderers had become more trouble than they were worth.

With a reward of thirty blankets each for their capture as added incentive, the Newittee turned against the three. In the attempt to bring them in, two were shot and one escaped. Not to be deterred by the lack of one body, the Newittee killed a slave to be used as a substitute, and three corpses were presented to the authorities at the fort. In true white-man fashion, the reward came not in the actual blankets but in a letter issued by Blenkinsop to Blanshard in Fort Victoria.

The Newittee murders destroyed Blanshard's career. Both he and the navy were rebuked for misuse of authority and vessels. By then, the British press had spread the details of the murders throughout Britain, making Fort Rupert seem a very undesirable destination for immigrants. The press reports came too late to deter the Gilmour party, however, for they were already enroute to the notorious

---

[14] It has only recently been discovered that Jean Gilmour was on the voyage. Genealogist Brian J. Porter reported that the Gilmours had baptised two children when they returned to Scotland, one born at the mouth of the Columbia River and the other in Victoria.

outpost, which by late summer 1851 was again peaceful and still without a significant coal discovery.

Eager to set to work, Gilmour proceeded to sink test pits but did not find a single seam worth developing. He became highly skeptical of Muir's knowledge of mining and expressed his skepticism in letters to Alexander Barclay, causing the Company secretary to wonder whether Muir was "entirely ignorant of the true indications of coal or ha[d] been deceiving the Company with his misrepresentations."

The Company's disillusionment with Muir had grown since his sons' desertions, especially when in May of 1851 Muir had refused to return to Fort Rupert without other miners. Since the only miners in the Colony at the time were his sons and nephews who had by then returned from California, Douglas had asked them to re-enter the HBC service. The errant miners were so convinced of their own innocence, claiming that they had only gone to California to seek justice, that they demanded wages for the nine months they were absent and half a crown extra pay for the time they were employed in shanking the pit at Fort Rupert. Since Douglas refused to give in to their demands and Muir would not return to the fort without them, the Chief Factor and the stubborn oversman agreed to Muir's being discharged from the service. He was to keep himself available if his services were needed anytime prior to the end of his contract. Off he went to Sooke where he leased a sawmill and put mining behind him for a time.

It only took a few days for Boyd Gilmour to dismiss Muir's shaft near the fort. He determined to bore for coal at Suquash, where the Indians had been so successful digging surface coal. There Boyd Gilmour, Robert Dunsmuir, Edward Walker, and others up to a total of about twenty people continued the search for coal all through that fall and winter. During that time as well the group was plagued by desertions both of miners and other Company servants.

Life was somewhat more civilized at Fort Rupert by then. Acreage had been cleared for a garden where planting various types of greens and potatoes had yielded good crops. This fresh produce was highly prized because provisions of all kinds and especially fresh ones had been scarce and expensive since the founding of the Colony. In March of 1852 it was still necessary to import flour and salt meats. Indians of course supplied all the fresh meat, earning themselves rewards in the only currency then available: blankets, cotton, tobacco, and beads.

To say that life had become more civilized, it is necessary to realize that two cultures lived side by side, each with its own definition of what it was to be civilized. Offense was usually caused by the whites and made worse by the Indians' taking it as an insult against the whole tribe. The outward manifestations of these differences and rumours of cannibalism struck fear in the hearts of uninitiated whites, but with knowledge came the realization that the Indians were mostly trustworthy and good neighbours. As Helmcken had said,

... among these people we walked and roamed and certainly, after having become accustomed to them felt less fear of molestation than I had often experienced when traversing the slums of London.

Recreation was of the homemade variety. Target shooting was popular although all the prizes went to certain Company servants who had been poachers in England. The arrival of some horses and cattle fascinated the Indians, who squatted on the beach to watch and applaud as some of the Kanakas fashioned rope bridles and mounted the horses. Some Indians ran away in terror when the riders galloped the horses straight towards the spectators.

It was not a place to give joy to the heart of a white woman, especially a young woman with small children. The only medicines available were peppermint, Turlington's balsam, jalap, salts, emetics, and Seidlitz powders.[15] The Indians demonstrated their different cultural values by once kidnapping baby James Dunsmuir for several hours. When the baby was found, his benevolent captors attempted to buy him from his frantic parents for sea-otter skins piled "to the height of a man," a handsome price indeed. Andrew Hunter's daughter Agnes was stunned when a returning raiding party tossed a bloody head at her feet as she walked on the beach.

Many of the Canadian and Kanaka company servants were married to Indian women from northern tribes. They had apparently made an admirable adjustment to their lives between the two cultures. Dressed in more or less European fashion, plump and comparatively fair by European standards, they had much to teach the white women by example as they sewed, made soap, prepared and tanned leather, washed, ironed, and mended. However, their admirable behaviour was not always rewarded with the respect of the Company officials, who never referred to them in official reports by their proper names.

[15] Balsam was a soothing aromatic resin called the "Universal Panacea" because it was used for cuts, wounds, coughs, colds and so on; jalap was a dried root used as a purgative; Seidlitz powder was a laxative named after a natural water with the same properties at Seidlitz (now in Czechoslovakia) and commonly used well into the twentieth century.

The white women were always called "Mrs.," the Indian women, "so-and-so's wife."

The boreholes at Suquash were yielding no more coal than Muir's shaft at the fort. Gilmour tried boring in every likely location. He bored directly behind the fort, and again further inland, where he was stopped by quicksand. Another attempt southwest of the fort was stopped at thirty fathoms; then he tried ten miles along the seacoast. Often the bores passed through coal seams but none was wider than six inches, an amount too narrow to mine successfully. Nearly all the boreholes ended when they reached whinstone. By late spring of 1852, Gilmour's patience was growing thin.

At the same time, his similarly unsuccessful predecessor had been summoned to Fort Victoria from Sooke. James Douglas had received Gilmour's journal and wished Muir to go over it with him. It was June of 1852 and Douglas was already aware that there might be coal in Nanaimo. He needed an expert to assess the chances of ever finding coal at the north end of the Island, and Muir was the best he had.

Whereas Gilmour had worked on the basis that whinstone was the bottom of any possible deposit, Muir insisted that it was merely a dyke intersecting the coal bed and that coal could well be found beneath it. But by July Douglas was prepared to believe Gilmour when he said that the indications for coal were very unfavorable. Gilmour had continued to sink bores, some through the whinstone even though they could only advance ten inches daily into its hard blue surface; north of the fort, south of the fort, inland, on the coast he drilled, and though there were plenty of surface beds, he never found the elusive mineral underground.[16]

In that same summer, the Indians stopped digging coal on the surface. It was by now necessary to dig down ten feet, and they were unwilling to go that deep. Gilmour continued to search until October

---

[16] Throughout the 1860's, various reports of fine coal seams at Fort Rupert reached Victoria and Nanaimo: an eight foot outcropping in 1861; six seams of coal found between McNeill harbour and Fort Rupert in 1864; the North Pacific Coal Company employing five men digging in a twenty inch seam sending forty tons of coal out by schooner in 1865; the Saaquash Coal Mine needing more workmen in 1868 to dig coal "superior to Nanaimo." Always the coal was superior and the seam bigger but the mines never lasted. The HBC, which had maintained the fort as a fur and salmon trading and missionary centre, made another unsuccessful attempt to mine there in 1875. In 1894, an English company found a five foot seam. The Pacific Coast Coal Mining Company found six feet of coal in 1908 and opened a mine of respectable size which was worked until 1915. In 1920 work resumed until the Company was liquidated in 1926. In 1952 Suquash Collieries Ltd. acquired the licenses but little mining occurred.

1852. His efforts included making a trip to Quatsino as Muir had done the year before and an experiment with cutting lines through the forest, which he hoped would enable him to examine the geological features of the area. This labour intensive but fruitless exercise was the last effort of a frustrated man who soon applied for a transfer and was sent to Nanaimo, where interesting things were happening and where he would confront his critic, John Muir, now back in Company service and in full control there.

Although Gilmour left Fort Rupert in December of 1852 taking four miners with him, the mining operation was not officially abandoned for a few months yet. Andrew Hunter stayed on another month waiting for the H.M.S. *Discovery* to transfer the virgin steam engine to Nanaimo. Edward Walker broke his leg in four places and was confined to bed for six months. He and Robert Dunsmuir did not arrive in Nanaimo until April of 1853. Whether Dunsmuir waited for his friend's leg to heal or whether their mutual arrival was a coincidence, Walker would be a friend to Dunsmuir for life, never in a position of power but always ready to move on to the next adventure and do what he could to make it work.

John Muir had returned to HBC favour and was in charge of the successful Nanaimo venture. His son Robert and nephew Archibald were with him. The rest of the family were in Sooke, having taken up land in that community near Fort Victoria. John McGregor joined his uncle in Nanaimo, where his own fiery personality and expertise would make him a man to be reckoned with.

Andrew Muir did not go back to mining. He turned his ebullience and righteous indignation to tending a piece of land in Sooke. Not long after his return from the gold fields, he and his brother John, Jr. had hatched up a scheme to bring out settlers from Scotland, including women of good character, presumably to provide much needed brides. Whether the scheme succeeded or not, he did marry a lady named Isabella Weir and supported her by becoming a Sheriff of Vancouver's Island, an ironic career choice for a man who spent part of his first year on the Island in jail. One day in January 1859, he was discovered dead at his office on the corner of Yates and Government Streets in Victoria. He was only thirty-two years old. The adventure would continue without him and the dream would belong to someone else.

CHAPTER II

STOUT, ABLE AND HEARTY YOUNG MEN

The coal is easily got at and might be advantageously worked if they would lay out a few dollars and cents upon it. But that is not the way the Hudson's Bay Company go to work; for a small outlay they expect large returns; a great mistake in the coal trade at any rate.

The British Colonist

[Miners are] by no means an industrious set of men, and seldom deliver more than a single ton of coal per diem... The oversman assures me that he has seen them dig two tons of coal between 7 and 10 o'clock in the morning and do nothing more for the rest of the day, which was spent in idleness, as we have no further claims on their time.

James Douglas, Chief Factor

By May of 1853, the least dissatisfied men in Nanaimo were Iroquois and French-Canadian axemen, Company servants living the life they had chosen. Their services were in demand and their finely honed skill with axe and adze much appreciated. Most of the rest of the inhabitants of this newest fort on the coast were apprehensive, discontented, or just plain uncomfortable.

Joseph McKay was a Company servant too, and the Company was better for it. Twenty-four years old and able beyond his years, he had been a Company man all his life. But now he was required to be clerk-in-charge of a coal mining operation, and that was something he knew nothing about.

Dr. George Johnstone knew something about medicine, but he had been unhappy ever since he arrived. The clerk surgeon lived reluctantly on his sailboat anchored in the harbour and practiced medicine uncomfortably on shore in a building with a leaky roof.

Andrew Hunter was on Vancouver Island by choice but still had not been given a chance to do what he did best. He was a steam mechanic in the days when that put him at the forefront of technology, yet the steam engine he had tended since leaving England in 1850 had yet to do a stroke of work. Now he had brought it to Nanaimo and still it sat idle.

Raymond, the blacksmith, knew how important he was to the operation of the fort, but he had forgotten his "toe iron" and was unhappy with the bellows. He had been told to give priority to work needed by the miners, but everyone needed Raymond, and a man could do just so much work in a day.

Robert and Archibald Muir, John McGregor, Robert Dunsmuir, and Archibald French comprised the entire force of properly trained miners. The number was miniscule and would generally be so for years to come. With such a dearth of skilled hands, the establishment was dependent on assistants, Company servants who worked alongside the miners and learned from them. They learned to mine, they learned their worth, and they learned to make demands for better pay and better hours.

McKay could not understand their attitude. Although they only got half the pay of the miners, they received equal bed and board and medical attention, and if they satisfied the oversman, they could be promoted. The regular miners impressed McKay even less. Because the coal was in demand they felt they should be paid more than the two shillings sixpence a ton agreed to in their contracts.

Oversmen for this motley crew were Boyd Gilmour and John Muir. Neither had been very successful in finding coal, and the fact that they did not like each other was making an uncomfortable situation intolerable. In addition, Muir had the Lowland Scot's aversion to "hillsmen" or Highlanders, a prejudice which included Orcadians, a species of Scot much favoured by the Company and in abundant supply in Nanaimo. When ship captains complained of the coal being dirty and containing shale and other incombustible materials, Muir blamed the problems on "the carelessness of the hillsmen."

This unhappy collection of human beings, numbering thirty-seven altogether, found itself in a small but growing collection of rough-hewn log buildings on the shore of a harbour protected by two islands, the larger one named Newcastle, the smaller one named Protection. The islands and the harbour sat upon an enormous body of coal. Joseph McKay had been the first white man to see evidence of this treasure just four years before.

Like the Kwakiutl up north, the local Coast Salish tribe knew the black rock existed; loose pieces lay on the beaches of the harbour. As the Snenymos made their migratory round each year, fishing in the spring at False Narrows, in the summer on the Fraser River, and in the fall from their villages on the Nanaimo River, and passing the winter months on the shores of Departure Bay, they were aware of the outcroppings of coal. But except for its use as a dye or for making jewellery, it was unimportant to them. It seemed to be important to the white men. They brought it all the way from the other side of the world in big ships so their blacksmith could make a hot fire with it. The black rock burned and made it possible for the smithy to make tools and fix guns. Che-wich-i-kan, an Indian from Nanaimo Bay, had a good look at some one day in 1849 when he was in Fort Victoria getting his gun fixed. He told the blacksmith that there was a lot of this rock lying around the beaches where he lived. The blacksmith got all excited and called for Joseph McKay, at that time a twenty year old clerk.

With the offer of a bottle of rum and a free gun repair if he brought back some of the black rock, the Indian paddled back to his home up Island. It was December and a bad time to be out on the water so he did not return immediately. Then sickness prevented him from returning until spring, but when he did he came with a canoe loaded with coal. He had spoken the truth.

In that spring of 1850, the Hudson's Bay Company (HBC) had been in the coal mining business at Fort Rupert for eight months. No coal had been found below the surface, and the miners were already making a lot of trouble. But that did not deter Joseph McKay from fitting out a prospecting party and proceeding at once to the harbour where Che-wich-i-kan lived. Eight days later, on May 8, 1850, they discovered the first of three Nanaimo coal seams and named it the Douglas seam in honour of James Douglas. Fifty-three years later at a Royal Commission hearing, an Indian named Dick Whoahkum remembered that day and said that when McKay saw it, he "started dancing on top of the coal for joy."

As joyful as McKay was, he was in no hurry to dig the coal. The Company still had nine years to run on the grant giving them exclusive rights to the territory, and they were sure to find coal any day at Fort Rupert. So the discovery was duly noted, Che-wich-i-kan got his bottle of rum and his gun repaired, and the Indians went back to fishing.

By that summer the Indians at Fort Rupert had already had their rights to the coal usurped. Acting on orders from London, James Douglas proceeded with no specific guidelines save that the natives were to be considered the rightful possessors of the land only if it were cultivated. "All other land is to be considered as waste and applicable to the purpose of colonization."

The arrogance of this assumption was probably lost on the Indians. Their concept of land use was entirely different from that of the Company. If someone needed to use the land it was theirs until such time as they no longer needed it; then it was everybody's again. The treaties that were signed between the various tribes of West Coast Indians and the HBC were meaningless to the original inhabitants. In February of 1851, the Kwakiutl were given lands between McNeill's Harbour and Hardy Bay and two miles inland. Although they were allowed to keep their village sites and enclosed fields, they relinquished their rights to areas that included coal. For all this they received 150 pounds sterling in trade goods. This was the first of fourteen treaties negotiated by James Douglas. The last one was with the Nanaimo Indians.

By then the Indians knew the value of the coal to the white men and expected to be compensated for it. Knowing this, Douglas was very careful as he began negotiations to "extinguish Indian title to the Nanaimo coal district." The peace loving Snenymos bargained hard before a treaty was finally concluded on December 23, 1854. The land from Commercial Inlet to twelve miles up the Nanaimo River was purchased for the British Crown. Five months later the HBC bought six thousand acres of that land from the Crown for one pound sterling per acre.

Although the Company was not ready to exploit the Nanaimo coalfield in the summer of 1850, the whole perspective had changed two years later. In May of 1852, McKay reinvestigated the Nanaimo coal beds; in August James Douglas inspected them for himself. Coal was found in three places, the last of which was a seam fifty-seven and three quarter inches thick — clean coal which rose above the surface of the water in a narrow cove which came to be called Commercial Inlet. From the Indians who had recently begun to work the coal they were able to obtain fifty tons in just one day.

Quickly realizing their value as labourers, the Indians made extravagant demands, but became well satisfied when they found that a day's work could earn them a shirt. Working on a cash and carry basis they received tickets which they could then exchange for small trade items such as powder and shot, gunflints, clay pipes, vermilion, bunches of large beads, tobacco, molasses, rough cotton, shirts, soap, barrel salmon, brass thimbles, and finger rings. Those with the will could also save up for blankets which cost eight barrels of coal each.

Having returned from California and settled briefly in Sooke, Robert and Archibald Muir were welcomed back into the HBC fold when they arrived at Nanaimo with John Muir on September 6th and were commissioned to open a shaft at the high water mark. To assist them and to protect them against the natives, they were sent a few French-Canadians and Kanakas. Among the many lessons the Company had learned from the Fort Rupert experience had been the importance of protecting the miners and of making them answerable only to the oversmen, not to the clerk-in-charge.

September came in unusually wet, emphasizing the dark and damp of the log huts where they lived, the walls and roofs lined and covered with cedar bark. But the coal was easy to find. Just ten yards beyond where the Indians had been working, the Scottish miners reached coal seven feet below the surface. The first shipment, 480 barrels, was loaded onto the H.M.S. *Cadboro* on September 10, 1852.

Included in that first party was Joseph Despard Pemberton, a surveyor for the HBC. With his assistant B. W. Pearce, he chose to camp separately from the others just where a "small rivulet" called Millstone Creek flowed into the harbour.[1] As was fitting, the area became known as Pemberton's Encampment. Here too, a thick bed of coal was discovered, this time in a steep bluff which hid the camp from the buildings of the new fort.

Muir said all the coal was good, the equal of English coal. Muir had been wrong before, but this time it seemed as though he knew what he was talking about. The Indians were getting such large amounts of coal out that there was an urgent call for more trade goods.

After the fruitless search at Fort Rupert it all seemed too good to be true. There were so many promising places to dig coal. Muir began another shaft one hundred yards further into Commercial Inlet, eight feet from the edge of the bank at the location where Che-wich-i-kan, who had now been dubbed "Coal Tyee," had found the first coal. The new mine was HBC Number One Shaft. With such success it did not take long for the Company to encounter a labour supply problem. There was just too much happening with too few men to go around. Muir required two steady men to work the winch. He would not use Indian labour for the job as they were likely to stop work without

---

[1] It would be more accurate to call the "rivulet" a river. It is sometimes referred to as "The Millstream."

warning, especially when possible enemies paddled into the harbour.

But even the white miners were unreliable. Boyd Gilmour, who had arrived from Fort Rupert in December, 1852, had not been in Nanaimo two months before he was quarrelling with the men under him. When James Douglas arrived on a tour of inspection in January of 1853, he was greeted by striking miners. "They brought forward a long string of petty complaints, which I disposed of in a very summary matter, and soon brought them to their senses."

Douglas was able to influence the men where Muir and Gilmour were not. With his air of dignity and his imposing presence, the Chief Factor could don a hard wooden face when necessary and was described as "grand," "majestic," "noble," and "of Cromwellian order of mind." He had proven capable of dealing with troublesome Indians by meting out severe but just punishment according to the white man's laws. If he could deal with troublemakers from another culture he certainly could deal with ones from his own.

Douglas had arrived in Nanaimo fresh from having pursued the Indian murderers of a Fort Victoria shepherd named Peter Brown. The trail, which had led first to the Cowichan Indians, ended south of Nanaimo near a small river, which was named Chase River for the unsuccessful bid by one of the culprits to evade the British marines who accompanied Douglas. Both murderers were quickly tried and hung on Gallows Point on Protection Island in Nanaimo harbour.

Douglas' decisiveness was needed again in June when he perceived a "general combination among the Miners to do as little for their pay as the law allows and as the overmen are making no extra pay they are equally inert." Joseph McKay, in charge of the Fort but not the miners, was very discouraged.

We have here 2 oversmen whose sole duty is to superintend 5 miners and half a dozen labourers and though a very small task is expected from these worthies, who have a magnificent field of coal to work on, they cannot succeed in delivering even that small quantity in a marketable state.

John Muir and Boyd Gilmour were probably quite capable overs-men,[2] and had they stayed at home in Scotland would have performed effectively. They were not, however, suited to the job they had been hired to do on Vancouver Island. Pemberton observed that the two men needed to work under direction and that someone else was needed to plan the digging and to survey the layout of levels and

---

[2] "Overman" and "oversman" are used interchangeably.

shafts. As their inadequacies as developmental colliers and geologists and their inability to deal with labour became apparent, so did their rivalry, a rivalry that had developed even before they met face to face. Now with both of them sharing the responsibility for finding and developing coal seams in Nanaimo, the rivalry became intense.

Gilmour's lack of success as a geologist had followed him to Nanaimo. He was assigned to the northwest corner of Newcastle Island where he unsuccessfully sank a shaft, then a borehole, and then gave up when he struck conglomerate rock which he took to be the floor of the seam. One month later, aided by the discovery of coal at Pemberton's Encampment and by the presence of loose coal on the beach, Joseph McKay found the seam that had eluded Gilmour.

Much discouraged, Gilmour made a special trip to Fort Victoria to ask permission to investigate a newly discovered outcrop at Flea Point, south of Nanaimo. The outcrop had been found accidentally by McKay and Pemberton during an afternoon's stroll. The seam was eight hundred yards from the coast in a steep bank twenty feet above the level of a stream; it was fifty-four inches thick. Despite the richness of the discovery, nothing was done to develop it until the 1880's, and, by May, Gilmour was exploring for coal at the head of Commercial Inlet. Douglas commented dryly:

Mr. Gilmour does not appear to be very successful in his researches for Coal and moreover appears much dissatisfied with his lodgings, and his treatment generally, as he evidently considers himself slighted, a circumstance which I much regret...[3]

Boyd Gilmour had started with so much enthusiasm but had met with so little success. To compound his feelings of discontent, he was living without his wife, for although she had accompanied him to Fort Rupert, she had gone to Victoria rather than live in Nanaimo. Her husband shared one of the small log houses with his nephew, Robert Dunsmuir, Robert's wife Joan, and their growing family.

June of 1853 was a turning-point for Gilmour as his exploratory work at the head of Commercial Inlet yielded fruit. Within three years, Gilmour's "level-free" would be worked as two small mines. The one developed by his nephew Robert came to be known as Dunsmuir's Level-Free and the other was called Park Head Mine.

[3] Douglas urged McKay to give Gilmour "no cause for complaint" and later to make a special effort to get him a small amount of wine even though there was none available for sale.

Ten years later the same location would be the site of a much larger mine called Douglas Pit, the first major producer on the Island and the gateway to a bonanza in coal that would last into the twentieth century.

Gilmour's animosity towards Muir was as strong as ever. While Muir was absent in Sooke on sick leave, Gilmour spread the rumour that Muir was attempting to engage HBC servants to assist his sons Andrew and John, Jr., who had remained in Sooke. John Muir was fifty years old that summer. In those times and in that place he was considered an old man. This did not prevent him, while on sick leave, from walking to Fort Victoria from Sooke to confront James Douglas on several occasions and to interfere *in absentia* with a number of Gilmour's decisions.[4]

Muir was absent in Sooke. Gilmour had been successful in finding coal. Now work in the Nanaimo mines began to proceed more smoothly. Despite the occasional problem with laziness and insolence among the assistant miners, production was increasing. By the fall of 1853, some miners were producing up to two tons a day.

James Douglas was delighted. After a visit to Nanaimo with the usual pomp accorded by HBC posts to a visiting Chief Factor, he reported that a "prodigious amount of work, for the hands employed has been accomplished here; the place has quite the appearance of a little village." Douglas' enthusiasm was tempered by Pemberton's observation that someone was needed to plan the digging and to survey the layout of levels and shafts. With each oversman working separately under a Company official who knew nothing of coal mining, development was uncoordinated and haphazard.

Right in the middle of the little village, on the shore of the inlet that almost encircled the townsite, sat the surface buildings of HBC Number One Shaft with a square chimney of quarried stone, built by Orcadian William Isbister, and a low square-hewn log building which housed the hoisting gear and the steam boiler. A pithead frame built by an expert carpenter because "great niceity [is] required in taking the measurements and fitting the Joints," supported Andrew Hunter's steam engine.

Ever since he had personally squired the steam engine from Britain

---

4 When Muir's contract expired in 1854, he moved permanently to Sooke where he set up a steam logging and sawing operation with his sons. Later he was elected to the first colonial legislature. Even there his leadership abilities were in question. He was described by his fellow legislator, Dr. Helmcken, as "one of the led . . . who said Aye or Nay when present."

to Fort Rupert in 1851, Hunter had been anxious to see it put to work. The time finally came after the engine arrived in Nanaimo escorted by the faithful engineer in May of 1853. It was then that Boyd Gilmour suggested that it be used to pump water out of HBC Number One Shaft. Once the proper frame was built and the corroded parts were cleaned, the engine was ready for use in the late summer of 1853.

It was with a great deal of ceremony that Hunter's beloved engine, now dubbed the "Lady McKay," was finally started in the presence of James Douglas and his wife. Miners, labourers, and hundreds of Indians came to see the miraculous machine pump water out of the mine. The industrial age had arrived in Nanaimo.

In Britain the coal industry had existed on a small scale for hundreds of years before the needs of the industrial revolution turned it into a large and efficient supplier of fuel. The first pits were shallow, ventilated by nature and good luck, and used primitive tools and methods for loosening the coal. It was impossible to dig deep pits because no technology existed to ventilate or drain them of water, and the coal could not be lifted to the surface. Nor was there a need for deep pits, there being enough coal available close to the surface to supply all the marketplace demands.

When the development of iron smelting and railways dramatically increased the uses for coal, methods had to be invented to allow the mines to go deeper. Thus timbering to support tunnels, ventilating furnaces to provide a surer flow of air, horse-driven gins to pull out water and coal, canal systems to supply transportation to markets, and even such basic elements as tracks for underground cars had to be perfected.

The first twenty or thirty years of mining on Vancouver Island saw the industrial revolution in microcosm. The shallow pits of the Indians at Fort Rupert and on Newcastle Island gave way in 1852 to the shafts of HBC Number One and later HBC Number Two and the tunnels of the Newcastle and Pemberton mines. The adzes and axes of Indian and Ayrshireman alike were soon replaced with the picks and shovels of the mining trade and years later by steam driven cutting machinery. The natural flow of air alone ventilated those small mines until a furnace was built in HBC Number One in 1853; the furnace supplied air until steam jets and later steam driven fans arrived.

Coal was first loaded "with Klootchman and a potato basket," as the Colonist put it, but by the end of the 1850's there were wharves for large ships to come alongside, and by 1880 there was a sophisticated mechanized loading system in place. Potato baskets were replaced first by "skiveys" or "Hurley's," whose bodies were made of cedar twigs which were heated, bent between pine stubs, and driven into auger holes made in the frames or bolted on to wheel axles. The skiveys moved along the tramway from the mine to a weighing platform and then to a knapsack in which up to sixty pounds of coal was carried on the shoulders of an Indian woman to a canoe. The canoe was paddled to a waiting ship where the coal was hauled up in small woven baskets hand over hand and stored in barrels. Later in the decade, the canoes were paddled to small barges or lighters which were tied to the large ship. In turn skiveys were replaced by a streamlined and substantial car strong enough to withstand the rigours of a mechanized haulage system.

Horses, the engines of the pre-industrial age, were used in Nanaimo mines very early. At first they were employed at the mine entrance as the power source for the gin which pulled up the refuse rock, the water, and the skiveys full of coal. As the mines grew larger and their gateroads could accommodate an animal below ground, mules and horses pulled the coal from the face to shaft bottom where in some mines the animals also lived.

The method by which a miner lighted his work was an emotional issue, charged as it was with the difference between life and death. In order to dig coal and earn a living a man had to see what he was doing. Naked flame, whether from a candle, which was used in Britain until the end of the nineteenth century, or from a fish oil lamp, the light of choice on Vancouver Island, could cause an explosion in the presence of methane gas.

Sir Humphrey Davy had addressed the problem of naked flame lamps in 1815 when he discovered the qualities of wire gauze. Since that date it had been possible to supply miners with a lamp that would give light and not cause explosions. But despite the development of hundreds of different models, all based on the original principles of Davy's lamp, no one was ever able to make a safety lamp that gave enough light to satisfy the working miner. Even in the Black Country mines of Staffordshire in the 1850's, in mines which had a lot of firedamp and only primitive ventilation, miners were reluctant to use the Davy lamp despite its availability in the area since 1817. As one observer noted, "the colliers believed in the lamp but preferred the candle."

The early shallow mines of the Nanaimo coalfield did not have the "least possible trace of firedamp," so the use of the Davy lamp was deemed unnecessary. It is likely that the first English miners in

Nanaimo were accustomed to candles, but the Scottish miners were used to oil lamps, and since the Scots were the first miners to arrive it is likely that their preference prevailed. In fact, a shortage of fish oil, which was extracted by the Indians from cod livers, nearly closed down the mines in 1853.

The first lamps made by the blacksmith drew complaints from the miners because the spout was only half the height of the lamp. This caused it to waste more oil than it burned and allowed the fishy extract to run down the forehead of the wearer. The Kilmarnock Lamp came to the rescue.

A tinsmith at Fort Victoria was instructed to copy a lamp sent down by Joseph McKay. It very likely belonged to either Robert Dunsmuir or Boyd Gilmour and was a great improvement over the homemade ones the men had complained about. A hinged lid fitted down snugly over a bevelled rim well soldered into place, and a two-layered spout allowed excess oil to run back down into the lamp. This homely little pot, its large spout functional but ungainly, was fitted onto the soft caps of thousands of Vancouver Island coal miners over the next sixty years. Dangerous but bright, these oil lamps were used until electric lights replaced them in 1917. By then Vancouver Island mines had become notorious for being "fiery" mines, mines which produced a large amount of methane gas.

If the steam engine brought the modern age to Vancouver Island mining, HBC Number One Shaft itself was a more primitive throwback. At first it was big enough to accommodate only two miners, but the galleries were quickly extended so that six men, four mining and two hauling, could work it. Within five months the mine could have accommodated one hundred miners had there been that many available. When Muir realized that the conglomerate rock forming the floor of the mine was probably also the roof of a second seam, plans were made to extend the shaft. Douglas commented dryly "I will not venture to detail the thousand and one theories that are hourly stated on the subject of the Coal beds..."

Six feet high and four or five feet broad, the main gallery was solidly lined and roofed with squared timber. The ventilation system was driven by a fire situated at the bottom of a second shaft lined with logs and clay, and connecting the workings with the surface. The fire caused the warm air to rise pulling fresh air through the mine. Furnaces were a relatively new development in Britain, but had already been replaced in a few mines by the steam jet, a development which would occur on Vancouver Island twenty years later.

With a shaft of only fifty feet, HBC Number One was a shallow mine, so shallow that the drifts sometimes came out on the surface, but it was a real mine and must have given John Muir a sense of vindication after all his unsuccessful efforts in Fort Rupert. The main gallery ran parallel to the Inlet through six to seven feet of coal with adits running off it at right angles. Each adit employed two miners.

In the meantime, John McGregor had begun HBC Number Two Mine just a little further into Commercial Inlet. When its workings came close to HBC Number One, the two were connected and the pithead frame of Number One was dismantled. Number Two was deeper and had a cage to take miners down and bring coal up to the surface.

McGregor replaced Muir as oversman when the latter retired in 1854, but Gilmour had no use for McGregor either. The tall and rangy man, by then in his forties, had a quick temper and a lingering reputation for being unreliable based on his flight from Fort Rupert to the California gold fields. His promotion changed the management situation very little. The oversmen were still at odds with each other, and the mining camp was still under the supervision of Joseph McKay, a non-miner. McKay was later succeeded by Captain Charles Edward Stuart, another alumni of the HBC marine service and not a mining man either.

But the Company had already realized the importance of employing a man skilled in mining technology and was recruiting in England as Boyd Gilmour's three-year contract ran out. It is not surprising that Gilmour did not renew his contract given his largely frustrating experience on Vancouver Island. His wife Jean was not anxious to remain either, and so in the fall of 1854 he joined her in Victoria to await the birth of another child. The Gilmours[5] then sailed to Britain on the return voyage of the *Princess Royal*, which had just deposited George Robinson and a party of Staffordshire miners in Victoria. A new boss and a new group of miners were on their way to Nanaimo.

The HBC was heartily sick of Scottish miners, especially since the last shipload had not even reached North America. Forty miners and their families had left Britain aboard the *Colinda* but had mutineed — a practice not usually associated with passengers — and had been deposited unceremoniously in Valparaiso, Chile. Only one of them

---

[5] Gilmour lived out his life in Riccarton, dying there in 1869, the same year his nephew Robert Dunsmuir discovered his own coal seam.

ever made it to Vancouver Island. It is not surprising that the HBC decided to look elsewhere for new miners.

The "Black Country" near Birmingham in England produced iron, coal, glass, and pottery, in its mines and factories. In 1854 the area was just recovering from a severe economic crisis which had resulted in thousands emigrating. Even without a crisis, there was much to escape from in the coalfields of the Black Country.

Coalmasters or tenants leased land from a landowner, established a mine, and provided the surface installations. They in turn contracted to "butties" or middlemen to organize the underground work of the mines. A good wage and other benefits were the butties' reward for achieving maximum production at minimum cost. They employed as much low cost labour as they could, boys and inexperienced men, and spent as little money as possible on equipment, ventilation, and other safety measures.

Dangerous and exploitive, the buttie system's most flagrant misdemeanor lay in the fact that either the mineowner or the buttie owned the public house or "tommy shop" where ale, usually of inferior quality, was sold. The only alternative source of liquor was through hucksters, who charged even higher prices. Due to the irregularity with which wages were paid, miners often ran up bills at the tommy, with the result that their money often did not get any farther than the door.

It did not take long for a man to become enmeshed in such a system. By the time he was old enough to marry, he had already been in the mines for several years in an apprenticeship which lasted until the age of twenty-one. When a man married, he soon had a child and then several more; he was locked into the buttie system for life. If he was going to break loose he had to do it when he was young, but that was only a dream for most men. In March of 1854, the chance to make the dream come true was offered to the people of the Black Country hamlet of Brierly Hill.

In that spring the HBC had inserted notices in many British newspapers. The notices dwelt lovingly on the beauties and virtues of Vancouver Island and offered very tempting contracts to "miner-colonists." Although many of the men who ultimately emigrated were probably illiterate and therefore unable to read the advertisements, it only took one literate man reading for them to let them hear the details. From then on, the persuasive powers of George Robinson, a local mining agent already signed on by the Company, convinced them that here was an opportunity of a lifetime. At the Swan Inn at

Buckpool, the possibility of emigrating to Vancouver Island was discussed by men who up to that time had stayed very close to home.

Young men were what the Company wanted — young married men with one or two children. Everyone who signed up filled the bill or was working on it except for Elijah Ganner, who was older and had six children and was not at all what the Company had in mind. But Robinson recommended him, saying he was a "stout, able man" who "thoroughly understands every system of mining adopted in this country."

The rest of the recruits fit the Company's description. There was Thomas Hawkes and his wife Mary, who brought three children with them and would have seven more. John Thompson ensured his eligibility by marrying Elizabeth just before the ship left. Because Elizabeth was literate she could read and answer letters for those who were not. Edwin and Elizabeth Gough were among the first to sign up and one of the few couples who did not change their minds and refuse to come. Some made up their minds at the last minute after watching several of their friends and neighbours waver in their decision and decide to stay at home. John and Jane Biggs, Thomas and Elizabeth Jones, John and Lavinia Malpass, and Elijah and Frances Ganner all made decisions in a very short time, decisions that would change their lives dramatically.

And there was jovial George Baker, who loved to break into song at a party, and his wife Maryann. There were John and Isabella Baker, and Joseph and Ann Bevilockway. There was George Bull, whose restless spirit contrasted sharply with his inability to stay awake on the job. Daniel Dunn's wife Eliza Ann danced beautifully, but died young and childless. And there were those who would not stay in Nanaimo long, like William and Ann Harrison, William and Sarah Incher, Thomas and Elizabeth Jones, and Thomas York and his family.

Charlotte Lowndes left England with her husband Thomas and came back on the return voyage a widow, Thomas having died enroute. John and Maryann Meakin got off to a bad start in their new home but soon became respectable. John would be a miner until the day he died in a huge explosion.

Matthew Miller could play the cello and would still be mining when he was seventy years old. Abraham Richardson, who liked to be called John, and his brother Richard brought their wives Seadonan and Elizabeth. The Richardsons would discover coal for the Company and coal for themselves. Jesse and Maryann Sage would see their daughter Selena marry Edward Walker, and Joseph and Naomi Webb would become hotel owners.

Musicians and dancers, singers and jokers, they came from Brierly Hill, Bromley, Pensnett, Wordsley, Kingsroinford, Grave Yard, and Brickmoor in Staffordshire; Dudley in Worcestershire; and Camerton in Sommersetshire. The Company had asked for "stout, able and hearty young men," and here they were with young wives and young families to match.

The man who assembled this group and dealt with the men who had second thoughts and encouraged and cajoled those who finally agreed to come was George Robinson. He was hired to replace Boyd Gilmour but was much more qualified for the job than his predecessor. Qualifications do not necessarily make a good leader of men, however, and Robinson had a short fuse, which confounded him on more than one occasion.

His first job was to help the Company write a contract and get the voyage underway. Each candidate was loaned fifteen pounds to facilitate his departure. Initially Robinson advised the Company to offer a good wage because at home in the Black Country wages were higher than they had ever been. Arguing that it could not pay them more than the Scottish miners were paid, the Company was able only to match the five shillings per day wage that the Englishmen were being paid at home.

Without the lure of better wages to entice them to leave everything they found familiar and reassuring, all the original recruits except four or five backed out. Robinson was not deterred. "I am trying to get them to believe that they are being favoured in being accepted, rather than otherwise and this at present seems to be a stimulant," he wrote Mr. Barclay. He sent a crier through some of the villages of the district "informing the miners of my wanting a few miners to go to America." By mid-May he could say that even if some miners backed out he still had six or seven in reserve.

Britain was, at that time, just emerging from a period of economic distress and social disorder. The barbaric practice of employing women and children below ground in coal mines had been outlawed, although boys over the age of ten continued to work below ground and women continued to labour above ground at the pithead. By the late 1840's a doubling of export trade and much railroad development had led to increased employment, increased coal production, and a marked jump in heavy industry.

Britain entered the second half of the nineteenth century with a new degree of social stability. Chartism, that working-class movement which demanded electoral reform, had foundered on the demand for universal male suffrage. The revolutionary fervor of Europe in 1848 was now only a memory. Although the economic hardships of the 1840's had caused many people to emigrate, by the 1850's there were jobs at home. Yet twenty-three Black Country miners signed their names or their marks to contracts committing themselves to five years service for the same wages that they were receiving in mines situated around their lifelong homes. Only a dream that even a coal miner could better himself could have made them leave.

The five years were to begin on the day of embarkation. In return for two shillings sixpence a day with victuals and rations for two, they were to make themselves useful on the voyage but were not bound to go aloft. On arrival in Nanaimo they were to build a wooden house for their family with materials supplied by the Company on one imperial acre of land rented for one pound per year.

The HBC had become more knowledgeable about mining and miners. The contract specified wages of seventy-eight pounds per year for the digging of forty-five tons per month and two shillings sixpence per twenty-one hundred pound ton of clean and round coal dug over and above that amount. There would be extra pay for sinking, stone mining, and labouring. The Company would furnish all tools. George Robinson was able to report with satisfaction:

I have read the agreements to them all before their signatures were attached and I also cautioned them to well weigh the subject in their mind before they did sign and I also particularly reminded them of the result of their failing to comply with the terms of the agreement.

The trip to London was paid for by the Company as was the fare to Vancouver Island and back unless the miner was dismissed through repeated absence or neglect of duty. If a miner died during his term of contract, his widow and family would be returned to England at the Company's expense. As twenty-three men and twenty-three women and a "quantity of children" boarded the brand new HBC ship the *Princess Royal* on the evening of June 2, 1854, some may have thought of death and the danger they faced, but they were young people with a sense of adventure which belied their restricted upbringing. The adventure was about to begin.

Ten Norwegian labourers and a woman with five children who was joining her husband shared the main hold with the mining families. Headroom was just six feet; dim lanterns provided the only light;

71

there were no berths or cabins for steerage passengers. Only George Robinson, his wife and two children, a maid, and another family were entitled to such comfort.

On June 3rd the seven hundred ton oak and teak barque *Princess Royal*, one hundred twenty feet in length and thirty-six feet by the beam, left the East India docks. When it anchored at Esquimalt five months and twenty days later, the survivors had been through a terrible time of trial. Before the ship even reached Cape Horn with its inevitable gale-force winds, three children had been born and three had died. The water was rancid and no washing was permitted unless it rained. The smell therefore was unbearable. Those who tried washing in salt water saw their skin break into running sores. They soon came to heed the sailors, who advised against washing altogether, saying that a person's skin kept best in salt winds if it were wiped with a towel when it broke into a sweat.

After the cold and tumult of the rounding of Cape Horn, the ship caught the prevailing winds, which took them to the Sandwich Islands. Honolulu, the main port, was a regular stop for HBC ships bound for the Pacific Northwest or the Far East. Though still an independent kingdom, the Sandwich Islands had served as a resting place for ships' crews of several nations engaged first in the Chinese fur trade and later in whaling.

In 1842 HBC Governor Sir George Simpson had described Honolulu as a "strange admixture of the savage and the civilized, stacks of warehouses rising amid straw-huts." There were sailors, mechanics, missionaries and consuls; Chinese, Malays, Africans, and, of course, Kanakas. Because European women had only recently become a part of the community, many men had native wives. It cost very little to live, but alcohol abuse and aimlessness were rampant.

As the beleaguered passengers on the *Princess Royal* viewed the city of Honolulu from the water it must have looked like paradise. The lush vegetation, the bright blue water, the scattered wood and stone houses nestled in the trees all looked restful and reassuring. When the boat docked, the seamier side of Honolulu was revealed. There were no sanitary facilities, no proper roads or bridges. There were derelict buildings on the shore and derelict men lying drunk on the beaches. But for those still able to be amazed after all they had been through, there was much to inspire wonder. The exotic mix of races, the thatched roofs, the coral, the beautiful shells — no one brought up in a British mining town had ever seen anything like this.

While the ship was in harbour, two adults died. Thomas Lowndes left a widow and two year old son, and Sarah Incher died in childbirth. They were buried there in Honolulu. Sarah's baby died ten days later at sea. Morale was so low that this dead baby was thrown overboard with no burial rites "and no more Notice taken of it than if it had been a ded [sic] cat." Six days later when Dick Richardson's tiny daughter Mary was found lying dead at her mother's side, she was given a proper sea burial. In that six day period, the spirit of the group and the will to survive had returned.

In keeping with the wretchedness of the rest of the voyage, the Straits of Juan de Fuca offered up a gale for their arrival at Esquimalt. The ship finally dropped anchor, having lost two adults and six children. Because the harbour at Nanaimo had not been surveyed, no one knew whether it would accommodate the keel of the *Princess Royal*, so the passengers were divided between the *Recovery* and the *Beaver* and were quickly on their way.

In later years, the arrival at Nanaimo would take on a legendary quality reminiscent of the pilgrims landing on Plymouth Rock. No doubt both events were far less momentous than the commemorative ceremonies would indicate, but it is hard not to feel a sense of occasion when the landing at Nanaimo is described.

On a cold, overcast day, November 26, 1854, the two ships pulled into the harbour. Before them on the land were a few buildings straggling along the shore and a line of sooty miners' cabins. A Red Ensign with "HBC" on the fly waved bravely from a small bastion of square-hewn logs, the fluttering flag and the white dovecot-like structure no match for the dark, tall trees which closed in behind the tiny town. The tenders were lowered and the mining families rowed ashore. In keeping with the mythic nature of the event, there was a large rock at the water's edge and it was onto this rock that they stepped. As the Gough family took its turn, the sun broke through as if in welcome. The entire white population of 151 people and "a goodly number of Indians" stood waiting to meet them.

The Indians were members of five communities of the Coast Salish known collectively as the Snenymos.[6] The people were smaller than those in the northern tribes and much less interested in fighting unless forced to defend themselves. Chinook was their language, but they communicated with whites by using Chinook jargon, the so-called Oregon trade language that was a composite of Nootka, Chinook,

[6] It was from "Snenymos" that the name "Nanaimo" evolved. Before that, the settlement was briefly called "Colviletown" after Eden Colvile.

73

English, and French. "At best it [was] a wretched means of communication, poor in expression and almost destitute of grammatical forms."

The alarming practice of flattening the heads of infants between two strips of wood bound with cedar bark gave the Indians a bizarre appearance not enhanced in the least in European eyes by their wearing apparel. A blanket made of white dog wool or from the inner bark of cedar trees was wrapped around their hips and legs. Indian women dressed the same with the addition of a killicoat which consisted of several strips of cloth or cedar bark hanging loosely in front and joined at the waist with a piece of seaweed or twisted bark. To this traditional garb the men had added shirts bought with credits obtained by working in the mines. When the women adopted European dress, they chose short sleeveless chemisettes and gowns in navy blue cotton, which the white people felt improved their appearance considerably.

On the high ground of a peninsula separated from the town by Commercial Inlet the Indian "rancharee" surveyed the scene. Several barn-like longhouses commanded the hill, which sloped down to a beach where canoes lay in readiness. Between the beach and the houses a collection of refuse festered, described by an appalled British gentleman as "cockle-shells, oyster-shells, fish bones, pieces of putrid meat, old mats, pieces of rag, and dirt and filth of every description, the accumulation of generations."

Each longhouse was one hundred feet long and thirty feet wide, made of split cedar boards fastened together with poles and willow twig withes and strips of strong bark. White visitors were especially offended by conditions inside. A dozen families lived together, separated by only low partitions. There were no floors, no windows, no chimneys. Beds were rude platforms. In the corners were piles of mats, fishing tackle, and rubbish; stores of dried fish and berries hung from poles. And in the midst of all this was an assortment of dogs, cats, and chickens, whose presence at once contributed to the naturalness and the chaos of the scene.

The women were pug-nosed and seldom had good features by European standards, but there was an intelligence in their dark eyes. Hard-working and better at receiving instruction than their men, skilled at cooking and sewing, these women were the core around which Indian life revolved. Since the coal miners had come, the women had added loading the coal to their responsibilities.

These industrious Indian women were also prized as mates for white men in a bride-poor frontier town. The marriages did not lend the women the respect of the white community, however, and their children were unable to gain approval from either the whites or the Indians. Captain Walter Colquhoun Grant, Vancouver Island's first settler, revealed the prejudice of his time when he said:

The union of the white man with the North American savage has seldom if ever been attended with good results; the offspring invariably possess all the faults of the savage, rendered only the more acute by the admixture of some slight additional intelligence from the white parent; the men are passionate and vicious, the women stupid and ill-tempered, and instances are rare of either sex doing justice to the seeds of instruction which are plentifully scattered among them by missionaries of various persuasions.

When two cultures meet there is always misunderstanding. This is nowhere so obvious as in the North American experience between Europeans and Indians. That the judgments made on either side were racist and full of stereotypes is easy to believe, given that these misconceptions still exist in large part in the relationship between the two races. Lack of understanding or of even the wish to understand resulted in much misery for the Indians. In Nanaimo during the 1850's this ignorance led to the misreading of their culture. In particular, lack of appreciation for the differences between tribes had prompted the building of a bastion.

In contrast to the Haidas and the Kwakiutls from the north coast the Salish were a peaceful people unless they were settling feuds among themselves according to time honoured custom. But the white newcomers became increasingly threatened as one Indian-related incident followed another.

In September of 1852, forty Cowichans murdered one Nanaimo Indian employed at the mines. Four days later a Sku-who-mish Indian was murdered in revenge for three Snenymous killed the previous winter. Adam Horne, a Company employee, had witnessed Haidas murder and decapitate Qualicum Indians and take others for slaves, a common practice amongst all the Coastal Indians. In this pursuit of slaves, the Haida were the most aggressive. They often appeared at Nanaimo in their large canoes by the hundreds or even thousands. When they left it was not uncommon to see a body floating in the harbour — often a body without a head.

But Indian fierceness had never been directed against whites. What they did to whites fell into the category of petty annoyance. The McGregors were cooking meat outside when an Indian stole it. Joan Dunsmuir found an Indian with a knife in his hand looking at her second son Alexander as he lay in his cot. The Indian grunted unintelligibly and left. Many whites were treated to the Indians' lack of appreciation for the sanctity of the home. They wandered in, looked around, stole small items and left. But the murder of Peter Brown in Victoria and the subsequent hanging of the perpetrators on Gallows Point in Nanaimo's harbour hastened the decision to build a bastion.

Construction began on a high point of land at the entrance to Commercial Inlet, while British warships patrolled the Gulf and the *Cadboro* lay at anchor in the harbour, primarily to reassure the Indian labourers. Logs were brought in by Indians to the shoreline, where they were squared off and then packed up the knoll to the building site. Although it was winter and there was snow on the ground, the Indians worked with their feet and heads bare.

The actual builders were French-Canadians who had already built the bastions at Fort Victoria and Fort Rupert. Leo Lebine and Jean Baptiste Fortier were marvellously skilled axemen, proud of their work. It was said that they boasted they had made the square sided logs so smooth that they would allow themselves to be drawn over them naked. While it was true that they did brag in this way, it was also true that they were drinking at the time. No one was foolish enough to insist that they prove their boast.

The Bastion rose on its low stone foundation and was finished in June of 1854. Two six pound carronades were put in place by the versatile Edward Walker.[7] They were used to give James Douglas a seventeen gun salute when he arrived on inspection tours four or five times a year, but were never fired in anger. "Once in a while a few shots were fired across the harbour into the woods on Protection Island, so that the Indians might note the damaging effects — see the havoc made among the trees."

Built as a fortress, the Bastion came to serve a much more homely purpose in the early mining town. The HBC office was housed on the ground floor, an arsenal was located on the second, and the third was reserved for people in case of attack. Only once, in 1855, was the use of the third floor thought necessary when a huge flotilla of Kwakiutls appeared in the harbour bent on revenge for three murders. The whites waited in the Bastion for three days while the Indians conferred. When the Nanaimo chief agreed to be executed in exchange, the northern Indians left.

[7] A carronade is a short light cannon of large bore, for use at close range, named for the town of Carron in Scotland where it was first cast in 1779.

Suspended from the Bastion was a crosscut saw which was beaten with a triangular piece of metal to announce noon time and supper time. The saw was later replaced by a brass tambourine in the hands of a man marching through town, and still later by a bell imported from England. The bell, which was installed on a thirty foot scaffolding outside the Company store, became synonymous with momentous events. Nanaimo would not have a steam mine whistle, a prominent feature of so many mining towns, until 1870.

The cold and wet of a Vancouver Island November made the provision of housing for the *Princess Royal* passengers an immediate priority. They were crowded into small houses, some of which were six hundred square feet and some only half that size. Two families shared each building with two rooms allotted to each. Years later, the survivors told Mark Bate what those houses were like.

They told me how roughly the houses were constructed, of the dreary look outside, and the cramped space inside; how the chinks between the logs and poles, through which the wind would blow with a shriek of triumph, were plastered up with clay or stuffed with moss; of the interior equippage of benches, boards and bunk-like bedsteads; of the Dutch ovens and baking and cooking; of the drugget rush mats and rugs made in part of dog's hair by Indians, used for floor covering.

With rough cedar shingles covering the roofs and squat little lamps filled with fish oil providing a dim light that was meagerly supplemented by the open fireplace, the rooms were cold and damp and dark. Still the houses were better than miners' houses in Nova Scotia or Britain. In 1854 there were fifty-two houses and six outhouses; there were three stores, one school, and no churches.

It was not until 1857 that any mention of regular church services appeared in the Fort Journal although visiting clergymen had given services before that time. The lack of haste in providing a place of worship reflected the attitude towards religion in Europe, where the established churches were losing strength. James Douglas was of the opinion that a clergyman might be useful, however. At least he would come cheaper than a policeman.

Douglas thought the clergyman should be a member of the Free Kirk of Scotland, "the Miners generally being of that persuasion, and not disposed to receive instructions from the Clergy of any other denomination." It was, however, the Methodists, perhaps closer to the working class, who provided spiritual guidance initially, first in the person of the young and earnest schoolmaster, Cornelius Bryant, and then with a real minister.

Arthur Browning was one of four Methodist missionaries who came to the British Pacific Coast in 1858. Browning found "the people, mostly Europeans were painfully in need of Gospel privileges... Primarily this mission presented a most melancholy and (spiritually) uninviting aspect... we even now lament the non-immigration of godly men." In a more secular mood, company clerk Mark Bate thought the advent of the Methodists made the town "dressier" because people wore their best clothes to church.

Well below the Bastion and fifty yards to the southwest, sat the big Company store built in 1852 on pilings and facing on Commercial Inlet. It stood above a large enclosure with a distinctive high picket fence, white-washed with lime like everything else in town. Between the pickets and the store ran a railroad track which led to a wharf built by Edward Walker. Vessels drawing sixteen feet could anchor close to the wharf. Below the pickets was a log wall with two heavy timbered doors to give access to the yard by boat at high tide and onto a beach at low.

A store with a monopoly does not have to treat its customers with particular regard. As the population grew it became necessary for people to wait in line outside for the chance to buy their sugar, flour, venison, molasses, butter, comfits, almonds, rum by the bottle or the half gallon, rice, dried salmon, brown sugar, barrel salmon, salt pork, salt beef, and potatoes. The amount of salmon and venison depended on how busy the Indians were loading coal and how difficult the crossings of the Gulf were when they went to the Mainland to hunt.[8] The flour was coarse and sold for six dollars per hundred pounds, the butter of poor quality, the potatoes scarce because no one grew them locally until the Indians started. But there was plenty of salt fish as long as there were enough barrels, and there were lots of seagull eggs.

Storekeeper Adam Grant Horne also stocked tobacco, blankets, clay pipes, knives, candles, tin kettles, horn combs, soap, powder and shot, gunflints, vermilion, beads, brass thimbles, and finger rings. He could refurbish a wardrobe with cotton shirts, drawers, druggets, thread, ribbon, Welty shoes, "Turkey" handkerchiefs, common cotton handkerchiefs, "flannell," and baise cotton.

Prices were stiff. The coal dug by each man went onto his account at the store and he drew on this account whenever he wished to

[8] Indians sometimes brought as many as sixty-three deer in a day from Sechelt or Jervis Inlet. If the weather was hot or wind from the wrong direction delayed their arrival, the venison spoiled before it reached Nanaimo.

78

purchase anything. It took a lot of coal to pay for some of the items. There were three price systems. Superior HBC officers paid thirty-three percent over cost; lesser Company servants paid fifty to one hundred percent over; the "cash price" to non-Company employees was regulated by the prices in California and constituted an approximate three hundred percent mark-up. Small wonder that gardens were soon planted. A person could supply himself with onions, lettuce, radishes, cabbage, and spinach, but only on a small scale because there was so little cleared land.

Crab-apple and cherry trees and other wild fruit could be found everywhere. The vegetation was lush and covered the forest floor, which was pristine and free from fallen timber. But the trees pressed in. Mixed stands of Douglas fir, hemlock, and red cedar, grown huge from never having known an axe, surrounded the small collection of buildings on three sides. Scrubby shore pine, alder, big leaf maple, and dogwood filled in the spaces. Exotic arbutus trees seemed to stand alone. Against this formidable army the settlers were puny. They cleared only enough land to set their houses. The felled trees were used for mine timbers, building logs and lumber, the slabs left from square-hewing were used for fencing, and the stumps were left to get in the way.

Narrow pathways ran hither and thither from the cleared space in front of one door to the cleared space in front of another. At night it was not safe to travel these paths without a lantern, so random was their course and so likely were they to be obstructed by a stump. At night the only person likely to be out was Jim Kimo, a Kanaka watchman who affected a bright red sash and a tasseled cap. It was his duty at midnight to fire off a gun and call out "all's well," the former sound somehow belying the latter reassurance. Jim also managed to strike a drum at the same time, which must have led to insomnia amongst the population. The fact that he often played the drum during the day, too, must have led many to wonder first, whether Jim Kimo ever slept and second, whether it was worth it after all to have a night watchman.

As for roads, there was only one and that was not blazed until 1858. It terminated abruptly at the Big Swamp, "quite a mile across either way," where wild grass was cut to feed the mine animals. There was really no need for roads because there were no wagons, there being no one about who knew how to build one. Timber was hauled by oxen, and everything smaller was carried by hand on the trails that led to each mine and wound their way through the town.

79

Eventually a railroad bed, built on piles along the side of Commercial Inlet and past the Company warehouse to the wharf, became a street appropriately called Wharf Street. The road to the Big Swamp became Comox Road, and the random trails which wound around stumps to the houses and mines became streets, and the streets were given names, and some of them led to other roads which led out of town, but not too far. But all that happened later. For now there were only trails and trees.

Under the trees the ground was covered with salal, its berry sweet and wholesome, and kinnikinnick, a shrub whose leaves had a slight opiate effect when dried and smoked in pipes by the Indians. The most common plant around was camass, its light blue, white, or pink flowers marking the location of its sweet bulb root. Indians regarded camass as a delicacy and lay in large stores of it in the fall, using the harvest as a reason for family gatherings.

On the trail out to the Big Swamp, Edward Walker had a small garden "which, being shaded all around by good-sized trees, was of little use to him." Gardening must have been one of the few things Edward Walker did not do well. By the time his contract with the Company had expired in 1855 he already owned a sailboat, which he used to transport refuse coal to Victoria and which he filled with flour and potatoes for the return voyage. He carried dispatches; he transported lumber to the mine on Newcastle Island and came back with coal; he screened coal. By 1856 he was carrying mail from Victoria in his new boat the *Sarah Stone*. He continued to mine on a contract basis and did carpentry jobs for the Company. The beacon on Gallows Point was installed by him as was the one on Satellite reef.

Edward Walker was almost forty years old before he married Selena Sage, still in her teens. They would have at least nine children, and she would go with him as he faithfully followed Robert Dunsmuir from coal town to coal town. Their first-born was Alfred. Alfred would lose his life working for the man his father idolized.

Robert Dunsmuir and Edward Walker finished their contracts at the same time. In October of 1855 both were granted the first free miners' licenses ever issued by the HBC. Some writers would have us believe that Dunsmuir received that license as a reward for refusing to participate in a series of strikes and desertions which kept Nanaimo stirred up for most of 1855. This can only be based on speculation. The records are so filled with the names of the troublemakers that there is little reason to mention a man who was quietly getting on with his work. The written record does not justify labelling Dunsmuir a strikebreaker or scab but he can not have endeared himself to the dissatisfied miners by refusing to participate in their actions against the Company.

Ever since they refused to "make themselves useful" on the *Princess Royal* voyage as their contract had stipulated, the Staffordshire miners had been discontented. In January of 1855, when they had been in Nanaimo only two months, James Douglas heard through a private source that they were

again dissatisfied and have been giving a world of trouble. Some of them are also said to be tampering with the Americans proposing to desert the Company's service for our rivals in business.

The American rivals were the Puget's Sound Coal Mining Association at Bellingham Bay, where coal had been discovered in 1852. Joseph McKay had visited the camp to find a small settlement of eight or nine log huts and a half-finished sawmill. Short of labour like every other enterprise on the Pacific coast, they set about luring miners away from Nanaimo by sending recruiters, who found a small group ripe for the picking. Even though the HBC had recently agreed to pay them more for the extra coal they dug, Thomas York, Jesse Sage, John and George Baker, and Dick and John Richardson were lured by "flattering tales" and "the Spirits that are also sent to them Gratis" and deserted for Bellingham Bay.

The departure of the six miners in January, 1855 stirred up trouble among those who stayed behind. Their boss, George Robinson, was unable to deal with the situation.

[The desertion] is now beginning to act most fearfully upon the works at this place and everyday seems to increase the evil, nearly one half of the miners are idling away their time, and most of those who pretend to work do not perform much more than a fourth of what they ought to do, and to remonstrate with them about it seems perfect folly for the one part of them will simply laugh at you for doing so, and others will make use of the most offensive and insulting language imagineable [sic] — to you, to me, . . . I have treated them with kindness and they take advantage of it — I have spoken to them determinately and they reply insultingly.

By May the miners who were left behind had returned to their work. July saw three of the deserters back at work and the return of the other three expected. But the fall brought another lure more tempting than coal. Just as it did the Fort Rupert miners and as it would again and again as the century progressed, gold drew coal miners away. This time the find was on the Pend d'Orielle River in

Washington Territory, and it cast its spell on eight of the Staffordshire miners, including John Baker and Thomas York from the first group of deserters.

John Baker and William Incher had suffered real tragedy since their decision to emigrate. Baker's baby daughter Anne Marie was born and had died on the *Princess Royal*; Incher's wife Sarah died in childbirth in Honolulu, and her new baby was callously thrown overboard when it died at sea a few days later. Incher and his two orphaned children had little to be thankful for in their new home.

Like Baker and Incher the remaining six deserters were young and impetuous. It may have been youthful impulsiveness which caused them to emigrate in the first place and which now caused them to desert as a remedy for their dissatisfaction. Joseph Webb and John Meakin would later make their peace with life in Nanaimo and become leading citizens. Thomas York and William Harrison were obviously men who were never to be happy there and made successful lives elsewhere. Daniel Dunn had no children to hold him back, and as for George Bull, he was just plain lazy.

Bull was singled out by manager Robinson as being the most indolent, discontented, and mischief making of all the miners. Perhaps because of his indolence, his job at the Pemberton's Encampment Mine was not digging coal but tending the gin horse which drove the hoist. This task included long periods of inactivity as the driver waited for the signal to haul up another load of coal or let down an empty car, and Bull often fell asleep. Thus when the men in the mine "telegraphed" their need for a hoist, they got no response and would have to come to the surface and wake the sleepy fellow. Even when he returned after deserting he continued to be a malcontent, and after the death of his third child with hydrocephalus he packed up his family and left for Australia.

Robert Dunsmuir, a man who knew the value of hard work, may have been approached by the eight men just before they deserted. His great-grandson credits him with counselling the eight against this foolish action. The advice, if given, was ultimately ignored but may have reinforced the story that he received his free miners' license because he refused to go along with strikers.

On September 11, 1855, the eight men laid down their tools and refused to work. The next day, a distraught and drunken Meakin threatened to shoot his wife. Charles Stuart, the officer-in-charge who had replaced Joseph McKay, attempted unsuccessfully to handcuff Meakin, who was finally dragged away by several of his compatriots.

Their proposal that there should be a "fair fight" instead between Meakin and Stuart was ignored by Stuart who described the conduct of all the English and one or two of the Scottish miners as "disgraceful in the extreme." He dismissed the strikers as being "too lazy" to work, and he was only marginally less disgusted with most of the other miners.

Two days later the eight men disappeared, leaving their wives and families behind. Stuart's first response was to issue eviction notices saying the Company required their dwellings. The combined impact of having been deserted by their husbands and threatened with eviction in a town with a shortage of housing must have been very difficult for the young mothers.

Over the next three months, the deserters trickled back. William Harrison was only away for a week. When he returned and asked Robinson for a letter of reference so he could be readmitted to the Company service his request was granted because he was the only one Robinson "could speak favourably of." However, the Company's policy of refusing to readmit deserters was meaningless in Nanaimo of the 1850's. There simply was not enough white labour to allow the employer to be too particular. By October all the miners except Thomas York had been to Victoria to be reprimanded by the Governor and reinstated, albeit on less favourable contract terms.

One week back at work at these new terms decided Incher and Harrison once and for all and they left, this time with their families, on board the brig *Leonesa* for California. They were not seen in Nanaimo again. Those who remained fell to work with admirable vigour for a time. Stuart mused somewhat smugly that the whole experience had "been productive of more good than the whole of the concessions made to the miners since their employment with the company."

The subsequent return of Thomas York for the second time brought all the remaining *Princess Royal* miners back into the fold for the winter, but when Mr. Reed of Bellingham Bay arrived by canoe the next spring to recruit miners, he found a ready audience. This time perennial deserters Thomas York, John Baker, and Joseph Webb settled their accounts properly with the Company and quit the town. Five days later a scow from Bellingham Bay anchored outside the harbour and took the three men's wives and families on board. By September Baker and Webb had had enough of the squalid conditions to the south and returned yet again to the arms of the Company.

Thomas York never returned but went instead to the Fraser River gold rush in 1858.

The Pend d'Orielle gold find had occurred near where that river joins the Columbia. Since then, gold seekers had gradually worked their way as far north as the Thompson River and then gradually south again until they found gold on the Fraser in the fall of 1857. By 1858 the word had reached Puget's Sound and California, and the leftover miners from the heady days of the California gold rush came in their thousands, by boat and overland, and by their sheer numbers changed the history of British Columbia dramatically.

In Nanaimo, the news of gold being discovered so close to home was an irresistible draw to some coal miners. When seven miners and three labourers left for the Fraser, George Robinson commented:

The workmen now here, are all of them, with scarcely an exception crying out for an advance for ages, and there is very little work being done, many of them declaring their intentions of going to the diggings as soon as they can.

Among the miners drawn by Fraser River gold was Dick Richardson. Although he had also deserted in 1855, he had returned and had worked as a miner in the intervening three years. An injury suffered when the Newcastle Mine roof fell on him had not distracted him, but gold did. In 1858, when he was forty-eight years old and should have known better, he left Nanaimo to make his fortune. The literate company clerk Mark Bate, a young man at the time, observed:

. . . he was not long absent from Nanaimo, but on his return represented that he had made his pile, and told his friends he would soon be off to the Old Country. He walked around for a few days with affected dignity, dressed quite stylishly, and assumed the airs that some persons do when suddenly becoming rich.

The "pile" turned out to be a small sack of gold dust obtained by selling the equipment that he had taken with him. Dick Richardson soon had to become a coal miner again.

By July many miners had put together an outfit and gone in search of quick riches, but in 1858 there was no shortage of labour in the colony. Not all the men attracted by gold were able to find it, and some were clever enough to realize that a gold rush opens up many opportunities even for those who go nowhere near the diggings. For a while at least the Nanaimo coalfields had all the labour they could use.

There was not all that much need for labour. The Company had not proved to be especially adept at the business of coal mining. As they experimented with various kinds of contracts and various methods of management, the actual operation of the mines was very much hit and miss. The first two men in charge of the Nanaimo establishment, Joseph McKay and Charles Stuart, had no experience in the business. When Stuart was removed for chronic drunkenness, he was replaced by Charles S. Nicol, an engineer trained as a land surveyor. Although he was given the dual role of general manager and superintendent of the mines, Nicol had no mining experience either.

The men with mining experience had troubles of their own. Right from the beginning, when John Muir struggled to run the mining operation in Fort Rupert with little cooperation and a lot of interference from McNeill and Blenkinsop, the various oversmen and foremen had battled to run the mines effectively. They had to deal with discontented men within the limits of their abilities and under the restraining hand of the Company.

By the time George Robinson was hired in Staffordshire, some valuable lessons had been learned. He was allowed a large input into the contract for the *Princess Royal* miners and his practical mining as well as management experience should have made him a more effective boss. The fact that the miners continued to be discontented and the mines themselves inefficient was due at least in part to Robinson's personality and to a private tragedy.

His difficulties began after his arrival in Nanaimo in November of 1854. His wife Ann died the following January, having given birth to a son who soon joined his mother in the little graveyard located on land set aside by the Company overlooking the Millstream. Although Robinson was soon joined in Nanaimo by his two nephews, Mark Bate and Cornelius Bryant, his niece Elizabeth Bate, and his sister Maria, and although he eventually remarried, this tragic personal loss so early in his tenure may have affected his ability to deal with the men and the situation. Or he may never have been especially adept at employee relations. Whatever the reasons, Robinson's personality clearly undermined his effectiveness as a boss. Certainly his handling of the drunken Meakin in 1855 was badly botched. The following year Robinson had a confrontation with John McGregor.

McGregor can not have been an easy man to deal with, as his past performance as one of the leaders of the Fort Rupert strike and his running away to California had shown. But despite his unstable past, he was an experienced miner and became an oversman. After opening up "McGregor's headings," as HBC Number Two Mine was commonly called, he supervised the development of the Pemberton's Encampment Mine and the Newcastle Adit. But his reputation as a troublemaker persisted. When Robinson took him to task for being slack and negligent, and working short time, his temper flared again.

A bitter exchange of words between the English mine agent and the Scottish oversman began at the top of the little rise beside the Bastion and continued as the two men progressed towards the blacksmith shop, followed by a group of onlookers. As Robinson turned to go and report to the officer-in-charge, McGregor hurled "abusive epithets like Liar Hypcrite [sic]." In a rage Robinson turned back to McGregor, grabbed a heavy hammer left by the smithy, and knocked McGregor down with a blow to the head.

Alarmed at his lapse of control, Robinson hurried away to report his action, his behavior vindicated in his own mind by his victim's provocative language. The hapless McGregor had his head bandaged at the surgery by the doctor, who said the wound was rather extensive but not dangerous "at least in its primary character."

Robinson was later to tell his family that he thought he might be sent away in disgrace over this incident. Instead it was John McGregor who was sent to Victoria to cool off. Although Robinson continued as mine agent until his contract expired in 1859, he was so unpopular that there were plans made to celebrate his departure by hanging him in effigy.

John McGregor eventually settled in Sooke, but when he died in 1866 his body was brought to Nanaimo to be buried. The McGregor family had a stake in Nanaimo. The original complement of three children who arrived with their parents in 1849 had grown to include at least six others. Two of the sons especially, James and William, distinguished themselves after becoming coal miners. James was elected Member of the Provincial Parliament (MPP) and appealed to both businessmen and labour with his reasoned approach. It was said at the time that, with his personality and family influence, James McGregor was hard to beat. William worked his way up to be manager of the new Number One Mine, the largest mine in British Columbia, and died in an explosion there. A respectable and influential family grew from the loins of the troublemaker, John McGregor.

There were more than a few troublemakers in Nanaimo in the 1850's. When a French-Canadian miner killed another worker in a fight, officer-in-charge Charles Stuart, acting as magistrate and coroner, called court into session to determine the cause of death and to try the culprit at the same time. Counsel for the accused was trader

Ovid Allard, whose sole legal qualification was that his father had been a notary in Quebec. Allard may have missed his calling. He surveyed the jury and found it wanting.

They're all sober . . . I base my objection on the Magna Carta . . . you see, it says that a man can only be tried by his peers or equals. Now these Scotsmen, Englishmen and Americans are not our peers — and there being no French-Canadian on the jury we are not on trial before our equals.

Stuart discharged the discredited jury and a second one, half of which was French-Canadian, was assembled. When this jury could not agree the accused was bound over to keep the peace and the case was never called again.

By far the biggest challenge to the rudimentary criminal justice system were the Indians. Petty thievery and intertribal battles tried the ingenuity of the magistrate. Stuart's punishment of preference was to tie the culprit's hands, lay him over one of the Bastion cannons, and flog him with a cat-o-nine-tails. Flogging without trial got Charles Stuart a reprimand, but putting prisoners in jail, Indians especially, usually resulted in the prisoner escaping, helped by his friends.

The first floor of the Bastion had become the town jail. Prisoners without the wherewithall to escape occupied the dimly lit and poorly ventilated cells. Although the settlement had no policeman, it did have a jailer, the first one being a former assistant miner named William Weston. With his "springy-swingy walk" and his preference for pants cut short to just above his boots he was a figure of fun not in keeping with the solemnity of his post.

The most likely way to become one of William Weston's charges was to overindulge in alcohol. Lacking proper licensed premises, the town was supplied through the clandestine sale of the miners' free allowance of spirits to non-miners. The spirits most often seemed to be rum, imported in puncheons[9] and obviously quickly consumed, for in 1858 the legislature of the colony noted with surprise that though no liquor licenses had been taken out by anyone for the District of Nanaimo, "it is very well known that large quantities of spiritous liquors are consumed there."

While the miners looked after the spiritous needs of other whites, American traders arrived in large boats to cater to Indian feasts. The

---

[9] A puncheon is a large cask of varying capacity (seventy-two to one hundred twenty gallons).

87

dreadful effect of alcohol on the Indians would become noticeable in subsequent decades, but in 1859 a small, stalwart group of whites was already sounding the alarm.

Religion and temperance were inextricably bound together in those days, and in Nanaimo at least, neither was particularly welcome. A letter to *The British Colonist* in Victoria complained that advocates of religion and temperance were treated as "black sheep" or unwelcome citizens. One young man was determined to change that.

Cornelius Bryant came to Nanaimo at the invitation of his uncle, George Robinson. He was nineteen, six feet tall, and red-haired. Formerly a railway clerk in Brierly Hill, he was by Nanaimo standards sufficiently well-educated to become the schoolteacher when the incumbent, one Charles Bayley, left for Victoria.[10] But Cornelius Bryant was a man with a mission. At the tender age of sixteen he had signed a total abstinence pledge and since that time had filled his diary with long, flowery fervent discourses on God, his salary, and temperance. Seeing the work of the devil in the way the miners lived and in their consumption of alcohol, he organized the Band of Hope to attract other citizens interested in temperance and to save the less dedicated from the evils of drink.

The lack of organized religion in the town was especially hard on the Anglican-raised Bryant, who tried to fill in the void by reading from the prayer book on Sunday to whomever would listen. When Methodism came to Nanaimo in 1859 in the person of Arthur Browning, Cornelius Bryant and several miners heard the call and received admission to the Methodist church.

In principal, miners were in favour of education for their children, but education on colonial Vancouver Island was paid for by the individual parent. Because a desire for learned children did not always transfer into cold hard cash, Bryant had a difficult time collecting fees from his students. Without fees there was no teacher's salary.

His predecessor Bayley had taught school in a little log building located on the main street and supplied free by the Company. When public schools opened in 1855, Nanaimo's had twenty-nine pupils

---

[10] Charles Alfred Bayley was twenty-three when he arrived on Vancouver Island aboard the *Tory*. His fellow passengers were the Andrew Hunter family. Three years later he married their fifteen year old daughter, Agnes, on board a ship in Nanaimo harbour. Because he was not suited for labouring, Douglas made Bayley the first schoolmaster in Nanaimo. He left in 1857, and although he became Nanaimo's MLA in 1863, he never lived in the town again.

and one teacher with no fixed income. Small wonder that Bayley had seen more opportunity in Victoria.

The little log cabin also served as a home for Bryant and as a post office, the arrival of letters and newspapers being a haphazard affair, depending on whatever boat happened to be coming north. When mail did arrive, the post office was open from 10:00 a.m. to 4:00 p.m., not late enough for some labourers who worked until 6:00 p.m., but too late for poor Bryant, who was never paid for his post office work in all the six years he held the job. Lessons were disturbed repeatedly by people arriving at the schoolhouse for their mail — newspapers six months out of date, letters bearing family news no longer relevant, mail delayed by the vagueness of an address which said simply "Vancouver's Island, British North America." This stale treasure was the only link with the rest of the world.

The rest of the world managed for the most part to get along without news from Vancouver Island. Even the mother government in Britain seemed to forget just how slow the lines of communication were, a fact which had been especially apparent during the Crimean War. Although war was declared on March 28, 1854, the news did not arrive in Victoria until July of that year. Russia and Great Britain, although refusing to agree in the Crimea, did agree on some rules of the game, including the neutrality of the Eastern Pacific ocean. But Britain did not get around to telling the Governor of Vancouver Island about this and Douglas, good administrator that he was, prepared to defend the Island from the Russians without any help from Britain.

The autumn of 1854 brought the news that although the Island was not in danger it was needed as a refuge for wounded from the seige of Petropaulovski and as a coaling station for ships of the Royal Navy Pacific Squadron. While one such ship was taking on fuel in Nanaimo, a sailor on board succumbed to his wounds. His body was buried in the little graveyard, his tombstone an exotic oddity in the tiny, isolated town where petty labour skirmishes and thieving Indians provided the only excitement. So while the rest of the world made war, marked the passing of despots, recoiled in horror at the Indian Mutiny, and read with amazement and alarm Darwin's *Origin of the Species*, little Nanaimo continued its daily routine with no knowledge of the outside world save that which was several months old.

The graveyard claimed fewer victims than might have been expected because the population was so young. Half the 151 people living in Nanaimo in 1854 were under twenty years of age. Owing to the British law that required a surgeon on every emigrant ship, Vancouver Island was well supplied with doctors, most of whom chose to stay. Some were eccentrics, some scoundrels, some merely incompetent, but there was a goodly number of young, able medical men with a sense of adventure, who found the challenges of a new colony invigorating.

After leaving Fort Rupert, John Helmcken had returned to Victoria to be medical officer there and to supply other HBC posts with medications. His no-nonsense attitude towards the care of the body set the tone for the maintenance of health. "The treatment of the interior [is] simple," he said, "an emetic as soon as a man fell ill, followed by a purge — then the man has to get well by simples."[11]

"Simples" did no good for an assistant miner who was injured in July of 1855. When Patrick Divine carelessly allowed his foot to hang over the side of the cage, it was crushed between the cage and sill of the pithead frame. A few days later the foot had to be amputated. While he was recovering from that trauma, some tainted food caused him to vomit violently and he struck his stump against the side of the bed, rupturing an artery. The poor man bled to death. It was tersely noted that the fact that he had been suffering from venereal disease for some months "probably aggrivated [sic] the case and accelerated the result."

Venereal disease had no cure but there was hope for the eradication of another killer. Smallpox vaccinations had curtailed that disease dramatically among whites, but the virus still found victims among the Indians, who had no defense against it. When Douglas heard of an outbreak of the disease on the American side, he ordered vaccinations of the Indians in the colony. It was the first of many smallpox outbreaks which would exact a terrible toll among the native population.

About the same time as Cornelius Bryant and Mark Bate arrived in Nanaimo, the town also received a new doctor. Alfred Benson, who had been replaced in Victoria by John Helmcken, was now sent to Nanaimo, having served on a number of HBC posts since his arrival in 1848. Benson was probably transferred from Victoria because he was a "radical" and a "grumbler," and had sided with Blanshard against Douglas and the Company in the dispute that began with the Fort Rupert miners' strike. In England he had been well-clothed and sedate; in the colony he was a disheveled eccentric, who wore sea

---

[11] Simples are medicines made from medicinal plants or herbs.

boots because of the mud, usually with one pant leg tucked in and one hanging out. He lived in a room crowded with Indian curiosities, bird skins, geological specimens, and tobacco.

Widowed after just two years' marriage, Dr. Benson stayed on in Nanaimo as surgeon to the mines after the Company was sold, the new owners paying him a retainer for a year and then giving him permission to practice on his own. In his spare time he built a sloop, the *Hamley*, which he sold to the Miners' and Mechanics' Benevolent Society, and involved himself in the development of coal lands for the Harewood Mining Company. When he retired to England he was remembered fondly by his patients, who honoured him by changing the name of the mountain whose arms enfolded the tiny coal town from the Indian "Wakesiah" to "Mount Benson."

The health of any community depends on the availability of good drinking water. Someone prospecting for coal had discovered the only water source of any size in Nanaimo — springs, which bubbled out under the rocks of the tidal ravine, whose long finger almost separated the town from the mainland. At low tide, older children were sent down the steep sides of the ravine to fill empty powder cans with water. Filling a bathtub for a work-dirty father at the end of each shift kept many Nanaimo young people extremely busy.

Above the ravine, huddled along its steep edge, were the twelve-foot square one room cabins, which housed bachelors or men whose families had not yet joined them. On the ravine side there was only one small window in each cabin, a small porthole really, fitted with a heavy wooden shutter which could be pushed up from the inside and fastened with a yellow strap on an iron hook. Indians camped at the so-called "Euclataw Ranch" across the Millstone River from Pemberton's Encampment Mine would come up the ravine looking for alcohol. They would scramble up the cliff, rap at the shutter covering the porthole, and demand that a bottle be handed out lest hostilities be declared.

The men who lived in the cabins were troubled by more than thirsty Indians. All night, mice ran over the beds and their occupants. As a result, most men owned at least one cat, and one fellow whose cabin was graced with a kitten cut two holes in his door. The larger door was for the mother cat and the smaller for the kitten. When asked why he had done this he is reported to have replied that he was not the kind of man to let the mother in and make the baby stay outside!

All the houses were close to the mines where the men worked, with the exception of the mines on Newcastle Island. To get to work each morning, those miners stepped into canoes and paddled north through the harbour towards Exit Channel, which separated the town from Newcastle Island. Past the Millstone estuary and into the Channel made dark by the tall trees which crowded to the water's edge on each side, they silently made their way. The Channel was narrow and very deep, deep enough for the steamers which loaded right at the dock between Shaft and Tyne Points at the north end.

Ever since Joseph McKay had proved Boyd Gilmour wrong in 1853 about the coal on Newcastle, there had been a mine into that second and lower seam. The outcrop curved around a small bluff just north of the bay named for an Indian midden and extended right across the Island's north end to the ocean on the other side, where McKay Point commemorated the discovery. Under John McGregor the so-called Newcastle Adit was worked until 1856, when the pit employed most of the miners in town. Even the method of mining was a joint effort, being a blend of the pillar and stall technique of the Scottish miners with the longwall most familiar to the Staffordshire men.

The blending of the two methods resulted in a more wide-open mine without the roof support normally afforded by the large pillars of coal left in the Scottish miners' system. The roof of the worked out areas was initially supported by upright timbers and ultimately by waste rock being shovelled back into the gob. The attempt to blend the two methods may have been the cause of a near tragedy in April of 1856.

Mary Hawkes knew something bad had happened when she was asked to go the Island. With her reputation as an able nurse, she was called whenever there was an injury at the mines. This time one of the injured was her husband, Thomas. He and Dick Richardson had been caught in a rock fall, but neither man suffered permanent injury. Thomas held no grudge against the mine and returned to the Island twenty-four years later to get the last of the coal in the upper seam.

The mine was closed soon after the accident. Men were needed at a new mine being opened for the Company by Robert Dunsmuir, and the horses were needed for Number Three Mine. Through the next decade, however, every two years or so, men like John Thompson and Joseph Bevilockway would come back to do a little contract digging in the Newcastle Mine.

The Newcastle Mine became a going concern again in 1868, when Jesse Sage and his son-in-law Edward Walker contracted to go into the old adit and sink a new slope at the back. They opened back out to the surface around the bluff north of the adit opening and took out several thousand tons of coal. It was handy for ships to take on Newcastle coal. The mine was close to the beach and the dock was in deep water, but the coal was not that good. When the Douglas seam was uncovered on the Island, just a few yards to the south on Midden Bay, the old mine was gradually phased out by the early 1870's.

The best year for that old mine on Newcastle had been 1856, when it employed the entire workforce of the town. But those men were needed for the new level-free mines at the head of Commercial Inlet. The mines were called "level-free" because they sloped into the coal at a slight upward angle like adits, thus allowing the mine to free itself of water by gravity.

The Park Head Level-Free was the first Nanaimo mine to be developed along Robinson's new policy that the roads would be high and wide enough to accommodate horses inside in an effort to make the Company independent of Indian labour. When they were not available for haulage, the Indians, because of their unpredictable comings and goings, caused mines to be closed.

Below and to the south of the Park Head Mine was Dunsmuir's Level-Free. Working as a free agent under contract to the Nanaimo Coal Company, as the HBC establishment at Nanaimo was now called, Robert Dunsmuir made a singular success of this venture. This despite the fact that the coal was only of moderate quality and the seam only four and a half feet thick. Just two months after he took it on he was able to supply enough coal to fill the needs of the *Otter*, a screw steamer belonging to the Company. Soon, in a request which seemed to prophesy the future, the market in San Francisco was specifically ordering "Dunsmuir" coal.

Dunsmuir's relations with his employees were also a prophecy for the future. Work went slowly at first, despite the expanded work force, as the Staffordshire miners objected to being employed by a contract miner. Perhaps it was just the identity of this particular contract miner which made them so reluctant. His hard working, hard driving methods may not have been popular. However, despite the unhappiness of the labour force, by 1858 the mine had become the most valuable and least expensive operation in town.

Not long after, a wharf was completed by Edward Walker, leading from the two level-free mines and extending a quarter of a mile into deep water. This wharf was a precursor to the long wharf that would service the big Douglas Pit, which would soon take over the steadily improving body of coal so well begun by Robert Dunsmuir.

New mines quickly became old mines. In 1863, with the Douglas Pit already supplanting it at the head of Commercial Inlet, the Dunsmuir level-free had become a nuisance. When miners drawing pillars from the back reaches of the mine had been allowed to kindle a fire against the face to warm themselves, the coal had ignited and burned for two years, getting worse as time went on. Smoke crept out from a crevice of rock fractured by the mine caving in and filled the air with fumes. Despite assurances from the Company that the fire was caused by accident not mismanagement — a subtle distinction — it was very annoying to those who lived nearby.

Another mine in town had caused nothing but trouble. HBC Number Three started as a small shank in 1855, but it took until the following year for coal to be struck at the fourteen fathom level. It was here on the shores of the harbour, underneath the houses of the miners, that the irregularity of Vancouver Island coal first revealed itself. Through the next hundred years, the faulting of the coal bed was the biggest problem that managers and miners had to deal with. Time and again the coal pinched down to nothing, necessitating expensive and frustrating exploration through rock to relocate the errant seam.

In 1856, however, the biggest problem in HBC Number Three was controlling the water, which would gush into the workings and stop all mining. The horses and gin brought from the Newcastle Mine could not keep up with the pumping; Indians were hired to pump, using gear lowered into the shaft, while the miners tried unsuccessfully to dam the water. Flooding rendered the mine idle for almost a year until the venerable little steam engine from the defunct HBC Number One Mine could be moved and installed in a new pithead frame.

While the flooded mine sat idle, William Isbister began quarrying the stone for the ventilating furnace. The whole town depended on Isbister for his stonework. He built chimneys for engines and houses; he lined furnace shafts; he even built a stone house which because of its permanent character served many purposes down the years. Isbister gave good value for money. His chimneys were built "thick enough for a battlement."

When Number Three Mine's pump was finally ready in early 1857, the water that had kept the mine idle for almost a year was pumped

94

out in eight hours. James Douglas was not impressed, however. The engine driver cost more to employ than a horse and gin arrangement and that made Number Three coal too expensive to mine. In addition, the engine made a terrible noise as it went about its work. A visitor remarked, "About the first thing that attracts the stranger's eye on nearing the town, is the engine at Number Three Pit, blowing and snorting away most furiously, but doing very little work." The illustrious steam engine that brought Nanaimo into the industrial era had lapsed into an ignominious old age, as had the mine below it. When it closed in 1863, no one missed its fine household coal. What people noticed most was the quiet.[12]

By the end of the 1850's Nanaimo was starting to feel like a proper place to live. The Reverend Arthur Browning would likely have attributed it to the arrival of the Methodists. In the last year of the decade he could proudly point to regular observance of the Lord's Day, a decline of drunkenness, a visible improvement in family morals and to Indians attending church regularly and being "attentive to their duties." "Our small society, taken from the ranks of the enemy, [is] growing in the Divine life," he exulted, "and we anticipate for Nanaimo a Methodistic future."

The arrival of George Robinson's earnest young nephews Cornelius Bryant and Mark Bate had no doubt improved the tone of the place. While Cornelius did his teaching and temperance work, Mark busied himself as Company clerk for the sum of fifty pounds a year plus rations. He was not above requesting extra perks such as additional pay for recording the shipping from Park Head Mine, request denied, and free passage from England for his "female acquaintance" Sarah Ann Cartwright of Worcestershire, request granted. They were married in 1859. As he began his rise up the ladder from Company clerk to Company manager, he recorded his impressions in a messy but authoritative hand.

Describing his reaction to first seeing the town in 1857 he wrote:

... clean, whitewashed row of houses standing on a rising eminence a little way from the waterfront, the grassy slope between the buildings and the harbour looking fresh as spring; the towering peak of Wakesiah mountain, under a heavy cloud, and the intervening tall timber, formed a sombre looking background, giving the place just then a rather weird aspect."[13]

[12] Despite the noise it made, Hunter's steam engine was still being used in 1884 in the Douglas Pit.

[13] Whether the houses were sooty or white obviously depended on how recently they had been whitewashed.

The British Colonist, exercising the patronizing prerogative of the representative of the larger town on the Island, said of the inhabitants that they were

extremely ignorant of anything that transpired in the outer world. In those days justice was administered with a big stick, and the place seemed inexpressably [sic] weird and lonely, wearing altogether a reckless and despairing aspect, as did also the inhabitants, who thought themselves exiled and far away from the abodes of civilization, very seldom heard of, and their very existence almost unknown beyond the precincts of the Hudson's Bay Company offices.

Robert Dunsmuir (1825-1889),
coal miner.   PABC 2695

Nanaimo Indians pose in front of longhouse.
NANAIMO AND DISTRICT CENTENNIAL MUSEUM

Andrew Hunter (1811-84),
steam engineer.
WILLIAM HUNTER COLLECTION

Elizabeth Gough (1823-99); *Princess Royal*
passenger, miner's wife, hotel owner.
NANAIMO AND DISTRICT
CENTENNIAL MUSEUM

Later photograph of large Indian canoe, main method of transportation in early days.
RAY KNIGHT COLLECTION, PABC 89071

Downtown Nanaimo in 1858
showing miners' square hewn
log cabins and HBC Number
One Mine on the right.
PABC 93857

Matthew and Caroline Miller,
Princess Royal passengers, with
sons Charles and William.
NANAIMO AND DISTRICT
CENTENNIAL MUSEUM

Nanaimo 1875. Note Bastion, first tripod for aerial tramway, bridge at entrance of ravine, higher ravine bridge with two-story Literary Institute at one end.   PABC 11292

Harewood Mine's ill-fated aerial tramway.   PABC 49576

Top-hatted Robert Dunsmuir poses beside saddle-tanked locomotive *Duchess* as his employees watch from coal wagons.   PABC 49566

With miners' cabins and Bastion in background, the *Maude* is moored at Gordon's wharf.   PABC 93353

Coal loading
wharves at Departure
Bay accommodate
sailing and steam
ships. Trains from
mines arrive via
trestle above.
PABC 49559

Lt. Col. Charles
Frederick Houghton,
commanding
officer of militia
which assisted
Sheriff during 1877
Wellington strike.
PABC HP 5859

Pithead buildings of Dunsmuir's Number One Slope, 1875.   PABC 93352

Haze from coal fires hangs over Nanaimo as seen from Commercial Inlet at high tide. Buildings of Commercial Street supported on pilings.   PABC 31578

Joseph Randle, Jr. and Tom Mills, oversmen. Randle's high boots, clothing and soft cap typical miners' garb. Fish oil lamp in right hand.   PABC 93988

Number One Esplanade pithead after explosion, May 3, 1877.
NANAIMO AND DISTRICT CENTENNIAL MUSEUM

Rebuilt pithead of Number One Esplanade, 1891. Locomotive *San Francisco* and coal cars which carried five tons each.   PABC 20627

William McGregor (1855-98); manager Number One Esplanade Mine.
McGREGOR FAMILY COLLECTION

Frank Little, Superintendent Union Colliery, and his boss, James Dunsmuir.
CUMBERLAND MUSEUM

With fireboss in lead, work-dirty miners leave Number One Esplanade Mine carrying lunch buckets. Mule drivers have whips over shoulders.   PABC 93993

Wellington Hotel in new townsite. Like its two predecessors, it burned down and was rebuilt.   PABC 31531

Wellington bosses pose in abandoned Old Slope.   PABC 11286

Cumberland's muddy Dunsmuir Street. Note Cheap John's with lodge meeting rooms above and Waverly Hotel.   PABC 41767

Coke ovens at Union Bay.   NANAIMO AND DISTRICT CENTENNIAL MUSEUM

Coal cars lie like abandoned toys between two ends of Trent River trestle. Workers pose by wreckage of locomotive Number Four.   PABC 55326, PABC HP55325

Joan Dunsmuir (Mrs. Robert)
(1828-1908).   PABC 2699

Robert Dunsmuir, British
Columbia's wealthiest citizen.
PABC 95143

Robert Dunsmuir's Craigdarroch Castle.   PABC 5445

The Green, often site of union meetings, witnesses farewell to Sam Robins, the man with the white beard in the photo below. Note coal trestle in the background.

NANAIMO AND DISTRICT CENTENNIAL MUSEUM

CHAPTER III

Drunkards and Skedaddlers

There were drunken miners and rowdy sailors, pugnacious Indians, and the officials of the Hudson's Bay Company were not fit to be trusted with holding a magistracy.

The British Colonist

There are two things the Nanaimoites can boast of — 'Children and dogs' — speaking of quantity and quality.

Captain Dundas of the *Fusi Yama*

If the presence of drunken sailors and itinerant scallywags turns a village into a town then Nanaimo was one; if a bank, a butcher shop, a Chinese laundry, and a dress and stay maker mean a town has come of age then Nanaimo had arrived; if a hotel owned by a real Frenchman and another housing a first class billiard table give a town prestige then Nanaimo had it. Nanaimo in 1865 had all those things and more. It had one thousand people, most of them men. It had businesses, celebrations, and churches; a Philharmonic society and a Stipendiary Magistrate; and a Literary Institute Building Committee.

But only forty or fifty of the people had any plans to stay; the businesses had better ads than merchandise; the Philharmonic Society could not find musicians; the Stipendiary Magistrate did not do enough to justify his salary; and the Literary Institute building sat unfinished waiting for windows. Still, things were happening in Nanaimo in 1865 because by that year the Vancouver Coal Mining and Land Company (VCML) had been in Nanaimo for four years.

Despite the magnificent body of coal available to it, the Hudson's Bay Company (HBC) had never been a mining company at heart, for it lacked the will to develop the mineral properly. But in 1861 a group of very repectable British investors, including Justice T. C. Haliburton, M.P. and John R. Galsworthy, expressed interest in British Columbia, the Fraser River Gold Rush having made the colony a popular place for investment.[1] Through Alexander Grant Dallas, a HBC man who had married the daughter of James Douglas and then succeeded his father-in-law as head of the Western Department of the HBC, contact was made. Dallas became a shareholder in a new company set up to purchase the coal mines of Nanaimo from the Company that employed him.

Two years before, Dallas had recommended that the HBC hire Mr. C. S. Nicol, Royal Navy (retired), as general manager of the HBC coal mines. The former engineer and land surveyor had no previous mining experience, or for that matter HBC experience, but it was he who supervised the sale of the coal lands, five shallow pits, two steam engines, a company store full of overvalued merchandise, and one hundred dwelling houses to the VCML. The HBC retained the mortgage against which the new owners borrowed.

While still employed by the HBC, Nicol also served as the financial agent for the VCML and succeeded himself as manager in the new operation. At first it was hard to tell the difference between the business philosophies of the two companies. Just as the HBC had attempted to reap large profits from a small financial outlay, so too were the shareholders of the VCML interested in maximum dividends with a minimum of expense.

Money had to be spent before profits could be made, but it took until 1864 for the message to get through. In that year stockholder dissatisfaction reached a sufficient level for a committee to be appointed to investigate Company management. Justice Haliburton having died, the new Chairman of the Board was the Honourable Charles W. Wentworth Fitzwilliam, and he tackled the Company's problems energetically.

Fitzwilliam was no stranger to Vancouver Island. He had visited Fort Victoria in 1853 and again in 1863. By the second visit he had become the Viscount Milton, heir to the Earl Fitzwilliam. He was five feet tall, slender, and epileptic, but he had made his second journey not in the conventional way by ship around Cape Horn but overland from Canada in the company of five other Englishmen. The harrowing journey across the prairies, through the Yellowhead Pass in the Rocky Mountains, and down the river valleys of the interior of British

---

[1] Thomas Chandler Haliburton had spent most of his life in Nova Scotia and had only recently taken up residence in Britain. Besides being a retired judge, he was a prolific author, best known as the creator of Sam Slick. Galsworthy was the grandfather of the novelist, John Galsworthy III.

Columbia was accomplishment enough for even a robust man. Fitzwilliam returned by the same route a year later, this time stopping in the Cariboo to witness the newest gold rush at first hand. Such an intrepid young man was not likely to be daunted by the management of a coal company no matter how poorly run.

With John Galsworthy's son and namesake as his right-hand man, the new Chairman of the Board instituted a policy of judicious expenditure. Money was to be spent in order to make the coal company into a paying proposition for the shareholders. He sold the Company store to a local entrepreneur and wrote off "6000 pounds of rubbish" acquired with it. Instead of high dividends, which had been promised to the shareholders, he created reserves, which were invested in bonds. Eventually, in 1867, he discharged Captain Nicol, who he said had made an unreasonable profit when he arranged the sale from the HBC.

Yet despite Nicol's questionable role in the purchase of the Company, he had improved productivity by upgrading equipment and introducing better mining techniques. By cultivating personal contacts in California and other west coast locations, he had raised yearly exports. Local expertise in the persons of Mark Bate as Chief Clerk and Robert Dunsmuir as superintendent of mining operations, gave a certain degree of management continuity.

However, it was the Company directors who hired a young Ayrshireman named John Bryden to provide Nicol with expert advice on developing the coal beds. The former coal miner, hired on as "Coal Viewer" for three hundred pounds per annum, arrived from Britain in 1863. An energetic, knowledgeable, and practical man, Bryden plunged into the daily life of the mines and the town with the vigour of one who knows his worth and is sure of his opinions.

Within a year of his arrival, Bryden was serving on committees to find a site for a new cemetery and a colonial school. His name could be heard in every debate about civic affairs. By 1866 he was assistant manager of the VCML, and in 1867 he cemented his place in the hierarchy of the community by marrying Elizabeth Hamilton Dunsmuir, eldest daughter of Robert and Joan.

For by the 1860's, Robert Dunsmuir was also a respected community leader. Since receiving his free miner's licence he had worked for the HBC as a contracted oversman and for the VCML as mine superintendent. Farming and real estate also occupied his time and enhanced the family income. Although he chose to exercise his political beliefs as an organizer and not a candidate, his name at the head of committees of nomination, incorporation, and organization was a stamp of respectability for each endeavor.

At a public tea meeting in 1864, to mark his retirement as manager of the Douglas Pit, the man who some miners had vilified for his lack of participation in the early labour unrest of the town was feted. Following an "excellent spread of creature comforts," a newly respectable John Meakin rose to present a testimonial to Robert Dunsmuir on behalf of the miners of Nanaimo. "As a token of the great respect they entertained for their late overseer" he was given a gold watch and chain with appropriate inscription. Dunsmuir's humble reply was followed by three cheers and "He's a Jolly Good Fellow" and dancing until midnight.

Dunsmuir was leaving the Company to become the manager of a new mine just outside the VCML lease. The Harewood Mining Company was financed by the Lascelles family, whose wealth was based on West Indies sugar plantations. Following the 1837 abolition of slavery in all British possessions, which "spoiled" the West Indies for English investment, the Lascelles fortune, like many others, had to be put to work elsewhere. The Honourable Horace Douglas Lascelles, youngest son of the late Earl Harwood and brother of the present Earl had money to invest when he arrived in the Pacific as a Royal Navy officer on the H.M.S. *Topaz* in 1861.

Lascelles was unselfish, kind hearted, hospitable, and generous as only a man possessed of a large amount of money can be. Just one of a number of wealthy young Englishmen serving in the Royal Navy, he was attracted to a new company formed in 1863 by Dr. Alfred Benson, who had applied for and received a land grant of three thousand acres in the Chase River area, above the VCML lands.

By the time Robert Dunsmuir took over as manager of the Harewood Mining Company, fifteen men were already employed and tools had been brought to the site. From the six foot ten inch seam, Dunsmuir ordered a sample of coal to be extracted and sent to Victoria for testing at the Gas Works. The blacksmith said it was good coal. A visiting expert toured the mine site and marvelled at its advantages. A tunnel straight into the hill would make it easy to remove the coal, drain, and ventilate. By August 1864, there were company houses built and enough men to justify asking a visiting minister to preach a sermon.

One year later, mining had still not commenced. Despite the enthusiasm of the blacksmith, Dunsmuir had reservations about the quality of the coal. Since his and his miners' incomes were to be determined by the amount of coal they marketed, manager and employees alike had a huge stake in the mine's success. But the operation was doomed from the beginning.

No matter how good the coal was or how much of it was dug, if it could not be marketed, the mine would fail. Crucial to the marketing of coal was to get it to tidewater, where ships could take it away to the buyers. The VCML was particularly fortunate in this regard. Its mines were close to the ocean and it owned all the foreshore in the area.

Included in the charter already acquired by the Harewood Mining Company was government permission to construct a railway to Departure Bay through VCML land. Although the older company did not use the land on that second harbour, it was in fact the best and deepest water frontage, and the Company was loath to give it up. Speculation had it that what the VCML really wanted was to have the Harewood docks situated right in town, as this would stimulate the sale of town lots, just newly offered on the market. Whatever the reason, the VCML petitioned the Legislative Assembly in Victoria, in protest over the granting of the railway corridor.

Opinion in Nanaimo was divided between those who saw the new mine as a boon to the economy and those who felt development at Departure Bay would scatter population and resources. It was better to concentrate all development in one place, they said. Besides, a downtown terminus would mean a shorter railway line with better gradients and would avoid crossing the Big Swamp, the Millstone River, and the ravine near Departure Bay.

By the time the Legislative Assembly had overruled the VCML objections it was too late to save the enterprise from collapse. The miners, having earned little, sought jobs in Nanaimo; Dunsmuir returned to the security of the VCML; Lascelles soon succumbed prematurely to dropsy, leaving his British Columbia holdings to his sister Maud; and Rory Cameron was hired to live at the mine as a watchman, where his tall tales about his prowess with a gun entertained and amazed the readers of the *Nanaimo Gazette*.

It seems that Cameron was sitting in front of his cabin enjoying a "midday muckamuck" when over a steep bluff came two deer, one with a panther on its back. The fall dislodged the panther, and while the buck held him at bay, Cameron created a diversion with his Enfield rifle and the buck escaped. "The panther, cheated out of a dinner of venison, determined to make up for it by a steak off a Highlander." With the animal a few feet away and prepared to spring our hero ... raised his rifle to his shoulder and fired, the ball wounding the animal in the *back*. Rory's gun must have been superior to O'Toole's pistol, which could perform no greater feat than shooting around a corner, while Rory's, like the Australian boomerang can describe a circle.[2]

Rory Cameron's suspiciously acrobatic heroism was read with amusement in a town that had received a boost towards autonomy in a decision by the Company to sell building lots. In what was undoubtedly the most popular gesture in a rather autocratic reign, C. S. Nicol had supervised the first sale of land into private hands in the towns' short history.

Following a town plan drawn up in London using a contour map, lots were set aside and offered for auction in Victoria. The Company said that the sale took place in the capital to test the value of the land but local people were suspicious that the real reason was a desire for the higher prices that city folk would be prepared to pay. Such a sale would place all the property in the hands of absentee landowners. In May of 1864, one hundred Victoria investors bought building lots in Nanaimo for one quarter down, and one quarter in each of twelve, eighteen, and twenty-four months.

The Victoria sale was soon followed by another in Nanaimo, and produced a change in the emotional attachment of the inhabitants to the town. Suddenly the miners could take pride in the little collection of modest houses because they had a stake in it. No longer would they go without representation in the Colonial Legislature because the only property owner was the Company. The new landowners could now add their voices to those of the homesteaders who had pre-empted acreages south and west of Company land.

The presence of bonafide farmers also meant that fresh produce, eggs, and milk were more readily available, but only when the farmers were able to get to town. By 1864 Peter Sabiston, William Westwood, and the "Cornishmen" Francis and Nichols could supply most of the town's produce needs from their farms to the west in the Mountain District. To the south farms belonging to Nicol, Biggs, Jones, York, Richardson, Ferguson, and Franklyn grew hay and worked the fertile land of Cedar. But getting to town with their crops was not a simple matter of hitching up the horses and climbing on the wagon, for the roads were almost impassable.

The road in from Cedar was "in a very rough and haggard state." "Stumps and hollows of no mean dimensions are frequently met with

---

[2] "Panther" is a synonym for cougar or mountain lion.

along the road." It was often obstructed by fallen timber or even standing trees. Added to these obstructions were swamps "where a man has to wade up to his knees or go a mile or two out of his way." The streets in Nanaimo were little better.

It is by no means pleasant to go over ground where you can never walk three yards on the same level, or to scramble and sprawl among stumps and stones like a crab among rocks.

For streets we have nothing better than the Indian trail. Boulders, stumps, ash heaps and sand-pits obstruct our path as we wend our way along the streets.

There is a heap of rubbish [on Bastion Street] consisting of old hoops, bottles and so on which would seem to be the refuse of the establishment under whose fence they lay. A stranger getting among these hoops would with difficulty extricate himself. He would no sooner get out of one than he would put his feet in another, and finally end the performance, perhaps by a dangerous roll among the broken glass.

The large number of pigs who prowled the streets and rooted up potato patches, turnips and fences, drove at least one frustrated gardener to attacking them with an axe. Innumerable dogs who filled the night with their howling and wolves who came down from the hills at night to clean up the carcasses of dead horses, made the streets unpleasant and often risky places to be, especially after dark.

As if the streets were not problem enough, bridges, or the lack of them, made transportation even more dangerous and difficult. The one across the Nanaimo River on the way to Cedar washed out on a regular basis. The Company finally built a rickety bridge to connect the main street with Victoria Crescent on the other side of the ravine, but there was no bridge further up the ravine even though there were houses on the other side.

It is no joke, if you have occasion to visit a friend on the far side of the ravine in the middle of the night, to have to sprawl down one bank, and up the other, to say nothing of a considerable probability of pitching with your head into a bog, and your heels in the air, and affording a respectable coroner's jury materials for a verdict of 'died by inversion in a quagmire.'

This ragtag collection of trails, rickety bridges, quagmires, and stumps had been dignified with street names when the Company offered lots for sale. Except for Front Street, Bridge (later Commercial) Street, Chapel Street, Wharf Street, and Bastion Street, the names honoured far away royalty, Victoria and Albert, and equally far away members of the Company Board of Directors. Some worthy

103

gentlemen were able to offer names to more than one street. Thus the new Chairman of the Board lent his name to Milton, Wentworth, and Fitzwilliam Streets and another board member with the imposing name of Prideaux Selby had two streets named after him.

Still, the new street names did lend a certain tone to the collection of colliery buildings and the "remarkably sooty houses" that made up the coal camp. The log walls of the houses still allowed the wind to pass through "with a shriek of triumph" and empty casks often replaced chimneys which "bulged and tottered." Mark Bate said the substitute chimneys resembled "the hat of a person addicted to hard drinking," but the town had gained a certain measure of respectability. The manager and the magistrate each built fine houses above the ravine, the latter's being constructed of real bricks imported from England, to the amazement of the mere mortals of the town and a resounding clatter of tongues.

A large fire in 1865 consumed eighteen miners' cottages owned by the Company but made way for construction of better quality replacements. Indeed a policy of systematic burning of derelict log houses had begun, providing fuel for giant bonfires ignited to commemorate such memorable occasions as the first visit of the new Governor, Arthur Kennedy.

The appearance of the town did not improve overnight to some people's way of thinking. Although there was now a variation in design and some people surrounded their homes with gardens, although some of the stores and homes were lit with the new Canadian invention of kerosene instead of fish oil and tallow, few houses had curtains or pictures or ornaments or even flowerpots.

By 1866 the *Nanaimo Gazette* could still bemoan the fact that the town was primitive, that the houses were widely scattered without design and were poor and uncomfortable. As for the inside of the houses,

the greater number present not the slightest appearance that their inmates intend a continuous residence ... without the slightest interest in the houses that shelter them or the town which they inhabit. Dark, dingy cribs are most of them, with furniture and utensils so few and so rude as barely sufficient to minister to the animal wants.

The morose editor was no doubt indulging in some of the journalistic exaggeration so common to Victorian-era newspapermen, but his comments also reflected the townspeople's lack of proprietary pride, a condition which would gradually change as the people began

104

to own their own homes and have an influence over their own political future.

Up to that time, the town's political life had been solely a matter of form, but even then it had provided some lively moments. In 1856 the British Colonial office ordered then Governor Douglas to elect the colony's first assembly, an election which was arranged with almost no knowledge of legislative procedure. A proclamation listed five electoral districts and assigned the number of members to be chosen from each. Nanaimo was to be represented by one man.

In order to vote, a man had to own twenty acres of land. Nanaimo had only one landowner and that was the Company, so Nanaimo's one vote was cast by Captain Stuart, the officer-in-charge. Being the only man qualified to stand as a candidate as well, Stuart became Nanaimo's member until his election was protested on the basis of his only being the representative of the property owner. He was replaced by Dr. John F. Kennedy, a HBC employee from Victoria.

When Kennedy died in 1859 a notice was posted on the door of the Bastion, calling for a meeting of voters and inhabitants at that very location to elect a replacement. The fact that the notice failed to specify a time for the meeting was immaterial, for there were still no other voters. Shortly afterward, another notice appeared announcing that Charles Stuart had voted for one John George Barnston, a lawyer from Victoria, this second electoral foray being summed up by a wag writing to the editor of the *Colonist* saying:

Thus as far as I know to the contrary, our electioneering is over, and as it was done peaceably, quietly and without any rioting or fighting, I hope your Victoria people will admit that we 'done it very nicely.'

Barnston refused the honour. Two months later when the election was reheld, the nomination of John Swanson, Captain of the HBC steamer *Labouchere*, had to be seconded by a non-voter. The assembled crowd of fifteen people watched as George Robinson climbed up on the steps of the Bastion where everyone could see him and made a speech about the disgrace of it all. He did not blame the authorities; rather he blamed the people, none of whom had bothered acquiring any land, although some had talked about it.

Andrew Hunter took over the steps and said "I wish the place was as good now as it was when I first came to it." Then Thomas Mills got up and asked how Swanson was going to represent them when he spent at least six months of every year up north, and Stuart rose to defend his choice and warn George Robinson that he may yet have cause to regret having made the aforementioned remarks. The two men exchanged heated words after which several people signed the document as witnesses, including the Constable who had just arrived and had not witnessed anything.

Mills had been right about Swanson. The good captain was up north near the Russian possessions, as Alaska was called in those days, and refused to take his seat or be sworn in because of the scandal evoked by the election. When the people of Nanaimo asked when the election of a replacement would take place, they were informed that Mr. A. R. Green had already been their member for three weeks. Since Green spent most of the session in the United States, he soon ceased to qualify as a member too.

Things should have changed by 1861, because by then the Nanaimo electoral district had twenty-one registered voters. "Nanaimo is no longer a rotten-borough with only a proxy vote cast by the agent of the company," the *Colonist* triumphantly announced. Mr. David Babington Ring, a lawyer who had been nominated by Dr. Benson, was supported by the majority of the electorate, but then Attorney-General George Cary tried to block the by-election. Rumours abounded that Cary was about to send up a candidate who would oppose the local favorite. "Almost numberless lampoons, ridiculous caricatures, and doggerel verses" materialized in the days before the election. Posters bearing a cartoon drawing of Cary and another man racing with springs on their feet could be seen all over town.

On election day there were twenty persons present in front of the Colonial School to witness the nomination of Ring and the anticipated electoral battle, but no other candidates appeared. The returning officer declared Ring elected and the voters signed a resolution to that effect. The new member returned thanks and made promises and "so ended another of our proverbially quiet elections." From the harbour came a thirteen gun salute and a "tiger" fired by the brig *Christiana Carnell*, whose captain had ordered her adorned with all her bunting in honour of the occasion.

Two years later, Ring was no longer the darling of the electorate. Nothing had been done to implement the promises he had made to build a road to Victoria or to obtain a reciprocity treaty with the United States. That made the new candidate, former Nanaimo schoolteacher Charles Bayley, a popular choice. The town finally had a native son, or at least a former native son, to vote for. There was, however, "every prospect of the Nanaimo election being a very small affair." Only half a dozen voters evinced any interest.

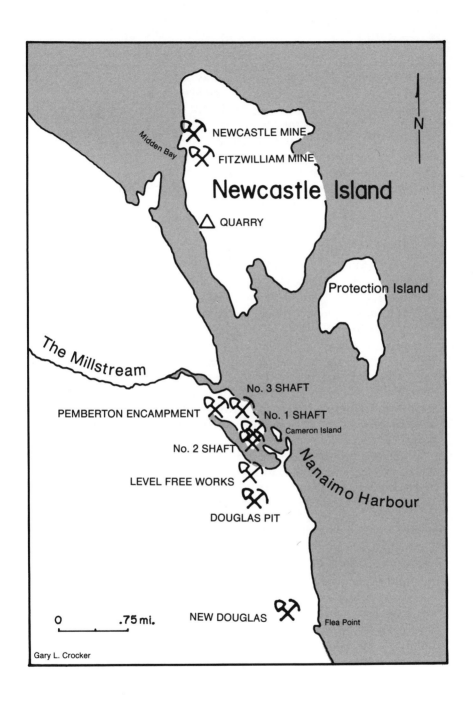

NANAIMO AREA MINES — 1852-1870

Bayley took matters in hand by covering the town with posters. On election day eight electors, six of whom were miners, gave Bayley a majority of two. D. Babington Ring was overheard to say that some miners were not fit to exercise the privilege of franchise.

Nanaimo voters had not given Bayley an overwhelming vote of confidence despite his former residency in the town and his being married to Andrew Hunter's daughter. And it seemed as though their lack of enthusiasm was justified, for he was seldom ever at the House of Assembly. One year into his term a meeting chaired by Robert Dunsmuir was called to overthrow the member. When only thirteen people appeared, Dunsmuir waited half an hour and then announced that it appeared Bayley had commenced attending to his duties, and they would let the subject drop until he erred again.

By 1865 Nanaimo was well and truly sick of being ignored in Victoria. Although money had been allotted to build a road from Nanaimo north to Comox, only eight hundred dollars had been set aside for public services in Nanaimo and nothing for the administration of justice or police protection. It was high time that Nanaimo's representative in Victoria was a real Nanaimo citizen.

Dunsmuir played an influential role by forming a Committee of Electors which asked Thomas Cunningham, a local storekeeper, to run. A few minutes before the election was due to take place at the courthouse, the whistle of the steamer *Diana* blew, and "numbers rushed down to the wharf with the dread expectation that the steamer was bringing in voters from Victoria in favour of Mr. D. Babington Ring."

While this proved not to be true, it did reveal another flaw in the Nanaimo electoral scene. The area across the Millstone River, the so-called Euclataw Ranch, where the Indians had camped a decade ago, was now called the Newcastle Townsite. It comprised land excluded from the Company coal lease and set aside as a future railroad grant. In 1860, several speculators from Victoria had availed themselves of an investment opportunity when lots were offered for sale.

Newcastle Townsite was a thorn in the side of Nanaimo. None of the landowners were interested in building there. No one lived there except for "a few Indian absqualators" who sometimes camped under the huge trees with which it was entirely covered right down to the shore. To add insult to injury, a thousand-dollar bridge had been built over the Millstream, a bridge to nowhere when bridges were needed desperately elsewhere in the town. The speculators from Victoria obviously had more influence with the government than did the residents of Nanaimo. In every election there was a fear that those investors would appear to elect their own candidate. But they did not come to the assistance of Mr. Ring in 1865, and in the show of hands on election day Cunningham received fourteen votes to Ring's six.

An 1866 "shot-gun marriage," which pleased neither of the partners, united the colonies of British Columbia and Vancouver Island under a government that consisted of nine magistrates nominated by the Governor and nine elected members. That the union of the two colonies was unpopular could be seen in the "blank apathy" which greeted the elections that year in Nanaimo. The coal town had completely lost interest in the legislative process. J. J. Southgate, a close friend of the Honourable Horace Douglas Lascelles but not even a resident of Nanaimo, was elected unopposed and in absentia. The ever-present and ever-eager Mr. Ring won the next election unopposed and took his place on the council in 1868, having earned by default the right to add the prefix "Honourable" to his name.

Victoria's neglect of Nanaimo continued. The oft-touted Comox Road was really only a trail "sixty miles long and ten feet wide," winding through enormous trees and eventually reaching the two solitary settlers who lived along its length. To the south of Nanaimo, the Victoria road was no better. It was so much quicker to go to Comox or Victoria by boat than to use the "highway system" of the Island. Any road improvements needed locally were paid for by the coal company or local private individuals.

One of the private road builders was Captain William Franklyn, who had hired workmen to build several miles of road from his farm south of town to tidewater. Franklyn was Nanaimo's magistrate, the first man not connected to the coal company to hold that office.

William Hales Franklyn had been in Nanaimo since he lost his position as captain of a Pacific and Orient steamer for throwing a passenger in irons. Described as "all British — bristled with it all over," he had earned the nickname the "British Lion." In keeping with his image, he had ordered that his house in town be built high above the rest of the community on the far side of the ravine, which seemed to guard the house like a moat would a castle. The handsome brick structure and his ability to finance road construction bore testimony to an income well beyond that of any coal miner.

The "British Lion" and his substantial income had been a topic of conversation ever since his arrival. Although he was at first unpaid, the Legislative Assembly soon assigned a yearly fee or stipend to the office of magistrate. "A stipendiary magistrate is no more required [in

109

Nanaimo] than a fifth wheel for a coach," fumed the *Colonist*. A citizen of Nanaimo agreed, saying it was just a way for the government to spend money on its pets. Another Nanaimoite defended Franklyn, saying that the state of the town had been alarming before he came but he was not sure that the job justified the 150 pound annual salary it drew.

The *Colonist* viewed the apppointment cynically.

Whether it is owing to the terror inspired by the Justice of the Peace resident here, or to the general contentment and prosperity of the people, vice is at a discount; every day bears the tranquility of a Sunday, only broken by the puffing of the engine, the gambols of the children and the singing and howling of the Siwashes over their departed friends, with the nocturnal sounds of their canine companions.

There was little enough to keep Franklyn busy. Someone worried in print that he would "die of having nothing to do" as there had only been one ten-minute case in the last five weeks. During the subsequent year, Franklyn also became Harbour Master, a position for which he received a salary as well and which appeared to have very few duties attached to it either.

As coal production increased, however, so did Franklyn's case load. Increased production meant more ships in the harbour, which meant more and more sailors roaming around town looking for trouble. A sailor charged with smashing the glass door at the French Hotel pleaded unconsciousness as a mitigating circumstance. A tar named John Williams attempted to gouge out the eyes of a well-known gent named Moses at the same hotel and was fined two dollars for being found in a drunken and helpless condition.

Drunken Indians and unscrupulous whiskey traders were more plentiful as well, the penalty for the former crime being a term in jail, and for the latter, a choice between jail or a fine. As the number of miscreants grew, so did the available supply of prisoner labour, which Franklyn commandeered to tend his garden. That their labour could have been well used improving the streets and that the only constable the town afforded was obliged to stand guard over them while they hoed and weeded, did nothing to temper the cynicism of the magistrate's critics.

Edwin Gough had chosen to become constable, reasoning that being in the fresh air and out of danger was preferable to digging coal. A kind man and slow to anger, the strong and well-built Gough was an ideal candidate for the job, but he cannot have known what was in store for him. In contrast to the generous salary collected by the

110

magistrate, Gough received no wages at all for policing the town and guarding the jail and had to support himself on the fees he received for serving summonses and attending court. Even so, he drew criticism for being a government favorite.

The next thing [that attracts the stranger's eye] is the bastion, built for the purpose of keeping evil away. Now alas! for Nanaimo morals it has produced a greater evil; it is now the county prison, in charge of one of the government's favorites.

The Bastion had fallen on evil days. It was unheated, dirty, and lacked proper security. Prisoners risked freezing in the winter and suffocation in the summer from the "bad air" that rose from the "convenience" below. The two cells crammed into the former bulwark could not accommodate the growing number of prisoners, the bulk of whom had to be sent at Nanaimo's expense to Victoria, where they were assigned to chain gangs for road work and other civic improvements. To have to pay for their export and be denied their labour was irritating enough. To be fired on from the shore, which happened more than once as the boats took the prisoners south, was insult indeed.

The few prisoners left in town were used for other work besides tending Franklyn's garden, but here again the underpaid constable drew criticism. One day Gough was in charge of three Indian prisoners who were removing a heap of ashes piled near the door of Gough's cabin, the entire neighbourhood having contributed to the dusty pile. Like most other streets in town, the one outside Gough's house had its share of stumps and it was on one of these that some wit posted the following:

Stumps, stumps, stumps,
Let the Constable move his own ashes,
And the Indians clear away these little chunks,
Against which a fellow's shin clashes.

In a less direct but more conventional mode of protest, a citizen wrote a letter to a Victoria newspaper criticizing Gough's use of chain gangs. Someone said Gough himself had written it to draw attention to the misuse of convict labour, but his inability to read and write made him innocent of that charge. When he was suspended for dereliction of duty and insolence, the *Nanaimo Gazette* pointed a finger at Magistrate Franklyn, accusing him of "scheming tricks" which had rendered Nanaimo without policemen.

111

Gough returned to coal mining, a job with considerably better wages and considerably less public scrutiny. His place was taken by a constable named Wenburne and a sergeant named Blake. Soon after assuming their law enforcement roles, the two men tangled with a species of gentleman becoming increasingly prevalent on the Island.

Bootleggers August Smith and James Hogan, a white man and a black man respectively, were found late one night in a boat containing two bottles of liquor, a large number of empties, and several spirit kegs also devoid of their former contents. In the scuffle that ensued when the bootleggers resisted arrest, one of them brandished a Bowie knife. The scene was conveniently illuminated by a light held by the Reverend Thomas Crosby, Methodist missionary, who knew a citizen's duty when he saw it. When the bootleggers were brought up before Magistrate Franklyn their defence was inventive.

... the two unfortunate bottles found in their possession were to be used solely by themselves as correctives to the extreme moisture of the atmosphere and Sergeant Blake was notorious for his antipathy to all the owners of all small craft who had a weakness for sailing along the coast with bottles and kegs for ballast.

About the time of the union between the two colonies in 1866, a retrenchment movement to save money began in Victoria. In response, a Nanaimo meeting chaired by John Bryden suggested getting rid of the Stipendiary Magistrate, as the office was totally unnecessary and a waste of public funds. Thomas Cunningham said they should have unpaid magistrates, who would be found "quite as efficient, though somewhat less despotic."

The days of Franklyn's stipend were numbered and he was soon dismissed from his position as magistrate following a debacle in the Legislative Council over the location of the colony's capital city. When Franklyn's intention to vote for New Westminster over Victoria became apparent, he was plied with liquor by the Victoria faction headed by Dr. John Helmcken. The Governor was so outraged by the unedifying spectacle that he dismissed Franklyn.

His replacement was Captain Warner Reeve Spalding, a bureaucrat who had served all over the united colonies and whose reputation as a former mounted policeman from Australia and a Captain in the Osmanli Irregular Cavalry in the Crimea lent him an air of mystery and dash. Spalding's responsibilities included being Assistant Commissioner of Lands, Collector of Revenue, County Court Judge, and Coroner, a combination which at first did not tax him. However, within the next ten years, the labour situation and the sudden increase in population would place his time in such demand that his integrity would be questioned.

Soon after assuming office, Spalding gathered together all the holders of liquor licenses in an effort to address a situation rapidly becoming a severe problem. The pub and hotel owners were asked to refrain from selling liquor to half-breed children. That the request should even have been necessary is an indication of the deteriorating condition of Nanaimo's first coal miners.

In the beginning, the Indians had provided a necessary service in the labour-short mines. Although their attendance could not be relied upon, especially when northern Indians bent on capturing slaves appeared in the harbour, there were always more Indians to take their place. They worked as miners in the early open pits, and later in the roadways of the underground mines as haulers, and in their canoes as loaders. The Indian women, or "Klootchmen" were especially hard-working and a very necessary part of the loading operation.

The white man's presence — his liquor and his diseases — changed that within a decade. "Whiskey may have killed its tens, but imported diseases its hundreds," observed Dr. Helmcken. Smallpox, measles, scarlatina, and syphilis killed many and left the survivors diseased and the women barren or their babies dead.

While a group of Indians from the north were visiting Victoria in 1862, several of their number contracted smallpox. Desperate and fearful, they fled back to their homes in the north, leaving their dead and dying in their nightly camps as they tried to escape the deadly disease. Having been infected with smallpox from blankets left at the northern Indian encampment near Nanaimo, two local Indians died. Even after their bodies were buried and their belongings burned, the fear remained, a fear shared by the white inhabitants.

Having just taken over the HBC mines, the VCML administered vaccinations to the Indian camp, aided by the Anglican minister, Reverend J. B. Good. Plans were made to relocate the Indians further south at the mouth of the Nanaimo River, well away from the town. Only new houses on a new location would wipe out the disease of which both white man and Indian were so afraid.

Two bales of HBC blankets and twelve barrels of lime with which to whitewash the new buildings was the price paid for the old land. Whitewashing was an effective method of controlling disease organisms and was used extensively in the white community. Reverend

Good, who had medical training, agreed to teach the Indians certain sanitary precautions.

The motivation of the Company was not altogether altruistic. The old Indian camp across Commercial Inlet sat on land that would make a perfect location for the deep-water wharves required by the Company if it were to attract the larger markets so necessary for survival. Indians in subsequent years had the small satisfaction of refusing to pay for the sports events that occurred on land below the trestles leading to the giant wharves.

The old camp disappeared in the rush to prevent the spread of the white man's disease and to make way for the white man's wharves. All that remained was the graveyard and then that was moved as well.

New graves were dug on a little side hill, and to these the remains were transferred. The holes however, were quite shallow, owing to the presence of a clay hardpan underneath. Next day a great outcry was made in the camp, and intense excitement prevailed, for most of the boxes had risen up and had come out of the graves.

A less scrupulous man of God might have tried to conjure a miracle out of that event, but the observer was Reverend Thomas Crosby, a sincere and forthright newly arrived Methodist missionary. Crosby had come to bring the gospel to the Indians, a mission begun by Reverend Ebenezer Robson, who would continue to minister to the white people in Nanaimo. In keeping with the practice of hundreds of Christian missionaries the world over, Crosby meant to eliminate heathen ways and bring the "savages" to a knowledge of Christ by transforming the Indians into white men.

Younger people were his main target, for he attributed the "sorceries, polygamy, domestic slavery, heathen dances, and etc." to the older members of the tribe. He described them as

a wild looking lot of little folk, with painted and dirt-begrimed faces and long, uncombed hair. Some of them were clothed in little print shirts, others had a small piece of blanket pinned around them, while some had no clothing at all.

If the appearance of the Indians seemed hardly Christian to the earnest young preacher, the living accommodations were the work of the devil. The new longhouses squatting by the shore, already surrounded by the refuse of daily living, were no fit place for Christian people to live. In contrast, the mission house with its pristine whiteness and picket-fenced garden was an inspiration to all who would be saved.

114

In 1867 several younger Indians were induced to build individual private dwellings. On a properly cleared and graded street on the hill overlooking the pagan longhouses, plots were marked out and white-washed frame houses built, each surrounded by carefully planted fruit and shade trees, their groomed domesticity a puny rebuke to the huge forest that pressed in from behind.

Having achieved a measure of external order, Crosby turned his attention toward two evils in particular — alcohol and the potlatch. If the longhouses were the work of the devil, then the potlatch was "the devil's high carnival."

Well, they used to have great big sheds, great big long houses and the middle of the roof was open. And they'd a great big fire there and what they were giving to various ones piled around outside and then they would do all their fancy dancing around. But the regalia and the stuff that they had, it was frightening sometimes.

The potlatch has been described as the "engine" of Indian society. In fact, it was the desire to accumulate surplus goods which could then be given away, thus commanding great respect, that had motivated Indians to work as coal miners in the beginning. But the generosity demonstrated by the host Indians was rarely understood by the white community. When thousands of Indians gathered in one place to feast and dance and howl and sing, white people could only assume that the devil was at work.

The Indians viewed the missionary's concerns with a delightful pragmatism. They offered to come to church and rest on Sunday if they could potlatch and dance during the week. Nineteenth century Christianity was not pragmatic. There could be no compromise. The fight to outlaw the potlatch was a long one, but finally, in 1893, the government yielded to pressure. Even then, enforcement was desultory at best.

Nanaimo Indians fared badly in their day to day contact with white people. An editorial in the *Gazette* said that justice for Indians was a mockery. Indian women were insulted by ruffians and violated and seduced with no recourse. They could count on no police assistance. If Indians were unable to pay the fines levied against them in court, their canoes, blankets, and muskets were seized and sold. An Indian was flogged for picking up an old platter on the street. Indians were jailed without charge. The editorial accused the magistrate of making up the laws as he went along. When an Indian employed by the magistrate complained when he did not receive his wages, he was locked up for a month.

The Indian who most deserved to be revered by the white community received the worst treatment. Che-wich-i-kan had been named Coal Tyee in honour of his having discovered Nanaimo coal, but he had become a pitiable figure soliciting for a handout or a drink, dressed in rags. No one knew how old he was. It was hard to tell by looking at him. One Sunday in 1865 he attended the service at St. Paul's church in town and was asked to leave because of "the fishy odour" that emanated from him, an odour which would not have been eliminated even with "the whole contents of the neighboring druggist's shop." It was pointed out that he could go to church on the reserve anyway.

On the subject of alcohol, however, there was much more a meeting of minds between the two communities. Indian leaders were as concerned as whites were. Native police officers were trained to search out illegal sales and caches of liquor, which in just a decade had grown to be a major cause of heartache in the Indian camp.

Ever since American traders first dropped anchor in Cowichan Bay, there had been a ready market for illicit liquor among Indians. As the decade progressed, the sale of "tangleleg" or "tanglefoot" increased greatly, so that some individuals were able to support themselves entirely on the illegal trade. By 1871 "firewater" was being manufactured by whites in Victoria solely for sale to Indians, the five gallon oil cans used for transport being seen on all parts of the coast. A missionary reported:

I have actually seen Indian canoes [in Victoria] pulling out from under the wharves with from 20 to 40 of these cans, under the gaze of the local police, whilst no attempt was made to stop the traffic.

In Nanaimo, however, the fight against illicit whiskey had been joined. Royal Navy steamers seized suspect boats. Reverend Crosby and the American owner of the limestone quarry on Newcastle Island were able to procure the cancellation of the licence of a notorious establishment on the shores of Departure Bay. The so-called "Whiskey Synagogue" made no pretence at keeping the law and sold to Indians and workmen at the quarry, thus disrupting commerce as well as the local native population. Even the more reputable pubs in town were occasionally caught selling their wares to Indians.

The battle never ended. Most police court activity was devoted to either drunken Indians or white whiskey traders. The bootleg product sold by the traders was particularly lethal to the Indian drinker.

For the Indian woman, the combination of white men and illegal liquor could only bring ruin.

On the outskirts of town was a "suburb" of about three hundred souls, where white men lived with Indian wives and half-breed children. In a town where the men outnumbered white women two to one, it was a situation to be expected, but it was a situation fraught with disadvantages for the Indian women.

The union of a white man and an Indian woman was regarded as an inferior one. This despite the fact that Lady Amelia Douglas, wife of Sir James Douglas, had an Indian mother herself. By 1865 Indian women were characterized as sensual and ignorant and in the relationship solely to get access to whiskey. The white men, so the gossips said, brought liquor to their "klootchmen," who drank some of it and sold the rest to their relatives.

With such a negative picture painted of these women it is refreshing to read the description drawn by an outsider who visited in 1871. Sophie Cracoft, niece of Lady Franklin, accompanied her aunt on a visit to Nanaimo during a world tour to encourage expeditions to search for her Arctic explorer uncle, Sir John Franklin. Miss Cracoft was entranced by the women she saw.

We passed a good many women neatly dressed in print gowns, with gay Scotch plaid shawls over their heads. Some were really quite good looking — probably some of the mixed race. A good many had been hanging about all the morning, on the wharf off which we were moored. The most remarkable things they wore, were earrings of brilliant mother of pearl — some square, others shaped like fish, and others with patterns engraved on them.

Enthusiasm for the Methodist mission grew as other white men joined Reverend Crosby to lure the Nanaimo Indians to the Christian god. Lay missionaries and benevolent townspeople ministered and raised money and donated food to the sometimes penniless Crosby. He was able to point with pride and satisfaction to his prize pupil, the young Indian David Salosselton (Salloselton, Sallosalton) who preached to his own people with amazing effectiveness before dying of tuberculosis at the age of nineteen.

The tug of war between the old pagan ways and the new Christian ones became more complicated as the evil aspects of white society were absorbed into the Indian one. After Crosby left Nanaimo in 1874, the mission was never the same again. It seemed to have been cast adrift. When Company houses and private hotels began to spring up in anticipation of the new Number One Mine in the early 1880's, their proximity to the Indian reserve brought the white community too close again.

But alas! after so much had been done, the mission was virtually abandoned; the missionary was sent to another field; a coal mining village sprang up in the immediate neighbourhood, and many of the poor, half-taught Indians, left as sheep without a shepherd, became an easy prey to the destroyer.

In 1885 a Methodist mission teacher named Susannah Lawrence was sent to Nanaimo, fresh from service to Indians further up the coast. She found the Nanaimo Indians still wedded to their old customs, to dancing, feasting, and potlatching. "The work here is very different to that up north," she reported. "We did not have the drinking to contend with there, or the dancing either... But here we have both and wicked white men to encourage them in every way."[3]

Wicked white men were in abundance in the 1860's too. The constable was kept busy arresting whiskey traders, and the magistrate found his miniscule case load to consist almost entirely of liquor violations. Even in the 1850's, when there were no official liquor outlets in HBC dominated Nanaimo, temperance groups were already alarmed by the potential for evil in demon drink.

To fight against this evil, schoolteacher Cornelius Bryant formed the Band of Hope Temperance Society. Reverend Ebenezer Robson joined the battle when he arrived in 1860. In just two years, a number of citizens were reported to have discarded every kind of malt and spiritous liquor from their houses and had enjoyed an abstemious New Year's Eve without the "scratched noses and black eyes" sported by the "wine-bibbers the next day."

There was, however, an air of hypocrisy lurking about the pious abstainers. Certain of the town's leading citizens obviously felt that temperance should be encouraged for the population in general, but was not necessarily a model for one's own behavior. Robert Dunsmuir, for example, had made no secret of his rum purchases when employed by the HBC and would continue to be a robust drinker all his days. What Dunsmuir did in private, however, seemed to have little to do

---

[3] By the 1890's, conditions among Nanaimo's Indians had improved. Many had steady jobs, including a few who worked in the mines. Mark Bate credited the missionary teachers "who have faithfully laboured among them, the younger generation are copying many good examples of their more highly civilized bretheran." The Methodists had also expanded their work in Nanaimo to include a Chinese mission in 1885.

with his public posture, for he was a notable member of the Total Abstinence Society as early as 1863.[4]

Despite the presence of a temperance sentiment, the institution of the miners' pub gradually gained a foothold once the HBC bowed out of the town. The men quickly made up for the Company's monopoly in liquor sales by patronizing each new establishment.

... notwithstanding the efforts of the clergy, the police and the Press, that so great an amount of drunkenness exists; where, sir, can be the necessity of so many "hotels" in so small a place as Nanaimo?"

At first there was just one hotel, and what a grand place it was too, complete with wallpaper and a resident Frenchman for an owner, the flamboyant Monsieur Pugol. In the next four years, the number of liquor outlets increased dramatically. *Princess Royal* miner Joseph Webb teamed up with one Richard Nightingale to open the Miners' Hotel on Bridge Street. Designating it "an old established house" they offered English and French wines, brandy, gin, ale (colonial and English), whiskey, Old Tom, and porter in a central location, only a two minute walk from the steamboat landing. It was an establishment with a table "well and liberally supplied" by Mrs. Webb, superior sleeping accommodation, and a first-class billiard table to boot.

Not to be outdone, Tom Peck and Peter Sabiston began to advertise the Royal Hotel before it was even completed. With fifty bedrooms, several good dining and sitting rooms, hot and cold baths, a fine view, and English and American pool every Tuesday and Saturday evening, it was pretty hard to beat even though it was located way out in the country on the corner of Haliburton and Finlayson. While waiting for the completion of the hotel, Peck and Sabiston kept the wolf from the door by offering for sale, as the sole Nanaimo agents, Bunster Beer. "Throw physic to the dogs," their customers were advised, "and DRINK BUNSTER."

Partnerships never lasted long in the Nanaimo hotel business. Webb and Nightingale parted company the same year they opened the Miners' Hotel, Nightingale building himself a hotel near the Millstream and soon receiving a fine of one hundred dollars for selling

---

[4] As a Scot and a miner, Dunsmuir came from a tradition of alcohol consumption. In Scotland, miners indulged frequently in alcohol even below ground. For example, liquor was consumed when a workable seam was obtained, when coal was hit during shaft sinking, or whenever a room was cut or assigned. On New Year's Day the master provided a bonus libation, and following even a minor accident miners usually took the rest of the day off, stopping for a "social glass" before heading home.

liquor to Indians. Peck and Sabiston split up too and became proprietors of two different hotels. Peck had one on Victoria Crescent and Sabiston was associated with the Miners' Hotel. Stone and Jerome, proprietors of the Old Flag Inn on Bastion Street, failed to agree, and Jerome departed, leaving Stone to offer in addition to London Stout, "Colonial ale bottled by R. H. Stone and in prime order" at twenty-five cents a bottle for home consumption.[5]

In an effort to educate the younger generation to the evils of drink, Mr. and Mrs. C. S. Nicol offered a "bountiful repast and entertainment" to seventy "juveniles" on the site of a former saloon. Dr. Benson showed slides with his magic lantern, several views of which were "suggestive, instructive and interesting illustrations to the youthful mind." Reverend Good, pastor of St. Paul's Anglican Church, expressed the hope that liquor would never again be sold in the premises and called for a public news and reading room.

The reverend gentleman was addressing a pressing need in the town. Ever since a fire caused by spontaneous combustion in mine debris from the old HBC Number One Mine had destroyed a small stage built at one end of the mill and carpenter shop, there was no place for the public to be entertained. There were no boards for travelling theatre companies to tread, no platform for the likes of blacksmith Jim Miller with his homemade dulcimer and his funny ditties and songs, and no dais for conjurist and showman Captain Jonas Hewett, master of the coal barge *Thames*.

Clearly, if the town was to avoid sliding into the abyss of boredom-induced alcoholism, it needed a Literary Institute. Literary or Mechanics Institutes were a product of turn of the century Britain. They were educational advancement halls fostered by the leading citizens of individual towns but governed and used by working class men. In the days before membership in the working class was a thing of honour among workingmen, the lecture halls and reading rooms were designed to hasten the worker on his journey into middle class respectability. Nanaimo was to have the first one in the two British colonies on the Pacific Coast. On November 25, 1862 the inaugural meeting was held in St. Paul's Central School and Hall of Improvement and chaired by the first President, the ubiquitous C. S. Nicol. Four reverend gentlemen of various denominations delivered themselves of speeches.

[5] An Occidental Hotel is also mentioned in passing. The most famous Occidental Hotel was not built until 1887 by Sam Fiddick, who was, however, in Nanaimo in the 1860's.

Because Reverend Good had encouraged the founding of the organization and because his church school was used for meetings, the society came to be known as St. Paul's Literary Institute, with Good, an energetic and determined man if ever there was one, as Superintendent. Overlooking the harbour, his little church with its graceful spire had been built and rendered free of debt in just one year through the inventive fund raising of its pastor. Good had organized a day-long excursion from Victoria to view the opening ceremonies, during which a plate was passed among the assembled excursionists and $120, an amount well in excess of the building debt, was collected.

With equal vigour Good took on the Literary Society, proposing a constitution which debarred men who lived in states of fornication, habitual drunkenness, or other gross immoralities. Another clause said the President should always be nominated by the Bishop and the Superintendent should always be the minister of St. Paul's Church.

Already the so-called workingmen's organization looked to be on dangerous ground. Workingmen would have little say in who ran the organization. Mark Bate protested that they must not bar men who had indulged in "gross immoralities but rather hold out for the possibility of rehabilitation." The membership voted for a change in the constitution, which took away Good's veto power and the position of Superintendent, to which Good replied that if he could no longer be Superintendent and no longer have a veto, the society could no longer use the school either. He was not interested in being Vice-President, the post offered in a conciliatory gesture.

Time soothed Good's ruffled feelings and he accepted the vice-presidential position and the new constitution. On land donated by the Company on Bastion Street right by the ravine, a two story edifice with a meeting room below and a reading room upstairs was to be built by the firm of David William Gordon and Jacob Blessing. The newly mollified Good was persuaded to start the fund raising off with a lecture entitled "Our National Proverbs, what we may learn from them." That the *Colonist* characterized the lecture as "a great relief during these monotonous times" gave some indication of how desperate the town was for entertainment.

With the cornerstone already laid by Governor Kennedy, fund raising continued in earnest. At the first concert the local Member of the Legislative Assembly (MLA), Charles Bayley, presented sixty-three volumes, including Shakespeare and other standard works, and a local songwriter wrenched this bit of doggerel from his breast.

Where is Columbia after all! or yet Vancouver Island?
Were it not for Nanaimo's wealth, her precious gem — black diamond:
The only place for immigrants and all dead broken miners.
The country soon would be "gone in," were it not for Nanaimo.

Slowly the building began to take shape, its progress governed by the flow of funds into the coffers. There were times when the seriousness of the membership was in question, as when the building committee report was compiled. "It was drawn up in a dramshop an hour before the meeting and left on the bar for the inspection of the members should they drop in."

Enough of the outer shell was completed by December of 1865 to allow for a Christmas party on the premises. Months later the withered remains of evergreen boughs still hung from the walls of the large unfinished rooms, bedraggled testimony to waning enthusiasm and a shortage of building funds. The officers that year were a blend of coal company executives, miners, and merchants, a mixture perhaps not as proletarian as the founders in Britain had envisaged, but a representative blend none the less.

The lack of inside finishing or even outside paint did not preclude the use of the hall for shows, concerts, and dances, but the reading room was little used even after the Board of Directors of the VCML donated fifty volumes of "theological, medical, political and poetical" works. The weighty tomes and the few six month-old British periodicals lying upstairs did not tempt many visitors.

Downstairs was a different story. The Douglas Pit Troupe often performed for the benefit of the building fund. Excellent singers, comics, imitators, actors, and musicians, all employees of the coal company, did their turn. Admission was twenty-five cents. The Nanaimo Glee Club made its debut in 1866, having observed the successful inauguration of the Philharmonic Society two years before. The orchestra gave its first concert in December of 1865, its two violinists, one flutist, two cornetists, one cellist, one pianist, and six singers attempting to make the sound of a full symphony ensemble.

All the entertainment was not local by any means. With a hall to accommodate visiting troupes, Nanaimo was now on the circuit. The Marsh Family gave what they called a "Parlour Entertainment," which included the farce "Betsy Baker," the Irish two-act drama "Andy Blake," and the world-renowned Toodles all for one dollar admission, children half price.

One dollar represented a lot of money in 1865. Although an experienced miner could make up to $1.32 per ton, conditions in the mines then were not conducive to mining very many tons in a day. The *Gazette* estimated that most men in Nanaimo averaged $2.33 per ten hour day based on a six day week. After 1866 anyone receiving an annual income over $727.50 was required to pay one percent of that in income tax. At an annual wage of $729 the average miner just qualified. "It is a sin and a shame to tax a man's labour when his salary is scarcely sufficient to bread and clothe himself and his family."

Wages were paid monthly, regularly, in cash and promptly, but it was a long time from one month to the next. The reliability of Company wages led most merchants to offer credit, for without it there would have been very little business done. Steady miners paid their bills on payday; transients skedaddled.

"Skedaddlers" or fugitive debtors were a source of great consternation. There was no way for a merchant to conduct business and yet protect himself from the unscrupulous itinerant workers who came and went every day on the ships becoming so numerous in the harbour. It was hard to know whom to trust. The editor of the *Gazette* cautioned against

the backbiting and slanderous spirit which is now abroad in Nanaimo...If you are gone on a jaunt, you have run away from your creditors; if you are seen to take a glass of grog, or of wine, you are a drunkard.

Itinerants had no trouble getting jobs. Nanaimo badly needed more labour. As the mines opened up and the Indians became less reliable, the lack of labour, skilled or unskilled, became acute. The *Gazette* worried that reports of the poverty in Nanaimo would get out to the rest of the world and drive potential colonists away. Those who did come seemed to be either potential skedaddlers or the idle sons of rich men. John Bryden would later state:

We had at that time a great many of the aristocracy; we had doctors', lawyers' and bishops' sons, and I must say their love of whiskey was greater than their love of work.

There was, however, a continuing if small source of skilled labour. At that time in Britain unions had gained nation-wide status and respectability. In order to lessen the competition for jobs at home and thus gradually improve the material state of their members, unions had instituted a plan to encourage emigration. Especially during bad economic periods in the middle years of the decade, they encouraged members interested in the New World to accept offers of free passage from North American mine owners.

Union executives favoured the colonies over the United States as a destination for emigrants. They feared that skilled workers going to America would provide competition for Britain whereas workers in the colonies would be sending raw materials back for manufacture, thereby increasing the number of jobs in the motherland.

An additional source of union men at this time and in the decades to come were British union leaders blacklisted after strikes. No longer able to get work in Britain, these men were assisted by their unions to emigrate. Slowly the number of experienced union men on the Island would grow — men accustomed to a generation of union membership in Britain, men who arrived on Vancouver Island to find that there were no unions.

The first strike of the decade occurred before the HBC was sold to the VCML. One hundred men stopped working on September 30, 1861, when a tax of threepence per ton was levied for adulteration of coal. The Company held firm and only five days later the miners went back to work.

A strike of considerably longer duration occurred from August 1864 to February 1865, when runners demanded three dollars a day. The demand was a popular one and all the employees of the mine walked out, the miners demanding twelve and a half cents per ton increase and thirty-seven and a half cents per day on shift work. It was said that some men could not make more than two dollars per day no matter how hard they tried.

Mining was not seen as an honourable profession by some in Nanaimo; indeed at a political meeting a government official had referred to the people of Nanaimo as "only beastly miners." An outsider who tried to look at the strike with an impartial eye offered moral support to the strikers. He regarded strikes as great evils, but in this case he deemed the miners just, though incourteous in their demands. He pointed out that the town lots recently offered for sale were small but sold for big prices, and he knew of first class miners who had left town before the strike because they could not earn more than two dollars a day.

In the past the Company had lured miners to Nanaimo with the promise of accommodation in the Company boarding house and now used the same bait to entice "turncoats." They were offered free passage on the Company boat, *Fideliter*, and accommodation on Company premises. The strikers, who had experienced the rudimentary washing facilities and cramped quarters of the boarding house, must have been amused at the offer.

Recruiting of "turncoats" did not go well. The colony was full of miners, but they were interested in gold and would rather wait in Victoria for the spring mining season in the Cariboo than work for low wages in dangerous coal mines. However, when the Company was able to recruit some Mexican miners the strikers appointed a committee to bargain. On February 13, 1865 the miners returned to work with nothing resolved. Their fate would rest on what C. S. Nicol would decide when he returned from a trip to San Francisco. The arrival of strikebreakers had been sufficient to break five months of resolve.

Short work stoppages punctuated the next two years and prompted the Company to look to a surer supply of labour, which came in the form of twenty or thirty Chinese who would work for a dollar a day. This radical new venture in Company hiring practices had been recommended by John Wild, managing director of the VCML, who had been sent by the Board in 1865 to investigate the labour situation.

John Bryden was still an undermanager when the first Chinese arrived. He kept a close eye on this new experiment, assigning the Chinese to outside work although he was aware that the Company planned to put them into the mines. A contractor named Clarke was the first to actually take them below, and he found that they made very good runners, learning quickly and working efficiently. Bryden was impressed as well and attempted to use them as miners until Mr. Nicol found out he was paying them the same as he paid whites. "Why this won't do," Nicol is reported to have said, "if we are to pay the Chinamen the same rate of wage as the white men there will be no use employing them."

White miners agreed with Nicol except that they did not wish to see Chinese employed at any price. Since the first large groups had arrived for the Fraser River gold rush, the Chinese had been viewed with suspicion. By 1864 there were over two thousand in the Colony, and that number continued to grow as the gold rush moved up the Fraser to the Cariboo. They looked different, they dressed differently, they spoke an incomprehensible language, and they showed no desire to change. Even worse than that, they worked hard and they worked cheaply.

It has been said that in the first few years, Chinese "did not attract the thoughtful attention of the people." In reality, they were welcomed by employers, ignored by most of the populace, and disliked by labour. As early as 1860 a Nanaimo miner was arrested in Victoria for shaking a stick at a Chinese man. Nor had the miners' attitudes changed by 1867 when the *Colonist* observed,

Considerable excitement, we hear, exists at Nanaimo in consequence of the introduction of Chinese labourers. The colliers threaten with violence the first Chinaman who forgets his Celestial origin so far as to descend to the "bottomless pit" of a coal mine.

In the discontented years of 1865 to 1867, the introduction of Chinese workers into the mines was bad enough, but when Bryden was ordered to pay them less than white miners, it made the Chinese more desirable as employees and threatened the very jobs of the whites. Rumours spread through town in May of 1867 that the mines would be closed due to troubles caused by white miners protesting the Chinese presence. The Company locked its employees out and the miners called a strike.

Two months later the Company was able to lure its miners back to work with the promise of an increase of twelve and a half cents per ton, free pick handles, and a ton of free coal per month per miner. "Running" would be handled by contractors who would hire their own men, but the door was left open to the Chinese, whose low wages would be highly attractive to any business-like contractor. Eleven years later John Wild would say that the few Chinese he had recommended hiring had become "swarms."

Nor were the labour problems of the sixties solved in 1867. There continued to be talk of strikes, talk that was tempered by the knowledge that by 1868 "there are thousands of poor fellows in California who would be glad to come up in their places and who need but little inducement to come this way."

With the exception of the small-scale operations on Newcastle Island, where Jesse Sage and his son-in-law Edward Walker were sinking a slope to the back of the adit in the old HBC mine, all VCML mining activity in 1868 was concentrated on the Douglas Pit. Into the seam developed under the supervision of Boyd Gilmour a decade before and worked as two small level-free mines, the Park Head and the Dunsmuir, the Company now had a major mine.

The shaft had been begun in 1861 by the HBC and completed in 1862 just before the VCML assumed control. There was considerable excitement over the quality of the coal. It was superior to anything yet found in Nanaimo and better for steaming than coal from Sydney, Cape Breton or Pictou, Nova Scotia. In fact, it was equal to most English coal for steaming; it stowed better than Welsh coal; and as if that was not enough, there was lots of it.

Three shifts of miners were put to work under the supervision of Robert Dunsmuir, the men doing all the tasks by hand while waiting for the arrival of machinery and a locomotive enroute from England. By September of 1863 they were producing 120 tons per day, the railway was almost completed, and the new locomotive waited to begin its tasks. The locomotive was a marvel for all to see but most especially for the Indians and the white children born in Nanaimo who had never seen such a grand sight.

Before the arrival of the small, standard-gauge locomotive with her saddle tank engine, the Indians had been told that she would do the work of one hundred men. When the *Pioneer* arrived, complete with her own engineer and fireman,[6] one hundred Indians volunteered to test her strength by pulling on a rope tied to the little engine. The white men had obviously underestimated the strength of this new wonder, for even one hundred Indians could not stop her progress.

As exploration crews pressed ahead with boreholes, the extent of the seam justified the large expenditure for machinery. In 1865 out of the surrounding forest a proper pithead rose, with elevated platform for screening the coal and, projecting from its side, chutes which led down to four-ton wagons below. The *Pioneer* could pull twelve of those wagons at a time across the elevated bridge, so huge it dwarfed its surroundings, and on to the new two hundred by five hundred foot wharves. Built on the peninsula and island expropriated from the Indians, the new wharves allowed several ships at one time to be loaded.

After each car passed over the scales on the wharf, it was tipped into a chute and the coal shot down into the waiting ship, the continuous sound made by the "shooting" of the coal punctuating the atmosphere and reminding one observer of raw recruits firing bad volleys.

Coaling ships presented a whole set of problems of their own. There seemed to be either too many or too few. When there were too few, less coal could be sold and more had to be stockpiled, but often there were too many. In 1863 alone, 353 vessels, brigs and barques of the foreign trade, sloops and schooners for coastal markets, and 71 naval steamers came to Nanaimo to load coal. When the harbour filled with ships, the extra ones had to wait for space at the wharf and tempers grew shorter and shorter the longer they had to wait.

In an effort to make the loading process more efficient, an engine called the *Euclataw* was imported in 1866 to remove ballast from the

---

[6] Harry Cooper, engineer, and Thomas E. Peck, fireman, were the first of their kind west of Ontario.

ships, a time-consuming process. Sometimes a vessel emptied of its ballast needed "stiffening" by adding a few tons of coal to prevent her from turning over. Sailing vessels, so beautiful under full sail, were rendered ungainly in close quarters and by a lack of wind, and so had difficulty approaching and leaving the jetty, especially at low tide. This necessitated a call for rowboats manned by VCML labourers to manoeuvre them to and from the wharves.

To keep a steady supply of coal available for the waiting ships, the mine workings were extended further and further to the south. For the first time, methane gas was a factor to be taken into consideration. This was a big mine and a deep one and would have extensive workings. Fortunately, a "superior ventilation" system kept the gas within controllable limits.

Three hundred men worked the Douglas Pit in 1866. They descended the shaft on a narrow platform and disappeared down the slope and into the levels, their way lit by fish oil lamps hooked onto their soft peak caps. Someone had discovered that mixing a little bit of kerosene into the fish oil made the lamp burn brighter. You had to have some experience to get the best out of them. Mule drivers learned that on a straight track when the animal built up some speed, a man's light could make his forehead feel like it was on fire, but it was just something he had to live with if he wanted to keep up with his mule.

There was a matter-of-fact acceptance of all aspects of mining which amazed an outsider allowed to descend the shaft one day.

... we came suddenly to an almost vertical incline some 240 feet in depth ... [where] the miners were pursuing their calling with as little apparent concern as if they were on the broad surface of the earth instead of burrowing like rabbits 450 feet beneath it. In some places they were stooped almost double and in others there was lots of space from floor to roof.

Gradually, the number of mine accidents increased. Where ten years before there may have been only a few per year, now there were a few per month. The more experienced a man was the less likely he was to be injured, but the mine was full of inexperienced men.

William Parkin was typical of the men working in the Douglas Pit. He had been a gold prospector in the Cariboo but had had little success, so he made his way to Nanaimo and got a job right away in the big mine. Nanaimo seemed like a pretty good place to live, especially after he met Eliza Malpass. She had come over on the *Princess Royal* as a litle girl and was now a blooming eighteen year old.

They fell in love and married right away. Within a year their first child was born. Then William was blinded in an accident in the mine.

The Company did everything it could. Parkin was sent to San Francisco to have his eyes treated at the Eye Infirmary. He was given half pay and half a ton of coal a month for the rest of his life. But nothing could be done for his sight.

Eliza and William were a remarkable couple, however. The nineteen year old mother opened a grocery store on the main street. Over the ensuing years she ran the store and William delivered the groceries, guided by his dark brown spaniel Carlo, a gift of his Cariboo partners. Parkin was also the family baby-sitter and could be seen walking around town with the youngest child on his shoulder. Since the couple had a total of seventeen children, he had that job for many years.

Groceries from Parkins' store arrived in a basket. Longer trips required a wheelbarrow, but the longest ones, those out to the Fitzwilliam Mine at the north end of Newcastle Island, were taken by pack horse, the horse's halter lead in Carlo's mouth and Parkin walking alongside. Man, dog, and horse were probably the only ones who used the bridge that crossed the Millstream to the Newcastle Townsite. From there a narrow trail that would eventually lead to Departure Bay meandered along the shore of the Exit Channel to the point of land across from Midden Bay. Parkin would shout across to the mine and a boat would come over for the provisions.

While all Nanaimo merchants did not provide such a far- reaching delivery service, the town had become a considerably better place to shop. Gone were the days when the HBC store was the only retail outlet and the Company required its customers to line up in single file outside the door to buy their goods. Alexander Mayer's Red House on the corner of Bastion and Chapel was full of "very cheap goods from Portland and San Francisco." Mayer himself had come from Portland with two large trunks of goods in 1861 but had been prevented from opening a store by the HBC monopoly, so he opened his trunks on a street corner and sold out in short order. He returned some time later and set up shop in the lobby of the Miners' Hotel and sold out again. With the proceeds he bought at the public auction a lot with a log building on it. The building was painted red and became a general store.

There were butcher shops and bakeries, smithies and hardware stores; Gee Hap ran a laundry and so did Mrs. Smallbone; P. Hume painted signs. Alexander and Company and David Cerf competed with the Parkins for the grocery trade, with some additional competition from George Tranfield who specialized in fish, game, and vegetables.

Ladies could keep up with the fashions in Victoria, the Irish poplins and French laces, through Mrs. Moyle or Mrs. Raybould, each of whom ran millinery and dressmaking establishments. Mrs. Raybould also made stays, but the ladies were warned that crinolines were going out of style "though there is a great desire to continue them." For the more up-to-date, Thompson's "new style of hoops" were also available. Bonnets and hats of every shape from the "picturesque helmet of the Crusaders to the iron pot of the trader — hats that sit fairly and squarely upon the head like an American wide-awake,[7] and hats that none but a professed mathematician could describe with any degree of accuracy" could be made by either of the two ladies who vied for the limited Nanaimo trade.

Mrs. Raybould's husband William joined forces with a Mr. Shakespeare for one year in 1866 to provide ready-to-wear. The "Nanaimo Emporium" advertised suits, coats, vests, pants, carlisle capes, and overcoats for men. To tempt the women, Raybould and Shakespeare offered paletots and mantles, dresses in silk and mohair and fancy winseys, striped skirtings and haberdashery like ribbons, threads, laces and needles. All merchandise was priced "cheap for cash only."

Mining families had to buy mostly on credit, so Raybould may have had to change his "cash only" policy. There was a lot of competition for the disposable income of the miners, so storekeepers stayed open long hours to get their share. But everyone took a half day off on May Day, and on the birthday of Queen Victoria the whole town celebrated all day.

The first Nanaimo celebration in 1863 of the birthday of that most sedate of monarchs was as raucous as it could be. "I cannot say the 'utmost decorum prevailed'," sniffed the *Colonist*, describing Nanaimo's holiday, "and there was an average number of disturbances and disorders, but to catalogue these cases would prove neither interesting nor profitable."

Three years after, however, having achieved a greater sense of decorum, Nanaimo celebrated in a more sedate fashion but with no less vigour. There was a cricket match between the Douglas Pit Eleven and the Town, wickets pitched at 10:00 a.m., a shooting match for a fat pig valued at ten dollars, a "pic-nic" for school

---

[7] A soft felt hat with a broad brim.

children and teachers, the opening dinner for the Nanaimo Cricket Club at the Royal Hotel, and an amateur concert at the Mechanics Institute Hall.

Somewhat later that summer, on July 4th, the town celebrated again, but this time the occasion was American Independence Day! Flags were displayed on all businesses. There was boating, cricketing, and foot racing all in honour of the country to the south which had just come through a wrenching Civil War and the assassination of its president, Abraham Lincoln.

Perhaps it was the realization of how damaging it could be for a country to pit brother against brother, or to see its leader shot down in his moment of triumph, but the citizens of colonial Vancouver Island reached out to the Americans on the Fourth of July and would for several more years to come. The editor of the *Gazette* reminded them, "I recollect the time that 'all Americans were brigands' and the people here used to close their doors the moment they saw them approach."

The anti-American sentiment had not been without cause. Americans were the first to trade whiskey with the Indians. Their coal mines competed with Nanaimo's and their politicians cast a covetous eye northward from time to time, hoping to include the colonies within their borders. Irish-American Fenians, mostly veterans of the Civil War, would soon threaten an invasion of British possessions in an effort to force Irish independence. Although Fenian raids occurred in New Brunswick, Quebec, and Ontario, no Irishman crossed the border of British Columbia in anger. However, the possibility helped strengthen the very new Nanaimo militia unit.

The Volunteer Rifle Corps had originally been formed in 1864 for protection against "domestic and foreign foes." Opinion was divided about how essential it was. Some thought it totally unnecessary, but others were frightened by a recent Indian war which followed a massacre of white people in Bute Inlet. As a result, thirteen Nanaimo men signed up "in defence of the civil power."

Very little happened to develop the militia, however, until the threat of "the Fenian banditti" in 1867 mobilized eighty-seven men to attend a meeting which elected C. S. Nicol as the Corps Captain. Thomas Cunningham was assigned the task of requesting arms and equipment from the Governor and Dr. R. W. W. Carrall was elected ensign, the ladies of Nanaimo presenting him with a regulation infantry sword. Only one year passed before the Nanaimo militia unit had collapsed as surely as the Fenian threat that had spawned it.

131

When the need for the militia arose again nine years later, Nanaimo would be woefully unprepared.

The town acquitted itself much more creditably when it came to the provision of schooling for its children. Although only about one third of the eligible children attended, the tradition of education begun in the 1850's continued. After 1862, there was a public supported colonial school for boys and girls—situated on land donated by the Company—and a Girls' School, begun at the insistence of Reverend Good. The young ladies would be accommodated in "extensive and comfortable" surroundings in contrast to the "unsightly and incommodious building now used as the Colonial School."

To remedy the dilapidated state of the Colonial School, a public meeting under Robert Dunsmuir's chairmanship convened to request government help in constructing a proper building. The colonial government had just recognized the necessity for public education by passing an act to establish state-financed "free schools." Surely a town like Nanaimo, which had already provided schooling paid for by the parents, would qualify. A committee was struck to select sites. Since there were ninety children between the ages of five and sixteen and a preponderance of them were girls, it was deemed "imperatively necessary" that separate compartments for each sex be provided.

The request for a free school in Nanaimo fell on the less than receptive ears of Alfred Waddington, the Superintendent of Education, of whom it was said "education did not flourish during his regime." Waddington was far more interested in the potential of Bute Inlet as a transportation corridor, and when the two colonies united, the new Governor, Frederick Seymour, refused to sanction any grant for any public schools anywhere.

Clearly Nanaimo was ahead of its time. The people of the town decided that they would provide the money and a "Committee to Secure a Free School-House" was formed under Robert Dunsmuir, whose growing brood provided a sizeable portion of the student body.

Schoolhouse plans which presented "a handsome and tasty appearance" were approved. The Company donated more land. Ground was cleared in a working bee but the tenders came in far too high and the building plans had to be shelved. The children were transferred from the dilapidated Colonial School to St. Paul's. One month later the old building burned down.

By 1866 the need for a public school was critical. Nanaimo students were crammed into a very small room at St. Paul's. Even worse, girls and boys shared the same schoolroom. Alfred Waddington visited and observed: "It is no wonder children looked with aversion and disgust on school as the old schoolhouse is an oppobrium for the Colony."

Three more years passed. There were only seven government supported schools in the united colonies, but the support received by Nanaimo was marginal. No building was provided and only $480 a year was allotted to maintain the one provided by the town, yet Nanaimo sent the same proportion of its young people to school as did the bigger more sophisticated cities. Teachers were appointed without examination for fitness or inquiry into character. Nanaimo's only teacher was of good character, but Cornelius Bryant's salary was miniscule, when it was paid at all.

As if to add weight to the argument of those who demanded more help to educate Nanaimo's children, the *Colonist*, with its usual tongue-in-cheek tone, called attention to Nanaimo's growing school population.

[The] ladies of Nanaimo are determined to hold the foremost rank in reproductiveness, and are furnishing more leige subjects for Her Majesty than any other locality in the Colony of equal population. By rapid home production we may be at last independent of immigration.

The neglect of education was just one reflection of the continued indifference of Victoria to affairs in Nanaimo. But the married men of the town, most of whom were miners, had a stake in the town and a stake in their children's futures. They had long since given up hoping that Victoria would provide proper roads and bridges, but they were prepared to fight for schools.

The trustees of the school had been paying Cornelius Bryant a salary "just above starvation point" by assessing parents fifty cents per month per child. There were no funds for any other school expenses. Only about one fifth of children of school age attended school, a ratio comparable to other cities in the colonies. Families too poor to afford schooling sent boys as young as nine years of age to the mines, and the rest roamed the streets.

Someone said that now that British Columbia was going to be a part of Canada, teachers had to have proper qualifications and Cornelius Bryant was to be forced out. Someone said it was the miners who had demanded a better qualified teacher. Since Bryant was about to enter training for the Methodist ministry, the forced retirement did not upset him unduly.

His replacement was read in the classics and had diplomas to prove it. Someone pointed out that after the new schoolmaster appeared, school attendance dwindled so low that the school was closed. Someone else said that the coal company had interfered, giving $250 to support a denominational school that only perpetuated "the class and caste system of the old country."

It was high time that the new government of British Columbia stepped into the fray. An Act was passed in 1871 to maintain and manage public schools. Teachers' qualifications were set and subject matter was to be non-sectarian. Lessons in morality without dogma were the order of the day.

By 1873 Nanaimo had a new school on a site commanding the sea on Crace Street near the Douglas Pit. Four years later the Sisters of St. Ann established a day school for children of all creeds, and two years after that they moved the school into their new convent, a two story building overlooking the ravine. Its mansard roof provided an old world touch in a raw new world setting.[8]

Just below the site of the new convent was the continuously running spring where everyone in Nanaimo had drawn their household water since the town began. Indians would carry the water for five cents a bucket, but in the summer when the Indians were away fishing, children could be seen staggering home with a bucket in each hand.

In 1864 the new Nanaimo Water Works Company offered two thousand shares at two dollars each. Although all the shares were bought up quickly, nothing came of the original plan to bring water from the Millstone River. Two years later, however, a flume that C. S. Nicol had rigged up years before to supply his own home with water was extended to a tank from whence water was taken by cart and distributed around the town by bucket. A gentleman who styled himself "Count Lusak" was in charge of the cart and the bucket and handled the latter with gloved hands in order to prove his gentility. The water company also purchased a large boiler around which it proposed to erect a bathhouse. The bathhouse was never built.

It was a funny little town at the end of the world, sitting beside the ocean, pulling coal out of the ground and sending it off to big cities that had never heard of it. Although it was possible to get a message from Montreal to New Westminster in four hours via American electric telegraph, it took two months for mail to get to Nanaimo from England. The newspapers and the letters would be brought ashore by

[8] Nanaimo did not have a high school until 1886.

134

the captain of whatever ship happened to be carrying them and delivered to James Harvey's General Store and Post Office in the former HBC store below the Bastion.

One day in October of 1869, Robert Dunsmuir was sitting in Harvey's store. Harvey was married to Dunsmuir's second daughter, Aggie. Jimmy Hamilton was there too. He was a harmless, kindhearted sort of a man who lived by himself in a cabin beyond the Big Swamp not far from Diver Lake, a small fishing mecca north and west of Nanaimo. He was about as different from Robert Dunsmuir as a man could be, but the two men enjoyed each other's company, so when Jimmy suggested a fishing trip Robert agreed to go along.

Hamilton went fishing, but Robert wandered off to do what he always did when he could get away from town and beyond the VCML lease. He looked for coal. He had become so knowledgeable about the geological formations in the area that he knew what sort of strata would lay over the third seam, the body of coal that lay beneath the Douglas and Newcastle seams, the one everyone said was there but no one had ever found.

That evening he told his wife Joan that he had found Wellington coal. Behind Diver Lake he had happened on a large ridge of conglomerate rock, which he knew overlaid the third seam. Jimmy Hamilton was not interested, so the next day Dunsmuir took his friend William Isbister, the stone mason who had been in Nanaimo as long as he had, to look at the site. Isbister confirmed the find, but he was not interested in sharing it either. Lots of people had found coal on the Island; very few had made anything out of it.

Dunsmuir then took with him two miners who dug down about two and a half feet, found nothing, and left discouraged. But Robert was persistent. He dug around and finally at the foot of an upturned tree he found black dirt. One and a half feet below the surface he found the coal outcropping. Two more men were hired to prospect and in three days they discovered a three and a half foot seam, thirty feet below the top of the ridge, dipping southeast one foot in six.

In November, Dunsmuir applied for a prospecting license with the right to purchase fifteen hundred acres north of and adjoining the Mountain District. His request was immediately approved by the Colonial Government, which had passed legislation several years before to stimulate speculation in coal claims. The legislation allowed prospectors working alone only five hundred acres, but Joseph Trutch, Chief Commissioner of Lands and Works, was impressed by Dunsmuir's experience and ability and allowed him more land.

There had been coal discoveries all over the Island in the intervening years. George Robinson found coal at Nootka Sound, John Muir found it at Sooke; it was found at Cowichan, Quatsino Sound, North Saanich, and Comox. The regulations allowed individuals to enter "freely" Vancouver Island and explore for minerals upon applying for a two year prospecting licence on five hundred acres for individuals and twenty-five hundred acres for a ten-man partnership. After the prospecting licence had expired, the land grant could be secured by payment of five dollars per acre plus proof of at least ten thousand dollars spent to develop the seams.

Finding coal was not enough, however. In order to successfully exploit the resource, an entrepreneur needed three things. He needed expertise to work the coal efficiently; he needed sufficient funds to finance the venture until it began to pay for itself; and he needed access to tidewater.

On November 7, 1869, Robert Dunsmuir was a passenger on the *Sir James Douglas* when it was caught in a gale on its journey to Victoria. A "fine little steamer" whose "screw thumps much more now than formerly," the boat was no match for the gale, and her skipper put her into Cadboro Bay to wait out the storm. Several of her passengers were too impatient to wait and set off on foot for Victoria, Dunsmuir among them. His business was too important. Six days later, the word was out.

"A GREAT DISCOVERY of coal," trumpeted the *Colonist*, which was usually more restrained when announcing coal discoveries,

has been made at Departure Bay, a mile or two above Nanaimo. The seam is five or six feet thick and crops out on the shore at deep water in a most excellent harbour. Mr. Dunsmuir has secured the lead, so we hear.

With a small part fact and a large part misinformation, the beginning of the Dunsmuir empire was announced. But Dunsmuir himself was not nearly as sure as the newspaper was. He had the coal and he had the expertise, but now he had to secure enough capital to develop the seam within two years and then be able to purchase the land from the government.

He approached the financial firm of Rosenfeldt and Bermingham of San Francisco, which loaned him his initial capital at a high rate of interest. He accepted the government's terms for prospecting but asked for more time to survey. Although he actually commenced excavations in January of 1870, he still was not convinced he had found the best coal.

136

With a work force of five men whom he hired with a promise of future wages, he sank a slope ninety-seven and two-thirds yards into the seam and removed five hundred tons, twenty-five of which were taken on board the Royal Navy gunboat, H.M.S. *Boxer*, for trial. When compared to the same amounts of coal from the Douglas Pit and the Newcastle Mine, the Wellington coal proved most favourable for steaming.

Determined to find the best coal closest to tidewater, Dunsmuir continued to send out prospecting parties. On one foray, the crew prospecting the same ridge where the coal had been dug found the same seam half a mile nearer the sea and about twenty-seven feet from the surface. A borehole just three-quarters of a mile from the beach confirmed that the seam extended that far, but it was also at the edge of the limit beyond which the government would not allow him to go.

He was not bothered by other prospectors staking claims on the borders of his land grant. The main prospecting interest was at Comox at this time, and no one seemed to be aware that Dunsmuir had struck an altogether new seam.

The future coal magnate proceeded carefully, deciding to extract coal from the second site, which lay closer to the sea by half a mile from the original Wellington coal find, high on the ridge back of Diver Lake. The Royal Navy was prepared to buy everything he could produce if he could get it down to the sea. The process was difficult in the extreme. Wagonloads of coal had to be teamed down the steep slope to the beach, where the coal was loaded onto lighters and the open barges were manoeuvred out to ships at anchor in the deep water of the bay.

In October of 1870 the miners working for the VCML had been on strike for three months, and although the Company had a lot of coal stockpiled, the *Sir James Douglas* chose to take on Dunsmuir coal at Departure Bay. Then the HBC ship *Otter*, returning from Wrangell, Alaska with a boatload of ninety miners from the Cassiar gold hills, took on Wellington coal too.

Wellington coal from the Wellington seam. There was enough of it to sell, but the cost of developing the coal and the cost of borrowing money from the San Francisco financiers could have stopped the operation in its tracks. In December of 1870 Dunsmuir requested that he be allowed to continue as an individual prospector but with more land. This request was denied. A dispensation had been made for the prospecting phase but would not be made for the actual mining.

Robert had to take on partners. He needed their names on a piece of paper to qualify for the right to more land; and he needed money, not short-term, high interest money but solid low cost money, the kind that came from English fortunes and was passed on from generation to generation.

Once again the young naval officers at Esquimalt came to the aid of the Island coalfields. Lieutenant Wadham Neston Diggle of the H.M.S. *Grappler* bought in for twelve thousand dollars. That was enough to get his name included in the firm's title, Dunsmuir, Diggle and Company. The other partners were Captain (later Admiral) Arthur Farquhar, Captain Frederick Wilbraham Egerton, James Harvey, S. H. Rickman, F. A. Herne, R. Williams, and John Tweedie. James and Alexander Dunsmuir had been in partnership with their father from the beginning.

Half the shares were owned by the partners, the other half by Robert Dunsmuir on the strength of his expertise and of his possession of the claim to the Wellington seam. The partners supplied the money, but Robert Dunsmuir was the man in control. He was the Managing Partner.

CHAPTER IV

The Managing Partner

They all came out. They were all miners. Dunsmuir too. And I'm trying to figure out how he was the one that decided to make money on the coal and the others were the ones that banded together, you know, they stayed poor.

Lewis Thatcher, miner

Mr. Robert Dunsmuir is a gentleman most admirably adapted for his post; and although he is exacting from all his hands; there is no man on this coast who is more respected or thought of, than he is by every man who is in his employ.

Nanaimo Free Press, 1874

There is an impression in the community that we are obliged to accede to the miners' demands: but for the benefit of those whom it may concern we wish to state publicly that we have no intention to ask any of them to work for us again at any price.

Dunsmuir, Diggle and Co.

In the summer of 1871, Robert Dunsmuir had a large coal lease with proven coal of fine quality in abundant supply. Although he had already determined where he would begin to dig the coal and indeed had caused several hundred tons to be extracted, he could still be seen striding restlessly over the lease as if not yet certain he had found the best location for his mine.

I chanced to come upon the root of a fallen tree, which I thought had a peculiar appearance. On examination I found coal sticking on the upturned root, and digging under it, I saw that coal had been there, but was now removed by the action of fire... I sent for 2 of the workmen, who brought picks and shovels, and in half-an-hour, we discovered a seam of coal left 3 feet thick, the top of the course having been consumed.

This was an even better location for his mine. Nine feet of coal lay very close to the surface and it required only the removal of about five feet of earth to lay it bare. At a conservative estimate, the field would yield seven thousand tons per acre, probably much more, and the

Navy was anxious to buy it. The problem lay now in conveying the coal to tidewater.

The land encompassed by the lease gradually narrowed to a strip one mile wide as it advanced toward Departure Bay, ending three quarters of a mile from the beach. From there, access by way of a corridor of land had been reluctantly granted by the Vancouver Coal Mining and Land Company (VCML). It was only fifty-six feet wide and very steep. In the initial phases of development, teams of horses and mules had pulled the first coal shipments to the beach to be loaded into lighters which carried the coal alongside the naval vessels. But no large-scale operation could continue to load coal in that primitive manner.

By September the construction of a wharf had begun in the deep water on the north side of the bay. On the five acres of foreshore allowed him, Dunsmuir ordered coal sheds built, and as soon as the first wharf was completed additional wharves were begun so that several vessels could load at once. A railway would have to be engineered somehow to handle the steep slope, but in the meantime a wooden tramway was devised to connect the wharves to the mine three miles inland and on much higher terrain.

Rails made of fir 4 x 4's topped with scrap iron switchbacked their way from the mine to the top of the narrow sloping access to the beach. Here a one thousand-yard gravity incline was constructed on a 5.5% grade with a wire rope "the thickest in this country" to lower cars loaded with coal, the weight of which caused the empty cars at the bottom to be pulled to the top. Mules and horses then switched the cars from the bottom of the incline to the dock.

Within the year, Diggle purchased two traction engines from the Admiralty, the addition of flanged wheels transforming them into locomotives which replaced six animals each at the dock and in the mine yard. By 1878 the traction engines themselves were supplanted by two small saddle tank engines named *Duke* and *Duchess*, which took the cars from the foot of the incline to the wharves. Replacing the gravity incline was not so simple. It remained in service for another year, its existence a source of much concern for the mine and the growing number of inhabitants of the area.

Printed notices posted in conspicuous places warned people of the danger of riding the coal wagons on the incline should the rope break. The newly appointed Inspector of Mines fussed in his report:

140

I would beg to state that it is my opinion that sooner or later, a very serious accident will occur, as many women and children are in the habit of riding the waggons running on this incline, although constantly warned by the colliery officials against doing so.

At first anyone wishing to make their way from Departure Bay to Wellington, as the new coal camp was called, had little choice but to ride the incline. Even when a road of sorts was built in 1874, the temptation to ride rather than climb the hill on foot was too much for most people.

A tiny village had sprung up in the middle of a triangle formed by three small lakes, all abundantly supplied with fish. On the north shore of Diver Lake, one Charles "Donnybrook" Chantrell set himself up in business as a publican almost as soon as Dunsmuir secured his coal lease. Chantrell had been a miner in Nanaimo since 1860, but soothing the thirst of other miners looked to be a much more congenial profession. Until he could secure a liquor license in 1875, he provided accommodation in his own house for bachelor miners. As soon as Robert Dunsmuir approved the license, he began to sell liquor and to build the Wellington Inn.

A particularly cold winter had provided Chantrell with a good supply of ice, "clear as water," which he stored in an icehouse on the lakeshore. Such civilized measures existed in stark contrast to the swarms of dogs, pigeons, hens, turkeys, and geese which the innkeeper kept in the yard and which made approaching the hotel fraught with potential mishap.

The history of the Wellington Hotel, or Chantrell's as it was also called, was as chaotic as the yard that surrounded it. By 1879 the building was up for public auction, Chantrell having gone bankrupt; no sooner had the new owner, Tom Wall, bought it than it burned down. Wall rebuilt it. It burned down again. A few hundred yards away, a new site was chosen for the next reincarnation. In whatever form, and with whatever owner, the Wellington Hotel had a unique position in the community owned by Robert Dunsmuir. For the town was on Dunsmuir land and his approval was needed for every liquor license that was sold and every business that opened and every building that was constructed. He only gave his permission to one other saloon and that was the Cosmopolitan, which opened one week before Chantrell did, with a Grand Ball on New Year's Eve 1874.

Dunsmuir knew what a problem liquor could be in a mining camp, especially one with a large proportion of unmarried miners. He was, after all, one of the first members of the Total Abstinence Society of Nanaimo. That he continued to consume liquor himself despite these concerns was an early indication of the paternal approach he took toward his employees. He acted on the belief that he knew what was best for them and would take steps to help them avoid what he considered to be bad.

However, the hotels located outside his lease limits were beyond his control. At the south end of Diver Lake, on VCML land, stood Brown's Lakehouse, with its ballroom, stage and dressing rooms, bowling alley, and outdoor facilities for quoits and skittles. And when the provincial government, spurred on at last by the developments in Wellington, agreed to turn the beginning of the Comox Trail into the six mile long Wellington Road, Mr. P. Parson marked the middle point with the Half-Way Hotel.

Some wag said there should be two roads, one going to each saloon, and that they should be called Boniface Number One and Boniface Number Two,[1] but the people of the area were glad to have one road, and traffic became heavy as the new mines developed and the demand for labour grew.

Dunsmuir was a new kind of boss. Unlike Mark Bate and John Bryden, who shared management responsibility and had to answer to a distant board of directors in London, Dunsmuir was the ultimate authority on site and he was determined to control every aspect of the operation right down to where and how the people lived. That point was driven home right from the beginning when he caused a gate to be erected on the provincial road where it met his property.

All the land that the mines and the houses stood on was tightly controlled by the Managing Partner. He would sell no property to miners or merchants, saying that mining was too unsure a business and he wanted to protect the men from investing money in something that could be rendered worthless if the mines closed. His control of the land, symbolized by the gate across the Wellington Road, would manifest itself when the men he was trying to protect demanded that they be allowed to think for themselves.

Midway through the decade of the 1870's, Wellington was going "full blast." Everyone lived around the pithead of Number One Slope in houses built and owned by Robert Dunsmuir and there were houses in every stage of construction. Mr. W. Akenhead, who had a

---

[1] "Boniface" means landlord.

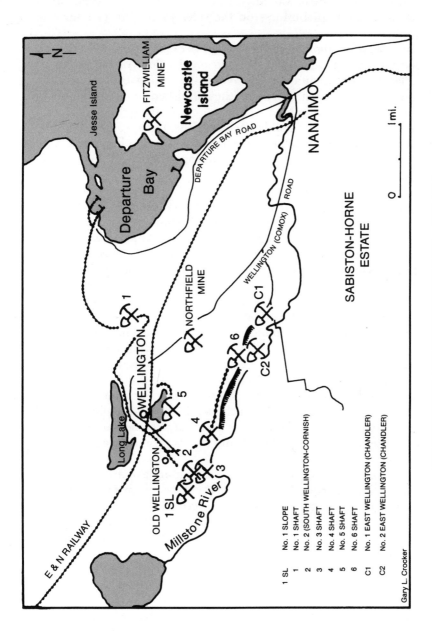

WELLINGTON AND DEPARTURE BAY — 1870-1900

N

Jesse Island

FITZWILLIAM MINE

Newcastle Island

Departure Bay

NANAIMO

DEPARTURE BAY ROAD

1 mi.

0

SABISTON-HORNE ESTATE

NORTHFIELD MINE

WELLINGTON (COMOX) ROAD

1

C1

WELLINGTON

6

C2

Long Lake

5

4

E & N RAILWAY

WELLINGTON

OLD WELLINGTON

1 SL

0 1 2

3

Millstone River

1 SL	No. 1 SLOPE
1	No. 1 SHAFT
2	No. 2 (SOUTH WELLINGTON-CORNISH)
3	No. 3 SHAFT
4	No. 4 SHAFT
5	No. 5 SHAFT
6	No. 6 SHAFT
C1	No. 1 EAST WELLINGTON (CHANDLER)
C2	No. 2 EAST WELLINGTON (CHANDLER)

Gary L. Crocker

boarding house which was already full of bachelor miners, ran a wholesale and retail business on the side. John Mahrer opened a bakery.

There were enough people in town in 1874 for a rousing May 24th picnic with sports and then dancing on the floor of the yet to be completed Cosmopolitan hotel. When the spring evening got too cold, everyone adjourned to one of the unfinished Company houses to continue the celebration. Mr. Dunsmuir was always generous with money to support these holiday celebrations, but specified that it be spent on sports. By 1876 there was a school, stores, a Forester's Hall, and a Literary Institute already equipped with an *Encyclopedia Britannica* donated by Captain Egerton.

Of the 150 men employed at the mine in 1874, only eight had families with them. Unlike the VCML, which preferred and indeed encouraged family men, Dunsmuir hired whomever was available. The overwhelming preponderance of unmarried men gave the community an unsettled air and a rough facade which Cornelius Bryant, by now a Methodist minister, compared to Nanaimo in the 1850's. "This is a place," said the good pastor, "with a population wholly engaged in coal mining, and as spiritually destitute as Nanaimo was, ere our Mission was begun there in 1859."

The devout were to be found, however, crowded into Akenhead's boarding house to hear Mr. F. J. Saunders read an essay on "The Creation Reviewed" at the request of his fellow workmen, or attending the Methodist picnic at Departure Bay at which three Indian babies were baptized by the minister from Nanaimo. Soon the Methodists built a church, but although by then more families had moved into the town, the money for the church came hard because a short strike had already occurred and another, much bigger one was brewing.

The mine had been in full operation, going as hard as the men could dig the coal, since 1873. In 1875 the slope was six hundred yards long and getting longer every day. Its length was divided by a straight row of timbers, leaving one side of the slope for the hauling rope and the other for the men to come up and go down. Soon, levels ate into the rich coal seam on both sides of the slope.

New boilers, seated in solid masonry quarried just a few yards away from the engine house, drove hoisting gear mounted on heavy timbers which led down the long slope to where the coal lay. Steam was the energy that drove the pumping, hoisting, loading, and transportation systems and that made the mine as modern as British mines of

144

the time. In a labour short environment, it was necessary to use as much machinery as possible.

The mode of ventilation was considered modern too, especially when compared to Nova Scotia mines of the time which were "ventilated by the miraculous interposition of Providence." A furnace was constructed by bricking in the walls of a shaft sunk straight down from the surface. At its base, which was connected with the workings of the mine, a hot fire burned, its insatiable appetite for oxygen pulling air down the slope and throughout the mine, sweeping methane gas and smoke from the blasting along with it and away from where it could harm the workmen.

The roaring fire of the ventilation furnace was tended by a Chinese, one of the few employed directly by the Company.[2] On an evening in October of 1876, the man in charge of the furnace piled on extra coal so it would last until morning and left the furnace unattended. At midnight the mine whistle summoned the Dunsmuirs from their beds to witness a runaway fire feeding on the coal on each side of the upper slope. By morning a flaming column one hundred yards high had burst its way through a cave-in in front of the mine office and roared defiantly for another four days before being brought under control.

One year later, the new Coal Mines Regulations Act would prohibit Chinese from attending ventilation furnaces, but Robert Dunsmuir and his sons did not take well to being told how to run their mines. They continued to employ Chinese in this capacity regardless of the fearsome fire that had almost destroyed their dream when it had barely begun.

The Dunsmuirs were not alone in their opposition to the new act. Mine managers from Nanaimo and Baynes Sound were united with them in their contention that the bill in its preliminary form interfered with the "successful prosecution of coal mining in this Province."[3]

In the fledgling province, only five years old when its politicians proposed the act to regulate coal mines, government interference was resented by men who had been writing their own rules for twenty years. When a coal inspector's branch was inaugurated in 1874 to gather production statistics and make routine colliery investigations, few people knew or cared about its existence. But during the election campaign in 1875, the alarming increase in the number of mine accidents had become an important issue to the electorate.

[2] In 1871, the Dunsmuir work force of forty men had included seven Chinese.

[3] The Baynes Sound manager, Archibald Dick, became government mine inspector in 1880, in charge of enforcing the very act he was now opposing.

In response, the government of Premier George Walkem introduced a bill to establish a Coal Mines Regulations Act in January of 1876. The attempt proved abortive, for the bill died a month later when the government was defeated. Its death was not mourned by a small but articulate group of miners whose spokesman, James Harold, criticized it at a gathering of miners, owners, and managers who met with David W. Gordon, the local contractor with political aspirations.

The miners said the new bill must be modelled on the British Act of 1872. No boys under twelve must work in the mines; boys over twelve must work only eight hours; miners should be allowed to appoint a check weighman; no owner or manager must act as an inspector; an inspector must have the power to shut down a dangerous mine; one hundred cubic feet of pure air must be provided for every man, boy, and horse.

There was one more demand made. "That no Chinese shall be employed in any position where his neglect or carelessness might endanger the limbs or lives of any man working in the mines." That demand was made at a time when there were relatively few Chinese employed, and most of those who were had been hired by the miners themselves. But the number of Chinese grew dramatically as labour unrest and mine expansion made any worker desirable to the owners. And as the number grew, the white miners' demand for their removal grew too.

The owners did not want an act regulating their activities no matter what form it took, but a petition to that effect was ignored and a new bill passed in the Legislature. It was scheduled to come into force on August 15, 1877. Had it been proclaimed sooner, its rules might have saved the lives of three miners killed in the VCML Fitzwilliam Mine in September of 1876.

The conditions in this mine on Newcastle Island, across Departure Bay from the Wellington wharves, were probably no worse than those in any other mine in the area. A furnace ventilated the workings; doors and stoppings directed the flow of air; miners had access to safety lamps to test for gas; but no one checked to see that the mine was gas free. No one impressed upon the employees the necessity of keeping those doors and stoppings closed. When the misdirected ventilation failed to rid the mine of methane gas and the resulting explosion killed three miners, the coroner's jury, which included miners' spokesman James Harold, found gross negligence on the part of the officers and superintendent of the VCML.

Coroner Spalding was probably correct when he disagreed with this verdict. He said that while management had been negligent, the men were as much to blame. They knew that their work places must be gas free, and they also knew that doors and stoppings must be kept closed. Accordingly, he ruled that from then on a sign stating that no man was allowed to enter before 6:00 a.m. without permission of the fireman must be posted outside the mine. There was no requirement, however, for the fireman to have done any testing for gas nor any assurance that all miners, whether white or Chinese, could read the sign. That one of the miners killed was Chinese and that another Chinese man had been observed leaving stoppings open when they should have been closed, added to the anti-Oriental sentiment that was simmering throughout the district. The Wellington Mine furnace fire one month later, a fire that was caused by a Chinese worker, cannot have improved race relations.

In 1876, however, Chinese workers in mines were a minor irritant. There was too much money to be made and too many mines needing labour to worry much about the odd explosion and fire. All someone had to do was stand on the big wharf at the Fitzwilliam Mine and look out on the Bay to see what was happening.

The harbour at Departure Bay was full of ships waiting to take on Wellington coal. Barques and schooners rode at anchor in the deep water, sheltered in the basin that enfolded the harbour like an ample mother with her arms out to comfort and keep safe.

But like boisterous, bored children, the sailors from the waiting ships chafed and made trouble. There was nowhere to drink in the harbour area. The Whiskey Synagogue which had so infuriated the owner of the Newcastle Island Quarry had been replaced by Harper's Departure Bay House which could not get a license to sell liquor. The homely little building sat there at the foot of the long hill like a symbol of what was not quite possible. Just beyond, the new road climbed the hill in the direction of Nanaimo, challenging the thirsty to make the long hike.

"This apology for a road" was narrow and almost impassable in winter. On the long hill that ran down to the point of land opposite Newcastle Island, a stream of water six to eight feet wide sometimes ran. The only alternative for the traveller intent on reaching Nanaimo was to take the ferry *Leviathan*, which ran twice a day with a stop at Newcastle Island going and coming.

Until 1876, the only other buildings at the Bay were a few shanties and the colliery sheds in back of the wharves. All there was for the sailors to do was sit on the beach, argue, fight, and wish they were somewhere else. Then the Wellington Colliery office was moved to Departure Bay, its "neat and tasty" appearance, large public room, and several private offices with their walnut fittings giving the harbour area a classier tone. Robert Dunsmuir moved his headquarters to this new building and left his eldest son, James, in charge of the mine and living in the fine family home, which was called "Ardoon," near the mine.

James Dunsmuir should have been a man for the New World. His birthplace was an immigrant ship aground in the mouth of the Columbia River; his first home was a rough cabin at Fort Rupert where he was kidnapped by Indians fascinated by his fair skin; the Nanaimo Indians were his fishing companions, the mines his primary teacher. His destiny until his father found his own coal had been to be a machinist in someone else's mines. To acquire some polish befitting the first son and heir of a successful entrepreneur, James was sent to the Hamilton Military Academy in Blackburg, Virginia. When he returned to Wellington in 1876 he had a southern belle for a wife, a fine home, and he was the manager of a large coal mine. He was twenty-five years old.

Although "Mrs. James" was popular in Wellington and well-known for her fine singing voice at village concerts, her husband could not claim the same popularity among all his employees. Despite his practical training, he did not appreciate the situation of the miners who worked for him. His father Robert was paternalistic and demanding, but he had sympathy for the miners' problems and attempted to improve working conditions as long as the men conformed to what he thought was best. James was stiff-necked and short-tempered and seemed unwilling to put himself out to produce a better working situation. The difference in the approach of the two men became apparent during the big strike of 1877.

But James was an able man and turned his machinist training to solving the problem of communication between the mines at Wellington and the wharves at the Bay. Working with his employees Abe Hamilton and master mechanic William Wall, and using information from the *Scientific American*, James fashioned a telephone out of two yeast cake boxes, copper from powder keg banding, magnets made of iron strips, and a diaphragm made of a tintype photograph.

It was the first telephone in British Columbia but not the first in the world. One year before, in March of 1876, Alexander Graham Bell had been granted a patent for the telephone, beating at least twenty other inventors by a matter of weeks. Later, Robert Dunsmuir was able to buy two phones in San Francisco to replace the makeshift one made by his three employees.

Father and son were always looking for more efficient ways of running the Wellington operation. After the furnace fire, the miners detected some more subtle changes. The boxes or skips which the miners filled with coal and which were weighed to determine how much each man would be paid, seemed to weigh less, even though they were loaded higher. The check weighman, although paid by the miners and in place to see that they got a fair deal, was by old custom a company employee and therefore in danger of losing his job if he angered his boss. Weighman Harrison said he thought the scales were weighing correctly, but the men disagreed.

The miners had some other grievances. They resented having to come outside to pick up their own rails, ties, and props. Each trip away from the face meant time lost from getting coal, and it was the coal they were paid for. A rule that there be two men in each "room" at the coal face angered them as well.

With resentment brewing, but with no formal organization to focus their grievances, the miners received shocking news in July of 1876. At a meeting called by Robert Dunsmuir, they were asked to take a twenty cent reduction from $1.20, the pay they received for each ton of coal. Rival companies in San Francisco had initiated a price competition to get rid of this annoying new source from Vancouver Island, whose coal seemed so popular with the California customers. Faced with having to lower his prices, too, and with the cost of shipping rising, Dunsmuir said he could no longer compete at the price he was paying his men.

To the miners' eyes, Dunsmuir did not seem to be suffering from the competition of the marketplace. He had built a big house right in the midst of the tiny two-room homes of the miners. Despite huge start-up and development costs, he appeared to be living well. The miners' impression of his affluence was more accurate than they knew. Within the next six years he would be able to buy out his partners at many times their original investment, open and develop several mines, and acquire new property to be held in reserve. Yet with all this financial success, he was asking the miners to accept a reduction in their small wages.

They refused and within a few days seventy of them were laid off, leaving thirty-six to work for another three weeks at the old rate. "I told them," said Dunsmuir, "they would give me as much coal as I wanted and they could go to work at $1.20 and the rest could play."

149

His tough stance alarmed the miners. For the next week he saw deputations at all hours, sometimes in the middle of the night. Some offered to work at $1.10. Given this offer, Dunsmuir fired the thirty-six men working at $1.20 and hired those who would work for $1.10.[4] Walking along the railway track on their way to a meeting to discuss this development, several miners happened to meet Dunsmuir. He told them that he regarded hiring these men at $1.10 as meeting the miners half way.

Next day, a deputation met with their employer to tell him they would not work for less than $1.20. In response, Dunsmuir said the mine would have to stand and put up notices in the mine yard calling for men to work by contract. Fourteen men responded and worked for two days.

On July 29, 1876, a "Notice to All Miners" appeared in the *Free Press*, a weekly newspaper published since 1874 from Nanaimo.

We, the Miners of the Wellington Colliery, Vancouver Island, British Columbia, being out on strike against a reduction of 12½%, do hereby notify all miners to abstain from coming to the above mentioned place, in search of work.

"The Miners of the Wellington Colliery" unfortunately did not represent any sort of an organized group. There was no sense of union solidarity to prevent any of the 240 men employed at the mine coming to Dunsmuir and saying they would work as cheaply as those on contract. There was nothing for the rest to do but agree to the new terms and resume work in August at one dollar per ton.

Almost without exception, the men at Wellington were of British origin. They came from a country where an era of bitter union battles had ended and where the union had been accepted as a fact of life. Though their fathers had been radicals, they were much more conservative, having seen the successes of capitalism and the absense of a viable alternative. The 1867 Reform Bill had given many of them the vote, and Prime Minister William Gladstone had overseen legislation in 1871 which accepted unions into the British scheme of things. An 1875 law brought in by Gladstone's successor, Benjamin Disraeli, had legalized picketing and abolished a law which made combining into a union a conspiracy.

Bad times in Britain in the 1860's had made the colonies seem highly desirable. Canada, although no longer a colony, was still

[4] No employer on Vancouver Island ever paid that much for coal again.

regarded as one and was certainly a desirable place to go, unless a man could stay in Britain. So they came in great numbers and some of them worked for Robert Dunsmuir, but there were no unions. They had tried to strike in the summer and had not been strong enough to keep other miners from returning to work.

Trouble brewed all through the fall and bubbled to the surface again in November. The scales were weighing the miners short. When complaints persisted into the new year, Dunsmuir decided that although he could find nothing wrong with the scales, the men must be compensated. He offered to pay each man for half a hundred-weight extra. That only two men actually applied for the compensation was explained by another miner who said, "I considered it beneath my dignity to go and get my coal made up."

Perhaps Dunsmuir belatedly understood the pride that went into the miners' decisions because he did agree to have the scales checked. Under the supervision of his son James, a box was placed on the scale and coal added gradually. Up to four hundred pounds, the weight was accurate, but after that mark the readings made no sense. An American miner named George Vipont suggested that the scales from Departure Bay be brought up to the mine. Vipont had been helped on several occasions by Mr. Dunsmuir and was making a positive suggestion to help settle the problem. James refused, saying that the scales were needed down there and they would repair the old one as soon as foreman Frank Little was feeling better. He refused to order a new scale from Britain because it would take two to three months to be delivered.

Vipont bent down and investigated the plates of the scale. He showed a reluctant James how the upper and lower plates rested on each other improperly. A blacksmith was called and the scale was fixed for a time.

A few days later, a miner named Haggerty complained again to James that the Company was cheating the men. James told him to get his tools and leave. Haggerty proposed they weigh four or five boxes and then take them down to the Bay and weigh them there. That was too much trouble for James. Haggerty offered to get several miners to do all the work and bear the expense. James still refused and Haggerty was out of a job.

When the men complained about Haggerty being fired, Robert Dunsmuir said he had not been fired at all but rather his contract had simply run out and had not been renewed. To Dunsmuir's way of thinking that did not constitute being fired, but Haggerty was still out of a job. In this Robert supported his son, but when Billy Baker told him that the men were growling about the scales, the owner said "Billy, I don't want anything but what is right, tell the miners to appoint a committee and get Little and see what is the matter with the scales."

Something was definitely erratic about the Wellington Mine scales. Discrepancies had been noticed the previous spring, but the errors found then had been in the miners' favour. The scales were four years old, but they had been checked only once and that was after the fire. Large mine scales required more frequent maintenance than that. When another complaint finally convinced Robert and James that they were inaccurate, Robert's second son Alexander was sent to Chantrell's to tell the men. It was too late. He was pushed out of the saloon by the miners as their wives and children looked on.

The miners had reached their boiling point. They had had their wages reduced to one dollar per ton and were sure that the scales were inaccurate. On February 1, 1877, at a meeting at Chantrell's, the miners demanded the return of the twenty cents per ton they had been docked the previous August. Dunsmuir refused but said if they went to work he would do something about the scales. This outraged the miners. Old grievances which had lain dormant suddenly surfaced again.

One such complaint was the price of blasting powder. Miners were required to buy powder from the Company and Wellington coal seemed to require an unusually large amount of powder to move it, sometimes two to three pounds per shot. Although Dunsmuir had promised in July 1876 to take fifty cents per keg off the cost of blasting powder he had not done so.

Dunsmuirs, father and sons, were visited by a deputation of miners, who issued an ultimatum giving the owners two days to reinstate their old wages and rehire Haggerty. The men in this deputation were more than mere miners. James Phillips, Alexander Hoggan, Henry Adams, and William Macdonald were union men. The first coal miners' union on Vancouver Island was about to make itself known.

Although Robert told them he would not change his mind, the men worked for the next two days. During that time the scales broke down again and the men were being assigned average weights for their coal. On the morning of the third day, when Robert was riding down to Departure Bay, he was told there was a strike. One hundred miners had walked off, throwing another 130 backhands, runners, blacksmiths, and pithead crew out of work.

Four days later on February 7th, at a meeting of miners from Wellington, Chase River, Harewood, Douglas, and Newcastle mines to discuss the new Coal Mines Regulations Act, a communication from the Wellington miners was received. Their request for moral and financial support was enthusiastically endorsed.

Like an outraged parent who had determined to wash his hands of his troublesome children, Robert Dunsmuir announced that all occupants of Company houses had one month in which to vacate the premises. Then he took his battle to the press in the following "card" which first appeared on February 14th.

There is an impression in the community that we are obliged to accede to the miners' demands: but for the benefit of those whom it may concern we wish to state publicly that we have no intention to ask any of them to work for us again at any price.

Signed Dunsmuir, Diggle and Company.

In the course of the next four months, that "card" appeared regularly in the local paper. Although all sides in the dispute used the newspapers in Nanaimo and Victoria to air their views, the way Dunsmuir used the press seems beneath the dignity of a man of substance. When George Vipont turned against him, Dunsmuir wrote to the *Free Press* describing all he had done for Vipont in the past and what an ingrate he was. He published long lists of wages of individual miners, surely a matter to be kept private between an employer and employee, and when the men protested, he explained and rationalized his actions again in print.

Having announced by his "card" that he would never employ the strikers again, he set out to provide the mine with new labour. Alexander Dunsmuir, a twenty-four year old whose talents in dealing with other businessmen had made him his father's contact man in real estate and politics, was sent to San Francisco to hire strikebreakers.

His ads in the San Francisco papers bore quick results. On Friday, February 23rd, thirty-three new men arrived at Departure Bay on the steamer *Etta White* and were met by Mr. Dunsmuir himself, who discussed the seam and the geological excellence of the place and told them that tools would be provided. He also mentioned that the mine had been hit by a strike, the first time that any of the new men had heard of it.

The thirty-three would later be called "Italians," but there were Englishmen, Frenchmen, and Irishmen among them too. They were housed in three shanties near the wharf. That night, some of the

Wellington men came to take the newcomers for a drink, but only some of the Irishmen accepted.

The next morning the Wellington men tried a new approach when the new miners were escorted up the hill on the Company railroad and taken to the mine. If they would not drink with them, would they come to a meeting? Strikers followed strikebreakers down the mine slope until Robert Dunsmuir stood between the two groups with his arms out and forbade the strikers to proceed any further. Dunsmuir's courage or the strikers' ingrained respect for authority made them turn around and leave the mine, but they waited outside for an hour until the new men emerged. In order to prevent contact between the two groups, the strikebreakers were quickly loaded into coal wagons and returned to Departure Bay. Some announced they would be ready to work on Monday, but others were not so sure.

Henry Stewart was an articulate and honest man. He had come from San Francisco to work, but now he wanted to know more about what was going on. He talked to the strikers and discovered that some of them were married, all were "practical coal miners," and they had been swindled by the scales, on the wages they had been promised, and on the price of powder. Stewart spoke for many of the new men when he said that they would leave the area if they got financial assistance.

The Wellington miners determined not to leave anything to chance. On Sunday at noon one hundred of them marched down to the Bay shanties to "encourage" the newcomers' quick departure. Some, like Stewart, went willingly, their baggage being carried by local men. Others went under duress.

R. W. Osborne, the apparent leader of the newcomers, became the special target of James Williams and Joseph Hoskins. Osborne and his large zinc trunk were half carried and half pushed down to the pebble beach where a canoe waited for the baggage and the occasional man unable to walk to Nanaimo. Such a man was Luigi Valliguzzi, whose sore leg made him a candidate for a canoe ride but whose strong arms made him a reluctant paddler for the short trip across the Bay and down Exit Channel to Nanaimo harbour.

In the confusion of old-timers and newcomers, the hollering of oaths, the push and the scramble, Christopher Loat, the Company bookkeeper, ordered a man to get a message to James Dunsmuir in Nanaimo, as fast as he could. The quickest route was the Departure Bay trail that ran up the steep hill and then along the water, but the messenger's path was twice blocked by strikers, forcing him to go around by a back road.

When James got the message, he headed for Departure Bay as fast as his horse and buggy would take him. Enroute he encountered the "Italians," as he called them, being herded toward town by the strikers. He demanded they turn around, but before they could comply the strikers surrounded them and forced their continued journey to Nanaimo, where the luggage canoe and its reluctant paddler had landed. Soon all the strikebreakers were in the main room of one of the hotels in Nanaimo which served as a boarding house for miners.

Now Henry Stewart said that when they got to Nanaimo "the chief thing done was drinking," but Henry was a reasonable man. There were a lot of new men in that public room who were not pleased with what was happening. Even though the strikers fed them dinner, they were outraged to learn that they could choose to go that night by canoe to Victoria, wait for the next steamer, or stay and work in Nanaimo, but they must never try to work at Wellington.

Eight men chose to stay. The remaining twenty-five were herded out of the hotel and toward the harbour through streets full of curious onlookers, strikers, Nanaimo miners, and Dunsmuir men. One rode a mule up and down the street trying to encourage the new men to stay, but the strikers pushed them away and on toward the harbour. Mr. Dunsmuir himself was there trying unsuccessfully to contact Osborne.

At the harbour's edge lay the luggage canoe with two more canoes rented by the strikers to accommodate the newcomers. As each man climbed reluctantly aboard, the canoes settled deeper and deeper in the water leaving very little freeboard. Luigi Valliguzzi sat in the luggage canoe until he could stand it no more. He got out and waded ashore, sore leg and all, only to be met by a man who said he was Dunsmuir's partner and would pay his board if he would rejoin the canoes and wait in Victoria until he was called. Diggle had a big stake in this strike, too.

From the overloaded canoes came another protest. They were all strangers to these waters. How could they get to Victoria without a guide? Four strikers were appointed to accompany them to their destination. James Knight, Henry Adams, Henry Smith, and John Jenkins soon paid for their willingness to serve as guides when they were arrested in Victoria and charged with intimidation of the strikebreakers.

Despite the inauspicious beginning, the voyage proceeded without incident to Saanich, the men continuing on foot the last eighteen miles to Victoria. Each man's pocket was enriched by the fifteen dollars given him by the strikers to cover his return to San Francisco.

Not all the new men left Victoria. Several were observed checking in at the Pacific Telegraph Hotel to await a recall from Wellington. Valliguzzi and several others stayed around to be Company witnesses when Knight, Adams, Smith, and Jenkins were brought to trial. Henry Stewart stayed, too, and testified very convincingly in favour of the four committee men who had volunteered to serve as guides.

In Wellington there was something afoot that had not happened before. The miners were organized and were presenting a united front. They were determined to behave in a responsible manner, but they were not going to back down. Their mature handling of the first shipment of strikebreakers sent warning signals to Robert Dunsmuir. On that very Sunday evening, as the three overloaded canoes made their way to Saanich through the sheltered waters of the Gulf Islands, an obviously unnerved Dunsmuir turned to his friends in high places.

He first wrote to the newly sworn-in Premier of the Province, Andrew Elliott, who also served as Attorney-General. It was in that capacity that Robert addressed him when he wrote:

For goodness sake act promptly in this matter, I am afraid that there will be bloodshed among us at this time; I know the miners as well, I think, as any one, and I can see that we have all a hard battle to fight. Diggle will, of course, tell you all.

Diggle seems to have become a glorified messenger. Before he left for Victoria he was dispatched to take a copy of the letter to Magistrate Spalding, who had demonstrated that he was a reasonable man by his firm handling of troublesome crews of visiting ships and his efforts to curb the selling of liquor to half-breed children. Many felt that he had been given too large a territory, which made him often absent from his headquarters for long periods of time, but his evenhanded action as the coroner during the inquest into the Newcastle Mine explosion brought him admiration and a reputation for impartiality.

Just one year later, however, with Wellington in the grip of a strike, the impartial Captain Spalding seemed to be firmly in Dunsmuir's camp. The fact that he was also lawyer to Company partner Admiral Farquhar reinforced this impression.

Diggle brought Robert's letter to Spalding and waited while he wrote a letter to the Lieutenant-Governor.

156

The miners [are] determined to proceed to extremities and have already committed such acts of violence as will necessitate the employment of an armed force to reduce them to order and compel them to respect the law. I would suggest that one of Her Majesty's ships should be dispatched as early as possible to this station, for the purpose of overawing the miners and, if need be, enforcing obedience to authority.

Diggle made his way south to Victoria on that Sunday night, carrying letters to the Premier and the Lieutenant-Governor asking for armed force and a naval vessel to deal with one hundred miners who had stopped working and had met the threat of blackleg labour by escorting the offending workers out of the area in a determined but peaceful manner.

The new week began with a flurry of activity on both sides. The Old Picnic Ground in Nanaimo was the site of a morning meeting of all the miners in the district. The *Free Press* reported that the strikers had the sympathy of the community. Included in a report given by Vipont on the scales was the bald statement that Robert Dunsmuir had lied.

As the fire of righteous indignation was fanned by the successes moderation had brought them that weekend, the rhetoric became more and more grandiose. James Harold said Dunsmuir should be ashamed of the men he had brought in, "the sweepings of the gutters, no miners, no nothings. He will sack them when the price goes down, and they will roam the country as robbers." When Uriah Hockyard had the floor, he insisted on the term "blackleg" over the objections of the meeting's chairman. "Any man taking tools into a mine where the men are on strike is a blackleg — in the old country they call them 'nobsticks'."

The call for a union went up, and the organizers were ready. When the motion was put and passed, an executive was elected with the following admonition to guide them in their conduct.

Organize and let us be as one man on this Island. Unions sometimes go too far but it is not the fault of the Union, but the officers, so you will have to be careful who you appoint as officers.

The newly elected president of the newly formed Coalminers' Mutual Protective Society was William Macdonald of Wellington. A. Mackenzie from Harewood Mine was elected secretary and Fred Wild from Nanaimo, treasurer. A working committee with two representatives each from Chase River, Harewood, Douglas, and Wellington Mines, and one from Newcastle Mine, was also elected.

By the time the meeting adjourned for lunch, it had accomplished with its morning's labours the founding of the first miners' union on Vancouver Island.

While the miners met in Nanaimo, Robert Dunsmuir exercised his prerogative as a property owner and closed the gate that marked the end of the public part of Wellington Road and the beginning of Dunsmuir land. The mine camp was isolated. Alex Mayer from the Red House store in Nanaimo had been supplying miners with cheaper groceries than they could buy in Wellington. His wagon was not allowed past the gate. Dunsmuir told Akenhead the butcher and Mahrer the baker, "publickly and in a friendly way," that it would not be worth their while to kill any beef or fetch any bread. The medical officer for the mine, Dr. Daniel Cluness, was told by Mr. Dunsmuir that "as his men had ceased to work he had no control over their usual monthly payment for doctor and would not be responsible for same."[5]

The brand new executive of the brand new union met in the afternoon of February 26th. They resolved to appoint men to collect money by subscription to reimburse the Wellington men for their expenses in sending the strikebreakers out of the country; they resolved to draw up a list of rules and regulations to be endorsed by the individual societies at each colliery; and they resolved that those men who wished to sign their names as members be allowed to do so. One hundred thirty-seven did just that.

Communications between Nanaimo and Victoria were rapid when canoes carried the messenger with letter in hand. Barely two days after Dunsmuir sent his urgent request to Elliott, a reply was on its way to Magistrate Spalding. A commission would be appointed and the gunship H.M.S. *Rocket* dispatched "to render assistance to the officers of the law should occasion require, and when called upon by you."

When Dunsmuir was informed of this reply by Spalding he wrote again to Elliott, begging him to hurry the commission. Still in a distressed frame of mind, the coal magnate said, "such a lot of men I never had to deal with before, and there will be no peace with them until they get a proper lesson and in haste." The fatherly lesson was to be delivered by government.

The arm of the law came down swiftly on the four committee men

---

[5] The miners paid a monthly fee to the doctor in return for unlimited medical care for themselves and their families.

who had helped the San Francisco strikebreakers just two days before. Adams, Smith, Knight, and Jenkins were arrested on Tuesday, February 27th, charged with intimidation by R. W. Osborne, and bailed out the same day by their provincial member, D. W. Gordon. At their trial in Victoria Police Court the following day, the judge apologized for any possible hurt feelings and allowed the prisoners to leave without any reflections on their character. The four men left the court room to the applause of the spectators.

Undeterred by this dismissal, the authorities in Nanaimo seized four more strikers on the very next day. Working in an orderly fashion with the townsfolk of Wellington looking on quietly, Provincial Police Superintendent Todd arrested Joseph Hoskin, John D. Edwards, James Thompson, and James Williams and charged them with preventing the strikebreakers from working. When the four were brought up before Magistrate Spalding, they refused to be tried by him and instead were committed for trial in Provincial Supreme Court.

One observer of the arrests was not reassured by the orderliness of the crowd. As the time loomed closer for the miners to vacate the Company houses, Dunsmuir fretted in yet another letter to the Attorney-General.

We are going to have trouble, if not bloodshed, when we commence to eject the miners from the houses... they say they will not leave, and that we cannot put them out.

So sure was he that there would be trouble that he offered to pay for a government bill, to be drawn up and passed immediately, which would eject the miners before the expiration of the notice period. Fortunately for the democratic process, the chief legal officer of the province ignored the request.

In the meantime, the H.M.S. *Rocket* had arrived in Departure Bay, its presence prompting a petition in protest signed by 106 miners. No breach of peace had occurred and none was intended, and the miners felt they had been disgraced as law-abiding citizens "to have armed force in their midst."

The "armed force" was purely symbolic. The *Rocket* was a small screw steamer built especially for use in the Crimean War twenty-two years before. Its maximum speed with a strong breeze astern was about five knots, so slow "that gentlemen on board have ample leisure to examine the coast in detail." A wit in Victoria described her as "decidedly the reverse of handy." With a gale ahead, she drifted leeward and a "half-hour's cannonading from her gun would probably have shaken her framework fatally." Despite her decrepit condition, however, her presence in the harbour was insulting to many citizens, even those who were not miners.

The strike was only three weeks old and already Dunsmuir had used many weapons in his battle with the miners. He had closed the town, excluding suppliers of food and medicine; he had given out eviction notices; he had imported strikebreakers, albeit unsuccessfully. He had advertised his intentions in the newspapers and called for legal and legislative help from his Victoria friends. The courts having refused him satisfaction so far, he determined to take the strike into the courtroom on a more personal basis.

George Norris was the owner, publisher, and sole reporter of the *Nanaimo Free Press* and had in the latter capacity attended the first union meeting in Nanaimo and reported on the proceedings. Included in his account was George Vipont's discussion about the scales and his calling Robert Dunsmuir a liar. Uriah Hockyard's remarks were also recorded at length. In his next tactic against the miners, Dunsmuir sued the newspaper, Vipont, and Hockyard for libel.

In Magistrate's Court three days later, on March 6th, the charges were dismissed against Vipont and Hockyard. Their testimony would, however, be heard when George Norris defended himself against Dunsmuir's libel charge one week later.

Magistrate Spalding was a busy man in the first days of March. On the third day of the month, he announced Premier Elliott's commission, which was earnestly desired by both sides in the dispute. Chief Justice Sir Matthew Baillie Begbie, whose reputation as the "Hanging Judge" had been made in the gold fields of the Cariboo, agreed to conduct the inquiry provided both parties would accept and abide by his decision. The union and Mr. Dunsmuir both agreed to this proviso.

Dunsmuir had hedged his bets, however. Forty-two miners from San Francisco were waiting in Victoria for the Company to decide on a propitious time to bring them to Wellington. Dunsmuir was distressed to learn that the *Rocket* had left Departure Bay and returned to Victoria. He wrote to Elliott on March 6th explaining that he had all these men in Victoria who were costing him money and he had to have protection from the government. He sent his son Alexander and his son-in-law John Bryden to explain matters in person, but he insisted that he must have the *Rocket* back immediately.[6]

[6] Bryden was at this time still employed as Mine Manager at the VCML mines, chief rival of Dunsmuir, Diggle and Co.

With the Dunsmuir family making demands on the government of the day, the miners found themselves a champion in the leader of the opposition. George Walkem had been Premier until his defeat one month before, and he would be Premier again. An Irishman who was educated in law at McGill University, he was a determined opponent of Premier Elliott, whom he informed in a letter dated March 6th that he had been retained to defend the miners. He asked to be notified regarding arbitration and to save time and "ruinous delay for both employers and employees" wished to be communicated with directly rather than through the miners.

Walkem's appointment was opportune and it is not unreasonable to question his motives in agreeing to represent the miners. It was certainly likely to keep his name in print for some months. A politically ambitious man, he had many critics who described him as a fence-sitter or a weathercock, likely to adopt any position that would ensure him a return to political power.

The strike was now being fought in several arenas. While the politicians exchanged insults through their respective Victoria journalistic mouthpieces (The *Colonist* for Elliott and the *Standard* for Walkem), the Nanaimo courts listened to the Norris libel case, and the *Free Press* published Dunsmuir's "cards" and citizens' letters on both sides of the fight. The eviction notice on the Company houses expired on March 8, 1877.

No one acted at first. The miners continued to live in the little cottages, the daily family routine played out against the backdrop of the idle pithead. Dunsmuir spent his days in the courthouse in Nanaimo defending the accuracy of his scales and pondering the ingratitude of Vipont.[7] When the libel case against George Norris was sent to the Supreme Court, Dunsmuir decided to withdraw his charges. His point had been made.

The only hope for a quick settlement was the Begbie commission of arbitration, and it was eagerly awaited. But then a member of the union committee met Mr. Dunsmuir in Mead's Barber Shop and discovered that the boss would not submit wages to arbitration. The conversation was reported to the miners' legal adviser. Walkem was

[7] Dunsmuir had loaned Vipont the money to bring his wife and children to Wellington and had assisted him when he broke his leg. Vipont applied for and received a contract for running coal from Dunsmuir and when unable to pay his men, Dunsmuir had paid them and given Vipont wages. Vipont had, however, repaid all the money Dunsmuir had loaned to him.

now in Wellington, and he recommended that the miners withdraw their acceptance of the commission.

With that avenue no longer a hope for immediate reconciliation, Alexander Dunsmuir was instructed by his father to bring the new San Francisco men up on Monday, March 12th. Robert had written to Elliott again asking that the Superintendent of Police accompany the strikebreakers. His letter made it quite clear, however, that though he was requesting government help, he would not accept government interference.

I expected that there would have been some one up before now to enquire into the disturbances. You must bear in mind that I would not allow anyone to arbitrate on our business as I can manage that myself, and in fact there is nothing to arbitrate on excepting the breaking of the law by the miners.

The steamer *Maude* arrived on Monday with the second shipment of blackleg labour. When the coal train arrived in Wellington bearing the new men, it was greeted by women with babies in their arms, women who asked if the men had come to take the bread and butter out of their mouths. The miners' wives knew what weapons worked best when dealing with men of good will. All the newcomers decided not to work and could soon be seen mingling at Chantrell's with the strikers "as though they had been friends for years."

Magistrate Spalding was in an unenviable position next morning when the outsiders appeared in his courtroom asking to be compensated for the damage and inconvenience they had sustained in coming to Wellington "as they averred they would not have come at all had a true representation of the facts of the case been put before them in San Francisco." When Spalding declined to take action, he left them with no option but to travel to Victoria, where the city gave them a few days' work to buy food.

With no hope of reactivating the mine, Dunsmuir played his last card. He applied to Spalding's court for possession orders on twelve of the Company houses. Deputy Sheriff Brown was dispatched to Wellington on March 28th to take formal possession. Acting on Walkem's advice, the miners refused to move. Again Dunsmuir wrote to Attorney-General Elliott.

The miners have defied the under Sheriff, and rumour has it that our friend Walkem has advised them that there is no law in the country to compel them to leave the houses. We are at last in a fix — cannot get possession of our property and the law is set at naught. Harris must send force, none can be got here.

Sheriff Harris, High-Bailiff of the County Court and Sheriff of Vancouver, was just the man to use force, but both he and Robert Dunsmuir had underestimated the resolve of the families in the Company houses.

It was the end of March. The strike was almost two months old. Dunsmuir had been frustrated in each of his moves by a well-disciplined group of men who generally had the sympathy of the community for their restrained but steadfast approach. But they did not represent all the miners in the district. An articulate letter writer spoke for the non-union miners when he pointed out that many followed the strike leaders because they were afraid of being called a "blackleg." Implying that the strike leaders were ex-gold miners who had come to the area to cause trouble, the writer said:

Gentlemen, you have done enough; we are quite satisfied with your efforts; but go back to your gold mines, and for God's sake stay there; and then we may have the peace and general satisfaction again, which we always enjoyed before you came amongst us.

A reply to this letter pointed out that the miners believed that the price of coal had recovered and the Company should therefore be able to restore their old wage rate. If this was not true then "let the proprietors be less arbitrary and the men less obstinate and the strike will not last a day longer." Dunsmuir responded by publishing the hours worked and wages earned by fifty of the men on strike.

On April 3, 1877, the *Rocket* tied up at Gordon's wharf in Nanaimo. Sheriff Harris and four deputies left the ship and made their way to Wellington to be greeted by a crowd of miners. They watched as Harris attempted to take possession of two homes and was thwarted because his deputies refused to work. In frustration Harris sent word back to the *Rocket* asking for volunteers from among the marines on board. With the assistance of twelve "blue jackets" he ejected the George Furness family and William Griffiths. The posse then retreated to the ship, which immediately pulled away from the dock, the hoots and groans of the crowd on shore ringing in their ears.

Having stayed behind to plan his next move, Sheriff Harris, followed by the derisive crowd, proceeded to the office of lawyer Theodore Davie. Robert Dunsmuir waited with Davie to confer with the law officer, the crowd subjecting them all the while to a traditional mining camp harassment by beating on coal oil tins and singing the "Death of Nelson." Three cheers and three groans were called for "the brave men who turned the women and cripples out of the houses."[8]

In a second attempt to enforce the eviction orders, the Sheriff succeeded only in exchanging "hard language" with the miners. He left Nanaimo promising to return "with a force sufficiently strong to force the orders of ejectment."

By refusing to leave their houses and by exchanging hard language with the Sheriff, the miners had defied the law. Letters to the editor in the *Free Press* reflected a growing impatience with the strike and a lessening of sympathy for the miners. Some people had no sympathy at all.

... if Dunsmuir will only send to the States he will get for the asking thousands of men out of employment... Here, I am sorry to say, the mania in favor of high wages is not yet cured. My advice... is to reduce their average wages to $1.50 per day; and if the men decline this to combine and bring out a few hundred good miners from Pennsylvania, Canada or even England.

When Sheriff Harris returned to Wellington on April 13th with fourteen young cadets sworn as special constables, a crowd of men and women, about two hundred strong, followed their wagon down the main road of the town, past Ardoon, across a bridge which spanned a small ravine, and up to the cottages around the pithead. Emotions ran very high that morning in Wellington. The Sheriff and his young cohorts, outnumbered twelve to one, were wary and prepared for a lopsided fight. The miners were incensed by the "young bloods from Victoria," mere boys who had been sent to do what the deputies, grown men, had been unwilling to do.

A feeling of inevitability pervaded the scene. The crowd knew that the warrants would be served and belongings removed from the houses. Behind a barricaded door Alex Hoggan, his wife, and a sick child waited for the confrontation they knew would come. The Sheriff ordered the door broken down. But when one of his assistants handed him an axe, the owner demanded its return. The Sheriff evoked the Queen's name, to which the miner replied, "I don't care a damn; the Queen never paid a cent for that axe."

---

[8] Theodore Davie was one of five present or future Premiers of British Columbia who were involved directly or peripherally in the strike. The others were Andrew Elliott, George Walkem, James Dunsmuir, and Edward Gawlor Prior, the first mine inspector, whose term began that spring.

The Queen won that round and the axe was applied to the door, which broke open, revealing a tiny room about fifteen feet square and Alex Hoggan, angry and ready to defend his rights no matter what happened. Harris demanded that he be given possession of the house, waving a warrant in front of Alex with the name "David Hoggan" written on it. Alex said that the name on the warrant was not his, but Harris ignored this technicality and repeated his demand two more times. As Hoggan lunged at the Sheriff, grabbing him around the waist and attempting to push him out of the house, Mrs. Hoggan came out of a side room and pushed the Sheriff against the wall. Shaking himself in indignation Harris told her, "This is the dearest day's work you ever did in your life."

Someone spoke to Hoggan and he calmed down, allowing the Sheriff to exit with some dignity. Leaving two helpers behind to complete the eviction, Harris came outside to find that the crowd had driven the rest of the young constables away by pummelling them with fists and pelting them with sticks and stones. Abusive language filled the air as Harris drove back over the bridge and down the road to the relative safety of Ardoon.

It was one o'clock in the afternoon. When the people saw where Harris was heading, they followed, herding the constables with them. Accounts vary as to how badly the cadets were treated. One claimed to have been thrown off the bridge and to have been threatened with death. Another said that one of the ringleaders, James Phillips, offered to fight him or any one of the cadets for one hundred dollars. The *Colonist* reported later that although some received "some hard knocks from sticks, stones and fists, they all returned free from any serious injury." One constable said Phillips had even protected him by keeping between him and the crowd.

The women made a special impression on a reporter from the *Standard*:

No sooner had he [a deputy] made an entry, than he was pitchforked out of the house and kicked and cuffed through a line of indignant Amazons, when he quickly beat a retreat...None of the parties were hurt, although they received considerable cuffing from the women who vigorously assaulted them.

In the late afternoon the bruised and beaten posse left Wellington, trailing a group of taunting strikers for the first mile or so. Having reached the relative safety of Nanaimo, the cadets cajoled the Sheriff into buying a keg of beer, and in comparative peace they assessed

165

their day's work. Seals had been placed on three houses; six people and their belongings had been evicted; in total only six houses had been emptied. The Sheriff's work was only half done.

Newspapers continued to provide a secondary battleground between Robert Dunsmuir and his former employees. The mine owner said he had refrained from publishing the wage lists earlier because the high wages would only have caused dissatisfaction among other miners. He only did it now because begging committees had been sent through the Island. The salaries were indeed fairly high, but Dunsmuir failed to mention that most of the men shared those wages with the Chinese helpers who worked for them.

Even good wages do not last forever. Robert Dunsmuir had forgotten very quickly what it was like to live on a miner's income. In one of his letters published in the paper he said:

Not a nail of the houses which they are asked to leave belongs to them, and every man can find land enough on the Island to build a house, and I think they have had ample time to do so since they quit work had they been so minded.

On April 20th, twenty more possession orders were issued, and Dunsmuir continued his haranguing of the Attorney-General.

If the law cannot be carried out, I shall shut down the works for twelve months; and if there is not something done next week, I shall do so. We have been put to too much expense for the want of a proper force....

Premier Elliott was not about to allow one of the largest enterprises in the province to close down. He had in fact taken steps ten days before to provide Dunsmuir with his "proper force." An April 12th "Notice to Militia" had alerted the clerks and merchants who made up the civil defence arm of the government that their services might be required.

A militia call out needed the signatures of three Justices of the Peace. They did not have to reside in the area, and it was not even necessary for a disturbance to have occurred. Dunsmuir would not have had to look far to find sympathetic officials. Of the seven Justices of the Peace in the Nanaimo area, only Joseph Planta was not directly involved in mining. Mark Bate and Thomas Bulkley were mine managers; Frederick Egerton and Wadham Diggle were directors of Dunsmuir, Diggle and Company; John Bryden was a mine manager, Captain of the Nanaimo Militia, and Dunsmuir's son-in-law; and the seventh was Dunsmuir himself. But he chose instead to go to three justices in Victoria.

166

Dunsmuir may have wished the order to have the appearance of neutrality or to look as if it came directly from the government. Whatever the reason, A. J. Langley, a chemist, David Leneveu, a merchant and director of the Baynes Sound Coal Company, and W. C. Ward, manager of the Bank of British Columbia, along with Nanaimo's Stipendiary Magistrate Warner Spalding, signed the requisition ordering in the militia. Although the militia order came at the request of a private individual, the government was certainly ready to be as helpful as possible. It approved the use of one of Her Majesty's ships to assist the Sheriff "in case of repeated outrage" and had already sent out a province-wide alert to the militia.

One militia unit was left out of the call up. Following the disintegration of the Volunteer Rifle Corps in 1868, the new Nanaimo Rifle Corps was organized in 1874, with thirty-six volunteers under Captain John Bryden and Lieutenant Edward Prior. From the beginning they were an unlikely group. Lieutenant-Colonel Houghton, Deputy Adjutant-General of the Militia for British Columbia, said of them, "There is not a single officer or man in the corps who knows anything whatever with regard to drill, much less is capable of giving instruction therein." The intervening years had brought no improvement, the absence of a drill instructor and the lack of enthusiasm of the corps captain making for a lackluster showing. On the annual inspection in November of 1876 Houghton arrived in Nanaimo to find that the inspection had entirely escaped Bryden's mind. The Colonel left without ever having seen the corps. In February of the next year, just as the strike began, Bryden pleaded a heavy workload and resigned. [9]

The absence of the Nanaimo Rifle Corps was hardly noticed. Houghton was pleased when the muster produced the names of fifty-six men. Having assessed the opposition, he estimated that one hundred strikers and "a very large majority of the men of the other coal mines in the vicinity [who] were known to sympathize with them," would face his "Sunday soldiers."

The Victoria papers watched and took sides. The *Colonist* fully supported the militia call out, seeing dire consequences to the miners' refusal to vacate their homes.

---

[9] In 1882 the Nanaimo militia company was split in two, with half going to Wellington. The Nanaimo contingent was mustered out two years later for lack of efficiency. The Wellington Company could not drill on weekdays because of work and were castigated by *Princess Royal* veteran Daniel Dunn for practicing on Sunday.

The outlook for Nanaimo and the Province is bad — very bad. Heretofore it had been supposed that law reigned supreme in British Columbia. Now it has gone forth that a mob of men who decline to work for high wages virtually hold possession of a piece of property that had been a source of wealth to the Province in general and of Nanaimo in particular and prevent its development. What security is there in these proceedings for capital seeking investment to come to British Columbia?

Not surprisingly, the *Standard* saw no such sinister consequences. "The miners have no intention of using violence in resisting the execution of the law." The paper pointed out that the first group of Sheriff's assistants refused to perform their disagreeable task and the second had been composed of boys who merely irritated the miners.

On Friday, April 27th, Premier Elliott asked Magistrate Spalding to meet the Sheriff at Departure Bay on the following Monday morning. A committee of the Executive Council having approved the disbursal of sixteen hundred dollars to cover expenses, the Sheriff would be attended by a contingent of active militia, Sunday soldiers eager for duty.

All that day the tension built, as the miners waited for Dunsmuir's next move. The seals had been broken on the empty houses and their former tenants were back in full possession. A rumour about militia units being sent was dismissed as preposterous. Of much more immediate concern was the fifty to seventy-five blacklegs reported to be on their way from San Francisco to work the mines.

Early Sunday morning, April 29th, the drill shed of the Victoria Militia was drenched with rain and lashed by a cold wind as two companies of Sunday soldiers mustered for the big adventure. Each man was given a haversack filled with provisions, a blanket and a mattress, and twenty rounds of ammunition. Houghton stood before them to counsel moderation. They were not to fire unless required to by the magistrate. If required to fire they must perform their duty "with coolness and steadiness, and in such a manner as to be able to discontinue your fire at the instant in which it shall be found that there is no longer occasion for it."

At Spratt's wharf the side-wheel paddle steamer *Maude* waited to take them to New Westminster to join the rest of the force. Departing at 11:00 a.m., they wound their way through the Gulf Islands and across the Straits of Georgia to the mouth of the Fraser River. Although they were behind schedule, they stopped at Ladner's landing to offer assistance to the owner, whose house was on fire. Ladner declined their offer, perhaps feeling that such a grand looking contingent must be bound for far more important duties than the saving of his house.

Thirty-one men of the New Westminster Rifles and the Seymour Artillery had been waiting on the dock at New Westminster all afternoon. They were a fine looking lot. Several had medals, including a sergeant, who had been decorated for service at Sebastopol in the Crimea. When the *Maude* finally pulled into view it was 7:30 p.m. While the Victoria men disembarked with orders to return at the sound of bugles, the patient mainland soldiers were given their supplies and indoctrination.

Fifty-one men, five officers, a doctor, and a "war correspondent" were aboard the *Maude* when she pulled away from the dock at 10:00 p.m. The little steamer was overflowing with soldiers — soldiers on top and underneath the saloon tables, soldiers on every available square foot of floor and deck. To add to the discomfort, many were seasick as the steamer rolled and pitched in a head wind, plowing her way across the Straits hour after hour through the darkness.

After a sleepless night, it was with much relief that the soldiers observed Entrance Island passing on the port side at 9:30 the following morning. The new lighthouse on the bare rock marked the beginning of more protected waters and the end of their voyage. At eleven o'clock, three hours behind schedule, they quietly chugged into Departure Bay where the *Rocket* lay at anchor with Sheriff Harris on board.

Waiting on the big Wellington wharves as the *Maude* tied up was Robert Dunsmuir himself, with Magistrate Spalding standing beside him. With the Seymour Artillery in the lead, the militia marched past, splendid in crisp uniforms, their boots polished and their weapons gleaming. A thousand yards away at the foot of the incline the dirty coal wagons awaited them. Parade perfect soldiers reluctantly climbed aboard the blackened cars for their journey up the hill. At the top, a saddle tank locomotive was ready with steam up and more dirty coal cars to take them to Wellington. The exciting outing, already marred by the rough sea crossing and a lack of sleep, seemed even less glamourous as the militia wearily clambered into the waiting cars.

Some had never been on such a thing before and some were in distress about the amount of pipeclay which would be required to clean up their belts and accoutrements. After the ride one young gentleman fell into tribulation respecting the accumulation of coal dust on his handsome face and on attempting to wipe it off was no doubt much comforted by the remark of a comrade that it was a first rate war-paint and that he looked ugly enough to frighten a Modoc.

War-paint was out of place in Wellington. As the train slowly made its way along the narrow arm of Long Lake and through the town to the mine, everything seemed abnormally quiet. One hour before, there had been a funeral for a small boy who had drowned in a well, and the atmosphere was subdued.

The rumour about the militia coming had been true! Word spread quickly as the soldiers climbed out of the coal wagons and formed up into companies. A crowd assembled to greet the newcomers with playful banter. "My God, what's them?" "Ain't there a lot of 'em too." "A dose or two of buckshot would clear 'em all out." "They've come to eat turkey till they bust."

The good-natured joking put the soldiers at ease and the occasional one was heard to laugh as they marched toward the Company houses, but the mood changed as the Sheriff proceeded with the evictions while the militia stood guard. The presence of soldiers in the little mining camp was more than any striker had bargained for.

Clumps of townspeople stood watching. Some women "raved and abused the Dunsmuirs," but no one talked of violence. Old Mrs. Haggerty pleaded to be allowed to stay in her house until her son returned home and told her where she could go to live. Her house was left untouched. At one point during the afternoon the evictions stopped for half an hour while two miners made an offer to leave their houses quietly the next day if they could stay that night. Those requests were denied.

Billy Baker did not go quietly. When his house was broken into, he yelled abuse and was dragged away by his friends. The enraged man broke away and returned to his house where he was next seen struggling with a bailiff over an axe. As Baker was handcuffed and dragged away again hollering abuse and accusing the bailiff of striking him, some women prayed that he would be quiet. He was led away to a shady spot and when he had cooled down he begged for the handcuffs to be removed. "He said the bailiff was about to break up the bedstead on which his wife had died and it was that that maddened him."

By 4:00 p.m. five families had been ejected and three miners arrested and charged with obstruction of the Sheriff during his last visit. The goods taken from the houses were carried to the railroad, loaded in cars, and taken off Company property. It took a long time to get rid of all the belongings. Crying women, their tears as much a sign of outrage as misery, watched their household goods disappear.

When someone said the Nanaimo men were on their way to help the strikers, Magistrate Spalding panicked and ordered Number Two Company to guard the mine all night. The soldiers accordingly were ordered to stack their rifles and go down to the boat to fetch their blankets. When they returned, the remaining troops climbed aboard the train to return to the Bay. Before the train could build up much speed the engine was thrown off the track. No one was blamed. No one was hurt. It was a strangely appropriate end to the first day of "battle."

The 5:30 bugle next morning did not come too early for the guards at the mine. All night the more nervous of their numbers had stayed awake, sure that wild animals were about to devour them. The identity of the "wild animals" was never determined. One sentry almost frightened a stranger to death when the interloper refused to answer his challenge quickly enough and had a bayonet pointed at his chest. As if the wild animals and strangers were not bad enough, when the other soldiers who had slept on the *Maude* arrived at the mine at 7:30, they were furious because they had not been left their fair share of blankets. When hurt feelings and wild imaginations were calmed, the soldiers returned to the business at hand. That day Sheriff Harris wanted them closer to him, although the military only watched as the business of eviction proceeded.

The first target was the house of Sam Harris. In his younger days Sam had dreamed the same dreams as Robert Dunsmuir and had found coal in the Cowichan area. The dream of riches had come to nothing, however, and now in middle age Sam Harris dug coal to make someone else rich. Pleurisy, asthma, rheumatism, and Bright's disease made every day a misery, but as long as he could dig coal he had to keep going. A man had to eat. That did not make Sam like it any better, and since the strike started he had been feeling more than a little put upon. A petty squabble with Dunsmuir had marked Sam as a troublemaker, but when the Sheriff arrived at his house, it was the neighbour women who caused the commotion, one regretting she had no rotten eggs to throw. "If times were not so hard," she said, "she would have thrown good ones."

Joseph Hoskin's house was barricaded with beams and sticks in such a scientific way that it could not be breached, so the Sheriff got in by completely shattering the back door. The Hoskin women refused to carry away any of their evicted belongings and muttered about slapping faces.

Despite the disgruntled women and the odd squabble, the day's work was accomplished in relative calm, the well-behaved militia setting the tone with their quiet forbearance. Reassured by the militia's presence, the Sheriff became almost benevolent. Beauchamp was allowed to stay in his house because his wife was sick. So was Henry Ross. Two other miners were given time to move their belongings out. While the Sheriff was resting from his labours, a four year old boy came up to him with a slice of bread and butter in one hand and a model of a club the size of a large match in the other. The Sheriff and the crowd laughed when the youngster said, "You old devil, I should like to thrash you."

Twenty families were evicted from their homes, three or four for the second time, but none resorted to violence. Police Superintendent Todd called the miners intelligent and law-abiding. The *Colonist* intoned:

The majesty of the law has been asserted at Wellington. The orders of the court have been enforced. The ringleaders in resistance are in custody; and the extent of their punishment may depend upon the future of their friends and fellow-strikers at Wellington.

Prisoners Alex Hoggan, James Thompson, and James Phillips were taken aboard the *Maude*. A permanent guard was assigned, with an additional sentry on the gangway and another double sentry at the end of the wharf, "both to guard against the escape of the prisoners and to prevent any of the Militia straying towards the town of Nanaimo... unless provided with a pass." The soldiers were finding Departure Bay as dull as the sailors did.

Wednesday dawned very hot. Having spent the day seeking shade under the larger sheds back of the coal wharves, the militia cannot have been unhappy when they left the Bay that evening bound for the mainland again. In the dark of a moonless night the boat struck a rock, a not unusual occurrence in the waters around Vancouver Island before proper navigation aids were installed. With only two small, ten-man lifeboats available, Houghton decided it was safer to remain on board. The expedition ended ignominiously the next morning when an Indian in a canoe picked up the soldiers and their prisoners and deposited them on a small nearby island to await rescue by a steamer.

The militia did not deserve this inglorious end to its first call out.

The Sunday soldiers had gone on the assignment in good faith and had acquitted themselves honourably and in good humour. Even so, the citizens of Wellington and Nanaimo must have laughed when they heard of the militia perched on an island awaiting rescue, for there was a general feeling among the people of the towns, no matter which side of the strike they were on, that the government had no business sending soldiers to settle a local issue. The local grand jury said as much on May 9th.

The archaic and now defunct legal institution of the grand jury functioned much as a preliminary hearing would in modern times. The accused were brought up before a group of fellow citizens whose duty it was to decide whether a valid charge or "true bill" existed. If it did, the accused were put on trial. The Nanaimo Grand Jury also took the extraordinary step of officially protesting the action of the government in sending in the militia. Foreman James Brown sent the following letter to Chief Justice Begbie.

That, no act of violence having been committed, and the law having been exceeded but in the retained occupation of the tenements, the stigmas cast upon this community by the calling in of the military, was caused only by the incapacity of the Sheriff in the execution of his duty, and that misrepresentations must have been made to have induced the government to proceed to such extreme measures.

Begbie immediately replied to Mr. Brown, noting the exceptional character of this communication and questioning why the strikers had resisted at all. Labelling them as misguided, he urged that their leaders induce them to return to work and "try to make amends for the loss and expense which the town and the whole Province have sustained." The Chief Justice, who was to have been the impartial arbiter of the aborted commission to settle the strike, concluded his remarks to Mr. Brown by expressing pity for the strikers and by making the startling accusation that they had gone against the advice of their legal advisers when they refused to vacate the Company houses. If the source of this last piece of information was the strikers' lawyer himself, then George Walkem was playing on both sides, for it had been he who advised the strikers to stay in the houses.

Nor did the unhappiness of the citizens of Nanaimo stop the provincial government from continuing to interfere. When Dunsmuir's next shipment of strikebreakers arrived in Victoria from San Francisco, the Attorney-General asked the Mayor of Victoria to allow two city policemen to assist the Superintendent of Provincial

Police when he accompanied the new work force to Wellington. The provincial government would reimburse the city. Thirty-nine new men arrived in Wellington on the *Maude* on May 24th and went to work unopposed. The mine was operating again after almost four months of inactivity.

In the meantime, charges against the arrested miners were changed to the more serious ones of conspiracy and assaulting officers in the execution of their duty. At the preliminary hearings in Victoria in early May a trial date was determined. Bail was set at $500 plus two securities of $250 each, well beyond the ability of any of them to pay.

When the Victoria Assizes convened in mid-May, the strikers were charged with "unlawfully and without legal authority compelling divers persons engaged by Dunsmuir and Diggle as miners to abstain from lawfully performing their work according to their said agreements." Hoggan, Phillips, and Thompson were to serve as scapegoats and be punished for the new union having disturbed the status quo. One of the judges intoned that "to sympathize with these laborers would be to introduce a system of communism into the community."[10]

Only Alex Hoggan was found guilty, and even then, the jury made a recommendation for mercy. Accordingly, the judge sentenced him to four months without hard labour. Hoggan had been upset when his house was broken into and had resisted on the technicality that the eviction warrant was in his brother David's name, not his own. There is little doubt that he was a union man and a striker but so were many others. It is not hard to conclude that Hoggan was the token prisoner, sentenced to provide atonement for all the others.[11]

[10] The reference to communism is interesting. Karl Marx had written *The Communist Manifesto* in 1848, but it was only read by a very small number of people in the next thirty years. *Das Kapital* was published in 1867, but the ideas expressed in it spread slowly and competed with anarchism for the hearts of young revolutionaries. The judge may have been referring to the communism of the Paris Commune, then very much in people's minds, but though Marx made a legend of the Commune in one of his pamphlets, it had very little in common with the ideas Marx discussed in his other writings.

Middle class opinion in Europe did tend to associate the excesses of the Commune with the International Workingmen's Association (First International) founded in 1864 and lasting until 1876. This may explain the strength of the opposition in many countries to socialism and other forms of working class organization. In any case, the miners of far off Wellington in 1877 were not likely to even be aware of communism in any form.

[11] There were three Hoggan brothers, Alexander, David, and William. Both William and David were shareholders in the Union Coal Company, which by 1881 had been sold to Robert Dunsmuir. David Hoggan continued to be a thorn in Dunsmuir's side when he opposed the inclusion of Newcastle Townsite in the railroad lands Dunsmuir was given as part of his deal with the government to build the Esquimalt and Nanaimo Railway.

Activities at the Wellington Mine were taking on a normal appearance. The arrival on June 3rd of thirty-one additional men made it possible to run three shifts again. But these men were not miners. They were described as "the most ragged, forbidding-looking lot of men that ever set foot in the Province, and not one has ever been in a coal mine in his life." Even so, Robert Dunsmuir was reported to have said "No" to forty other applicants who applied for work because he had all the hands he required. Six days later, John Stara from Calliano Italy, aged thirty-five, was killed in the mine. He was one of the most recent arrivals.

Wellington Mine, like all the mines on the Island, was becoming a large producer of coal and employer of men. As the miners invaded the coal body farther and farther and at a faster rate, and as production figures increased and markets developed, the mines were becoming more and more dangerous. Firedamp, until about 1875 only rarely encountered, was now an almost daily occurrence in some mines. The new inspector, Edward Prior, begged mine owners to take a lesson from experiences in other countries, where some of the worst explosions had occurred in mines considered safe.

Prior was fighting an uphill battle. He had to hound managers of all the mines to obey the Coal Mines Regulations Act. Repeated reminders to avoid the use of iron tampers, which could cause sparks, went unheeded in mine after mine. Even when managers paid attention to Prior's admonitions, he invariably found on his next inspection that things had gone back to the way they had been before.

The Act provided for each mine to post "Special Rules" which applied to conditions unique to that mine. These rules seemed to be a particular anathema to John Bryden of the VCML and to the Dunsmuirs, who resisted posting them for several months.

The Act was resisted or at best disregarded by the miners as well. In 1878, Prior reported that although plenty of timber was available, many miners would risk a fall of rock or coal rather than take the time to prop the roof. The number of serious injuries and deaths from cave-ins was beginning to grow, although the number of accidents in relation to the amount of production stayed about the same. In addition, no miners in any of the mines had availed themselves of the provision in the Act allowing for gas committees to check the working places for firedamp. In this case, however, it is likely that the lack of pay for work on the committee was what made it unattractive.

The beleaguered Prior, only twenty-five when he took on the Inspector's job, met his nemesis in the opposition of the Dunsmuirs.

When he brought James to court for failure to report an accident, he was accused of malicious motives and personal malice. Dunsmuir also stated that "he did not care for or think anything of the Mining Act as it was altogether unconstitutional and he would prove it shortly in a higher court." Dunsmuir swore that the accident had not occurred in his mine. After the case was dismissed because of the absence of the witness who had seen the accident happen, Dunsmuir was heard to admit that the accident had in fact occurred in his mine.

Several months later Prior resigned and moved to Victoria to set himself up in the hardware business. His future lay in politics and reached its zenith when he succeeded James Dunsmuir as Premier of British Columbia in 1902. Like Dunsmuir, he later became Lieutenant-Governor of the province as well. But in April of 1879 he still had an onerous duty to perform in the mines.

With the Coal Mines Regulations Act less than two years old and still being fought or ignored by most mine owners, with miners more interested in production than safety, with the mines developing faster than experienced miners could be found and many of the inexperienced men being unable to speak or read English, and with markets opening up and ships standing in Nanaimo harbour and Departure Bay waiting for coal that had not yet been dug, it was only a matter of time before a disaster of major proportions occurred.

Shortly after work resumed in the Wellington Mine, the Number Ten Level was begun. Eighteen months later there was still only one heading because the level had been gassy right from the beginning. A small explosion had occurred when it was being driven, but the furnace ventilation of that mine was impressive, so no one was worried about the gas. By April, nine stalls had been driven upbrow in the heading. When the coal in Horne's stall took fire on the night of Tuesday, April 15, 1879, all the miners left their own work and fought through the night and the following day to contain it.

Robert Dunsmuir took charge of the fire at 3:00 a.m. Wednesday morning and stayed there until late afternoon with only a twenty minute break for breakfast. He ordered a curtain installed so part of the air could drive away the smoke and part of it could sweep away the gas in the heading. On the curtain written in large letters in chalk were the words "No one allowed to pass here — FIRE!" The last word was very large and underlined.

The day shift foreman was John Dixon, "as good a pitman as ever stepped." He had been qualified as a fireman or lower level boss for about a year and "knew every twist and turn" of the ventilation system. On his way into the mine he was stopped by John Dick, a recently certificated manager who was employed elsewhere in the area but who had responded, as all qualified managers did, to the need for as much expert advice as possible in time of a mine crisis. Dick asked Dixon to go into the heading "for his sake," and Dixon reluctantly agreed.

Wellington Mine in 1879 was full of Chinese. They worked for individual miners as loaders and were also employed directly by the Company as runners and furnace men. In fact, white miners had been placed in the position of having to employ Chinese helpers because the Chinese runners employed by the Company would not bring as many boxes to white miners employing white helpers. Robert Dunsmuir said it was natural for Chinese to assist their own people. He also said that Chinese were as safe as anyone else in the mine even if they could not speak or read English, but he was very strict with the men of this race. If he caught one leaving a door open, the offender was called to the office, fined ten dollars, and fired. On this particular day, he took no chances and ordered all Chinese out of the fire area.

At noon, John Dixon passed Robert Dunsmuir in the level and grumbled about John Dick being afraid of gas. He resented being ordered about by a man who was a stranger to the mine. Dunsmuir cautioned Dixon not to let anyone go behind the curtain.

He gave the same message to the afternoon shift when it arrived for work at 3:00 p.m. Each man was told individually not to go through the curtain. Johan Henry Westfeldt translated the instructions for a recent German immigrant. Obeying instructions to the letter, the night shift fireman, George Churchill, did not check behind the curtain for gas. All through the evening and into the night the coal was kept wet and the fire seemed to be under control. Indeed, the men continued to use the naked flame lamps that were standard for this mine.

At the 6:00 a.m. shift change on Thursday, April 17th, George Churchill watched as John Dixon went down the slope carrying a Clanny safety lamp. The dim light was supplemented by the naked flame oil lamp attached to his cap and burning brightly. Churchill also overheard the supervisor of Chinese workers send two Chinese down because a miner was growling about having no boxes and no one to run them. Thirty minutes later the mine whistle began to blow fearfully. There had been an explosion. As soon as the inspector was informed, he hurried to the mine, familiarized himself with the plan, and descended the slope.

It would be more than thirty years before there was breathing apparatus available for rescuers and supervisors whose duty it was to go into mines right after a disaster had occurred. Edward Prior and the Dunsmuirs went down unprotected. From the Number Seven Level down, there was evidence of a "fearful blast." As Prior descended to the Number Nine level he found

an overcast blown to pieces and the roof had caved in badly. At the mouth of Number Ten level . . . I found a lot of coal waggons piled up in a heap, all the stoppings blown out, roof blown down, and rails torn up and twisted; in fact a perfect chaos and shewing every sign of there having been a large body of gas ignited.

In a mine disaster all mining men, whether owners, inspectors, or diggers, have common cause and for a time are united by a single purpose. The managers of the South Wellington, Nanaimo, and Chase River mines worked alongside the inspector and the Dunsmuirs and miners from all over the district to restore the flow of air, rid the mine of chokedamp, and find the bodies. Above ground, the women waited to receive the injured and the dead and to identify their loved ones. Elizabeth Thompson was cited especially for her care of the injured and attention to the dead. Since her arrival on the *Princess Royal* she had developed a reputation as an able nurse who did not shrink from the horrors of a mine disaster.

For several days the atmosphere was charged with steam and afterdamp — steam from the water being played on the coal and afterdamp from the explosion. No flame could be seen but the water that came off the coal was nearly boiling. Despite opposition from Robert Dunsmuir and John Bryden, the inspector insisted the mine be flooded to ensure the fire was extinguished. A creek was diverted into the slope, and the mine slowly filled with water. When it was finally pumped out in January of 1880 the badly burned body of a Chinese was found within fifty feet of the level face.

It was the first major British Columbia mining disaster. Eleven men died as the gas that had accumulated behind the curtain in Horne's stall was ignited, probably by a naked flame lamp. Probably the lamp was on the cap of a Chinese. Whether it was or not, the explosion was blamed on the Chinese and became part of the growing belief that they should be excluded from the mines altogether.

Four Chinese died in the Wellington Mine that day in April. They were not named, nor was anything known about them. There was also one Italian, one Irishman, one American, and three Englishmen.

One victim was born in Nanaimo. His name was Reuben and he was the son of Elizabeth and Edwin Gough. His father had died four years before, having returned to mining only to lose a leg in a mine accident in 1871. Reuben was fourteen when he died in the Wellington Mine.

John Dixon left a wife and six children in Wellington town. His body had been found behind the canvas curtain with the bodies of two Chinese. There was only one reason for an experienced man like Dixon to have gone inside the curtain — to order the two Orientals out of the forbidden area. The other eight victims were either killed directly by the force of the explosion or asphyxiated by the afterdamp.

Inspector Prior had much to say about the use of naked lamps in fiery, that is gassy, mines. Gas could usually be rendered harmless with good ventilation but

circumstances may at any time arise when a large body of gas may be suddenly encountered, at which time the ordinary amount of air circulating becomes totally inadequate... Then, disaster is sure to follow if naked lights are around.

After making several other recommendations, Prior closed his report with the opinion that he would never be able to influence either managers or miners to use safety lamps. Miners found the light too dim and owners found the lamps too expensive. Exactly thirty years later, after another explosion, another inspector would recommend the use of safety lamps in another Dunsmuir mine, but this time thirty-two men would be killed.

The fire and the strike and the explosion had made Wellington, in its brief life so far, a town full of anger and sorrow. A lot of coal had been dug and a lot of money made by the investors. Besides the original mine, which soon came to be called the Old Slope, there was a shaft close to the boundaries of the lease about fifteen hundred yards from Departure Bay. Although it was first sunk in 1874, problems with the rock and soil structure and the presence of a heavy water feeder had made it difficult to mine.

But the only difficulty in the Old Slope was a shortage of miners. Despite large purchases of machinery and the latest steam technology, there was still need for many men to blast and timber and load in the narrow confines at the face. There was never enough labour available, even with the increasing number of Chinese arriving from the defunct gold fields of the interior and the completed railway projects of the United States.

Given this ever increasing need for labour, Robert Dunsmuir was not able to make good his declaration that no one who joined a union would ever work for him again. Archibald Cowie was still working for Dunsmuir in 1883 even though he was listed in the *Free Press* as a striker in 1877; so was John Edwards, and he had even been charged with intimidation of the strikebreakers. George Furness, Thomas Goldsworthy, Walter Griffiths, Edward, Joseph, Richard, and William Hoskin, James Knight, James Phillips, Henry Smith, James Thompson, and James Williams all continued to work at Wellington despite their involvement in the strike. Even George Vipont and union president William Macdonald were able to work for the man who had said he would never employ them again.

Most notably, the Hoggan brothers — David, William, and Alex — remained Dunsmuir employees. Two months after being sentenced to jail, Alex had been transferred to Nanaimo from Victoria to be nearer his family. Less than a month later his sentence was remitted and he returned to work at the Wellington Mine.

Sheriff Harris did not fare so well. A petition was circulated saying "he is totally unfit first from want of education, second from want of gentlemanly deportment and third, as was shown in court, he stands at the head of his class in beastly vulgarity." Lieutenant-Colonel Houghton fared much better. In March of 1879, the forty-one year old Deputy Adjutant-General of the British Columbia Militia married Marian Dunsmuir, the twenty-four year old third daughter of Robert and Joan Dunsmuir, and sailed away for his honeymoon on board the *Maude*. The marriage was in keeping with the Dunsmuir facility for acquiring useful and influential sons-in-law.[12]

Though Dunsmuir continued to attract relatives and friends in high places, he still had the loyalty of an old friend from simpler times. Edward Walker had followed Dunsmuir to Wellington. There Robert used Edward's experience and skill to prepare the groundwork for his first pithead and to build one of the wharves at Departure Bay. As the number of mines grew, Walker, no longer a young man, could be seen working at the surface around Numbers Three and Four mines. His first love was still sailing, however, and he competed in local races in his newest vessel *Quickstep*.

Jimmy Hamilton had been an old and loyal friend to Dunsmuir as well. It had been he who suggested the fishing trip to Diver Lake

---

[12] Houghton was later transferred to Manitoba and was part of the force opposing Louis Riel in the Northwest Rebellion of 1885.

which resulted in Dunsmuir finding his coal seam. He was a harmless, kind-hearted man with no big ambitions and chose to remain in his cabin near the lake while his friend drove himself to prove and develop his find all through the winter, spring, and summer of 1870.

In that year, as Dunsmuir strove to make his dream come true, the entire Island coal mining industry stood at the brink of labour unrest. And Jimmy Hamilton's life, which had been lived so quietly, would end in a violent act that would presage the strife about to envelope both Wellington and Nanaimo.

Jimmy shared the solitude near Diver Lake with his neighbours, Mr. and Mrs. Smallbone — she a laundress and he a bootlegger of some renown. One day in September 1870, two Indians visited Smallbone's illicit groggery and, finding no one at home, broke in, stole several items, drank all the beer, and left three empty glasses and a naked footprint on the table. As they passed Jimmy Hamilton's cabin, he protested their noisiness. They hit him on the head, cut his throat, dragged him into the cabin, and set it on fire.

At the Nanaimo Assizes in November of 1870, Judge Begbie presiding, a true bill was found against the two Indians for murder and burglary. It was determined that the only way to get a confession was to offer one defendant immunity from the murder charge so he would testify against the other. Thus the Indian Quinam testified against his friend Jim, who, after a lengthy trial, was found guilty and sentenced to be hanged. Quinam pleaded guilty to house-breaking and was sentenced to three years with hard labour.

Feeling was so high in Nanaimo, it had been hard to get unbiased jurors. After the trial, a public meeting condemned the Crown for accepting Quinam as Queen's evidence, he being the guiltier of the two in the opinion of the citizens. So incensed was public opinion that it was necessary for the government to assign the gunship H.M.S. *Sparrowhawk* to remain in the harbour until the hanging took place.

As Robert Dunsmuir announced to the world the news of the Wellington coal discovery, his friend's murderers were brought to justice under the watchful eye of the Royal Navy. But there was another reason for the presence of the gunship. The miners of the VCML had been on strike for a month and the Board of Directors in London were determined that "any outrage to life or property will be punished with promptitude and severity." Big time coal mining and big time labour trouble had reached Nanaimo.

CHAPTER V

Celestial Colliers and Bunster Beer

Nanaimo is a straggling village without any regularity in the laying out. So you wander about, round green knolls, and up and down hill, after a fashion more picturesque than after the fashion of other towns. The Clergyman, the Doctor and the Magistrate are I believe the only people of the upper class — the rest are shopkeepers and miners.

Sophia Cracoft, niece of Lady Franklin

This strike lasted for seven months during which time practically everyone in town was out of employment, and the stores refused to give any credit, which was a great hardship to people with several children. Young men, like myself could go fishing, or clam digging, and thus eke out a living.

Reverend Charles Montgomery Tate

Eighteen year old Charles Tate, son of a Northumberland sea captain, was destined to be an adventurer. In 1870 he left his mother in Blyth to travel to Liverpool, where he boarded a boat for New York. From there, he travelled across the great North American continent on a series of American railroads to San Francisco. He was bound for the gold fields of British Columbia, and he hoped he was not too late to get his share of the wealth.

The ship landed at Victoria, where Tate learned the bad news. There were more men returning from the gold fields than going there. From the disillusioning stories they told, he realized he had better change his plans. The Victoria newspapers were full of ads appealing to the returning gold miners to consider coming to Nanaimo to dig coal. Now Tate was no miner, but he was from the north of England and that made him seem like one. Since Blyth was not far from Newcastle, maybe a little of the coal know-how of that area had rubbed off on him. The coal company in Nanaimo seemed to think he would do, and Charles Tate found himself in charge of a pithead engine at one of their mines.

Then the Board of Directors of the Vancouver Coal Mining and Land Company (VCML) in London issued a pronouncement which would make Tate's career at the mine a shortlived thing. Ever acutely aware of the shareholders' primary concern that dividends be paid and on time, the board had to draw on the Company's financial reserves when prices for coal in San Francisco dropped. Even so, they were only able to pay a dividend of fifteen percent, down from the previous year's twenty. In order to replenish the reserves the board in faraway London voted to reduce miners' wages.

An ocean and a continent away, Nanaimo miners were told that as of August 1, 1870, the price they received for digging one ton of coal would drop by two and one half cents. The August wage cut was accepted reluctantly, but when they were told that the price would be reduced a further ten cents as of October 1st, the miners would tolerate no more. The loss of "one bit" per ton was too much.[1] Strengthened by the determination of most of the other Company employees who were to have their wages reduced in proportion, the miners called a general strike on October 3rd. Even the Chinese and Indians, who by their very presence in the mine had agreed to accept lower wages, walked off the job.

Company executives telegraphed London requesting instructions. In the increasingly threatening atmosphere of Nanaimo, they felt outnumbered. As the board deliberated from the safety and comfort of their London headquarters, local managers and clerks huddled in the converted boarding house at Haliburton and Finlayson that served as the Nanaimo office, waiting for their instructions from so far away. The board in London stood its ground. With twenty-five thousand tons of coal stored in bunkers on the docks, they could afford to be firm.

The precarious situation of management personnel on the scene was worsened when, on October 5th, the wharfmen joined the strike. No coal could be loaded without them. The resolve of the strikers was so strong that when mine superintendent John Bryden ordered that one engine be kept going to keep the Douglas Pit free of water, he placed his engineer in jeopardy.

Andrew Hunter was in a position of responsibility. Having spent twenty years on the coast and having achieved a reputation as a conscientious, if somewhat cantankerous, citizen, he had a duty to ensure that the mine would be workable when the strike was over. For his trouble Hunter became the scapegoat when some of the more desperate miners resorted to violence and threw a bottle containing powder and a fuse through the window of his house. That the

[1] The Company received $6.50 per ton at the pithead for the same coal.

explosion failed to occur due to the neck of the bottle breaking off did not lessen the impact of the message it was meant to convey.

As anonymous threats of more violence created a climate of fear among non-striking Company employees, the government in Victoria responded by issuing a proclamation that

all persons found using threats, resorting to force, or otherwise illegally interferring [sic] with those who desire to continue the pursuit of their lawful occupations, will be persecuted [sic] with the utmost rigor of the law; and that any outrage to life and property will be punished with promptitude and severity.

The Governor's point was made vividly when the H.M.S. *Sparrowhawk* dropped anchor in the harbour. The ship would be there for two or three weeks, it was said, to preserve the peace threatened by the strike and by the trial of Jimmy Hamilton's murderers.

Despite gunships and proclamations, however, the "disposition to insubordination" continued on the part of some miners. Just before Christmas one miner stabbed and seriously injured another. The H.M.S. *Boxer*, fresh from having tested Dunsmuir's new coal find, replaced the *Sparrowhawk* in its harbour guard duties. A miners' deputation sent to see the managers was offered certain terms if the men would return to work. They rejected the Company's offer.

As January settled in cold and wet, miners' families began to experience real distress. A three man delegation sent to Victoria to solicit subscriptions for relief announced their presence in the capital city with an appeal published in the local newspapers. One of the three men was Edwin Gough, no longer the town constable and newly returned to the mines until the strike cut off his livelihood.[2]

There was little money to be solicited in Nanaimo itself. Every wage earner was either employed in the mines or ran a business dependent upon the miners' custom. The one exception was the Newcastle Island Quarry, which employed fifty men and was expecting thirty-seven Chinese from San Francisco to augment the work force. The quarrymen gave $91.50 toward the relief of the destitute families.

It was necessary to go further afield and so a begging party was organized under the leadership of one Billy Sampson. Included in his

[2] Edwin Gough had done well since his return to mining. Just before the strike he had completed the building of a large house and had leased his former home to the Good Templars.

184

crew was Charles Tate, who had been using his idle time to teach Indians whom he met on the beach to read and write.

During the winter we organized a begging party to wait on the few settlers on the various islands between Nanaimo and Victoria. We hired an old Indian named Kwal-alkup, with his large war canoe, and picked up potatoes, and other vegetables, besides an occasional sack of flour, some groceries, salt meat, and other edibles.

Tate had already established himself as a religious man. Having joined the Methodist church in Nanaimo for lack of a Presbyterian one, he discovered that he felt very much at home with his new religious colleagues. When the begging party found itself on Saltspring Island on a Sunday, Tate refused to continue the trip on the Sabbath. "This raised a storm among my compatriots who talked of using force." They finally agreed to stay for the day if Tate would conduct a service, and by the next Sunday were back in Nanaimo with "a canoe load of provisions which were divided according to the needs of the people, and all unmarried men were counted out."

Ominous rumours circulated that "celestial colliers," as *The Colonist* quaintly described them, were being engaged to work the mines, and there were one hundred more Chinese on the way. But the miners still held out.

Edwin Gough, who had returned to Nanaimo from Victoria, John Malpass, and a Mr. Wilkinson decided to leave Nanaimo for Bellingham in search of employment. Conditions at the American mines were so primitive that when Gough broke both the bones between the ankle and knee of one leg, there was no medical attention immediately available. By the time he was seen by a doctor, the wound where the broken bones pierced the skin was swollen and the leg could not be realigned. Soon amputation was necessary, ending for good the sporadic mining career begun with such optimism on the *Princess Royal*.

When a work stoppage was of sufficient duration to threaten the economy in a wide radius, armchair experts emerged. Each one had a considered opinion either for or against the strikers and many found it necessary to express themselves in letters to the editor. Such an expert was the writer in March of 1871 who compared Nova Scotia miners to those on Vancouver Island.

"Our miners wish to make out that they cannot live," he began. He quoted figures from Nova Scotia which showed that after deductions for physician, school master, lamps, and powder, the eastern miners received one dollar per day. In British Columbia by comparison the colliers make it a rule not to pick up more than $3.00 a day for eight hours, and they are furnished with fuel free of charge. Laborers are paid $1.75 per day, and are allowed to purchase coal at a nominal price. To sustain a competition with Australian coal at San Francisco our coal companies must be enabled to sell at a considerable abatement in price... The miners are too well paid already. If I am correctly informed there are five hotels in Nanaimo, maintained almost entirely by the mining population, yet if you meet one of these men he will tell you that he can barely make wages sufficient to live on.

Three dollars a day. An expert miner in Nanaimo could indeed make three dollars a day if he had been assigned a good place. However, the writer made no reference to the deductions which reduced the sum to two dollars. British Columbia miners did make more than Nova Scotia miners, but this did not make them well paid. They were more fortunate than the easterners too in that there was no Company store which would have required them to take part of their pay in "over-valued goods or beer." Ironically, if the Company had had a store that employees were required to patronize, it could have paid the shareholders' dividends from the profits.[3]

What the Nanaimo miners resented was having to bear the burden of the competition faced by the Nanaimo product in San Francisco from coal that came as ballast in Australian ships sent to the United States to pick up grain. The miners of one small coal mining community were unimportant in the game of markets and price cutting, but despite their insignificance they were determined to hold out as long as they could.

But the Company still had coal stockpiled and the children were hungry. Although the Chinese strikebreakers never materialized, the Company held firm too. Ships still left Nanaimo loaded with coal, and many miners had left for the most recent gold rush at Omineca in the interior of the colony.

Miners' meetings adjourned with no decisions made. Rumours of negotiations with the Company kept everyone stirred up. Finally on April 18th, six and one-half months after the strike began, the miners reached an agreement with the Company, whose twenty-five thousand ton pile of coal was now reduced to three thousand tons. The reduction in wages held but the Company had made a concession on the issue of screening.

Prior to the strike, rock and slack had been screened from the good

---

[3] When the VCML sold the HBC store soon after acquiring it, Nanaimo miners were inadvertently spared the tyranny of the "tally-shop" or "pluck-me."

coal below ground at a piece rate charged to the individual miner. This would now be done on the surface at the Company's expense. Having accepted this compromise in good faith, the miners returned to work only to see the mine gradually return to the old system of screening.

It is said that 'all things have an end', and so the hungry miners, and their hungry families hailed the glad day when the steam whistle called the men to work, and the rusty wheels of the machinery once more began their busy work of lifting coal to the surface, and sending back empty's [sic]. With the rest of the men I marched boldly into the office, to sign on for my old job, only to be told by the office Boss that they were letting out all the young men, and none but the men with families were to be employed. And now what? I had no money to go elsewhere, the shack in which I batched belonged to the coal company, and if I didn't pay the rent at the end of the month I would have to 'get out.'

God works in mysterious ways. The Company had chosen this time to pursue its policy of giving employment preference to married men. Men with wives and families were probably more stable and less likely to cause trouble. But Charles Tate was no troublemaker and he was able to get a job as a teacher at the Indian school. What started as a job became a vocation. He became fluent in the language of the Indians including "an unusual command of Chinook jargon." First as a lay worker and later as an ordained Methodist minister, he worked for the rest of his life as a missionary to the coastal Indians. The chronicler of the Nanaimo strike of 1870 and '71 found his true calling.

That the Company was able to be so exclusive in its hiring practices in 1871 was the direct result of a sudden dramatic increase in immigration to British Columbia. Whereas in 1870 English families were being offered free fares to come to the colony, and the VCML was actively encouraging miners from the north of England, in 1871 labour, of the single male variety at least, was arriving on the coast in large numbers, attracted by the possibility of a railroad.

Conservative politicians in the government of Canada's first Prime Minister Sir John A. Macdonald were even then concluding an agreement with a delegation from the west coast which included John Helmcken, now an influential and controversial Victoria politician. The Canadians wanted British Columbia to join the new Dominion, at that time a young and rather dull youngster of four years of age. Sir John was a visionary. He saw the vast Northwest Territories with the mountainous Pacific colony beyond as a hinterland of resources and markets for Canadian industry. Some Americans had the same vision, and Macdonald was determined to be the one to see his dream come true.

In order to ensure that the colony on the Pacific joined Canada and not the geographically more logical western states, Sir John offered the delegates from British Columbia a railroad. It was a preposterously grandiose proposal but one that struck a chord with the westerners. Farming and mining were developing in the Fraser Valley and the Interior and the primitive wagon roads that had serviced the various gold rush communities were an expensive and cumbersome method of transporting large amounts of produce to market. A railroad through the entire province would be just the thing, especially if it was financed by the taxpayers of Canada.

A second attraction to the railroad lay in all the employment it would provide. Thousands of men would be required to build a railroad through terrain only marginally less difficult that that of the Canadian Shield, which would also have to be breached to build an all-Canadian road. No one had ever built a railroad so long and over such difficult terrain. The American trans-continental route completed two years before was a thousand miles shorter, was composed of the lines of several different companies, and had been financed by a population many times that of the Dominion.

But the deal was struck. On July 20, 1871, British Columbia would become the sixth province in the Dominion of Canada, and within two years of that date a railroad was to have been started from both ends of the incredible stretch of territory from Lake Superior to the Pacific Coast.

Word travelled fast. Ex-gold miners, ex-farmers, adventurers, layabouts, Canadians, Americans, Chinese made their way to British Columbia to build the railroad, but no railroad appeared. Surveyors combed the valleys and rivers of the province searching for a likely route, politicians argued, financiers schemed, scandals broke, and elections were lost, but not a foot of track was laid.

The glut of labour did not last long, however. Even without the railroad, the economy of the new province began to expand. In Nanaimo, established mines were pushed farther and farther into the coal body and new mines were developed. Robert Dunsmuir had discovered his own coal seam. Experienced coal miners were very much in demand and inexperienced ones would do as well.

"Miners who know anything about coal working will find steady and remunerative employment at Nanaimo," announced *The Colonist* in 1872. By December the paper proclaimed that there was not an idle man except from choice. A steady flow of Nova Scotia miners came west via the American railroad and north from San Francisco by ship. In March of 1873 there were four hundred men employed in Nanaimo and Wellington — Englishmen, Scots, Welshmen, Irishmen, Americans, and Cape Bretoners.

Miners make high wages and most of the old hands are looked on as very good workmen. In fact, experienced coal workers are constantly finding their way to our mines, meeting at once with steady jobs.

Among the inexperienced hands who also flocked to the coalfields were many Chinese. They had come to North America to mine gold and build railroads, but they would shift to the coal mines and work for the low wages already being paid to a small number of their compatriots brought in by the Company a few years before. It did not take long for the white miners to realize that they could train a Chinese helper, mine twice as much coal, and only have to pay him half the wages. Abuses began to occur until some of the whites would go down in the morning only long enough to set their Chinese helpers to work and then leave them. The practice was ended quickly by John Bryden when Chinese began to suffer more injuries than was usual.

By 1877 there were eighty-seven Chinese employed in the area mines, not including the ones hired by individual miners. Because they constituted almost a third of the work force they were viewed with hostility by the whites even as they employed them. Their increasing numbers only exacerbated an animosity which went back to the days when there were only a few Chinese to be found in the coalfields.

In the 1871 election a candidate for the Nanaimo seat promised that "he would not let the tawny Mongolians work." The promise proved as empty as most made by politicians, and over the next few years the number of Chinese increased considerably, as did anti-Oriental incidents. Certain men of Nanaimo staged a raid on two Chinese wash houses; they broke into Si Sing and Company store and pitched boxes of tea and china into the street, the glass cutting one Chinese in the face. As similar incidents continued to occur, each one was blamed on outsiders.

The *Free Press* chided, "Although the Chinese are anything but a desirable element in our midst, yet while here they should no more be treated with abuse than any other inhabitants." The attacks continued with a raid on the gambling house at Number 84, Winfield Crescent.

Anti-Oriental sentiment was expressed in an official way as well. When one Chinese and one white were arrested for selling liquor to Indians, the white man was given the option of six months in jail or a fifty dollar fine, but the Chinese man was sentenced to six months' hard labour.

Though there were hundreds of Chinese already in Victoria, it was not until the building of the railroad, when thousands of them were imported at once, that Victorians became incensed by their presence. In Nanaimo they were resented from the beginning, probably because they were brought in to replace white workers. As *The Colonist* remarked, "probably in no other community does the question [exclusion of Chinese] excite so much interest [as in Nanaimo]."

There was no Chinatown then. The Chinese lived among the rest of the town's inhabitants. In their unusual clothes with their hair dressed in a pigtail, they stood out, and their customs marked them as different. The white population looked on with a mixture of fascination and derision to such events as Chinese New Year.

Would you be surprised to learn it is a general holiday here? "Pig hangs high," a large boiler used in former times by the Co. to boil cattle-feed, has been rigged and the Heathen Chinee is hovering round it intently watching the contents.

And there was among the Chinese the occasional law breaker. Although it was not illegal in British Columbia to use or manufacture opium and opium smoking was an accepted practice among the Chinese and indeed among many white gentleman, too, it was illegal to import the drug into the United States. In an effort to stop the flow of opium coming from China via Canadian ships, fifteen watchmen were employed at the mail dock in Nanaimo to catch Chinese longshoremen smuggling opium ashore in the thick soles of their shoes.

The people of Nanaimo at the beginning of the 1870's were a peculiar blend of the ordinary and the exotic. The overwhelming majority of the six hundred whites were British, and observations on the "Englishness" of the place were often made. Even the two hundred or so temporary inhabitants who came and went on the ships were mostly of British stock. Each year the population increased by half or more, but each time most of the new people were from Britain.

In contrast to the white British folk were one hundred or more

190

Chinese men and a large population of Indians, still numerous despite the continuing depredations of white men's diseases and white men's vices. Although John Bryden preferred them as runners and would still have employed them in the mines, he found it hard at any price to interest them in being mine workers. The third "exotic" component in the population was a significant number of "coloured" people.

The majority of the blacks were probably part of the six hundred who emigrated from California to Victoria in 1858. Despite some discrimination, especially from expatriate Americans and from Cowichan Indians, who considered the blacks to be inferior and therefore fair game as targets for molestation, the black experience in British Columbia had been generally favorable. Although many had moved to Saltspring Island to farm, approximately forty of them with their wives were living in Nanaimo in 1870.

The mines were booming: markets opened up; more and more coal was discovered, the process enhanced by the new diamond drill boring machine; the demand for labour exceeded the supply despite the constant influx of men; Chinese were hired by both management and miners, their willingness to work for a dollar a day outweighing the reluctance of the whites to bring them into the mines.

John Bryden shared the job of managing the VCML mines with Mark Bate. Both men had become influential in the community in the years since their arrival but the two were as different as two men could be. Bryden had been associated with mining since he was eighteen, first as a miner and later as a "coal viewer," in which capacity he had come to Nanaimo in 1863 and been charged with developing future resources. Bate's arrival six years before Bryden's had been at the urging of his uncle, George Robinson, then in charge of the Hudson's Bay Company (HBC) mines. His expertise lay in clerking, and he had used it to work his way up to manager of the VCML.

The gregarious and community-minded Bate was in charge of the clerical and financial functions of the Company and was to have no part in the actual operation of the mines when he took over from C. S. Nicol in 1867. The mines were the domain of Robert Dunsmuir until 1869 and then of John Bryden, his new son-in-law. As Bate's increasing involvement in community affairs kept him away from the mine office more and more, Bryden's responsibilities and resentment grew.

Given the unsettled nature of the Company management and the necessity of reporting to and awaiting orders from a board of directors in London, it is amazing that the VCML mines developed as much as they did in the 1870's. In the beginning of the decade, the only mine of

191

any consequence was the Douglas Pit, its large pithead, railroad, and loading grounds dominating the town on its south side, the Park Head Swamp at its doorstep, and the tall fir trees behind. In 1872 it was already the "Old Pit," ten years being a venerable age for a coal mine in those days.

"Old Pit" or not, it still was a producer. A large winding engine, driven by steam from furnaces and boilers that were deemed "models of their kind," could haul nine tons of coal up an incline nearly two hundred yards long at an angle of thirteen degrees without any trouble at all. At the pithead the coal cars were impelled along a tramway by gravity alone, to a scale, where the weight of each car was assigned to the miner whose tally hung inside the top edge. The coal was then tipped onto a screen with a large wagon underneath to receive the lumps. Smaller lumps were caught on a second screen and the dross was captured to feed the furnaces which drove the engine.

But old age was creeping up on the Old Douglas Pit. On New Year's Day 1873, a large cave-in blocked off the lower works. Water began to accumulate in the mine, rising day after day and reducing the horse roads to knee-deep mud. The cave was draining a large swamp and the Company had to employ many men to drain the offending bog and throw branches and rubbish into the crevice to stop the water entering the mine. Pumping the works dry took several years and used up an entire year's dividends. Other problems included bush fires which often threatened the surface facilities of the mine so closely surrounded by the primeval forest. In addition, as the works extended to the south the mine became difficult to ventilate.

One mile south of the Old Pit, a new mine was opened in 1875. It was to be a "model pit in every respect." A two mile long tramway enabled the New Douglas mine to share the loading facilities already in place, just as a connection in the workings underground facilitated a shared ventilation system. Eventually the Old Pit became an upcast for the newer mine.

The body of coal it tapped had been discovered twenty years before by Joseph McKay and James Douglas, investigated by Boyd Gilmour, and finally proven by borehole in 1870. It was said the coal would last for thirty years. After 1877, the New Douglas Mine with its connections to the Old Pit would be called the Chase River Mine in recognition of an operation on its southern edge begun in 1870 around the original boreholes. The workings advanced relentlessly, finding more and more coal in the most southern reaches of the Company lease limits.

Like the Dunsmuir mine a few miles to the north, the VCML mines were equipped similarly to British collieries of the time with steam equipment for ventilating, pumping water, and hoisting and loading coal. But whereas Dunsmuir tended to purchase American equipment or, in later years, salvage equipment purchased from defunct partnerships, the VCML bought British machinery. Machinery, however, could not replace hand labour at the face; nor could imported machinery, with the long delays in delivery, replace local ingenuity.

In 1876 a miner employed in the Old Pit invented a new hand coal boring machine which would drill a blasting hole five foot six inches deep in twenty minutes. It was celebrated as a great labour saver which was also less costly, but the inventor's name was not remembered.

Nanaimo mine owners preferred British equipment, but Nanaimo miners liked California powder. It may have been that British powder was just as good, but by the time it arrived via ship it was often waterlogged. And the pits south of town required "heavy shot" — a charge of one to one and a half pounds of gunpowder — to move the coal.

Such a heavy charge scattered the coal widely though, and if the brattice was close enough to the face to direct fresh air properly, the blast would knock down the brattice as well. In the standoff that resulted when the mine inspector insisted that the brattice be closed, and the miners insisted it be back at least nine feet to avoid its being knocked down, the miners prevailed, thereby increasing the risk of explosion.

By the close of the decade, the workings of the Chase River Mine crept out under the harbour, separated from the sea by 350 feet of sandstone and conglomerate. Water percolated down through the roof, but anyone tasting it knew it was fresh water and there was no cause for concern.

At the other end of the harbour on Newcastle Island, the Fitzwilliam and Newcastle mines drew coal on a much more limited basis than did the VCML mines to the south. Like the Chase River Mine, the Fitzwilliam Mine tapped both the Newcastle and Douglas seams, giving upper and lower working levels. With its large wharf projecting out into Midden Bay and positioned very close to the pit mouth, the mine was a convenient place for ships to take on coal.

As the H.M.S. *Boxer* test of Wellington coal had shown, the qualities of coal varied from mine to mine within fairly close proximity. Fitzwilliam coal was purer than that from the Douglas Pit, though not so highly bituminous. It burned exceedingly well when a hot fire was maintained and made a clinker which did not adhere and was therefore not destructive of grates and boilers.

The Fitzwilliam Mine had the unenviable distinction of being the first area mine to lose lives due to an explosion, and soon after that it began to experience major problems with its ventilating system. For several years it was mined sporadically, including one period in 1880 when Thomas Hawkes and Elijah Ganner, no longer fresh young men from the *Princess Royal*, were included in the small work force.

The mine was also a training ground for Edward Gawlor Prior who at the tender age of twenty-one was hired as assistant underviewer. The future mine inspector and later Premier of the province celebrated his twenty-first birthday in a way sure to make him popular with his fellow employees and future constituents. A cask of ale was broached in the centre of town, and everyone was invited to partake.

The young man who was given charge of the Fitzwilliam Mine in its last years was also popular. William McGregor was the son of the volatile John McGregor, he of the abortive Fort Rupert strike and colourful language, who had died in Sooke in 1866. The widow Mary had brought her husband back to Nanaimo to be buried in the little cemetery above the Millstream estuary and had settled in Nanaimo with her large family. Two years later, thirteen year old William had entered the VCML mines and had worked his way up through every position until he was now, at the age of twenty-five, supervisor of hauling and shipping at the Fitzwilliam Mine.[4] Four years later, he would be manager of the new VCML Number One, the biggest mine in British Columbia.

The earliest miners on Newcastle Island lived in Nanaimo, but as the Fitzwilliam Mine increased production the Company deemed it advantageous to build houses at the mine site. In 1874, contractor D. W. Gordon, soon to be elected Nanaimo's Member of the Provincial Parliament (MPP) and later Member of Parliament in Ottawa, built miners' houses on the ridge just above the beach and adjacent to the mine portal.

The first white people to actually live on the Island were probably the occupants of the bunkhouses at the quarry, half way up the Channel, the population of single whites and Chinese fluctuating

---

[4] William McGregor married Amanda Meakin, daughter of John and Maryann from the *Princess Royal*.

194

with the market for sandstone. In 1874, a contract was secured to provide sandstone for a new penitentiary at New Westminster on the mainland, and in due course the schooner *Industry* came alongside the quarry dock to take on the huge blocks of building stone.

This was the first visit to Nanaimo for the schooner and her captain, Jemmy Jones. Jones liked what he saw and he liked even better what he heard. Harewood Mine was reopening, and the new owner was looking for a ship to take the first load of coal. T. A. Bulkley, a surveyor by profession, had purchased the mine from Lady Maud Lascelles. She had inherited it from her brother and can have had little interest in the seemingly worthless mine on a far-away island in the Pacific.

Captain Bulkley was sure he could solve the problem of getting Harewood coal to tidewater. The nine thousand acre lease secured, he let the contract for tunnel development. Houses were built, again by the redoubtable Gordon, and construction was commenced on an elevated wire tramway supported from the harbour to the mine on large tripods.

The Harewood aerial tramway was such a wonder that even though it only actually functioned for less than a year, it is revered to this day as a symbol of coal mining in Nanaimo. Its success as a symbol contrasts sharply with its success as a practical means to convey coal. It was doomed from the beginning by the failure of the machinery to arrive and by "other accidents." Thousands of dollars were invested in two-hundred pound capacity buckets and on a replacement for the original cable, which began to stretch as soon as the buckets were loaded.

The three and a half mile long replacement cable arrived from San Francisco one year too late. The tramway had already been shut down. The customs officer confiscated the four thousand dollar rope in the name of the Crown and slapped a duty of one thousand dollars on it. When an agent for the Company broke open the padlocked door of the customs shed and attempted to load the cable onto a waiting steamer, he was stopped just in time. The duty was eventually paid.

In its short working life the aerial tramway caused so many problems that a crew of men had to be hired just to keep it running. As the cable stretched, the buckets would pile up between the tripods and occasionally fall to the ground. When everything was working correctly, the tramway could carry thirty tons an hour, but everything was seldom working correctly.

Captain Jemmy Jones, by now a resident of Nanaimo, was a prankster, and he could not resist the possibilities offered by the tramway. His celebrated journey perched in one of the buckets has been told and retold — how the tramway stopped at noon just as Jemmy's bucket passed over Albert and Wallace streets; how a crowd gathered and began to harass him; how he threw coal back at his tormentors; and how the Constable happened to be in the crowd. When Jemmy's bucket arrived at the mine the constable was waiting for him. He was arrested and fined for trespassing, public mischief, disturbing the peace, and being drunk.

Captain Jemmy Jones knew a thing or two about being drunk and he made a reputation for himself as a sea lawyer defending sailors on intoxication charges. After his sailing days ended in the sinking of his vessel off Trial Island in 1878, Jemmy lived for another four years, adding to his legend all the while. He was true to form on May Day one year when he and a group of American sailors paraded through the town playing accordions and penny whistles and calling themselves the "Calethumpians." They managed to enrage many of Queen Victoria's loyal subjects by carrying the American flag.

But Jemmy Jones lasted longer than the Harewood Mine under Captain Bulkley. Although there were still people living at the mine in 1877 the tramway was long since defunct, and the tunnel roof, full of slips and potholes, was deemed too treacherous to work. Pleading bad markets, management closed the mine. The tripods remained for another twelve years when the VCML, new owner of the large Harewood coal lease, had them taken down.

Despite being outraged at Jemmy Jones' parading of the American flag, Nanaimo's citizens loved parades and celebrations. Although May Day, that traditional festival of spring, had been observed on Vancouver Island since at least 1867, it is not likely that it had the labour significance it acquired by the 1890's. Before that it vied with the Queen's Birthday three weeks later as the first big celebration of the summer. There were sports on the Green under the shadow of the loading wharves, and water sports on the harbour, for the benefit of spectators who sat on the wild grass where the slope of the land made a natural grandstand just off Front Street.

The Queen's Birthday always overshadowed the July 1st celebrations. British Columbia's entry into Confederation had been quiet and would be quietly marked in succeeding years as befitted a marriage not of sentiment but of convenience. But May 24th symbolized the strong ties Nanaimo felt to Great Britain, and everyone had to contribute to make it a success. Subscriptions were requested through ads in the *Free Press*, miners giving a dollar each and the hotels offering prize money. One year there was a half-mile race scheduled in June to pay off the $18.50 still owed by the Queen's Birthday fund. The entrance fee was a dollar and the race, to be held on Wellington Road, was open to all horses except Jack Cade and Sleepy Dan.[5]

New Year was the best celebration of all, the preponderance of Scottish miners in the early years probably explaining the importance of this holiday over even Christmas. As the old year gave way to the new, as households welcomed as their first guest of the year a dark-haired man bearing coal in one hand and whiskey in the other, the air was full of sounds. The booming of the cannon at the Bastion, the sharp cracks of rifles and pistols fired in the air, and the resonant clanging of the Methodist Church bell all promised that this year would be better than the last.

It did not take long after British Columbia entered Confederation for the rest of the country to label the province as the "spoiled child of Confederation." The citizens of British Columbia were demanding, dissatisfied, and split into warring factions. The citizens of Nanaimo, the third largest city in the province, were especially dissatisfied because, as had always been the case, they seemed to have little say in government and received a very small portion of the revenues due to them.

Since the beginning of the colony, Nanaimo had been represented by outsiders. The tradition had begun when there were few property owners eligible to stand for election and it continued as leading provincial politicians came to regard Nanaimo as a seat available to anyone who needed it.

The last election before Confederation was fought between John Robson, editor of *The Daily British Colonist* and one Arthur Bunster, a brewer and protegy of Amor de Cosmos. Although de Cosmos was the founder of the *Colonist*, he was now Robson's rival. Bunster was told by the people of Nanaimo that they wanted a working man like themselves to represent them in Victoria. But the choice was already made, and neither of the candidates were what the people had in mind.

Many obstacles stood in the way of the two candidates. They both lived and worked in Victoria; the riding was large and included

---

[5] Sleepy Dan was a legendary horse who pulled a butcher cart except for the month before May 24th when he was in training for the annual horse race on Haliburton Street. Once he raced on Columbia Street in New Westminster, and according to his fans — and they were legion — he always won.

Nanaimo and Comox in its boundaries; the method of voting was by a show of hands and had to be conducted in the two centres on different days to accommodate the returning officer.

Before the federal Liberal government instituted the secret ballot in 1877, elections were shady affairs. Free beer was an integral part of the proceedings. In Nanaimo and Comox in 1870, the situation was ripe for manipulation. Nominating meetings took place simultaneously in the two centres on November 5th; polling was to take place in Comox on the 12th, after which the returns were to be taken to Nanaimo by Indian canoe before the polls closed there on the 14th.

Bunster had boasted he could buy Nanaimo with beer, and it was rumoured that he had already sent up a barrel of his own brew to Comox. The voting was very close there. Bunster had a lead of only seven votes. When this information was conveyed to him in Victoria, he realized that more than the presence of Bunster Beer was needed in Nanaimo. It was reported by his rival's newspaper that he left Victoria in great haste galloping up the Saanich Penninsula "on the outside of a horse" and continuing on by canoe to the hustings.

At 2:00 p.m. on the 14th, Robson was ahead in the balloting, and it was he who observed that "about this time canoes were sent to Big, Newcastle and other Islands in the vicinity and a large number of men were brought over and voted." He charged that many of these men were former American soldiers and non-residents and demanded that all voters be challenged and duly sworn.

Bunster won the election by twelve votes. Robson said that fifty illegal votes had been cast for his opponent. "Bunster's men were well 'primed' and free liquor was furnished for his supporters," the loser charged in print. He demanded further scrutiny. De Cosmos was jubilant over Robson's defeat, especially when the scrutiny confirmed Bunster's victory. The battle fought and lost, John Robson conceded graciously. He won the next election and later became Premier of British Columbia, arguably achieving greater distinction than his worthy opponent whose name lived on in Bunster Beer.

It was not until 1876 that the voters of Nanaimo were given the opportunity to vote for a "working man." John Bryden followed Robson as MPP. When Bryden resigned pleading pressure of work at the mine, James Harold was encouraged by his fellow workmen to run against D. W. Gordon, contractor, and Peter Sabiston, proprietor of the Miners' Hotel. A large number of miners attended the election meeting. Indeed forty percent of the names on the voters' list were miners, and another twenty percent also belonged to the working class. In a show of hands, Harold received the largest number of votes, which surprised Sabiston, who demanded that a poll be taken. This time the winner was Gordon.[6]

James Harold was a miner from Australia who had made his reputation in Nanaimo when he led the miners' opposition to the Coal Mines Regulations Act as it was first proposed. He was so articulate in speech and in print that some suspected that he was an outside union agitator sent in to infiltrate the local scene. As a member of the inquest jury for the Fitzwilliam explosion, he had found the Company responsible, a decision which was overruled by the coroner. In the year following the election his time was well filled with the Wellington strike, as a member of the miners' deputation, and as a frequent writer of letters to the editor.

Despite his obvious influence among the miners, he chose not to run in the 1878 election. Instead he and some other miners were among those who signed the nomination of James Abrams, a local clothier running with George Walkem, leader of the opposition, who had won the miners' support by representing them during the Wellington strike. The constituency was obviously not deemed ready to be represented by a real member of the working class.

James Abrams must have been in a strong position. His association with Walkem probably worked to his advantage. Abrams must have been perceived as a threat by Robert Dunsmuir, because he took a challenge of Abrams' right to vote all the way to the Supreme Court. When the ballots were counted, Abrams had defeated the incumbent Gordon.

Having elected a member who was perceived to be at least sympathetic to labour, the miners had their first taste of political power. That would have to content them for some time to come, for the day had not quite arrived when a sufficient number of the working class could be convinced that they could be effectively represented by one of their own. In the meantime, they showed their group strength in other ways.

Since the early 1860's mining men had provided for their own medical and funeral coverage by following the tradition of self-help begun in Britain at the turn of the nineteenth century. Each man contributed a set amount each month towards a fund which paid for a doctor's visits, hospital stays, time off work due to sickness or injury,

---

[6] To qualify as a voter one had to be a man, over twenty-one, a British citizen, a resident of the province for one year, and in the constituency for two months.

and funeral costs. Some funds were administered by the coal company and some by various lodges such as the Independent Order of Oddfellows, which arrived in Nanaimo from the United States in 1863 or the Ancient Order of Foresters, which came to Nanaimo in 1875 and Wellington in 1876. Most men belonged to more than one benefit plan.

It was in the hiring of doctors that miners had their opportunity to exercise a certain measure of power. In order for a doctor to secure a decent living, he needed an appointment as a fund doctor. Miners' funds hired and fired doctors by majority vote. A doctor therefore had to keep the majority of fund members happy to maintain his position.

No doctor in recorded history has ever made all his patients happy, and coal miners' doctors were no exception. Someone always had a complaint about a refusal to make a house call or about an ointment which failed to do the job. Repeatedly over the almost one hundred years that miners' funds hired doctors there were incidents of volatile meetings where the merits of the incumbent doctor were discussed heatedly.

Dr. Loftus R. McInnes was reputed to have great surgical skill and good common sense. He had practiced in Toronto and New Westminster before he came to Nanaimo as medical officer to the VCML, succeeding Dr. William McNaughton Jones who was leaving to be the medical superintendent of the New Westminster Lunatic Asylum. McInnes had been colliery physician for two years before he first became the subject of a Sick and Accident Fund meeting. Although some miners were unhappy with his services the majority were content, and McInnes continued to practice.

Then in 1879 his professional reputation was again a subject of debate when he took on the additional burden of the South Wellington Mine fund. Miners pointed out that he was also doctor to the Department of Marine and Fisheries, he was not young, and "of somewhat a corpulent nature and slightly short in wind." Although no one quarrelled with his medical abilities they knew about his troubles with the Nanaimo miners, and besides, he wanted "three men's pay." Having endured the ordeal of having his income, age, girth, and breathing capacity discussed in an open meeting by his potential employers and by the local press, McInnes was in fact hired.

Nanaimo had no hospital until 1876, when an epidemic of typhoid fever and typhus left bachelor miners dying unattended in their cabins. A group of citizens took the problem in hand and set about raising money to rent several of the old HBC bachelor's cabins on the edge of the ravine. Money was raised by public subscription and entertainments and by raffling a large Raymond sewing machine at the Old Flag Inn just across the street from the cabins. The beleaguered Dr. McInnes offered his services without charge for twelve months.With a bit of shuffling around and carpentry, a hospital emerged in the shape of an "L," with a narrow opening between the two arms to allow access to the ravine and its water supply.

At a time when most people preferred to be nursed at home, only bachelors needed the hospital. The cost of hospital care could be covered by membership in the St. Joseph Hospital Society begun by the Sisters of St. Ann. For an initiation fee of five dollars and one dollar per month dues, patients received free hospital treatment, free medications, and the doctor's visit at a reduced rate. Four years later in 1881, the coal company donated a piece of land at the top of the town on Franklyn Street, on which the first proper hospital was built.

Although the makeshift hospital accommodated a wide variety of ailments — general debility, thoracic aneurism, a fractured tibia, syphilitic rheumatism — communicable diseases were the chief medical concern. Typhoid fever, typhus, and smallpox, despite the possibility of vaccination, caused fear and hysterical responses in the authorities and the general population. When one white child contracted a case of smallpox, a clean-up of Indian and Chinese houses was ordered. When an Indian woman in the Euclataw camp across the Millstream was reported to have smallpox, she was taken away and her house and belongings burned. It later turned out that she did not have the disease after all.

So marked was the fear of communicable diseases that a pest house was established on Harewood Road for the accommodation of infected individuals. That little is known about its actual functioning reflects the abhorrence with which it and its occupants were viewed. As settlement crept nearer and nearer to it, the pest house ceased to be used as a hospital and the Company took it over to store pit props. [7]

Epidemics or supposed epidemics caused a ripple of excitement in a town that probably had more tumult than most towns its size. To the already volatile mix of Indians and Chinese, too many bachelors, and

[7] In 1892, an outbreak of smallpox caused the Mayor of Nanaimo to look for a new location for a pest house. A site opposite Jesse Island in Departure Bay near an old lime kiln was selected, to the horror of ships' captains who used a site nearby to take on fresh water, and of vacationers who camped there. Wellington and Departure Bay residents said it was a deliberate attempt to boycott Wellington coal, and Mrs. Dunsmuir got an injunction stopping the city from using the site.

a thousand people living too close together was added the constantly changing supply of sailors, sometimes as many as two hundred at once, ripe for a good time on shore after weeks and months at sea on coaling ships.

The *Newbern*'s people, as usual, left some of their spare cash in return for which some got dry goods, and others being dry, drunk.

A mutiny aboard the coal ship *Commodore* resulted in the captain brandishing a double barrelled shot-gun and shooting two members of the crew superficially before finally hiding himself in the coal.

A fight occurred between two quarry workers in a saloon in which a nose was bitten off.

The captain of a visiting vessel destroyed $200 worth of property in a saloon and then called his crew to clean out the town; he was repentant in front of the magistrate.

Constable William Stewart of the Provincial Police was the sole person responsible for policing this unruly lot. In his capacity as arresting officer and custodian of the jail, he met with constant frustration. The jail was still inadequately housed in the Bastion, which was described as "about the size and style of an ordinary farmer's hen-house, elevated on wooden stilts and insecure." The difficulties in being the only law officer were obvious to anyone watching in December of 1871 when Constable Stewart attempted to arrest two whiskey sellers.

The redoubtable Stewart commanded his prisoners to follow him to our gaol, and he led off with exalting pride. But, Lo! on reaching the prison door he found he had no following.

Having acquired a temporary assistant, Stewart again attempted the arrest. This time, the constable and his assistant were reduced to wrestling in the street with the two malefactors.

The lack of a proper jail symbolized the neglect of Nanaimo by Victoria. The jail was in disrepair; the constable, on duty twenty-four hours a day seven days a week, was overworked; and the stipendiary magistrate had too large a territory and was therefore away far too frequently and for far too long a time.

Four Grand Juries, two of them chaired by Robert Dunsmuir, called attention to the need for more than one constable, and for heat and a secure fence for the jail. A proper jail was finally built and a prison guard hired, making it possible for the first time for Nanaimo's convicts to stay at home and work on the city chain gangs. Far from making the taxpayers of Nanaimo happy, however, the presence of the chain gang doing road work only gave them new cause for complaint. They were making the roads too wide! Roads that were too wide cost too much money.

That first prison guard went on to become Nanaimo's first Sheriff. Samuel Drake was a former prospector and miner. There was a rumour that he was descended from the brother of Sir Francis Drake, having been born in Devon just six miles from the mansion of the dashing Elizabethan adventurer. Possibly being kin to Sir Francis did not put food on the table, and Drake set out for the New World to pursue a young man's dreams.

He crossed the United States during the Civil War, trying to pay his way by working in a silver mine but losing out when the owner of the mine died without having paid his employees. He arrived in San Francisco in an old wagon, flat broke until he met a man who agreed to stake him to come to British Columbia.

The Cariboo was the place for a young man to go, and Sam spent several years there digging for gold. One day he met an Anglican minister who told him about Nanaimo. Sam was not making much as a gold miner, so he thought he would try coal for a change. And so it was that he came to the Island.

A man of many talents, Sam played the coronet for the church. One day he looked up into the choir and saw Rhoda Malpass, the daughter of Lavinia and John, born the year after her parents arrived in Nanaimo on the *Princess Royal*. "I marked that little lady for my own," he told his grandchildren years later. Nineteen year old Rhoda married thirty-six year old Sam in 1874 and produced eleven children.

With a growing family to support, Sam looked for something a little more prestigious than coal mining and settled on becoming a law enforcement officer. And he did it in fine style. A white shirt with a string tie and a frock coat adorned his person and on his head was a black silk top hat. Sam Drake served his adopted city as Sheriff for thirty-two years. His fellow law officer, William Stewart, died in 1904, still Chief Constable and Gaoler after thirty-five years.

The roads and bridges of Nanaimo needed more than the long awaited convict chain gangs. Nanaimo's streets continued to be "much as they came from the hands of nature," and the rocks on Commercial Street were so numerous that a cow had been killed falling over them. Victoria Road, running beyond the Old Pit towards the Chase River Mine, particularly enraged one man who fumed, "It's simply murdering Queen's English to call it a trail. Stumps, stones, quagmires and streams reign supreme."

Bridges, or the lack of them, continued to be a major source of unhappiness. Makeshift bridges built across rain-induced chasms washed out after the next storm. Holes went unrepaired in the larger bridges. The Long Bridge which connected Commercial Street to Victoria Crescent was unsuitable for pedestrians. T. E. Peck and Arthur Bunster remedied that by building a footbridge to facilitate the progress of beer drinkers across the ravine to imbibe Bunster Beer at Peck's Hotel.

A bridge had finally been built across the Millstone River on the road to Comox. Because that road now led first to Dunsmuir's new mining camp, it was more commonly called Wellington Road. It was a road in name only. Just nine feet wide on average, it was too narrow for wagons to pass each other.

The increased traffic between Nanaimo and Wellington over what was really no more than a trail had played havoc with the corduroy bridges which crossed several low and marshy spots. It was sometimes necessary for teamsters to spend an hour or two repairing these bridges if they were to deliver their freight the six miles to Wellington.

With such terrible roads, it is not too surprising that there was no regular mail service connecting Wellington, Harewood, Chase River, and Nanaimo. All mail came on a weekly basis to William Earl's second hand store in Nanaimo. Having taken over the job of postmaster from James Harvey, Earl took his job seriously. He waited until two or three bags of mail had accumulated, then took his place inside the wicket he had specially constructed in his store. The crowd was required to wait outside. "Like a schoolmaster calling the roll," he would call out a name, the recipient would reply "Here," and the letter would be passed to him. With only a weekly service, a letter took five to six days to get to Victoria even though boats plied the route several times a week.

That trip to Victoria took twelve hours. The *Maude* had replaced the *Sir James Douglas*, which had been declared totally unfit to carry passengers, but the *Maude* had a peculiar propensity for running aground. In 1872, she ran aground on a rock in Departure Bay within one hundred yards of the Dunsmuir wharf at a tide so high that she had to stay there for two weeks until another tide occurred high enough to float her off. Fortunately the rock was flat enough to accommodate her comfortably, and Captain Holmes, her resourceful skipper, used the time to build a beacon for the offending rock.

In 1874 the *Maude* was replaced by the *Cariboo Fly*, a bigger and faster boat, which was able to accommodate thirty passengers in its large upper deck saloon. The *Maude* continued to give service as required and continued to run aground.

Billy Lewis remembered his trip on the doughty old vessel when he arrived on the coast as a young boy.

We left Victoria on the steamer called the *Maude*, and left at seven o'clock in the morning, and I remember we ran aground and took quite a while getting off, and then on our way up to Salt Spring Island, there was a little trouble there, and when we got to Dodds Narrows, the tide was against us. The old *Maude* could only make six knots, the Dodds Narrows was running at eight, so we had to wait for the return of the tide, arriving in Nanaimo at twelve o'clock at night.

Although some ships seemed to have a special affinity for hidden underwater reefs and sandbars, there was nothing unusual about running aground. The provision of buoys and beacons was a haphazard affair. Despite efforts by the Royal Navy and private individuals like Edward Walker, weather, wind, floating ice, and careless mariners continually removed the markers, and the government was slow to replace them.

Nanaimo was named a port of entry in 1863, making it possible for foreign ships to come directly to her harbour without first stopping in Victoria, but despite the official designation, maintenance of the aids to navigation did not improve. Individual ship captains, the coal company, and even concerned citizens installed and replaced markers as their need became apparent, their existence and location passed on to mariners by word of mouth.

With Nanaimo an official port of entry, ships could come in ballast directly to the coal towns and wait for their turn at the loading wharves. Ships of all descriptions lay at anchor, their holds waiting to be filled through loading chutes which swung out over the ships' hatches. What a wonder those chutes were. They could be raised and lowered by a winch to suit the level of the tide and size of the vessel. After years of awkward loading procedures, of wharves falling down and burning down, of too much coal and too few ships, and then too many ships and too little coal, these new loading facilities promised better days to come.

The land end of the loading process was often delayed by the yard locomotive. Once the locomotive ran over a cow and another time it had too much steam up and jumped the track, pushing cars ahead of it through the end of the trestle and almost onto the vessel waiting below. Delays could also occur when there was not enough coal to fill a ship. Some ship captains threatened to go to Departure Bay instead. This would have availed them little as Dunsmuir had the same loading apparatus and did not stockpile coal; it was his firm policy only to mine coal that had been ordered in advance. But Robert Dunsmuir was quick to see the possibilities in the unhappiness of the ship captains. He offered to load a boat in three days at the same price offered by the VCML, whose office manager, Mark Bate, anxiously kept detailed track of activity at his rival's wharves.

Bate's and Bryden's fragmented management of the VCML had begun to seriously affect the Company's ability to supply coal. Miners were often on strike; equipment often broke down and could not be fixed until spare parts arrived from England; the Company's buyer in San Francisco, John Rosenfeld, would telegraph that a newly arrived ship must be given priority over those that had been waiting in the harbour.

Under ideal conditions, a ship could be loaded in two to three days, but conditions were seldom ideal. The *Thrasher* had been there for six weeks before she was finally loaded. However, because there were no tugs available to tow her away from the docks, she continued to lie alongside, making it impossible for another boat to take on coal.

Even after finally leaving Nanaimo harbour, her troubles were not over. Word arrived that the *Thrasher* was "hard and fast on Gabriola Reef" and taking on water rapidly. Instruments, furniture, and sails were removed. The coal that had taken weeks to load was thrown overboard in an attempt to save the ship, southeast winds making it impossible to pump or to fix the leak. Finally the Captain abandoned her and went to Victoria to offer the wreck for sale. It is doubtful he had many good things to say about the experience of loading coal at the VCML.

Not all ship captains left Nanaimo cursing the docks and their unruly crews. Captain John Freeman had been coming into Nanaimo harbour since the 1850's, and he appreciated the steady if uneven progress of the loading procedure. Captain Freeman was like most ship masters. He had a wife and family in Liverpool but was never home for long. His wife was very young when he met and married her in Manchester. Every two years or so, the good Captain would arrive back in Liverpool for a short visit. When he left his family again for the sea, his wife would be expecting another baby.

It was not until Freeman happened to take sick while in Nanaimo that he decided he liked the place well enough to stay there. Having acquired the job of Harbour Master, he wrote his wife to tell her the good news that at last he was settling down, and she could come and bring the seven children. This was not good news to Mrs. Freeman though. She dragged her feet. Her husband went back to Liverpool to try to convince her, and another child was conceived. It took another trip and another pregnancy before the Freeman family embarked for Nanaimo to join the Captain.

Two of the Freeman boys, Harry and John, had inherited a large portion of their father's adventurous nature. On board the ship to Halifax they locked a younger brother in the ship's paint locker and pretended he had fallen overboard. Accordingly the captain of this ship took the two in hand. He had the first mate teach them four hours of seamanship and mathematics every day.

From Halifax, the family journeyed to Montreal, where they were stranded for several months before they boarded the immigrant train, which only went as far as Calgary. From Calgary they had to travel by stagecoach through the United States, the boys making so much ruckus inside the coach they were compelled to sit on top all the way to the coast.

Even the captain of the ship that took them to Nanaimo had trouble with Harry and John. While the ship lay at anchor in the harbour waiting for wharf space, the boys' behavior forced him to put the family ashore on Protection Island to await their father, who was delayed by bad weather from coming to get them.

Finally, the family was reunited and settled in Nanaimo. But the parents, who had never lived together for any length of time, found they could not get along. They parted ways, Captain Freeman going to Victoria and becoming skipper of the *Glory of the Seas,* a collier which came often to Nanaimo, and Mrs. Freeman staying in her new home to raise her large brood of children. Her son Harry, perhaps benefitting from those mathematics lessons on board ship, became a mining engineer and a mine manager respected by both his peers and his employees.

Mrs. Freeman had been loath to leave the bustle of Liverpool for the isolation of Nanaimo, so far from the civilization and culture of Britain. But that is not to say there was no cultural life in Nanaimo. Lectures and readings of Charles Dickens' works were particularly popular. Dickens wrote his novels in serialized form, each installment anxiously awaited by his readers, including readers in Nanaimo who had to wait for each installment to be carried across an ocean and a continent.

207

And music was important, too. Local choirs and soloists entertained at every function. To the already established Philharmonic was added a Brass Band, whose founder Reverend Raynard would recruit Sam Drake in the Cariboo gold fields. By the time Sam arrived in Nanaimo, the band was a going concern, but two years before, in 1872, it had been founded on faith alone. The persuasive Raynard had managed to convince potential band members that they could learn the rudiments of music without instruments. The instruments had been ordered but like everything else worth having in Nanaimo, they had a long way to travel. When they did arrive in July, the Nanaimo Brass Band had been practicing for several months using their imaginations.

Public lectures at the Literary Institute continued to be a popular form of entertainment. Titles such as "Peculiar People," "Funny Folks," and "Demonology, Spiritualism and Fascination" drew larger audiences than the religious subjects of a decade before. Despite the popularity of such functions, a boast that the Institute had ended the year 1871 in the black had a hollow ring. The building was still uncompleted and had never been properly furnished; the library was badly in need of books; the reading room was ill-supplied; and the coal company was owed $1059.

As if to belie its declining fortunes, the Institute building was finally painted in 1874. The formerly dismal exterior of the town's largest edifice was transformed with lemon yellow walls and brown trim. Surely now, membership would grow. Surely now, more and more people would find the monthly fifty cent fee a bargain if it bought association with this stunning structure.

It was not to be. Though the public attended lectures and parties in the large room on the main floor, membership in the Institute continued to decline. The reading room upstairs went unused. Would-be seekers of knowledge may have been discouraged by the outside stairway which provided unprotected access to the second floor. In a town with so much rain, that alone could deter people from improving their minds.

In 1887, the venerable dowager that was the Literary Institute building began a second career as Nanaimo's second City Hall. Her predecessor for the honour of housing the city administration was a homely little thing with a checkered past.

The "Old Stone House" was a small, rough stone cottage which would have reminded a Shetland Islander of home. It had been built by an Orkney Islander, William Isbister, in 1852, to be the HBC guest house. Within its stone walls many a "good feast and good bottle had been enjoyed." But buildings were at a premium in early Nanaimo, and the stone house had to serve as a school part time.

Education was one thing, but when the Company needed office space, the stone house became the domain of Captain Stuart and George Robinson and later C. S. Nicol, until 1867, when the Company offices were moved to the former Company boarding house on Haliburton Street, closer to the Douglas Pit. For the next eight years, the Old Stone House or Tyhee House as the Indians called it, was a private residence, but its central location on Front Street made it a prime candidate for city hall when the town finally became incorporated in 1875.

Ten years before, the *Nanaimo Gazette* had demanded that Nanaimo be incorporated. Only in that way would a decent proportion of the taxes collected from the citizens be spent in the town. A meeting chaired by John Bryden passed a resolution in favour of municipal government. Those present at the well-attended gathering asked their representative in the Legislative Assembly, Thomas Cunningham, to present a bill of incorporation which would, among other things, allot property taxes to the town.

While the House of Assembly discussed the Nanaimo proposal, a faction that opposed incorporation emerged. The coal company general manager, C. S. Nicol, despite taking an active part in framing the bill, now decided to sign his name to a petition in opposition. He said it was important to wait until the two colonies of Vancouver Island and British Columbia were united.

No sooner had the Legislative Assembly received this petition than it was followed by a second petition saying the first one was fraudulent. It contained names of non-residents, including people known to be in England and San Francisco, and names of people known to be for incorporation. The counter-petition bore 179 signatures representing the majority of landholders and including thirty names which had appeared on the anti-incorporation petition. The meeting that generated the counter-petition voted seventy-five percent in favour of incorporation and ended with three cheers for Cunningham and the *Nanaimo Gazette*.

Demonstrating what they thought of incorporation, the opposition party placed a "Charter" in a tin box, which they sealed tightly and carried in procession through the streets, preceeded by a group of musicians playing out-of-tune music. When they reached the Long

Bridge, the box was lowered and disappeared into the thick oozy muck that comprised the bed of the ravine at low tide.

When the Select Committee of the Legislative Assembly in Victoria perused the two petitions it was found that the number of signatures exceeded the total number of adult males in Nanaimo. It confirmed the accusation, too, that the anti-incorporation petition contained names of people who no longer lived in Nanaimo or, in fact, never had. However, if the head of the Coal Company supported this petition it was obviously necessary to take it seriously. The committee then determined to see which petition represented the most property.

It was no contest. By far the largest property holder was the coal company, and C. S. Nicol had cast his vote on behalf of the Company in opposition to incorporation. The Company had only recently allowed private property ownership and obviously was not prepared to relinquish control of the affairs of the town just yet. The Select Committee in Victoria decided Nanaimo was not yet ready for incorporation.

Just how powerful and influential the Company was in the life of the town can be seen in this battle. Company officers had been influential on both sides. John Bryden, then a pit boss, and Robert Dunsmuir, mine superintendent, had been active on the original committee. Company clerk Mark Bate had been the Company mouthpiece through whom the original demand for incorporation was made in the *Gazette*.

Bate's avocation as a newspaper writer began when the *Gazette* started publication in 1865. It was through the editorials in this paper that the idea of incorporation had been introduced. It was not surprising that the *Gazette* was seen by certain influential people in town to be under the domination of the Company. They demanded that the newspaper sever those connections.

Ever eager to comment on Nanaimo concerns, *The Colonist* entered the fray. Was this an attempt by the "magnates of Nanaimo and their syncophants to gag the *Gazette*?" Was the paper "Too honest for the 'upper ten' of the busy hamlet?" Without knowing the identity of the "magnates" of Nanaimo, it is possible to guess that one of them owned the building that housed the newspaper. The printer, Joseph McClure, was ordered to vacate the premises. He barricaded the door and carried on as before, aided in his defiance by some of the town's miners.

On publication days, the miners would go to the office, drive the bailiff and "two or three vendors of tangleleg" away from the door, and pick up their newspapers. Sam Waddington, a disabled miner, continued his practice of collecting subscription money by going from door to door. Public sympathy seemed to be with McClure and "they bring him wine and all kinds of good things to cheer him up in his confinement."

Despite the support of the miners, however, McClure could not hold out under economic pressure. In late June of 1866, he opened the door to the bailiff and allowed the equipment to be removed to Victoria. There it was sold at auction to one C. W. Wallace, who returned it to Nanaimo and commenced printing a new weekly paper whose masthead said "Nanaimo Gazette" with "Nanaimo Tribune" in a box below it. *The Colonist* was very disparaging of this new venture. The *Gazette* was a "literary footpad," "an invalid paper," and "a sickly concern not worthy of being called a newspaper."

In contrast to its predecessor of the same name, the new paper was certainly not pro-company. When it died one year later, the New Westminster newspaper *The British Columbian* attributed its demise to abuse by the Governor; *The Colonist* disagreed, saying the paper was in fact an organ of government and died as a result.

Ten years later, no outside newspaper, no government, not even the coal company could prevent Nanaimo from getting a newspaper and a City Charter. In 1873 a meeting to discuss incorporation was told by George Walkem, then Attorney-General, that he and Nanaimo's representative John Robson were not on good enough terms to discuss the financial needs of the area. Robson, as editor of *The Colonist*, "stigmatised Walkem and his colleagues as rogues and liars and," opined Walkem, "this may be the reason why Nanaimo did not get justice."

But the intervening years had wrought a change. British Columbia was now a province; there were many more people in Nanaimo, and many more of them were property owners; the Coal Company was now co-managed by John Bryden, who had continued to believe in the necessity of incorporation. While still the most influential landowner, the Company was not in the position of power it once had been. Not only was the management fragmented and therefore weaker, but there was a second major employer in the area in the person of Robert Dunsmuir.

Dunsmuir had always been in favour of incorporation, and it was his son Alexander who, in a letter-to-the-editor in the brand new *Nanaimo Free Press*, announced a new petition to reopen the issue of

211

incorporation. Alex Dunsmuir was just twenty-one, but he had been his father's "contact" man since he was nineteen, and he spoke for his father in this issue.

The petition was greeted with the usual charges of false signatures and false pretenses, but the time was right. The provincial *Gazette* of December 26, 1874, announced that a bill to create the City of Nanaimo had been passed. The business of the new city, under its first Mayor, Mark Bate, would be supervised from the homely little stone cottage built by the HBC twenty-three years before.[8]

In the first few years after incorporation, Nanaimo prospered. An outsider noted that it had all the amenities, was beautifully located, and bore little resemblance to the dark colliery villages of England. Newcomers continued to arrive in great numbers and house construction was brisk.

In downtown Nanaimo, wooden sidewalks kept ladies' dresses out of the mud. Of course, the city council had to be reminded to deal with the nails that worked their way up and caught on hems, and when the ladies had to cross the street those same hems got muddy anyway, but progress was being made. One could still shop for hats and stays at Mrs. Raybould's and almost anything in dry goods at Alex Mayer's or William Parkin's. Romano and Quagliotti's across the Long Bridge on Victoria Crescent was not quite so respectable because they did so much business with Indians. Indian patronage must have been lucrative for Messrs. Romano and Quagliotti, however, for they stayed open from seven in the morning until midnight if there were any customers around, and they required their clerks to be able to speak Chinook.

The employment base of the town was becoming diversified to some extent. Besides the Newcastle Island Quarry, there was the Dawson Whaling Company and two sawmills. Robertson and Company Sawmill had a steam whistle which could be heard in Wellington, too, four times a day beginning at 5:15 in the morning.

Down on the Millstream was another sawmill owned by a Yankee named Chauncey Carpenter. His employees lived in old HBC blockhouses, each square logged building having two stone fireplaces and iron-bound shutters over the small windows. Inside were rows of

---

[8] When City Hall moved to the Literary Institute building in 1887, the Old Stone House became the Bank of British Columbia for two years. For another three years it was the office of Police Magistrate Joseph Planta. In 1893, after serving as a steam laundry for less than a year, the little cottage was torn down.

bunks over which rats scampered all night long. A man had to cope with the rats and provide his own bedding, but the food was good. For an eleven and a half hour day you could make thirty dollars a month and board. That was not as good as you could get in the mines, but it was a lot nicer than going underground.[9]

One of the men working for Chauncey Carpenter was a nineteen year old straight off the boat from the Shetland Islands. The *Manitoban* had carried Eric Duncan away from Scotland as a steerage passenger with no assets but his youth. The boat required its steerage passengers to supply their own tin plates, billy cans, and cutlery, but Duncan thought the food was good — porridge with black treacle, meat and potatoes, good bread and butter. The butter turned out to be mostly suet, but he had no complaints. He landed in Quebec and took a train to Sacramento, sleeping on slatted seats and buying food at stations for thirteen days. Then followed a boat trip from Sacramento to San Francisco. The sun beat down on him the whole way, and the only remedy for the thirst was a hogshead of yellow river water.

The *City of Panama* out of San Francisco was the "narrowest boat for her length" Duncan had ever seen. When she turned broadside and started to roll, a fellow passenger touted brandy as a sure cure for seasickness. Soon, however, he was seen "flat on his back in the scuppers, bawling like a calf, with vomit all over him, and the bottle rolling and dancing beside him." The passengers were confined to the open deck for the four day trip. Meals consisting of over-peppered soup, low grade meat and vegetables, and broken hardtack were eaten standing up at a swinging table suspended from the top deck. They slept in hammocks which were stretched between the stanchions every evening and taken down every morning. Duncan's destination was the farmland around Comox, but he stayed in Nanaimo long enough to work for Chauncey Carpenter and witness the fire of 1878.

Sooner or later, a town surrounded on three sides by tall timber was a sure candidate for a major fire. Every year, people dreaded the hot, dry summer days when bush fires threatened the farmland and often the town itself. In 1872 the bush fires south of town could be seen leaping from treetop to treetop. There were bush fires north of town

---

[9] Carpenter would later build the barque *Nanaimo* to ship his lumber abroad.

that year too, as far north as Qualicum. All summer the air was filled with smoke.

Despite the ever-present danger of fire in the summer, Nanaimo had no fire department, and though the Nanaimo Water Works had been formed in 1866, water was still obtained from the spring in the ravine and distributed throughout the town by bucket. The town consisted entirely of wooden buildings except for City Hall and John Hirst's new stone warehouse near his dock at the foot of Wharf Street.

From Hirst's warehouse, Wharf Street ran along Commercial Inlet and into Commercial Street, and all the buildings on the Inlet side rested on pillars at the back and dry land at the front. The lower side of Commercial Street was "practically a string of saloons" — the Britannia Hotel, What Cheer House, and Elizabeth Gough's Nanaimo Hotel among them. On the afternoon of April 20, 1878, there was a strong northwest wind which fanned a fire started by sparks from a chimney. Soon the buildings with their backs to the Inlet were a mass of flames.

The fire quickly attracted hundreds of people — people to fight the flames and people to gawk. Chauncey Carpenter gave his employees at the sawmill a holiday to see it, and many of them confiscated the liquor bottles being thrown out the windows of the burning saloons. But some people tried to fight the fire, and others were able to help the victims save a lot of furniture and stock from their stores.

Someone called for blankets to be soaked and spread over the nearby buildings not yet touched by the fire. Alex Mayer, proprietor of the Red House store, supplied rolls of them, while John Hirst refused to relinquish a single blanket, even though his store front was charred black by the fire across the street. "There were loud comments on the generous Jew and the skinflint Englishman."

The victims of the fire included What Cheer House, Mrs. Ekstein's store, the Sturton residence, the Nanaimo Hotel, a fruit store, Wing Sing wash house, and Canessa's fish store and jetty. Alex Mayer had a damaged blanket sale, offering stout green blankets for $1.50 each. Many of Chauncey Carpenter's millhands got drunk on the purloined liquor, and could be seen late that night chasing one another with axes over Chauncey's lumber piles. Chauncey, however, was pleased. Now he had a market for all that lumber.

One month later the Black Diamond Fire Company was organized. The What Cheer House was replaced by the Royal Hotel. Elizabeth Gough, though recently widowed, rebuilt the Nanaimo Hotel and stayed in business until she died in 1899, having rebuilt the hotel a second time after another fire.[10]

Most bachelor miners lived in hotels or boarding houses. They were a transient lot and only stayed in town as long as there was work, or until the Constable ran them out for misbehaving. Until 1876 there was little regulation of the pubs beyond the requirement of a license. It was town councillor Peter Sabiston, a hotel owner himself, who proposed that pubs be closed on Sunday. From then on only medicines and, presumably, medicinal alcohol, could be sold on the Sabbath and then only between one o'clock and five.

Before the fire, the Black Diamond Saloon, the Identical Saloon, and Peck's Hotel on Victoria Crescent, the Miners' Hotel, Nanaimo Hotel, and What Cheer House on Commercial, the Britannia Hotel down close to Commercial Inlet, and the Old Flag Inn — strategically situated across from the Literary Institute — were in place to offer liquor, and in some cases bed and board, to all comers.

Since Robert Dunsmuir had severely limited the number of saloons in Wellington, travellers to that town were given every chance at lubrication in two new conveniently situated saloons. Newcastle House, sitting where the Wellington-Comox Road began at the Millstream Bridge, received its license in 1876. Two years later, George Mitchell opened the Quarterway Pub, so named because it marked one quarter of the six-mile journey to Wellington. After being refreshed at the Quarterway, a traveller heading north towards Wellington might take a side journey down the East Wellington road to see the big things that were happening there.

The trail came over the brow of a ridge, and down to the valley of the Millstream River. It was farming country. The whole valley had been owned by William Joseph Westwood, who bought it for one dollar an acre in 1864. When the farm buildings were destroyed by fire in 1871, and William died of apoplexy, he left his widow with five of her own children and five children from William's first marriage.

Robert Dunsmuir's discovery of coal just north and east of the valley led a lot of people to believe that there was coal under Mrs. Westwood's land. She was perfectly amenable to letting other people search for and mine whatever coal they found and gradually sold off most of the acreage to Robert Chandler, through his agent Ralph

---

[10] Elizabeth Gough must have been a formidable woman. When Edwin died she was left with seven children and would lose her youngest son, Reuben, in an explosion in Wellington in 1879. Although illiterate she successfully managed the family hotels right up to her death at the age of seventy-six.

Wingate. The price for six hundred acres with the coal rights was one hundred fifty thousand dollars cash.

To find the coal Chandler hired John Dick, an Ayrshireman who had arrived in the area with his brother Archibald over a decade before. He was among the first group of mine managers to sit their manager's ticket exams in 1878. If anyone could find coal it was John Dick. He had already proven himself working for the VCML looking for Chase River coal. Now he found East Wellington coal for Chandler.

Dick also found coal for Adam Grant Horne and his partner Peter Sabiston. The Sabiston-Horne Estate consisted of four hundred acres of valley land south and east of Chandler's property. The storekeeper and the saloon owner had no expertise, so they formed a company with building contractor Jacob Blessing and John Dick. Blessing would handle finances and Dick would remove the coal. The company operated a slope for three years in six feet of fine hard coal until Robert Dunsmuir and Sons purchased it from them.

This was not the first time Dunsmuir had bought out a smaller operator nor would it be the last. Setting a pattern that he repeated several times in the next decade, Dunsmuir shut the mine down and used its equipment elsewhere. A decade later the mine was reopened under the designation "Wellington Collieries Number Two Slope," and coal was extracted from it for just one year. The mine is interesting only in the nickname it was given for its brief life. It was "facetiously styled 'Jingle Pot'," the first time that this name is mentioned in the records. The rights to the coal would be purchased in the early twentieth century by another entrepreneur, the mysterious Alvo von Albensleben, and the nickname would stick, spawning a number of theories as to its origin.[11]

Sam Francis and Thomas Nichols were known as The Cornishmen, and they owned the Cornish Estate which nestled in close to the ridge of land on the west side of Dunsmuir's lease. In 1876 they discovered coal on their farm. Sinking a shaft they proceeded to mine night and day using exclusively Chinese labour.

The Cornish Mine or South Wellington Mine as it came to be called — it being south and west of Dunsmuir's Wellington Mine — received a great deal of cooperation from the VCML. Mark Bate loaned the Cornishmen some small ballast cars to help in the construction of their road. The Company gave them permission to cross

[11] See the author's book *Boss Whistle*.

its railroad grade when they built the three and one quarter mile long railroad to the wharf directly opposite the Fitzwilliam Mine on Newcastle Island and not far from the old building on the road to Departure Bay called Peck's Synagogue.

They obviously planned a major operation, purchasing the locomotive *Premier No. 1* from San Francisco and planning a pithead of some size. Rumours flickered throughout the district. The ventilation so far was totally inadequate; the shaft had to be timbered all the way down; an explosion blew the head gear down. John Bryden watched with great interest. The Cornishmen's property could give the VCML access to the Wellington seam.

Then, late in the year 1878, Thomas Nicholas announced that the company was broke. Sam Francis was reported to be away making financial arrangements. There was no money for payday. When Nicholas absconded and Francis tried to follow suit, the Estate was put into insolvency. Robert Chandler came forward with money to pay the men, and it was revealed that he had already helped the Cornishmen once before and held a mortgage on the property.

Chandler's help notwithstanding, Thomas Nicholas was forced to declare insolvency in March of 1879. At the auction of his property, Chandler was the only bidder. He appointed his agent Ralph Wingate to manage this mine as well.

Despite seventeen years of management experience, ten of them on the coast, Wingate could not run the mine to suit the Inspector. There was no brattice in the pit, insufficient air at the face, no fireman's report book; non-working levels were not fenced off; there was no barometer or thermometer, no brake on the winding engine or indicator to show the position of the load in the shaft. Firedamp, albeit in small quantities, occurred often; the roof was treacherous and required a large number of timbers.

By this time John Bryden of the VCML was becoming disenchanted with his longtime employer, and at about the same time he began to lose his enthusiasm for the Company acquiring the South Wellington Mine. Family loyalties were tugging at him. Mark Bate obsessively reported in his VCML Director's Diary each meeting Bryden had with his father-in-law, including fishing trips taken and visits to the office by Dunsmuir inquiring for Bryden. Bate's paranoia was understandable. His management partner was fraternizing with the enemy.

Robert Dunsmuir had also been keeping a close eye on activities at South Wellington. In fact, the mine was like a rat nibbling at his vitals, situated as it was on his flank, dangerously close to encroaching

217

on his lease. In addition, there was the annoyance of Mr. Quagliotti's saloon.

The enterprising Quagliotti had built his pub 240 feet from the mine and forty feet from the office where the men were paid. The inspector had frequently called manager Wingate's attention to this dubious situation, but Wingate seemed strongly in favour of it. Such tolerance was soon explained when Wingate was revealed as co-owner of the drinking establishment.

In November of 1879, two months after announcing the discovery of a good coal seam, Chandler sold the former Cornish Mine to Dunsmuir, explaining that the seventy-five cent tariff recently imposed by the American government had broken him. Not only had Dunsmuir acquired two of the three mining operations on his western flank, but he had also acquired the problem of Quagliotti's saloon. Writing to the Inspector of Mines, he said:

It is impossible to keep some men away from drink when it is so easy of access, and, as you must be aware, a very little taken on surface will make a man intoxicated when he gets below.[12]

The Inspector recommended to the Minister of Mines that a law be passed forbidding the sale of liquor within 440 yards of a colliery. Since a thirsty man will walk a great deal farther than 440 yards for a drink, and since future mines did have saloons close to the edge of mine property, it is likely that his suggestion was not acted upon. However, Quagliotti may well have moved his business elsewhere since Robert Dunsmuir was a man whose fatherly interest in his miners' welfare brooked no interference.

The decade began and ended with a strike, and there had been several in between. Even the Chinese employed by the VCML struck the mine in January of 1872. They contended that the temperature outside was too cold to work in and refused to work again until it moderated. The last strike of the decade was set against the deteriorating management and difficult mining conditions at the VCML.

John Bryden had been a close observer of the 1877 Wellington strike. He felt his own VCML miners were being paid too much, and if Dunsmuir was successful in getting a reduction in wages, then Bryden could get the same in his mine. But a reduction was mightily resisted by the Nanaimo miners. They said that the Wellington miners were as well paid at seventy-five cents per ton as the VCML

---

[12] This assumption is not supported by modern day miners.

miners were at one dollar "owing to our coal being worse to get and requiring more powder."

But the Board of Directors in London was demanding a wage reduction. Acting in accord for once, Bate and Bryden had resisted calling the miners together. They feared that such a meeting would lead to other meetings with other mines. The two managers preferred to "attack them section by section, to prevent combining, which we have done and with general success."

Just about the time they were going to reduce the wages in 1878, there was a large exodus of Indians and Chinese to the Fraser River fisheries for wages higher than the mines paid. The Chinese who remained were "very independent and did not feel like going to work at a reduction." Bryden eventually persuaded them to accept a twelve and a half cent reduction to one dollar and twelve and a half cents per day. Since the Chinese generally left Nanaimo in the spring for the gold mines and returned in the fall, Bryden hoped he could get them to work for a dollar when they returned.

Bryden made this observation knowing that many Chinese were refusing to work as runners, complaining that the work was too heavy. Those who would work preferred to work for Dunsmuir because he paid $1.25 per day. The VCML continued to lose white miners to Wellington as well. Dunsmuir paid less but the coal was much easier to get, Nanaimo seams being faulted and narrow.

Late in the fall of 1879, John Bryden still feared a strike too much to risk a general reduction in wages.

Strikes sometimes occur when least looked for, and a spirit of opposition is often developed in those whom one would have supposed to be the most easily managed. And in dealing with our men during some of our strikes we have not always been as firm with them as we should have been, and especially during the last one when they compelled us to discharge an efficient Doctor, and accept one who was at the time a cripple, and when they had accomplished this they boasted that they were master of the field and could make their own terms with the company.

And so, John Bryden, a man beleaguered on all sides — his employers demanding a wage reduction, his men flexing their muscles, his partner in management distracted by his other job as Mayor — vowed to deal with this crisis by giving the impression of great firmness. "I will tell the men there will be a reduction on January 1 and will start in the thick coal first."

219

CHAPTER VI

A Few Mostly Mischievous Fellows

The poor miners get barely enough recompense to keep themselves and families from the ills of abject poverty. The merchants, grocers, etc. in the town seem almost to share the same condition.

A. J. Woodman, Nanaimo resident

I do not however, like [miners'] meetings, as there are always some present who are ready for mischief.

John Bryden

Errors in men's time last month were numerous and serious. Too much time is given in some instances — and in others too little and in some cases none at all is returned for men who say they have been at work all the month!

Mark Bate

The Vancouver Coal Mining and Land Company (VCML) in 1880 was in a sorry state. The management team, bound together unwillingly, had to answer to the Board of Directors in London who in turn had to provide the largest possible dividends to demanding shareholders. In the scale of importance, dividends came first, followed by colliery improvements. Miners' wage increases came a poor third.

The coal body currently being mined by the VCML was heavily faulted, a liability exacerbated by Bate's insistence that they persevere in trying to work through the faults instead of seeking coal elsewhere. The new loading wharves were plagued by minor problems, each slowing down the marketing process. From a high of one hundred four thousand tons in 1879, production figures would fall to thirty-five thousand by 1883.

The two managers worked at cross purposes to each other — Bryden, the intolerant but experienced manager who allowed no changes in policy or instruction and Bate, the former office clerk and now popular Mayor of Nanaimo who could be persuaded to overrule Bryden and who, as some of the men knew, could be manipulated.

At the insistence of the shareholders, the new decade and the new year began with the announcement of a wage reduction. This had been mightily opposed by the miners who attended the preliminary meetings held to induce them to accept. Bryden's reluctance to call these meetings was probably justified. Only three years before, there were unions at all the mines in the area. Even though Robert Dunsmuir's strength in opposing the union at Wellington had resulted in the disappearance of all the locals, a new crisis could easily bring about their restoration.

Just the previous year the Workingman's Protective Association had formed in Victoria under Noah Shakespeare, a former Nanaimo coal miner from Brierly Hill who was also president of the Anti-Chinese Society. Unions were becoming something that an employer could not ignore, but the miners of the area were timid after the failures in Wellington. The VCML men had tried to get all the miners of the district to meet, but the Wellington miners seemed reluctant to attend meetings even when they were held in Brown's Hotel so close to Diver Lake.

Using a variant of "divide and conquer," Bryden had determined to ease in gradually his policy of lower wages. Having first made sure that a good supply of coal was on hand ready for shipping, he offered new stalls at eighty cents a ton with no allowance for narrow work. The Douglas mines were full of narrow seams, but after some delay a group of miners agreed to take the offer. Then Bryden notified the men in the Chase River Mine that there would be a twenty percent reduction starting March 1st.

Some complained bitterly and their complaints were justified. Reverend Cornelius Bryant observed privately that he did not see how they could live on the rate being offered. Others said little. Bryden began to think his plan would work until he saw a notice calling a miners' meeting. Having been refused in their attempts to have the Wellington men join them in a general strike, VCML miners determined to go it alone.

Some men quit work on March 1st, and by the 15th everyone was out. "Meetings of the men have been controlled and carried by a few mostly mischievous fellows, some of whom never even worked for us, but are at present idling about the town," Bryden said peevishly. His sources told him that quite a few men had opposed the strike but were outvoted. Any miners who were determined to work seemed to be leaving for jobs elsewhere.

Bryden wrote to the secretary of the Board of Directors in London suggesting he hire strikebreakers. "It won't be any use to try and get white men," he wrote.

There is I believe a good many Italians in San Francisco, and many of them are good miners, and if we find it necessary to get fresh hands, I think we should try them, as they are a class that would not be easily advised or intimidated.

John Bryden's reference to Italians not being white men may have been a slip of the tongue, but it did reflect the opinion current at that time with regard to Italians. The first group of strikebreakers to be brought into Wellington in 1877 were referred to as "Italians" even though the majority were not of that nationality. And it was Italian strikebreakers who would help defeat the union in the Pennsylvania coal strike in 1888.

This reputation had its roots in the origins of Italian immigrants. Until 1870, there had not been a political or cultural Italy. In that year Rome and Venetia finally joined the collection of separate states which had gradually united under King Victor Emmanuel II. The political unity of the new state was a fragile thing, maintained only by avoiding large issues. With the lowest literacy and highest birth rate in western Europe, with too many unskilled labourers for too few jobs, and with compulsory military service for all able young men, Italy had become an impossible place for many of her male citizens to survive.

Emigration was the solution for the most enterprising. The young men left to get work in North America, hoping to save enough money to pay off the family debts and provide dowries for their sisters. They had every intention of returning to Italy eventually, and the ties to the family in the Old Country remained very strong. In the New World their lack of family gave them mobility, which made it easier to move quickly to where the jobs were, especially in a strike situation. But this very bachelor state labelled them as less stable and therefore less desirable as residents of towns seeking repectability and permanence. Their status in the coalfields ranked only slightly above the Chinese, another group of itinerant bachelors.

The first Italians to come to North America were skilled miners from the industrial north. By 1870 there were over eight hundred Italian miners in North America, and by 1877 a few of them at least were on Vancouver Island. Among the dead in the explosions on the Island in the nineteenth century were Italians from the industrialized northern cities of Turin, Genoa, Parma, Piacenza, and Venice. Later, the poorer agricultural southern states would send out their young men, unskilled and desperate, to compete in the mines and factories of North America.

It is easier to document their continent-wide reputation as strike-breakers than to find a solid reason to explain it, although several have tried. Most were so poor at home that they were never in a position to bargain if they wanted to eat. Those who had jobs worked under a hierarchical system that accustomed them to be submissive to a boss. Because the strongest and most enterprising were the most likely to emigrate, expatriate Italians were apt to exaggerate a national tendency towards individualism. Coming from one of the most depressed areas in Europe, they found their situation in Canada good by comparison, so their lack of real grievances made them poor candidates for union recruitment.

Although there were enough Italians in Wellington by 1884 for one third of the dead in an explosion to be of that nationality, none of them had arrived as strikebreakers for the VCML strike in 1880. John Bryden's decision not to bring in strikebreakers may have been prompted by a directive from London, but perhaps his attention was simply diverted by another problem. For suddenly his time and energies were entirely taken up with a fire on the Company premises.

Every night it was the custom to bank and tamp down the fire in the machine shops located near the loading wharves. Once this was done, the employees left for the night, leaving the building unattended. It was not thought to be necessary to hire a night watchman, the shops being in a very public place with people passing often, especially when there was a vessel at the wharf. Besides, the city watchman checked all buildings for possible fires, and Bryden himself lived so close by, in one of the fine homes on the Esplanade, that he could check the shops from his bedroom window.

Up until the time of the strike, it had never entered anyone's head to worry about arson, the VCML work force being considered friendly by management. But on the night in question Bryden was restless. He had offered the striking miners a scale rate according to height of the seam but had been refused. As he paced restlessly in his bedroom he glanced out the window from time to time. About 4:40 a.m. he checked once more and then finally fell asleep, only to be wakened twenty minutes later by the strong glare cast off by a fire which burned the machine shops to the ground. Despite Bryden's suspicions that the fire had been deliberately set, he was not able to prove it.

By the end of April, however, Bryden was feeling more optimistic. Some of the miners were reported to be trying to get others to return to work. Then the Board of Directors interfered again. A telegram arrived from John Rosenfeld, the Company's agent in San Francisco. "Directors leave decision to me, I advise you to resume work immediately on best terms."

The same board that had caused the strike by its insistence on lowering wages had ended the strike by yielding to the men's demands. It was too much for John Bryden. The Company had gained little and "the men are naturally emboldened by their success and will be ready to work us further mischief." His letter of resignation was addressed to the man with whom he had been corresponding for some time — Samuel Robins, secretary to the Board. "I fear," Bryden wrote, "that my influence with our men will be very much lessened, and consequently my usefulness to the Company very much impaired." When he left to become manager of the Dunsmuir collieries, it surprised no one.

John Bryden had been correct about the mischief makers. Nanaimo labour was emboldened by its victory in 1880. A second strike occurred in the fall of 1881 as the Company, managed solely by Mark Bate with William McGregor supervising the day to day work in the mines, continued to experience major difficulties. The market was weak, there was more water than usual in the mine, and a fire in the Chase River Mine burned for four weeks, losing the Company orders which were quickly picked up by Dunsmuir. The Fitzwilliam miners had walked out in March of 1881 in a dispute over free coal for miners' homes; winch men demanded and received a twenty-five cent increase in May; in June the Company's solution to the problem of loading coal in a very steep area angered the miners; that summer the Number Four level men wanted compensation for dirty coal. And each time Bate had given in.

When most of the miners walked out in September 1881, however, the board instructed Bate to take a tough stance. With three thousand tons of coal stockpiled, a strike would free up capital for the development of a big new mine that just might solve all their problems. By the end of October, the striking miners had returned to work.

Exploration had started the year before, using the diamond drill boring machine that the Company had been using since 1875. A ripple of excitement spread through the town when it became known that a huge body of coal had been located close to the beach half a mile south of the shipping wharves, six hundred feet down, eight feet thick, and very hard. The sinking of a shaft commenced in May of 1881.

Workers made an open cut twenty feet deep in from the beach, then sank a shaft twenty-four feet in diameter a further twenty feet through alluvial gravel and clay until they hit solid rock. Building from the bottom towards the surface, they lined the sides of the shaft with timber blocks two feet six inches long, butt end to the shaft, leaving an opening eighteen feet in diameter. Clay filled the space between the blocks and the wall. When the crew pumped the water out they found the shaft stayed almost dry.

Now the sinking proper commenced, using a compressed air drilling machine with shots fired off electrically. Good progress was made until half way down the proposed six hundred feet. Then water began to flow in freely. At first a double direct acting engine with two sixteen-inch cylinders receiving steam from two boilers handled the amount of water, but later a larger engine was erected, a double engine with thirty-inch cylinders and winding drums fourteen feet in diameter. This, the largest engine in British Columbia, was imported from England aboard the Hudson's Bay Company barque *Princess Royal*, which was still in service and still allied with coal miners.

Clearly, this was not just another mine. No expense was to be spared in what must have been a desperate move on the part of the directors to make the Company start to pay. Invitations were issued to observe the "monster" engine, as it had been dubbed, being lowered into place. So much steam was needed to get it running that its start-up had to be postponed.

Once the water problem was under control, sinking resumed. For a while things went fine until the water coming out of the rock became strongly impregnated with gas so painful to the eyes that "the greater part of the sinkers had to leave off work at times." Even with the installation of a fan to supplement the one already in use, the sinkers could only stand to work for three-hour shifts.

Harry Biggs worked on that contract sinking Number One. He was born in 1856 right there in Nanaimo and grew up in a log house on the 160 acres his coal miner father had preempted across the harbour from where they were sinking the shaft. His father died wealthy and respected in 1899, having converted passage on the *Princess Royal* into a tidy fortune in livestock, but his sons Harry and George were coal miners just like everyone else.

The problem of the gas encountered by the sinkers was relayed to London. The board did not believe that a little gas could be such a problem, so they sent Sam Robins out to investigate, or that was the reason people chose to believe for the appearance of so eminent a personage.

Of all the men at the VCML office in London, there was no one as well informed about Nanaimo as Samuel Matthew Robins. Nor was there a man more likely to find a solution to the management problems plaguing the Nanaimo operation. From a background in managing both mines and manufacturing establishments he had been hired by the London office in 1869, the same year that Robert Dunsmuir discovered coal on the other side of the world. The two men were to become bitter enemies.

The same John Rosenfeld who had recommended the end of the strike recommended that Sam Robins should come to Nanaimo on an inspection tour in July of 1883. The gas problem notwithstanding, a fine camaraderie had developed among the sinkers and a friendly rivalry between the three-hour shifts as to who could bring up the most buckets. The "Old Stiffs" challenged Big 'Lijah Smithhurst's crew and beat them soundly.

On October 26, 1883, at ten o'clock in the evening, Douglas seam coal was reached in the shaft. Four days later, a bullock was roasted whole to feed the three hundred invited employees and guests who filled the upper and lower levels of the Institute Hall for the traditional "Winning the Coal" banquet. Surely this mine meant the beginning of better times.

Replete with dinner, the assembled guests listened as Sam Robins, undeterred by the euphoria of the event, made a hard hitting speech. He did not wish to review the dismal company record of the past five to six years. "It would be a gloomy task, and we will let the dead past bury its dead." He knew that the general opinion in Nanaimo was that the VCML "was a stupid old company and the proprietors had more money than brains," but he believed the Board of Directors had been deceived in the past. Things would be different now.

By year end the shaft bottom had been made secure with large timbers, some twenty-four inches square. Two drifts had been driven away into the coal for some considerable distance. Both drifts lay beneath the harbour, the one to the south in a seam which gradually thickened to eleven feet and the one to the north staying at about seven feet. The head gear was under construction, railway sidings were laid, and ships already waited for coal.

No one knew just how extensive this mine would be, for its coal lay primarily under the sea, but the Company had big plans for its development. Such a large mine would need an extremely effective ventilation system, but just how large and powerful it had to be was a lesson learned painfully.

A second shaft, or updraft, is necessary to ventilate any mine. Just seventy-five yards away from the main or downcast shaft of Number One Mine, the updraft shaft reached coal, but there still had to be a connection between the two. Before that connection could be made an explosion occurred, an explosion in which four men were burned and two were killed.

New mines are especially gassy, as the methane which has been trapped for millions of years within the coal is released. The ventilating system must be strong enough to sweep the gas away before it can explode. Number One was so gassy that open flame lamps, the ones preferred by miners for the bright light they gave, could not be used. Instead Davy and Geordie safety lamps gave their safe but dim illumination. In addition, firebosses were required to check the workings for gas before the miners could go to work. All these precautions were rendered meaningless, however, by the fact that some of the safety lamps "drew gas."

Until the two shafts could be connected, the mine was ventilated in a makeshift fashion. A pipe extended down the main shaft from the surface to the bottom to bring in fresh air. Nearby, a manually operated fan sucked the air both fresh and foul from the mine floor through a system of ten-inch-square air boxes installed to within seven feet of the working face.

Manager William McGregor was just twenty-nine years old. Although he was an able young man, he had no experience in new mine development, especially on such a large scale. Inspector Archibald Dick was a qualified colliery manager and had been inspector for four years. With no other coal mining areas yet developed in the province, he was able to live in and devote full time to the Nanaimo-Wellington area, and he guided McGregor step by step as the new mine developed.

The brattice was too far back. There were potholes in the roof where gas could collect. The ventilation system was not strong enough for the amount of gas being released. Gassy areas should be fenced off and a notice posted to warn miners. Gas at the face and in the potholes should be brushed out. The mine was exceedingly dry. There were too many men in the mine for the amount of ventilation. The warnings and directives from the inspector mounted.

On February 19, 1884, in a drift full of gas, an explosion burned the face and hands of miner Ah Hin. Inspector Dick investigated, told acting oversman Joseph Randle that the air pipe in the shaft did not come close enough to the fan, and wrote up his recommendations in a letter to McGregor which he then mailed! The letter did not arrive for four days, one day after a far more serious explosion had occurred in exactly the same place.

On February 22nd, Joseph Randle, in his capacity as acting oversman, instructed Joseph Guthro, a fireboss, to push the heading through as fast as possible to connect with a heading coming from Number Two shaft and thereby complete the connection that would give the mine a proper ventilating system. Guthro was told that he was in charge of checking for gas, brushing out any potholes, and firing the shots for his crew, which consisted of Randle's father, Joseph Sr., David Hardy, and Sam Harris.

Sam Harris should not even have been there. His health had been terrible for years even though he was a relatively young fifty years old. Despite his altercation with Robert Dunsmuir during the 1877 strike, he had continued to work in the Wellington mines until he had almost died in a fall of rock in 1883. By then Number One Mine in Nanaimo was hiring and Sam tried his luck there.

Perhaps it was his experience that made McGregor take Sam on, or perhaps there was such an acute shortage of men that even a man as sick as Sam was of some use. His chest was so weak that his cough almost prevented him from walking home from work each night. His friend Sober Tait said, "I thought he would have died long ago." Sam was not fooling himself. He knew that one day one of his spells would carry him away, but a man had to put food on the table. And so he worked.

Sober Tait was working nearby, frustrated by his Geordie safety lamp. "I couldn't see anything with it . . . you couldn't see much with it at best." The crew had Geordie and Davy safety lamps, and Guthro used one to check for gas in the drift. The rest of the miners' lamps sat on the floor beside them, casting a dim glow as Hardy and Randle drilled into the coal and Harris turned the fan.

Hardy tamped the hole, charged it, and lit the shot with touch paper ignited with a match struck by Guthro. A match in a gassy mine can be as lethal as knife to the heart. Afterwards someone tried to explain their foolishness by saying "It must have been clear [of gas] or they could not light the touch paper with a match." The oversman

228

said that Guthro did not do his duty; he ought to have brushed out all the gas. But Guthro had been placed in charge and "we put all confidence in Guthro."

From his sickbed Guthro would say that he expected he was to blame for the explosion. If he knew that the safety lamps were drawing gas or that the fan was not pulling enough fresh air, then he was indeed responsible. But the roof was too high to brush properly and should have had a brattice curtain to direct fresh air up to it, and there was in that roof a fifteen-foot-long pothole which may have had some gas lurking in its upper reaches. Those things were discovered at the inquest into Guthro's death two months later.

The small crew had moved back about forty yards for the firing of the shot at 1:15 a.m. An explosion immediately ripped through the drift, which according to one witness "was making gas pretty free." David Hardy saw a momentary flash, and then flame scorched the exposed flesh of his face and hands.

Henderson Davidson was the bottom man for Number One shaft, on duty one hundred yards away from the explosion. It threw him on his back for two or three minutes, but he was not burned, and when he came to his senses he reached for the small stick tied to the rope to signal for the bucket to be dropped. The bucket was used to raise and lower men and material until a permanent cage could be installed. Someone at the top of the shaft heard the signal and lowered the bucket. Then he received the signal again and again.

Davidson waited in frustration at shaft bottom. Despite several pulls of the signal rope, no bucket appeared. In the complete darkness following the explosion he could not see what the problem was. He could hear the cries of the injured miners as they screamed for help in putting out the fire that burned their clothing, and he knew that afterdamp would be filling the drift and creeping toward shaft bottom, but still there was no bucket.

In the darkness Guthro called "if there is any person not burned for God's sake put out my clothes." Hardy's, Harris', and Randle's clothes burned, too. Sober Tait and Alfred Miller braved the afterdamp to extinguish the fire, but the damage to the men's faces and hands had been done. Guthro said he felt like he was burned inside. Miller and Tait and George Biggs helped the four to the shaft bottom.

Still there was no bucket. On the surface, the headworks had been destroyed, but William McGregor and two helpers were able to pull the bucket up. They climbed aboard, determined to find out why Davidson kept signalling from the bottom. At a point several feet above Davidson and the waiting injured miners, the bucket stopped, its descent impeded by rubbish. Once this was cleared away, the bucket was able to descend.

But it had been half an hour since the explosion. Afterdamp was strong in the drift. The burned miners moaned and shivered as their shocked and assaulted bodies began to feel the pain of the severe burns. As soon as the bosses climbed out of the bucket, Hardy, Randle, and Guthro were loaded aboard. Poor old Harris had to wait another ten minutes for the second trip because the bucket could only take three at a time.

As soon as Joseph Randle, Jr. heard about the explosion he hastened to the mine and descended the shaft, not realizing that his father was one of the victims. He checked for fires and then returned to the surface and headed for home. It was only when he reached there that he found that his father had been burned.

Fortunately, the burns suffered by Hardy and Randle, Sr. were not severe, and they were able to resume their normal routines in a few days. Hardy, however, could not bring himself to return to the mine. Five days after the explosion, Sam Harris succumbed to death "by shock to a worn out constitution." His funeral, under the auspices of the Knights of Labour, drew a large crowd which followed the cortege to the graveyard and slowly filed by the grave, each man dropping a sprig of evergreen onto the coffin.

When word of a disaster spread through a mining town, it was common practice for all the doctors in the area to converge on the site. In the wee hours of February 22nd, one of those who arrived at Number One had been Dr. William Wymond Walkem, the colliery physician for East Wellington. Guthro had asked him that night if he would attend him, but Walkem had said, "You have your colliery surgeon, he will attend you." In the rivalry that accompanied doctors' mine appointments, the patient did not always receive care from his physician of preference.

Dr. Daniel Cluness was the colliery physician hired by the Number One miners. McGill trained and faithful to his charges, he had nonetheless made himself unpopular with some people since his arrival on the Island. By refusing to live in Wellington when he was colliery physician there, he lost the miners' confidence and they voted to replace him. His purchase of a drug store in Nanaimo, while not unusual, struck some people as a conflict of interest. His propensity for strong drink, which ultimately caused his death from a cirrhotic liver, may have prejudiced some of his patients against him. Whatever the reason, his appointment to care for the miners of Number One was not universally popular.

Joe Guthro needed medical attention desperately. Following the custom of the time, Joe was cared for at home by his wife and his mother-in-law. To assist the women in the round-the-clock, seven-days-a-week task of caring for the severely burned man, his boss, Mr. McGregor, hired three of his fellow miners.

The unlikely nursing team consisted of Michael Corcoran, Sam Waddington, and Johan Henry Westfeldt. Westfeldt was a Dutch-man who was no stranger to mine accidents, having witnessed the 1879 explosion at Wellington and having himself been injured twice in falls of coal.

With surprising tenderness and dedication, the miners' nursing team administered morphine, physic, and laxatives, changed bed clothes and dressings, and straightened burn contracted fingers. But despite the care and the daily visits by Dr. Cluness, the patient's burns became infected and the man began to have terrible nightmares. When the doctor himself became ill and could no longer attend the patient, the family turned to Dr. Walkem, the man they had wanted in the first place.

The Guthro home with its small rooms and single floor with only a carpet to prevent the dust and wind from leaking in between the boards, was not a perfect place to care for a sick man. When Dr. Walkem entered the bedroom he was appalled by the sight that met his eyes.

The room stank. There was oil everywhere. Guthro's temperature was 105.5 degrees, and his pulse raced at 154 beats per minute. Dead skin putrefied on his burns, and the edges of the sores were dark coloured and sloughing. When the doctor sat the patient up he saw a carron oil dressing and several bed sores. The wasted and pain-wracked body lay on filthy sheets contaminated with fecal material.

In consultation with Cluness' partner, Dr. Robert O'Brian, Walkem ordered a complete change of treatment. The room was stripped of carpet and curtains. The importance of frequent linen changes was stressed. A regimen of carbolic oil dressings, quinine and iron, small doses of calomite, and brandy and milk mixed with glycerine and water caused the symptoms of blood poisoning to disappear over the next ten days. Having proved himself to be the more effective physician, Walkem successfully blocked Cluness' return. But the patient's improvement was short-lived.

On March 22nd, Johan Westfeldt went to Dr. Walkem's office in the doctor's home for instructions for the night. He was given some powders and a bottle of brandy. He asked the doctor what he thought of Joe. Walkem said, "Joe is all right." Westfeldt said, "Doctor, I believe Joe is going to die." "Yes," said the doctor, "and so are you but it will take a long time yet." Westfeldt returned to his patient and gave him a mixture of brandy, sugar, and water. Joe Guthro died twenty minutes later.

At the post-mortem performed by Dr. William McNaughton Jones, newly returned from his labours at the New Westminster Lunatic Asylum and now quarantine officer for the port of Victoria, Westfeldt was required to identify the body. He had cared for his fellow miner every night from 6:00 p.m. to 6:00 a.m. He had seen him suffer and rally and die. His flat-voiced testimony confirmed Joseph Guthro's identity and hid what he felt as he looked down at him.

I saw the post mortem examination made by Dr. Jones. I saw the dead body today. I saw the dead body buried. I saw the Coroner and Jury at the grave where the dead body was. It is the same body that was buried. It is the body of Joe Guthro.

On the day after the explosion that ultimately took Joe Guthro's life, William McGregor received Archibald Dick's letter telling him that the brattice was too far back in the drift to effectively get rid of the gas. The letter had been mailed two days before the explosion. Also on the day after the explosion, the connection was made between the drifts of the upcast and downcast shafts. The gas disappeared in ten minutes.

The death of Joseph Guthro put the medical care of injured miners in stark relief. The first help a man received after an accident was from his fellow miners, untrained in first aid and dependent on their wits to save a life. Aside from the obvious step of pulling fallen rock or coal off the man or extinguishing a fire on his clothes, miners watched each other routinely for signs of distress. A man drowsy from inhaling carbon monoxide would be helped to fresh air; a man injured or dazed from an explosion would be helped to outrun and outsmart the afterdamp as it crept through the mine. Often the only thing that could be done while the men waited for the doctor was to give comfort. This sometimes came in the form of pouring cold tea from their lunch boxes on the man's face to refresh and soothe him.

The preference for home care over hospital care was universal. Hospitals were places where people died. The hospital was even referred to as the "dead house." Even if a man was a bachelor, he preferred to be nursed in his boarding house if his landlady was amenable. It was also the landlady who prepared his body for burial if he succumbed.

Home for the Chinese miners was a shack shared by four or five friends, who could be counted on to nurse each other if the need arose. Once the mine doctor had given initial treatment, the Chinese miner was hustled home to be treated "properly" by the Chinese doctor. Besides the obvious comforts opium offered to a man in pain, Chinese "medicine" included wine which they rubbed on sore areas and took internally. When asked by an inquest jury how Chinese wine differed from the usual, the witness said, "Chinese wine all same white man's wine."

Probably the Chinese culture contained just as many effective and noneffective methods for treating the sick as did the white culture. However, there was a tendency among Chinese mine workers to disregard or even undo what the white doctor had prescribed. This resulted in several slow and painful deaths for Chinese men in the little shacks clustered around each pithead.

The Chinese had become a significant part of the work force in Nanaimo and Wellington. Not only were they desirable to mine owners as runners, but they were now employed as backhands by many white miners. Although not trained or experienced as diggers, the Chinese had observed the mining process, and some were now in a position to dig coal on their own. It is not surprising therefore that the presence of Chinese in the mine became the major issue in the 1883 strike in Wellington.

The union movement in all mining communities had been suppressed effectively in the years since 1877, but after 1881 there was a resurgence of organizing activity, probably encouraged by Mark Bate's less than firm management policies. First there was a secret union and then the Miners' Mutual Protective Association (MMPA) was reborn. In April of 1883 the Wellington miners felt themselves sufficiently strong to hold a mass meeting to consider the formation of branch associations in Nanaimo and East Wellington.

The primary area of concern was the growing work force, which included many unqualified men, men whose ignorance or carelessness could cause the death of others. Wages were going down and land prices were going up as more and more men arrived to work in the rapidly expanding mines.

By August it was very apparent that Robert Dunsmuir and Sons — as the firm was now called since Dunsmuir bought out Diggle's share

233

in May of that year — was discharging union members again. A strike was called on August 10th and on the very same day the Company gave notice to the strikers to quit the colliery houses before September 19th.

The old pattern repeated itself. Robert Dunsmuir took to the newspapers again to make the public aware of his position. He published lists of wages and pointed out that most miners did not work very long hours. After they charged the blasting holes, they left their Chinamen to do the work. "Nearly all the miners at Wellington employed a Chinaman," he said. "One miner went on holidays and left his Chinaman to do the mining and still managed to clear almost three dollars a day."

The union did not counter this allegation. There was an awareness that the miners themselves had been responsible for the Chinese learning the mining trade. There were other problems, too, which the miners had brought on themselves. In an effort to gain contracts for running levels, they underbid each other so much that the low bids simply "gambl[ed] their muscle away."

Some members worried that it might be too soon to start the union. Others advocated temperance, saying "we must start with ourselves and shake off the great curse of intemperance, for in this community that is the curse of our cause." Despite a new awareness of the need for temperance, few of the miners at the meeting agreed. However, Robert Dunsmuir had been heard to say that if the men got more money they would only spend it on alcohol.

Dunsmuir was a determined man when it came to strikers. He requisitioned special police, paying for them himself as the law allowed. Rumour said that the policemen were there to make the Chinese work and that those who refused would be told to take their blankets and get out of town. Only thirty or forty Chinese and a few whites were left to work the Wellington mines by September.

Having come to the realization that the employing of Chinese helpers weakened their cause, union men unanimously agreed never to employ Chinese "in any capacity, under any circumstances, or conditions whatsoever." At a public meeting someone pointed out how quickly the Chinese had become a part of the economy. After a few men had employed them, others were forced by economic considerations to do the same; even miners' wives hired them to do washing and bought vegetables from them at a good price.

Unions were stronger than they were in 1877. When Alexander Dunsmuir arrived in Departure Bay on board the steamer *Alexander* with fourteen strikebreakers from San Francisco, the newcomers refused to work when the union men told them about the strike. One said, "I am a union man to the back bone." Some left, some got work in Nanaimo. They said the facts had been misrepresented to them in San Francisco.

John Bryden, having resigned from the VCML at the close of the strike in 1881, was right back in the middle of one in his new job as manager of the Wellington Colliery. In November he advertised for miners. The union told Dunsmuir that the issue was now the Chinese, not wages. Dunsmuir sent them to see Bryden, who would only meet with them as individuals, not as a union delegation. When Dunsmuir promised to rehire men if they came as individuals and promised to gradually remove Chinese from the face, uncommitted men started to return to work. By November 7th there were 140 miners at work, including forty Chinese who had formerly worked for individual miners but now worked for Dunsmuir.

Though the MMPA floundered and died, the impulse to combine did not. One month after Dunsmuir hired the Chinese miners, the Calvin Ewing Local Assembly 3017 of the Knights of Labour was organized in Nanaimo. It was the first Knights of Labour local in British Columbia, and it became the focus of union activity north of Victoria.

James Young signed the notice for the first meeting at the Foresters' Hall in January of 1884, but the chief organizer was Samuel Myers, an Irishman who had come to British Columbia for the Fraser River Gold Rush and had been rambling around the province ever since until he settled down in Wellington in 1877. Forty-five years old in 1884 and unmarried, Myers had been initiated into the order in San Francisco just the year before.

The Knights of Labour has been called "the most daring labour experiment of the age." It began in Philadelphia when Uriah Stephens, leader of a small group of garment workers, formed a secret society with oaths and elaborate ritual. Claiming to be "more than a trade union," its idealistic program stressed education, cooperative economic activity, and land and money reform. It favoured political action over strikes as a way for labour to improve its lot.

By the time the Knights of Labour arrived in Canada in 1881, it had dropped its secrecy and begun a period of rapid expansion. Local assemblies took anyone who worked for wages but specifically excluded lawyers, bankers, doctors, and anyone in the liquor trade. In its quest to improve the condition of labour, it sought to improve the

235

individual labourer. Instead of reading dime novels or popular religious tracts, members were encouraged to read social criticism. Temperance was promoted as a mark of working class independence. Ritual and symbolism was used to give members a sense of working class worth. In some communities the Knights of Labour even replaced church going, as members gathered for "labour sermons" instead.

Perhaps because the Knights of Labour did not encourage strikes, Robert Dunsmuir agreed to be interviewed by a member in October of 1884. In that interview, the increasingly powerful and wealthy coal baron candidly stated his opinions. Half the men at Wellington could not make a living without a Chinese helper. However, he did not like Chinese at the face, nor did he like them as loaders, for they "fill too much dross and rock, and the miner always excuses himself by blaming the Chinaman."

Dunsmuir said he needed the Chinese as runners though,

> but as soon as I get another mine open which will enable me to give every miner a place to himself and still produce the necessary amount of coal to fill my orders, I shall then stop the miners hiring Chinamen to load their coal. John cannot dig coal at all, at least not my coal..."[1]

Robert Dunsmuir had been "getting another mine open" with a vengeance since 1880, and especially since May of 1883 when he bought out his last partner, Wadham Diggle, for six hundred thousand dollars. He then renamed his company Robert Dunsmuir and Sons. His flagship mine, Number One Slope, had developed rapidly and now had several openings to the surface, including a connection through to the South Wellington Mine, which Dunsmuir had purchased from Robert Chandler in 1879 and converted to an adit level to drain all the water out of the big mine. Close by the coal camp of South Wellington was Number Three Pit, which had developed from a ten foot seam struck in 1881 in the Millstone Valley on the western edge of the lease. A trestle brought the coal from the mine portal on the valley floor up seventy feet to the top of the Bluffs close to where Number Four Shaft was sunk in 1881 through the tough conglomerate rock that formed the cap of the ridge and where Dunsmuir had first found evidence of his seam.

One man had died sinking Number Four Shaft. In order to make sure there was no gas present, Henry Adams — a former Wellington

---

[1] "John" was used to denote any Chinese. White people seemed unable either to remember or to understand the use of Chinese names.

union officer — and two fellow workers had foolishly lowered a naked light in the bucket. Having heard no explosion they hauled the bucket up again, climbed aboard, and lowered themselves down three hundred feet. Sixty feet from the bottom there was an explosion. Adams was killed, and William Craven and John Robinson were severely burned.

While Dunsmuir developed the coal body lying beneath the Bluffs, Chandler, undeterred by having had to sell the South Wellington Mine to his larger rival, persisted in trying to develop the coal to the west of the Bluffs in the Millstone Valley. The East Wellington mines, situated on the former Westwood estate, had excited interest in the whole community for their proximity to Dunsmuir's rich coal body.

On the nightshift in the early hours of January 16, 1883, work was well along in the sinking of Number One Shaft of the East Wellington Mine. The sinkers were taking a supper break in the little cabin at the top. Dick Williams, Bill Davis, Ben Rough, Duncan McLeod, Mark Churchill, and Sam Lowe ate quickly, and then sat talking for a while. When Sam could not sit still any longer, he got up and went out, taking his lamp with him.

Everyone liked Sam. He had come to the Island from Amador, California a few weeks before and already belonged to the Ancient Order of Foresters and the Order of United Workmen. Thirty-four year old Sam had a teenaged wife, Elizabeth, and two baby daughters.

Right beside the cabin where the men sat, the partially completed shaft plunged into the earth, divided vertically to allow for return ventilation. Ten minutes after he went outside, Sam's fellow workers heard a noise and rushed out to investigate. Sam was nowhere to be seen. Ben, Dick, and Bill clambered into the bucket and lowered themselves to the bottom, where they found Sam's body lying in a broken, lifeless heap.

When they brought Sam up, they carried him to the carpenter's shop and called the superintendent. At the inquest convened for later that day in the same carpenter's shop, each man was asked to testify. Dick Williams told his version of what he thought had happened.

This is my story to me how he went into the shaft. I should think that he went into that part of the shaft nearest the cabin door. The shaft is partitioned. I think he mistook the shaft door for the cabin door. They are only about three feet apart. The entrances to both places are similar. The cabin is a little wider. The deceased was in his usual spirits — his spirits were usually good.

The funeral at the Methodist church in Nanaimo was well attended by Sam's lodge brothers, who watched the young widow as she stood by the open coffin and gazed at her dead husband. All Sam's friends were there but she felt terribly alone. When she had returned to her new home she wrote the following to her sister Mrs. Agnes Childers, somewhere in the United States.

Vancouver Island, B.C.
Nanaimo, January 19, 1883.

Dear Sister

I scarly know how to tell you of the Sad death of my porr Husband but I cannot tell you I will Send the paper and that will do as well So do write me Soon as I feel the want of some relation in time of troubel God help me to bare it on a count of my Fatherless children Dear Sister I hope you will never have to go through what I have since last Tuesday it is so hard with Strangers.

from Elizabeth Lowe

One of Sam and Elizabeth Lowe's daughters was named Effie Galena. Over a decade later, when she herself was a mere teenager, she married Robert Kilpatrick, a former miner then well into his thirties. At the time of Sam Lowe's death in 1883, Kilpatrick was still a miner, having been born into a mining family in Sydney Mines, Cape Breton, and having come with them when they emigrated to the Island. He had been injured in a loose powder burn in Wellington Mine and would be one of the strikers against Dunsmuir later in 1883.

Being a man of vision and ambition, Kilpatrick soon realized there were safer ways to make money in a mining town. He and his brother Daniel supplied timber to the Wellington mines, they rented out horses and wagons, and they opened undertaking businesses in Wellington and Nanaimo. As Cumberland, Extension, and Lady-smith were developed in succession, they extended their undertaking parlours, livery stables, and sawmills to each town.

When Robert Kilpatrick died of stomach cancer in 1902, he left behind three young children and a very young, very wealthy widow. Effie Galena Lowe Kilpatrick was not going to be like her mother, however, raising small children by herself in a little coal town. She took her money and her children and moved to Victoria, where she bought herself a grand home on Fort Street. Her subsequent marriage to a lawyer did not bring her happiness. Nine years after Robert Kilpatrick had died in his prime in Ladysmith, his wife committed suicide by swallowing carbolic acid.

The rapid increase in development of mines continued to produce widows and orphans in the decade of the 1880's. In the tiny village of

South Wellington, whose houses clustered around the pithead and trestle of Number Three Mine, and whose miners worked Number Three and Number Four, seven women became widows on June 30, 1884.

It had been two months and sixteen days since an inspection had been done in Number Four Pit. Inspector Dick was very busy as he was also assistant government agent, but he reminded anyone who mentioned it that he was only required to inspect each mine every three months. Had he been in the mine more often he would have realized that it had become a practice in Number Four Pit for miners to have a safety lamp and a naked flame lamp at the same time, the latter defeating the purpose of the former by its very presence.

New mines produced a lot of gas. Inexperienced miners caused more accidents. Miners and owners were anxious to dig as much coal as possible and both became careless about the danger in the mines. When accidents occurred people were cautious for a time and then they became careless again. Only four months had gone by since the explosion in Number One in Nanaimo had killed Sam Harris and Joe Guthro, but in the accelerated atmosphere of Vancouver Island in 1884, four months must have been long enough for people to forget the danger.

The details of this explosion have been lost in the bureaucratic maze. All that is known is that gas was ignited by a naked flame lamp and that a fireboss was ordered to stand trial at the Assizes for culpable neglect. That the Victoria Assizes found "No Bill" against the fireboss, and that the *Free Press* laid the blame at the feet of careless and thoughtless overseers *and* incautious workmen, can have meant little to the families of the twenty-three mine workers who died that day.

Seven Italians were among the dead. Seven married men also died, leaving thirty children fatherless. John Gill's wife and two children arrived from Ayrshire on board the steamer *Rithet* just in time to see his coffin lowered into the grave. Many of the families were newly arrived, having spent all their savings just getting to Vancouver Island. A public meeting was called to organize relief.

From subscription lists sent all over the province and beyond to Washington and California, came fifty-five hundred dollars in just three months. Each widow received a fixed sum and an amount for each child according to age: the younger the child, the more money received. But the families of the single men from Pennsylvania or California, Turin or Parchanza, London or Swansea had only a distant memory of a son or brother who left for a better life in the Pacific Northwest and died young.

And Number Four took more lives. A fire in December could finally be extinguished only by flooding the mine in February of 1885. A connection with Number Three Mine was made and the Millstone River allowed to flow in. When the fire was extinguished and the water pumped out in April, the bodies of John Paul and a Chinese were found. Paul had been the first miner to be alerted when the fire was discovered, and he had raced off to warn other miners. When he tried to retrace his steps he became lost and died with the unknown Chinese workman by his side.

In that tragic and busy year of 1884, Dunsmuir also opened his biggest mine. On the western shore of Diver Lake sinkers reached thirteen feet of good hard coal at a depth of 234 feet on August 20th. In just two more weeks the shaft was completed, headgear and upper works were in place, and a railroad connected the mine to the Wellington Colliery track. Coal was also struck again up on the Bluffs in 1885, and the mine was given the designation Number Six.

This vast network of mines, their workings interlocking like a jigsaw puzzle, feverishly extracted coal from the Wellington seam. A network of railway lines, a three track arrangement which could accommodate both a two foot six inch gauge and a three foot one, drew coal from each mine starting on the Bluffs with Number Six, passing Number Four, and reaching the top of the trestle at Number Three.

The Wellington Colliery Railroad then curved to the east toward tidewater, meeting a branch from Number One Slope on the one side and a branch from Number Five on the other, before it made its way along the thin arm of Long Lake. From there the line struck out across country, gradually descending the height of land almost to where Number One Shaft provided an escape outlet for Number Five Mine. There a horseshoe-shaped corner was necessary to accommodate the steadily decreasing slope of the land. The locomotive that had pulled the coal cars this far was uncoupled, and one that had come up from Departure Bay was attached, it being impossible for a single engine to negotiate the turn.

The train with its fresh locomotive now made its way back almost paralleling the upper track and gradually swinging toward the water, crossing the trail to Departure Bay and staying on the height of land above the wharves. It was necessary for the track to go past the wharves, where the cars could again be switchbacked down to the loading area. Five locomotives, 150 wagons, and ten miles of track made up the total system.

It was still necessary to post signs warning would-be hitchhikers of the dangers of riding the coal train. Despite the warnings, there were frequent accidents, including one in which an Indian lad jumping from car to car fell between two of them and was cut in half. It happened at the Horseshoe Curve.

If anything, Departure Bay was wilder than it had been a decade before. A tiny resident population was outnumbered by a very large "foreign and migratory element" composed of sailors and deserters from ships. The only really respectable buildings were the Company office and the Dunsmuir home not far from the wharves. Joseph Harper ran a saloon which catered to the rowdy crowd. Sailors indulging in drunken fun fired revolvers and stampeded horses. It was not uncommon for the sun to rise on a body lying dead on the beach, another victim of a night's revelry. When two seamen asked Sam Fiddick for a ride in his buggy, held him at pistol point for a short time, and then jumped off, he considered himself fortunate.

Wellington was peaceful by comparison, and it made much more sense to have a jail in Departure Bay where it was needed. In 1881 Sheriff Drake and his chain gang constructed one close to the coal wharves. "Bummer's Hall," as it came to be called, consisted of one room with rings embedded in the wall to attach the chains of the prisoners, cells being considered an expensive luxury.

The lack of a jail in Wellington did have tragic consequences for a sailor arrested for disorderly conduct during a sports day. He was chained to an upright support in the stable of the Wellington Hotel. During the course of the afternoon, with people celebrating noisily outside, the sailor decided to attract attention by starting a fire. The stable burned so quickly that rescuers were unable to get inside to free the poor wretch before he was burned to death.

Sailors passing through Departure Bay were up to more than just drunkenness, commandeering wagons, and the occasional murder. Smugglers continued to use the coal ships to transport opium to San Francisco. In 1886 the steamer *Wellington*, one of Dunsmuir's colliers, was searched in San Francisco harbour. Eighteen packages containing ninety boxes of opium valued at nine hundred dollars were discovered in the forecastle. The perpetrators were never found and no one was arrested.

Wellington was a quiet collection of miners' homes and a few businesses. Most of the houses were so close to the mine, some miners went home for meals during their shift. The main road led right up to Number One Slope past houses built so close together it was almost possible to reach into a neighbour's window. Towering over the little cabins of the miners, the Dunsmuir residence with its two stories and twelve rooms called attention to how far the former coal miner had come.[2]

Although the town reached its peak population in 1885, it lacked many of the amenities of Nanaimo. The school was described as "a disgrace to any civilized community." The Methodist missionary complained that with a congregation of only sixteen, he had little to do. The Literary Institute no longer existed, and there were only two hotels. The lack of entertainment facilities contributed to the success of events like the Good Templars' socials and Fourth of July celebrations, Wellington being the only coal town to still celebrate the American holiday.

Dunsmuir continued to control the liquor outlets on his property. Wall's Hotel, formerly Chantrell's, dispensed alcohol on the shores of Diver Lake, close by the branch railroad track to Number Five Mine. In 1888 Wall's was renovated and reopened as the Wellington Hotel. Nearby, a bandstand was built to accommodate the new nineteen member Wellington Brass Band, its members, including both union men and management, resplendent in uniforms with caps bearing torches.

A story which lingers yet in the lore of Wellington says that in the early days Dunsmuir would occasionally drink too much at the hotel and have to be carried home by some of the miners. When the drunken party reached Dunsmuir's door he would say "Now all you sons of bitches be at work on Monday morning."

As he gained in stature and importance, his drinking sprees were more often conducted in Victoria and San Francisco, but he was never regarded by his family as having a drinking problem. The same could not be said about his son Alexander, who lived in San Francisco and gradually became more and more dependent on strong drink. He died an alcoholic at the age of forty-seven.

Just outside the northern boundaries of Dunsmuir's lease and thereby beyond his control, stood Somerset House, since 1880 the ideal location for heated discussions about "the master." The *Free*

[2] For a time, this house, called "Ardoon," also contained the colliery physician's office, the mine office, and the only telephone in town. Dunsmuir called his home in Nanaimo —situated by the bridge that crossed Commercial Inlet at Victoria Crescent— Ardoon as well.

Press took "the master" to task for not taking interest in the men's social intercourse. For a man whose paternalism had been overbearing at times, who refused to sell building lots because he did not want the miners saddled with useless land should the mines close, and who restricted liquor outlets for the public good, Robert Dunsmuir was remiss in not providing alternatives for culture and socializing.

Wellington never had a stable population in its years as a mining town. Dunsmuir's policy of only mining coal when there was a buyer meant that the miners were laid off when the markets were poor. A series of fires and floods caused several shutdowns, especially in Numbers Three and Four Pits. The insecurity of employment coupled with the Dunsmuir control of the town made for a constantly changing population. Cornelius Bryant, by then a Methodist missionary, described the situation when he wrote:

As the Coal Co. owns the whole town, and the people are only tenants, and, therefore, have no personal interest in the place outside of their wages, there cannot be other than a floating pop. here. Twenty-five families leave this year and are replaced; unmarried men constantly come and go.

There were some families who came and stayed, or moved to some nearby coal camp: Balagnos from Italy, Doumonts and LaBarrs from Belgium, Greenwells and Kilpatricks from Cape Breton, Hilliers from West Virginia, Littles from Illinois, McMillans and Polens from Nova Scotia, Parnhams from Wales, Treloars from Iowa, Wards from California. Legend also places Pancho Villa in Wellington digging coal. If the story is true then the Mexican revolutionary leader was eleven years old at the time.

The population of Wellington became somewhat more stable after 1887 when the new Esquimalt and Nanaimo Railway (E and N) reached the town, and a roundhouse and repair depot were built between the Wellington Hotel and Diver Lake. For the next twenty-seven years, until the railroad was extended to the Comox Valley, Wellington was the end-of-track and provided steady work for the men who serviced the engines and manned the roundhouse.

It is no accident that the E and N terminus was in Wellington, for the railway was another Dunsmuir project. Canada's Prime Minister needed someone to build the short line, and Robert Dunsmuir agreed to do it. He was the right man in the right place at the right time.

The story of how Robert Dunsmuir came to build the E and N and receive as compensation a reward out of all proportion to the task begins in 1871, when British Columbia joined Confederation on the

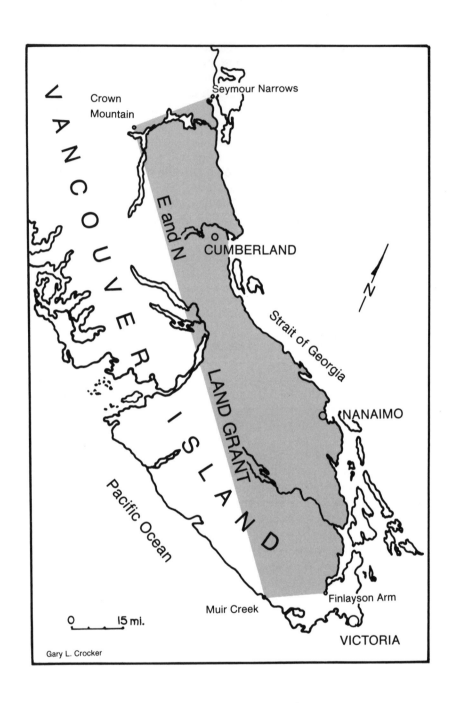

Crown
Mountain

Seymour Narrows

V A N C O U V E R I S L A N D

E and N

CUMBERLAND

Strait of Georgia

NANAIMO

LAND GRANT

Pacific Ocean

Muir Creek

Finlayson Arm

VICTORIA

0   15 mi.

Gary L. Crocker

N

E AND N LAND GRANT

strength of a federal promise to begin to build a railroad within two years. All British Columbia had to do was grant a twenty mile belt of land on each side of the line.

No one knew which route the railroad would take through the mountains. There were several alternatives and each had its supporters and detractors. Surveying crews clambered all over the interior investigating possible routes, but there was no doubt in the Vancouver Island delegates' minds where the terminus should be. The San Juan Islands had just been granted to the United States, and many saw them as an impediment to Canadian sovereignty, guarding as they did the entrance to the Gulf of Georgia. If the railroad terminus were on Vancouver Island, that sovereignty would be much more secure, to say nothing of the prestige and economic benefit which would accrue to the Island should the Bute Inlet-Seymour Narrows route be chosen. The railroad would then run down the eastern shore of the Island to its southern tip.

Just one day before the expiration of the two year period during which a start to the railroad had been promised, Sir John A. Macdonald announced by order-in-council that the terminus of the new transcontinental railroad would be the naval base at Esquimalt near Victoria. Although politically expedient, this announcement was stunningly premature, given that the route through British Columbia had yet to be decided. There seemed to be fairly general agreement that the mountains should be breached at the Yellowhead Pass, but mainlanders and Islanders disagreed sharply over the route through the province. Mainlanders wanted the Fraser River route; Islanders regarded Bute Inlet and Seymour Narrows as the only possibility.

During the next decade very little was done to advance a railroad. Macdonald's Tories lost power in a scandal involving Americans financing railroad construction. All through the term of the Liberal government which succeeded the Tories, Prime Minister Mackenzie dragged his feet. The idea of a transcontinental railroad was fiscally ridiculous, and the penurous Scot would have nothing to do with it. British Columbians, who had given enthusiastic endorsement to the railroad-based Confederation agreement, were by 1874 thoroughly disillusioned over the lack of progress.

In the spring of 1878, George Walkem, the miners' lawyer during the strike of 1877, was elected Premier of British Columbia as the man who would fight Ottawa. That summer Sir John returned to power in Ottawa, and this time he was the Member of Parliament for Victoria.

Macdonald had come to believe that the Fraser Valley route was the best one for the new railroad, it being the easiest to defend against the Americans crowding in to the south and the Russians lurking to the north from their Alaskan base. But as a blast of dynamite at Yale in the Fraser Canyon signalled the beginning of construction in May 1880, the citizens of Vancouver Island were very unhappy, and Vancouver Islanders made up a good proportion of the population of the province.

Ottawa and Victoria continued to fight. Ottawa wanted compensation for unarable land included in the railway grant and threatened to withhold subsidies; Victoria threatened secession and sent a petition to Queen Victoria. Although not the first to be sent to the monarch, this one finally impressed London and Ottawa. The all-red route to the Orient, the life-line of the Empire, was threatened if the docks and coal of Vancouver Island were lost to them.

In September of 1882 the Marquis of Lorne, Governor-General of Canada and husband of Queen Victoria's daughter, Princess Louise, visited British Columbia. Having watched and been impressed with the progress of railway construction in the interior of the province, he was stunned to find out how unhappy Vancouver Islanders were about the terminus.

The Governor-General quietly went to work to induce the reigning capitalist in the province to build a little line from Esquimalt to Nanaimo. Since Robert Dunsmuir had already made overtures in that direction, the task of inducement was easy indeed. All that need be decided were the terms. In the Settlement Act of 1884, the twenty-mile strip of land on either side of the railway line was transferred from the federal government to Robert and James Dunsmuir and John Bryden of Nanaimo and a group of American backers: Collis P. Huntington, Mark Hopkins, Leland Stanford, and Charles Crocker, the so-called Big Four of American railroads. The federal government also contributed $750,000 toward construction costs.

The E and N land grant consolidated the Dunsmuir fortune. Only the land already pre-empted by bonafide settlers was excluded from the vast tract of land that stretched from Seymour Narrows inland to Crown Mountain, straight down the Island to Muir Creek near Sooke, and across to Finlayson Arm. The east coast of Vancouver Island formed the other boundary. Included in the grant were all the surface rights including timber and all the sub-surface rights with the exception of gold and silver.

The passing of the Settlement Act in April of 1884 was celebrated

246

by some in Wellington. John Bryden gave a group of miners fifty dollars to toast the momentous event, and they announced their intention to go first to James Dunsmuir's home and give a cheer. When James sent word that they were not to come, there being a sick child in the house, they went directly to the pub for unlimited beer on Bryden. The Company pay clerk also contributed ten dollars. But a letter to the editor said that 99 percent of the local people opposed the bill and referred to the celebrants as "blacklegs and nobsticks." The acrimony of the previous year's strike could not be soothed by fifty dollar's worth of free beer.

What most interested Robert Dunsmuir about building the railway may well have been the coal lands he acquired. The lands adjacent to the southern border of the VCML coal lease well beyond Nanaimo were showing some promise. Having purchased mineral rights from James Beck, who had been there since 1868, and Sam Fiddick, who had preempted land in 1872 and again in 1884, the E and N opened the Alexandra Mine and named it in honour of the Princess of Wales, wife of the future King Edward VII. Within a year the mine was closed, but the valley would see many more miners in the next two or three decades, for this would be the site of the Black Track Mines.[3]

The first stake for the E and N was driven on May 6, 1884, and the last spike ceremoniously tapped in by Sir John A. Macdonald just two years and three months later at Mile 25, Cliffside Station, on the shores of Shawnigan Lake. The official train then proceeded north, taking its illustrious passenger, his wife Lady Macdonald, and Robert and Joan Dunsmuir to dine at the Royal Hotel in Nanaimo. For the two men, the combination of an interest in the finer details of coal mining and a mutual desire for a little whiskey was frustrated by the presence of the wives, until Dunsmuir suggested a mine tour. Six hundred feet below the surface in Number One Mine, the flagship mine of Dunsmuir's rivals, the capitalist and the politician, clad in overalls and liberated from the ladies' company, finally toasted the completion of the E and N.

The railroad was extended to Wellington in the following year, giving travellers a choice of two modes of travel between the two towns. By then, Wellington Road had shed its disreputable image and

---

[3] The mine was incorrectly called Alexandria for many years. Although Sam Fiddick sold his mineral rights to the E and N, his family acquired more through Sam's wife Elizabeth Grandam Fiddick, and mined the coal themselves until 1910 when they sold the rights to the Pacific Coast Coal Company.

was a "splendid gravel road." Elijah Ganner's son Joseph ran the Daily Mail Stage along its length and also offered his special spring wagon for parties or picnics at a nominal fee. The daily stage made regular stops at the Half-Way and Quarterway Hotels "to rest the horses" from their onerous task of pulling the wagon the six mile distance between the two towns. It was always suspected that the driver needed the "rest" more than the horses did.

Lavinia Malpass had occasion to travel the Wellington Road on board the stagecoach. Although small and delicate, the *Princess Royal* veteran could be formidable when necessary. She had once chased a large Indian man with a broom when he had walked into her house unannounced. In her middle age she was the mother-in-law of Sheriff Sam Drake and grandmother to a steadily growing number of grandchildren, thanks to her daughter Rhoda. Although she was tiny in stature, Lavinia Malpass was not a woman to be taken lightly.

Mrs. Malpass boarded the stagecoach in Wellington, where she and her husband John now lived. When the coach stopped at the Quarterway Pub, a desperate looking young man ran out of the woods and clambered onto the coach. He said someone was after him, and Mrs. Malpass thought he looked like a nice young man, so she allowed him to crouch on the floor with her voluminous skirts to hide him. When the police came looking for him — for he was an escaped prisoner from the chain gang — she threatened them with her umbrella if they did not leave immediately. The police obliged her.

Soon the driver reappeared, having refreshed both the horses and himself, and proceeded in the direction of Nanaimo, across the Millstream and through Company land thickly wooded on either side. The prisoner tapped the driver on the shoulder and asked him to stop the horses. He disappeared into the woods, leaving behind Mrs. Malpass to deal eventually with her outraged son-in-law, Sheriff Drake.

In the short six miles of the Wellington Road from the relatively "dry" Wellington to the wide open Nanaimo, it took two pubs to ease the traveller in need of a drink. In Nanaimo, although each hotel served two purposes, as a liquor outlet and a boarding house, it was in the sale of alcohol that these establishments excelled. In a town overflowing with single men, the fact that the rooms were "not very tempting places in which to spend the night" was immaterial. The hotels were there to provide strong drink and even did so at picnics and sports days, which were now deemed incomplete without a liquor stand peddling its wares alongside where the candy and fruit were sold.

It started to seem to a lot of people that there was too much liquor being peddled and consumed. The temperance movement, which had bided its time through the past two decades, blossomed as organized labour became aware of the harm that alcohol was doing to its members.

Management knew the great harm that liquor could do to the safety and efficiency of the mines. In a speech in 1882, John Bryden said, "Unanimity, constant care and above all temperance, in the officers in charge would materially assist in furthering the prosperity of the collieries." Union meetings in 1883 acknowledged the "great curse of intemperance." As the decade progressed, the Methodists, Good Templars, and the Women's Christian Temperance Union experienced a rush of interest and a growing membership. New groups like the Royal Templars of Temperance were formed; temperance groups built halls and filled them to capacity. At the forefront of the new drive towards sobriety were the Knights of Labour.

An equally important facet of Knights of Labour philosophy was the involvement of labour in the political process. As the qualifications for being a voter were gradually relaxed and broadened to include every Canadian man and every male British subject who had been in Canada for one year, politicians began to woo the working class vote. The Grits and the Tories had been ready to welcome the newly enfranchised working class into the fold. Being political neophytes, the workers were easily led to vote for the candidates chosen by the traditional parties. This traditional choice is best illustrated by the fact that Robert Dunsmuir was twice elected to the provincial legislature.

At a dinner in February of 1882, held in his honour before he left on a trip to Scotland, Dunsmuir mentioned his possible candidacy. In the subsequent election that July, he won the seat *in absentia*, his son-in-law James Harvey campaigning for him while he continued his European trip. For a man like Dunsmuir to be elected for the first time and not even have to bother to be there for the campaign, seems almost impossible given the animosity felt by many working class men towards him.

But in the heady atmosphere that pervaded the Island mining communities in the booming new decade, the working class vote had not been sufficient to defeat the absent Dunsmuir. Indeed, it is likely that many miners voted for him. He was a successful authoritarian figure and may have been seen by many as the kind of member no party in power could ignore when it came to getting government largess for his riding.

Four years later Robert Dunsmuir stood for re-election, but this time he was opposed by a labour candidate. The Workingman's Party, by now seven years old, decided to concentrate its efforts in Victoria and Nanaimo, and ran two candidates in each city. James Lewis, a former miner and now a Gabriola farmer, and Sam Myers, Knights of Labour organizer and miner, ran against Robert Dunsmuir and William Raybould, a city alderman.

Although the two labour candidates finished last in the polls, their defeat was partly due to a continuing lack of labour solidarity. Raybould had supported Abrams, the miners' candidate in 1878, and probably drew labour votes in 1886. Robert Dunsmuir also drew labour votes. Indeed a requisition asking him to run and signed by three hundred people included the names of J. B. Greenwell and Sam Fiddick. Clearly, the time had not yet come when most miners felt comfortable being represented by one of their own.

The day was not far off, however. Later in the same year, William Raybould died, and in the by-election called to replace him, James Lewis was elected, Sam Myers having stepped aside in his favour. The labour votes garnered by Raybould in the initial election now went to a candidate chosen by the labour movement.

And labour continued to pour into the province. "Come to British Columbia" said the government pamphlets of the decade. "The demand for labour is great and the wages are high." Comparing the province to Washington, Oregon, and California, the pamphlets boasted, "the climate is more healthy, there is more and better coal, taxation is immensely less, there are free unsectarian schools and the laws are better carried out. Every man who is able and willing to work with his hands and women unafraid of hard work are preferred over professors, clerks and high grade servants." This was the land of opportunity for the working class.

The VCML continued as well to advertise for miners in Great Britain. The ads were the stuff of dreams. Men who came to Nanaimo prepared to work hard and live frugally could expect to be able to buy land, build a house, plant a garden, make a decent wage, and raise a family in clean, open surroundings.

The pamphlets and advertisements said this was a land where dreams might come true. "A large free way of life prevails... men produce much, they consume much, and they spend much. No coin of less than ten cents is current." It was hard to resist the lure of land, housing, clean, open surroundings, and money.

The coins mentioned in the pamphlets were a recent addition to the currency of British Columbia. There were gold coins in twenty, ten, five, and two and a half dollar sizes, and silver coins in one dollar, fifty, twenty-five, and ten cent sizes, the latter being called the "short bit." Before the Canadian Pacific Railroad spanned the country in 1885, the most common currency was paper notes issued by the Bank of North America and the Bank of British Columbia. Before that, a mixture of American and Canadian currency had replaced the British money used since the earliest days on the Island.

Robert Dunsmuir used nothing but gold and silver once it was available. He kept a stock of five, ten, and twenty dollar gold pieces and sent rolls of gold coins to the purser on one of his boats, who used them to pay Dunsmuir's bills in Victoria.

Most of the people involved in the Island mines settled for considerably less than rolls of gold coins, however. Boys and Indians were paid $1.50 per day; white mine workers received between $2.00 and $3.50 while the Chinese still earned between $1.00 and $1.25. Contract miners, the elite workers in the mine who were paid by the ton, averaged between $3.00 and $4.00 per day.

There were, of course, deductions from that pay and some initial investment for equipment. To start work a miner needed a machie needle and tamper, a squib box, an oil can, two powder cans, an axe and a saw, the total package costing about forty dollars. Every month a man had to allow for the price of a new file to sharpen the drills, new squibs at fifty cents for one hundred, and oil and powder. Nanaimo mines needed a lot of powder to move the coal and Wellington mines needed even more. An 1870 Canadian duty had added fifty cents a keg to the price of powder, meaning an additional dollar to a dollar and a half each month per miner. This duty had been briefly removed in the early 1880's and reinstated in 1883. There was also a thirty percent duty on picks and shovels, which the miners also had to purchase themselves.

... any stranger would think some of the miners here are travelling tinkers, with their two powder cans, a fixing like an eight-day clock, and not forgetting the grub tins, all hung around his neck.

For the increasing number of family men living in Nanaimo, the pay earned in the mines after deductions was spread thinly unless there was more than one wage earner in the house. Miners received free coal and could get it hauled for a dollar under a special arrangement made by Mark Bate before he left the Company. Chinese miners avoided even that charge by picking up coal spilled along the Company railroad, a practice that became dangerous when white families started sending their children out to do the same.

A single miner lucky enough to find room in a boarding house or hotel could get board and room for six dollars per week. As the demand grew, the number of boarding houses increased, it being an acceptable way for women, and especially widows, to earn a living. There were hotels that catered to abstainers and those that catered to particular ethnic groups like Giuseppe Guffoti's Italian Boarding House on Haliburton Street, which opened in 1884 promising "Clean Beds! Good Meals! Free Bath!"

Free baths were a luxury only a long-time resident could really appreciate, the first proper waterworks having been built only in 1883. Wooden pipes made with a special auger that bored a four inch hole through small fir logs, ran across the Bastion Street bridge outside the railings, embedded in long boxes filled with sawdust. Still, there was a shortage of water in the summer.

The town had spread to the south where miners' houses now lined Haliburton Street, which had been just a cart track bordered on either side by a strip of green turf used as a footpath, until Number One Mine was developed. Tiny houses, poor and mean but many with bright flower gardens in front and vegetables in the back, sheltered large families.

Downtown Nanaimo's beauty depended upon the eye of the beholder. A disgruntled resident saw it as "a dirty, sprawling mining centre, the main street lined with flimsy wooden buildings and split with a rickety bridge over a stream filled with slime." This description outraged another citizen who pointed out that the main street was lined with various fine stores with plate-glass show windows and that the salt-water tides rushed up the Inlet twice a day filling the ravine and presumably covering the "slime."

The town was connected to Victoria and the mainland by a telegraph and a regular ferry service to New Westminster and the upstart Vancouver, the latter newly founded and about to usurp the former as the preeminent mainland city. The boat providing the service was the *Robert Dunsmuir*, called "Dirty Bob" by the locals because it carried coal as well as passengers.

Because the Literary Institute had closed its doors, reading material was even more at a premium, but the town had an Opera House, three stories high and built of brick with a facing of galvanized iron and cement. There was an auditorium forty feet wide and fifty-seven feet long, with a stage and dressing rooms, and an adjoining hotel with twenty-eight parlours and sleeping compartments. The entertainments presented there could hardly be called "opera," but they included the best that the circuits had to offer.

Picnics and sports days were by far the most popular entertainments. People of all ages watched and participated in "Climbing the Greasy Pole" and "Walking the Bowsprit," quoits, glass ball shooting and races, including a special one for married women and another for old men.

These were boom times and Nanaimo stretched and adjusted and cheered and gasped at the antics of newcomers and oldtimers alike. Cornelius Bryant was appalled. The redheaded giant of a Methodist minister sported red whiskers in his middle age. A temperance advocate since the age of seventeen and full of concern for the drunkenness and immorality he saw in his Indian parishioners, Bryant also found the white men he observed distressing. The leaders of the community, "those driving along in their fast carriages and their children... riding their fast horses and some of them I fear having their fast habits also" did not escape his censure. He was appalled by the profanity of the children in the streets and complained that even Sunday School children insulted their teachers and abused every unfortunate Chinaman they met enroute from Sunday School until they got into a "regular scrimage."

Jesse Sage was another oldtimer who did not like what was happening. Everyone knew who Jesse was. He had had one of his legs broken three times in the mines and it was now a couple of inches shorter than the other. This gave him a distinctive gait and made him easy to recognize as he stumped around town fuming about the dogs that were killing his sheep. "It would be advisable for all parties having valuable dogs to keep them at home during the next few days," he warned in a personal ad in the newspaper.

Sam Fiddick seemed to like the new influx of people just fine. The new E and N station drew them up Fitzwilliam Street, where Sam had built the Occidental Hotel on the corner of Fitzwilliam and Selby to cater to those making the long steep climb on foot or those newly arrived from Victoria. Of course the more fancy people heading for the Windsor Hotel downtown and its Delmonico Restaurant were met at the station by a free bus and missed Sam's establishment altogether.

Joshua Martell had been in Nanaimo for several years when he happened to meet Robert Campbell, who was newly arrived from Alaska but came originally from Cape Breton, where he had known Martell as a boy. Joshua had been in love with Campbell's sister, Barbara, years before and had lost her to another man during one of his frequent absences riding shotgun for wagon trains bound for Salt Lake City.

As he approached middle age, Martell was still a bachelor, but he had settled down from a life of adventure to work the new Number One Mine in Nanaimo. He was an experienced man, having mined coal in Nova Scotia and Ohio. Although he was employed as an oversman, he had qualified as a certified manager in 1883. Campbell told him that his sister Barbara was now widowed with one child and still living in Cape Breton.

Although Joshua made his living in the mines, he was articulate and wrote with a particularly fine hand. He penned a proposal of marriage to Barbara in the form of a five verse poem, which chided her for not waiting for him before and ended:

If the cap does not fit you just toss it away,
And say I'll have nothing to do with this sorry lad,
But if you should think you were fitted quite well,
Just drop a short note to Joshua Martell.

Barbara came west as soon as she could without even replying to the proposal. When she and her child reached San Francisco she sent word that she was on her way, and she married Martell in Victoria.

The boom in mining had brought many new people to the Island, the opening of Number One Mine being the most obvious manifestation of that boom. Although the huge coal body had been discovered under the management of Mark Bate, and he had supervised the development phase, the success of the mine and the steady recovery of the Company was due to another man entirely.

Sam Robins arrived in Nanaimo to stay in the spring of 1884. He found that the VCML company office, which also contained the manager's private residence, had burned to the ground leaving only the safe and the chimney. The fire had been bound to happen sooner or later. The two story building, the former unsuccessful company boarding house, sat immediately adjacent to track used for hauling coal cars to the wharf. Sparks from the locomotive had set the building on fire many times before. With this most graphic example of Company bungling effectively vanished, Robins set about to make the VCML an effective operation both for the shareholders and for the men he employed.

The condition of the VCML mines was a challenge. The Old Douglas Pit, former jewel in the Company crown, was effectively abandoned, its old and shaky pithead frame sitting like a decrepit monument to the beginning of big time Island mining twenty years before. The New Douglas Pit or Chase River Mine, while relatively safe for miners, was expensive to work and had an uncontrollable water problem. In 1885 the level of the water forced removal of pumps and rails from the lower workings. As water continued to rise toward the upper levels, miners worked against time to remove as many pillars as possible before the mine filled with water. By the next year the Company had conceded defeat, and water had filled the mine.

South of the Chase River Mine lay a whole new field which extended to the edge of the Company limits and beyond. Appropriately called Southfield it really consisted of a series of mines, as new openings were made and abandoned in the search for the best access to the large coal body lying there. The latest opening in 1884, called the New Slope, was situated between the Chase River and the original Southfield mines. Within the next six years the Company had added Number Three Pit (Chase River) and Number Four Southfield to its roster.

All through the 1880's, the VCML continued to explore for new coal, limited only by the boundaries of its lease. Mark Bate's interest in Robert Chandler's activities in East Wellington had resulted in company boreholes being sunk to Wellington coal in the so-called West Field. Not far away, another borehole into Wellington coal at the northern edge of the lease would lead to development at Northfield.

Vigorous pursuit of new coal was a preoccupation of other companies as well. By the end of the decade, the Oyster Harbour Coal Company had sunk two boreholes on the northwest side of Oyster Harbour fifteen miles south of Nanaimo. And far to the south on the easternmost island of the Gulf of Georgia, the Tumbo Island Coal Company had installed pithead gear in the hope that its boreholes would find coal extensive enough to make its promoters rich men.

After a two to three year market slump in the middle years, it was now possible to sell all the coal that could be produced. A good year was followed by a better year. British Columbia was the top supplier to the large San Francisco market. Markets were so good that producers could make money despite the onerous American coal duty.

That duty had haunted British Columbia coal producers, and by extension its miners, for decades. In 1870, before British Columbia joined Confederation, the editor of the *Colonist* expressed the belief that the Americans continued to charge duty in the hope that they could starve the province into joining the United States. By the end of that decade, Island coal was finding its way to California ports even further south and to Portland, Seattle, Mexico, Hawaii, and Hong Kong. Steamers of several navies and several mail services also ran on Vancouver Island coal.

Small operators could not have survived the fray. The Inspector of Mines reckoned only Robert Dunsmuir's abilities and the VCML's length of tenure had made it possible for them to sell coal in poor markets. Their chief competitor was the mines at Seattle which did not have to pay the seventy-five cent per ton American import duty on coal, nor the Canadian duty on tools and supplies. They had lower shipping charges as well. Despite these advantages, however, the superior character of Island coal made it the most desirable in the San Francisco markets.

When markets were bad, something had to give and that something was usually either miners' salaries or miners' jobs. When markets were good, there was a lot of making up for lost time and money. Both company and miner wanted to get out as much coal as possible. In the rush to do that chances were taken, corners were cut, and lives were lost.

Miners continued to die regularly in falls of rock and coal. Almost without exception these falls occurred from roofs that were improperly supported or supported not at all. A miner was supposed to prop the roof as he worked until he had advanced the face far enough for proper timbering to be installed. Finding the right prop and cutting it to fit took time away from digging more coal, and coal was the only thing a man got paid for.

By 1887 there had been a mine inspector on the Island for ten years. Most of the time that man had been Archibald Dick, and every year he commented in his report on the lack of timbering. Included in his report of 1880 to the new Minister of Mines, John Robson, was this admonition addressed to a mine owner.

256

Without any wish to interfere with your duties I would beg to be allowed to draw your attention to the desirability of impressing upon your foreman the stern necessity of being strict with the men under his charge in regard to setting of timber in their stalls. Some of them do not seem to be sufficiently alive to the danger of such a treacherous roof as they were working under.

By 1882 Dick had seen little improvement but had grown weary and somewhat fatalistic.

So it would seem that the number of accidents in and about the mines can only be lessened by greater care and more intelligence on the part of the miners and also of strictness on the part of the manager. But, as long as there are mines, there always will be some accidents which no human care or foresight can prevent.

Chinese miners had entered the mines in sufficient numbers by 1883 for them to figure in the fatality lists quite significantly. With the growing union restiveness regarding Chinese and indeed the strike in Wellington that year in which the Chinese were a major issue, the Minister of Mines had specified certain underground jobs that were not to be done by Chinese. The ostensible reason given was that they could not understand English.

The Inspector inquired of the Minister whether he included English-speaking Chinese in his dictum and was given an affirmative answer. By now there were sufficient inexperienced men being hired that blame was also tending to be placed upon them for the increase in numbers of accidents. Dick put these accusations into perspective when he reported:

... casualty happens not to the inexperienced miner only, as the most careful and experienced miner will sometimes be caught, and at a time when he thinks he had used great caution. But there is a class of men employed in the mines around here which I do not expect to know much about mining, although they learn something about it, after being in some time, so that they can do light work. This class is the Chinese.

When Inspector Dick wrote his report at the end of 1884, gas had become his primary concern. Number One Mine had suffered a series of small explosions and one large one in which Joe Guthro and Sam Harris had been burned so badly that they later died. Then in June twenty-three miners had gone to their deaths in Number Four Wellington Colliery. After dealing with the events and his subsequent investigation in a businesslike manner, the weary inspector allowed himself a small diatribe in expression of his frustration.

257

Any Tom, Dick or Harry who may come along gets a job, even though he does not know the first thing about mining. The ventilation is not carefully attended to . . . Even the daily examination is done in a perfunctory manner, and the inspection is but superficial and incomplete. Meanwhile the workings extend and the dangers grow greater, gas begins to accumulate in the old workings, but this goes on, generally so gradually as to excite little or no alarm. Gases may accumulate, dangers may gather and all be apparent but so long as nothing happens no special care is exercised.

Response to the inspector's concerns varied. Robert Dunsmuir blamed the Coal Mines Regulations Act. He could take the Act to the Supreme Court, he said, "and drive a coach and six through it." The VCML ordered a larger fan to power its ventilation system. The inspector continued unsuccessfully to urge miners and management to form gas committees to test for gas on a regular basis. Unskilled miners continued to be hired.

Some are careful and learn quickly; others will not be advised by anyone, although they are ignorant of the dangers they are exposed to any minute; they give the manager and all the officers under him anxious thoughts about them and other men employed in the mine.

And the big new mine on the shores of the harbour pushed its way out under the sea. Two double-decker cages stabilized by large cast-iron weights carried three shifts of men to the main slope, which by the end of 1886 had advanced one thousand yards under the harbour. Above the heads of the miners there was 850 feet of rock and then the sea, but inside the slope there was almost no water. In fact, Number One Mine was surprisingly dry, and the new suction fan, the largest one available, made it even drier.

It was particularly dry on the new Diagonal Slope. Miners there were driving through coal so thick it was sometimes not possible to see either the top or the bottom of it. It was good to work in a place like that; a man could dig a lot of coal in a hurry.

CHAPTER VII

Shot off the Solid

Now we have entered on another year I hope we shall enjoy still greater immunity from accidents, and that everyone engaged in and about the collieries will use the greatest caution, so that, if possible, no list will be required for accidents, and in making out my report at the end of the year it will be a chapter short... and I trust that the year before us will be a prosperous year to the mining industry and workmen in common.

Archibald Dick, Inspector

I know what blowing out shots are like... a great deal of coal dust is made to rise. I have seen a blowing out shot sometimes extend in flame about ten feet from the face.

James Malcolm, miner

I have read about coal dust being explosive. This I say theoretically as I have no practical knowledge of it.

Joshua Martell, oversman

On a sultry July evening in 1886, coal trimmers worked at the docks of the Vancouver Coal Mining and Land Company (VCML), loading the *Queen of the Pacific*. A rush of coal sliding down the chute caused a draught in air heavy with coal dust. The coal dust ignited in an immense sheet of flame as the forward section of the boat exploded. Twelve men were severely burned.

The inquest concluded that coal dust was explosive. This came as a surprise to many, but not to the man who visited the offices of the *Free Press* shortly afterward. Mark Bate, by now a Provincial Assessor and Collector for the District of Nanaimo and no longer associated with coal mines except as a member of the Board of Examiners, had collected information on the explosiveness of coal dust and now made it available to the editor.

In an August 4th editorial, the *Free Press* published a synopsis of the findings of a French inquiry into an 1875 explosion that had occurred without the presence of gas. The conclusions were as follows:

259

Very fine coal dust is a cause of danger in dry working places in which shots are fired. In well ventilated workings it may of itself alone give rise to disasters. In workings in which firedamp exists it increases the chance of explosions.

The next issue of the *Free Press* on August 7th quoted the President of the Newcastle Institute of Mining Engineers. He said that while he did not know how important coal dust was, he wished to warn that it could suddenly be ignited by flame and distilled into gas and could explode simultaneously over miles of excavations.

While mining people in Europe had been examining this new phenomenon for several years, mine managers in North America only became aware of the possible explosive power of coal dust when a disaster in the mines at Pocahontas, Virginia was attributed to an explosion of the fine waste coal. The *Free Press* published in serialized form a paper on the subject presented to the American Institute of Mining Engineers. All investigators agreed that coal dust was explosive, especially in newer mines where new technology had drastically improved the ventilation systems.

Number One Mine on the Esplanade was a well ventilated coal mine. A monster fan crouched beside the upcast Number Two shaft, its thirty-six foot wide hulk housing a twenty-six inch cylinder engine with a thirty inch stroke. Its arrival from England had been greeted with relief by the Company, which had been dependent on a primitive furnace-steam jet arrangement to move air through what was already becoming an extensive mine.

It almost did too good a job. "Sometimes we could not keep our lights burning in the strong current of air in the upcast." When shots were fired at the shaft bottom, it was necessary to slow the fan down, and the strong flow of air lowered the temperature inside the mine to the point that men were cold if they stopped working for a minute. Although the law required a mine's ventilation system to supply one hundred cubic feet of air per man, the monster fan at Number One Mine sometimes delivered five hundred to six hundred cubic feet for every man working.

Half that air was directed to the new diagonal slope being driven from the bottom of the main slope with levels going off each side. That slope tapped a body of coal so thick it was a wonder to behold, but that slope was gassy and needed good ventilation to drive away the firedamp.

The miners working in the diagonal slope did not consider the gas to be dangerous and resented the occasional lost time when mining had to stop for gas to be cleared laboriously from each stall. That had happened in April of 1887 and they had lost half a shift. No one wanted an explosion, but what was a little gas when they had all that ventilation?

We have lit feeders occasionally in the coal with our lamps — sometimes they are lit by the flame of the shots — we have to put them out to prevent them setting fire to the coal.

I never heard of any gas in anyone's place and I never went into anybody's place but my own. I never talked to others about the gas there as I never saw any to hurt and so I never spoke about it. The ventilation was the best I ever saw. There was too much air in there.

But the manager of Number One Mine, William McGregor, did not think there was too much air in the diagonal slope. He had been in coal mines all his life and knew the value of a good ventilation system. This new mine was to have the benefit of all the latest technology, and the huge fan was certainly an example of that. While McGregor had heard of coal dust explosions, he did not think his mine was sufficiently dusty to be dangerous. He said later he did not apprehend any danger from the coal dust that was there.

The dust lay thick on the floor of the diagonal slope; sometimes when a shot was fired the dust rose in great clouds. When a miner was shovelling it, the dust would billow up and be carried off by the current of air. The dust was also in the roof and in the stoppings, put there intentionally by the miners.

The roof of the diagonal slope was uneven. It varied in height from eight to thirteen feet. Timbers lining the rib of the tunnel supported stringers making a roof six and a half feet high. Above that artificial roof was a space that had to be filled with timbers or dross or "anything we could get hold of" to prevent gas from collecting. Miners used long-handled shovels to throw the dust or dross up into the space. When it came back on them they reckoned there was enough in there.

The stoppings were also filled with dust. Although some stoppings were made of brick or stone, those on the diagonal slope were constructed using two lines of upright timbers placed two feet apart and lined with boards on the inside, the ends of which were carved into the coal at either end. The space between the boards was filled with coal dust piled up to the roof and made tight. When the dross settled, as it always did, more could be added by removing a loose board at the top.

261

And coal dust did indeed settle. Because it was by its very nature fine and dry, it worked its way down. Every time a shot was fired some leaked out, adding to the dust in the air and leaving behind it a space for gas to collect.

There were other uses for the dust as well. Miners are practical people, and they use their environment to their advantage. The necessity to find material for tamping shots illustrates this well. Whereas in other coal mining areas of the world a mixture of soapstone and fire clay was used, the miners in Number One used coal dust wetted with water or left-over tea to fill the four to five foot hole that they had drilled to set their gunpowder charge.

Shots were fired by the miners themselves in Number One Mine, even though the Coal Mines Regulations Act required shot firing to be supervised. McGregor chose to interpret the clause as only applying to mines using safety lamps. Ever since the connection between the two shafts had been established, no one used safety lamps in Number One, with the exception of the firemen who used one to check for gas. But Archibald Dick had drawn McGregor's attention to the need for shot firing supervisors in 1884, pointing out in his letter that the clause applied to mines where flammable gas was present. Dick had observed that without this supervision, the incidence of second firing was high. Second firing was what probably happened in the newest crosscut of the diagonal slope at 5:55 p.m., Tuesday, May 3, 1887.

May had begun badly. The spring had been dry and cold, a sharp frost at the end of April stopping all growth. Then the new month began with winter storms — "tree-crashing south-easters with torrents of rain." It was a relief to get down inside the mine and away from this freakish weather.

Fireman James Price arrived at work at 11:00 p.m. May 2nd, for the night shift. The mine was different at night, quieter, with fewer men about. Price checked all the stalls for gas, pushing his safety lamp up where there was an opening, using a stick to extend his reach where necessary, checking for firedamp wherever it might be lurking in the roof, in the stoppings, in old workings, and in the stalls whose roofs were higher than that of the slope and were a trap for gas. As each place proved clear, he chalked his mark on the coal or on a timber or on the blade of a shovel. Back at the fire station at the top of the slope he entered "clear" in the book for the day shift.

Day shift miners needed the fireman's consent to pass the station and proceed down the slope to their stalls. With the diagonal slope reported clear of gas, the new crew began work in their places. Samuel Hague, William Griffiths, and William Thompson had been working right at the lowest end advancing the face of the slope. A few days ago they had left off working on the face to begin a crosscut which would serve as part of the ventilation network of the mine.

The dust was damp there at the crosscut, but three yards back up the slope it was dry, and it got drier the higher up the slope it went. In April, water had been applied to the dust with a hand pump, but it had dried very quickly. Mr. McGregor said he was waiting for a shipment of pipe to install a proper watering system.

Most miners did not know why it was necessary to water that dust. Even George Churchill, the day shift fireman, had no idea that coal dust could be dangerous. Other miners had heard bits and pieces of information, but no one knew enough to make them feel concerned.

The crosscut was lower than the slope and nine feet wide. Sometime during the morning, he was not sure exactly when, William Griffiths had fired a shot to loosen coal at the face. The shot had liberated some gas which had accumulated in a pothole over the roof timbers. A little flame had run fifteen feet along the roof and come out between the timbers, before extending into the slope between the lagging and the rib and running up the slope ten to twelve feet, perhaps more.

Many mining men would have called this a blowing out shot, but not Griffiths. If it had been a blower, he said, the naked flames of the miners' lamps would have ignited it and caused an explosion. According to Griffith, this was just a feeder. Later, other miners would agree with him, saying they had never seen a blowing out shot in Nanaimo mines. But blowing out shots by definition caused a flame to extend out at least ten feet from the face — this one extended about twenty.

Feeder or blower, there was no explosion. Griffiths reported gas; the area was cleared of miners; Churchill checked after three hours and it was clear; work resumed in the crosscut. Other miners in the slope had noticed gas that morning, but no one had said anything. Gas was not unusual, and if you told the bosses you lost time, time to dig coal, coal which was the only way to put bread on the table at home.

At 2:00 p.m. fireman Churchill made an entry in the book. "I examined mine. Bar. 29.95 — found all places clear vent. good." The evening shift took over at three o'clock that afternoon. At 5:35 p.m. oversman Richard Gibson met fireman Andrew Muir coming out of the diagonal slope. Muir was a careful man of considerable experience, and Gibson thought he would have reported gas if there had been any.

The events of the next half hour can only be speculated upon because all the participants died in the explosion. But when the blast area was finally reached in mid-May, it was possible for the investigators to form a fairly clear picture of what happened.

The crew at the face of the crosscut drilled a hole four and a half feet deep. They should have made a ten inch cutting in the centre of the face to allow some give in the coal, but wishing to save time, they did not. Almost certainly, failure to do this would result in a misfired shot in which all the force of the powder went to shooting the tamping back out the hole and no coal was broken. Miners called this a shot off the solid.

If no coal was broken and if the coal was making gas, the drill hole would fill with it. The miner would now be faced with a decision. He should drill a new hole and set a new charge. Of course, this would take extra time, time when he could be getting more coal. He would know that there might be gas in the first hole and he would also know that there was probably unexploded powder left from the first shot in there too. If the mine had employed shot firing supervisors he would have had no choice but to drill a second time, but this mine did not. Many men had taken the risk of a "standing hole shot" or "second firing," and the gamble paid off—no explosion and time saved.

If the miners in the crosscut gambled with a standing hole shot and if there was residual powder still present from the first one and if the coal had been making gas, as it had been earlier in the day, then this was the beginning of the explosion.

But this alone would not have caused 148 men to die on May 3rd in Number One Mine. It took a combination of conditions, as the inquest verdict said, "each of which may be in itself comparatively harmless [to] create a power that becomes terribly destructive and beyond human control."

Some time shortly before 5:55, at the top of the fan shaft, engineer William Miller increased the number of fan revolutions per minute. The already strong air current became even stronger.

In the crosscut 850 feet below the surface, the second shot was fired at 5:55 p.m. A blower of great magnitude shot out of the hole which was drilled at such an angle that the flame travelled well up the crosscut and into the slope before it hit the roof. The roof was filled with coal dust. The air was full of dust too, dust made extremely dry by the ventilation and suspended in the air by the force of the current

264

and the impact of the shot. The flame and concussion of the blast that followed travelled up the slope, fed by gas trapped above the timbers and in the stalls.

Coal dust explosions gather momentum as long as there is something to support them. Once started, the strong current of air increased the volume of the blast; it leaked around a curtain known to be less than airtight at the top of the slope, then spread to the rest of the mine, gathering power as it went. No stopping could be built strong enough to confine such an explosion to one area of the mine.

People at home eating dinner, people closing businesses for the day, people walking on the streets felt a thump under their feet. Off-duty miners knew what had happened right away. They ran back to the mine, followed by women and children, the whole town running pell mell down the hilly streets, the continuous roaring of the mine whistle filling the air and matching the roaring in their heads and hearts.

The first thump was followed by a second and the shafts belched smoke, pieces of wood, equipment, and then flame — flame shooting hundreds of feet in the air. The engineer saw it and stopped the fan. One minute later the fan itself ignited and was quickly consumed, leaving a mass of distorted iron. The fire had destroyed the huge engine as if in retribution for what it had inadvertently caused.

Jules Michael was having supper in a little cabin just off the bottom of Number Two shaft. He heard a sound

like a heavy fall of rock . . . and I felt the wind coming from it up the slope, I remember when the volume of air struck me. When I felt the rush I said, "My God! boys! What is coming on us now?"

James Stove was just sitting down in the mine engine room nearby. When he saw a red flame coming into the room he pulled his jumper over his head and lay as flat as he could. One minute later he saw another flash which nearly smothered him. When he thought it safe to rise, he left the engine room and found John Smith lying in the middle of the slope, both arms broken. He picked him up and propped him against a post. It was completely dark. Looking around he became aware of a faint glimmer in the engine room and was able to find his hat and lamp. He relit his lamp at the fire which was just breaking through the brattice.

Now he could see better, and he found John Jones, whom he brought to where Smith lay. Smith would die before he could be brought to the surface. Jack Lynch was lying not far away, and a Chinese was nearby with his leg broken. Just then Stove heard the

265

cage coming down, and as he ran towards the base of the shaft he was suddenly aware that he himself was burned and injured as well.

Sam Robins, William McGregor, and Archibald Dick with several others came down as soon as the cage could be lowered, loose timbers in the shaft having caused a slight delay. As the cage touched bottom they saw coal cars both empty and loaded lying piled up and twisted like carelessly thrown children's toys.

Fire from the engine house was beginning to make headway up the level. Attempts to slow its progress with buckets of water passed from hand to hand in the smoke and heat had little effect until the hand fire engine belonging to the city was brought down. On the surface, shifts of men had organized to dig a ditch in from the sea so that salt water could pour into the shaft to drown the fire. Sailors from waiting coal ships in Departure Bay and Nanaimo harbours dug with the other volunteers.

On the surface, too, the townspeople were gathering. Wives in clean white aprons donned for the evening meal, children crying, off-duty miners, and ex-miners and non-miners milling about waiting to do what they could, everyone wanting to hear the fate of their husbands and fathers and brothers and friends, but knowing that the news would be bad. Everyone who lives in a mining town knows that the afterdamp was even then spreading its lethal way throughout the levels and slopes and stalls of the mine. A well constructed stopping could fend it off, but the men trapped behind would die eventually unless help was brought to them.

Help could not come until the roadways of the mine were safe for the rescuers, and Number One had been grievously wounded. Some of her tunnels had caved and her ventilation system was in ruins, the brattice torn and the mighty fan a useless hulk. Without the ventilation system the afterdamp could not be swept away, and the afterdamp produced by a coal dust explosion was especially lethal.

The only survivors lay in a forlorn little group by the engine house where James Stove had gathered them. Besides Stove, of the 154 men on the evening shift only George Davis, Richard Gibson (Nanaimo's Mayor), John Jones, John Lynch, Jules Michael, and one Chinese survived.

By midnight Robins and McGregor were joined by the managers and miners who had arrived to help from other pits. With Frank Little, John Bryden, and Robert Scott from the Wellington mines, they descended the shaft to begin a sad routine which would be repeated day after day for weeks on end as they looked for bodies, replaced stoppings, and gradually restored the ventilation network.

The first victims were found soon after the search began. Among them was William Cochrane, whose stepbrother William Craven had also been killed and whose stepfather ran the Half-Way Hotel. Samuel Hudson's body was also recovered. He had been off duty when the explosion occurred and had died when he went into the mine to help in the rescue.

In the dark of that May night, twelve dead miners were brought to the surface and identified by friends or relatives. Volunteers treated the injured and received the dead in the cheerless atmosphere of the old schoolhouse. As one man helped wash the bodies for burial, his own relative was brought in. He laboured long to restore him to life; then, realizing the fruitlessness of his efforts, he gave up and got drunk. Others like James Harvey worked there all through the night.

Samuel Robins had a reputation as a fair and compassionate employer. He captured the imagination of novelist John Galsworthy to whom he described the events after the explosion. The writer, in a fictionalized rendering of Robins, told how he worked for thirty-six hours without a break and only stopped then because the men operating the cage refused to take him down again. As he drove his horses home, he halted several times on the street to speak to women asking him for news of their husbands and sons.

The task of searching for bodies stretched on and on. On May 5th, they found fifteen year old Michael Lyons, whose cousin on seeing him became hysterical and died several days later herself. Included in the forty-one dead found on May 6th was *Princess Royal* old-timer John Meakin and Johan Henry Westfeldt, who had nursed Joe Guthro so faithfully just three years before. With Westfeldt and Meakin was Andrew Muir, who like his namesake was from Ayrshire, and Robert and John Stove, sons of James who had survived, and seventeen year old James Isbister, and twenty-four year old Herbert Bevilockway — the list reads like a roll call of Nanaimo pioneers. William Lukey aged fifty and his twenty-seven year old son and namesake were found that day, too, and fifteen year old Andrew Hunter, who should not even have been down the mine at his age, and Alex Hoggan's son James, aged twenty-one. Joseph Forrest had been married for ten days and died near his new father-in-law and brother-in-law, John and Copley Woobank. And the bodies of "Chinamen 89, 100, 95, 84, 123, 117, 102, 104, 86, 87, 105, 97, 88 and 92" were brought up as well.

On May 8th, Sunday morning, rescuers were 1360 yards in along

Number One Level when they found thirty-five bodies behind a barricaded door — bodies of men who had survived the blast and succumbed many hours later to the afterdamp. Twenty-five white men sat in a row in almost natural positions, and a few feet away "Chinamen Numbers 107, 128, 136, 106, 108, 112, 90, 93, 96 and 101" had arranged themselves in a circle.

A damp whitish mold grew on the timbers of the mine, and some of the thirty-five had written in it with fingers or sticks. Over the heads of the white men on the caps of the timbers was written "13 hours in misery — John Stevens" and "1,2,3,5 o'clock — W. Bone." Nearby, the Oriental workers had written Chinese characters on three of the uprights. A dinner bucket was found in the space between the two groups. The bread and cake in it had not been touched.

Among the thirty-five dead was George Simmonds, a young civil engineer employed to help sink the shafts and establish the levels of the new mine. His widow Fanny would later marry William Bray, also an engineer. Bray would be killed in Protection Mine in 1896.

As the searchers pressed further into the mine, still battling the fallen timbers and caved in levels and still mindful that the fire continued to burn, they found graphic evidence of the force of the blast. A three to five ton rock had fallen from the roof and had been carried twelve to fifteen feet further up the slope. One man's body was pinned up against a post by his box. His feet were uphill and he was not touching the ground.

Above the mine the weather continued rough and stormy, as if in keeping with the terrible things that had happened below. A long poem appeared in the Colonist, the Victorian hyperbole for once seeming appropriate.

Can this indeed be May
That month so green and fair?
Surely November at its worst
Could scarce with this compare.

The poem described clouds of blackest hue, trees uprooted, and fences flying, and then went on:

But these are trifles. Ah!
What real trouble springs
Where Death's dark angel hovers low,
With close and stifling wings!

Woe for the stricken town!
Woe for the homes of gloom,
Which husband, son or father's face
Shall never more illume!

Of the twenty-two bodies found on May 9th, twelve had been trapped behind a cave-in. By now the bodies were decomposing and becoming hard to identify, but among them was Michael Corcoran, who like Westfeldt had been one of Joe Guthro's nurses, and Sam Myers, unsuccessful politician and successful Knights of Labour organizer. Archibald Muir was found that day too — "My Man Archy," who had survived the rigours of Fort Rupert and the gold fields of California and who had opened the first Nanaimo mine with his uncle John and his cousin Robert. Although Muir had bought land in Sooke, he had eventually returned to the mines in 1867, married Julia Bevilockway in 1871, and had lived in Nanaimo ever since.

The searchers continued their unenviable task, working their way slowly toward the diagonal slope. Three bodies were found on May 11th and another three on May 13th. Finally, on May 14th, they came upon the area where the explosion had originated. The scene that greeted their tired eyes was at once commonplace and terrible — commonplace because most of the fourteen men looked like they had just sought cover as they always did before a shot was fired, and terrible because the bodies were so disfigured and burned that they were recognizable only by their clothing and in some instances only by the articles in their pockets.

Relatives still kept their hopeless vigil at the top of the hoisting shaft. It was no longer possible to bring the bodies to the surface on stretchers, such was the state of decomposition. Now coffins were necessary. As fewer and fewer bodies were found, and the numbers of coffins grew less and less, the numbers of watchers diminished. June 20th, one body; July 28th, one more. Two Chinese men were found on October 15th and two more on December 10th.

Some families watched in vain. Three stalls that opened off the diagonal slope airway held seven bodies, imprisoned after several large cave-ins in late May made the area very dangerous for the rescuers. They tried to reinforce the roof. They even tried cutting a new heading from the face. But the seven bodies remained entombed. Jonathon Blundell was thirty-three; he was the father of five and married to Mary Ann Malpass, daughter of Lavinia and John.

George Biggs was twenty-seven; he, too, had been born of *Princess Royal* pioneers, and his brother had helped sink the shaft of that very mine. Thomas Dawson was thirty-two; he had left his wife and two children in Colorado while he made enough money for them to join him in Nanaimo. Welshman Thomas Hughes was thirty-two as well; he left a widow and two or three orphans to carry on without him, as did Robert Nicholson, who was thirty-four. No one in the white community knew who Chinamen 143 and 145 were, but their bodies were trapped with those of the five white men.

Legends grew up round the seven unfound bodies. The location of their bones was pinpointed by someone as being under the Balmoral Hotel. Years later — one man says in 1912, another says in 1923 — miners were ordered to reopen that section of the mine. "There was coats and everything hanging on nails and buckets; found buckets, coal oil lamps. Everything was well preserved but you could just brush and it would fall apart...." George Biggs' nephew, Herschel, says they found bones and clothing. The remains were quietly removed and buried again in the proper manner.

One hundred forty-eight men died that third day of May, 1887. The majority of the victims were buried following a mass funeral. Among the hundreds of mourners at the cemetery was a young boy holding tightly to his father's hand. John Sampson Freethy watched as a man on horseback met the coffin-laden wagons as they approached the graveyard, each driver giving the rider a list of names, which he carried at a gallop back to the mourners waiting by the holes dug in the green sod and the black earth.

Coal mining communities were used to coping with tragedy, even a tragedy of this magnitude. A relief committee was formed to administer the money that began pouring into Nanaimo almost immediately. Comprised of merchants whose numbers belatedly included the "licensed victuallers," who had at first been inexplicably forgotten despite their past history of generosity, the committee eventually collected $102,000 from places as far away as London, Montreal, and Virginia City, Nevada. Donors also included young John Fraser, a ten year old deaf boy whose mother was dead and whose father worked in the bush. John looked after himself and earned money running errands. He gave fifty cents to the relief fund.

The relief package was announced in July. Each widow would receive twelve dollars per month; children under five, four dollars; children between five and ten, six dollars; and older than ten, five dollars. After age fourteen a child no longer received money from the fund. To those parents of single victims who had supported their mothers and fathers, payments were also made. Since the Company gave free houses to some widows, they had five dollars deducted from their relief payments each month, as did women who owned their own homes. Families with savings received four percent less per annum.

Forty-six widows and 146 orphans were left to rearrange their lives. Some wished to return east or to Britain, and these were given tickets. In return, their allowances were reduced by half until the cost of the ticket was repaid. So many children left that the school population dropped drastically, causing the Sisters of St. Ann to convert their school to a hospital for a few years until a boom in the late 1890's increased the number of school children.

Mrs. Roderick Macdonald was not about to accept a monthly dole without a fight. She and at least one other widow requested a lump sum payment, and when it was refused wrote the following to the committee.

Since you thought it wise to refuse my most reasonable request, will you kindly extend your great generosity and deep interest in my welfare further, and obtain me some employment or start me in a private boarding house? You give me no chance of bettering myself elsewhere, and as I certainly shall not grow younger, and will have to support myself and my family long after this fund will be a song of the past. So the sooner I start to earn my own livelihood the better for me.

The careful if paternalistic management of the fund extended its life to include even the widows of another explosion in 1898. The money lasted until the last widow died. One reason for its long life was the fact that many widows forfeited their allowance when they remarried. For when all was said and done the best solution was another wage earner in the house, and there were a lot of men around who wanted a wife.

So Fanny Simmonds married William Bray, and Rosinda Woobank Forrest married William Bennett, and Julia Muir married Edward Brown and added three more children to her brood of three, and Mary Ann Blundell married Richard Rowe, who took on her five children and added three more. Rowe was a butcher, and so Mary Ann did not have to worry about loosing another man to the mines.

There was hardly a family untouched by the disaster. Almost everyone in town had a son or a son-in-law or an uncle or a father among the dead. Because of the common practice of two brothers or a father and a son working together in teams, some families were hit

271

several times over. John Woobank and his son Copley; Henry Lee and his son Hudson; the two William Lukeys; David and Arthur Ellis; brothers William and James Davey and Robert and John Stove all died side by side.

The inquest lasted for weeks. The few survivors and all the men who had worked the previous shift in the diagonal slope were questioned. Archibald Cowie had mined for thirty-five years off and on in Scotland and California before he came to the Island. He said he had seen a handful of dust thrown over a lamp in California, and even though there was no gas present, it had exploded. Joseph Randle, Jr. had already seen what gas could do in Number One when his father was burned three years before. He said he had talked to William McGregor a few days before the explosion about an article he had read. It said that after a coal dust explosion dust will be caked and lying on the walls. There certainly had been caking in some of the stalls on the diagonal slope.

When the experts testified, there was the same mixture of knowledge and ignorance about coal dust. William McGregor, though conscientious and experienced, felt that the little he knew about coal dust explosions did not apply to Number One because the mine was not sufficiently dusty. He had only ordered watering pipes as a precaution after the *Queen of the Pacific* explosion. Archibald Dick had read a lot about coal dust explosions and how they gathered momentum if there was anything to support them, but he did not feel he had any reason to call the management's attention to the danger of dust.

John Bryden seemed to be the most knowledgeable. "I dread coal dust more than I do gas," he testified, but he felt that watering created a new danger by causing spontaneous combustion to occur in mines with iron pyrites present. He knew of hundreds of mines that had caught on fire this way, and since all the Island mines had iron pyrites he considered it foolish to water the dust.

Because coal dust required a long, strong flame to be ignited, Bryden dismissed the possibility of naked flame lamps being partly to blame for the explosion. He also said the men used too much powder, a fact which McGregor corroborated but with which the miners disagreed. They were not likely to waste powder when they had to pay so much for it. Bryden concluded fatalistically, "To make coal mines absolutely safe you would have to close the mine."

One hundred years later in discussing coal dust explosions that occurred in Nova Scotia in 1878 and 1885, historian Donald Macleod made the following observation:

Working at breakneck pace to make a living wage, miners too often stemmed charges carelessly, frequently with the coal dust they found lying by their sides. Some repeatedly "shot off the solid" — the often risky practice of blasting the face without first cutting vertical "shears" into the coal — and thus produced "flaming shots." Others used excessive amounts of gunpowder, a practice rarely discouraged by those mines that sold miners their explosives. Existing rules had proven to be powerless in preventing the blown-out shot.

The rumours started soon after the explosion. "A foolhardy miner opened his lamp," chided one eastern newspaper, to which the *Free Press* indignantly replied, "There are no safety lamps used by miners in our pits." The daughter of one of the survivors would say years later:

...some old gentleman had a pipe and he took his matches and he went to light his pipe to have a smoke while he was resting and it was five minutes to six in the evening — we heard the thunderous sounds from our house.

When questioned recently, a modern day miner gave his judgment.

I would say that it was a lack of ventilation, I would blame the company in the first place — what lit it up I don't know, but I think the company didn't have sufficient air in there to dilute and render the gas harmless.

The most pernicious false conclusion as to the cause of the 1887 explosion had its beginnings several years before the explosion occurred. The groundwork had already been laid to make the Chinese the scapegoats for the disaster. Then on May 15, 1887, only one day after mine officials first reached the site of the explosion and well before any rational conclusions could have been drawn, there was a meeting of Wellington, Nanaimo, and East Wellington miners on a patch of green grass near Craven's Half-Way Hotel. There was only one reason for the meeting and that was to discuss taking steps to prevent the employment of Chinese in the mines.

Soon after, Mr. D. W. Gordon, M.P., rose in the House of Commons in Ottawa to answer a question from another Honourable Member who had asked, "Are the miners of Nanaimo restricted to using the Davy Lamp?" Gordon replied:

I think there is an understanding that such is only to be used, especially in certain parts of the mine, but as miners get better light and can consequently do more work when using a naked lamp, it is quite possible that some Chinamen may have violated the rules and caused the explosion.

Forty-eight Chinese men died on May 3rd and not one of them was found in the vicinity of the diagonal slope. The repercussions visited on the Chinese for their imagined involvement in causing the explosion were based entirely on fabrication. Chinese may well have caused their own and other people's deaths in the mines from time to time, but on May 3, 1887, they were totally blameless.

Some of the miners who had worked the diagonal slope on the shift just before the explosion left mining for good. By July, few men had returned to work in Number One, although many had promised they would. James Knight never came back; he chose farming instead. William Griffiths retreated to Gabriola Island and never mentioned the mines again, even though he had spent thirty years of his life in them. Though young Seriol Williams spent his summers with Griffiths as a boy and regarded him as close as a grandfather, he was not aware of Griffiths' coal miner past until he was an old man himself. One day, while looking at the inquest records of the explosion, Williams saw a signature as familiar to him as his own. It was only then that he knew that William Griffiths had fired the controversial shot on the shift before the explosion, the one he insisted was just a "feeder" shot but that would later be labelled a much more lethal "blowing out shot."

As May gave way to June, the unseasonably cold and stormy weather succumbed to a spell of blistering heat. All that summer the sun beat down on flower gardens which drooped and died for lack of moisture. Vegetable crops were sparse and stunted.

Archibald Dick was so busy with the inquest that he had no time to inspect other mines. The inquest verdict was vague and gave no guidelines for preventing another explosion.

That a combination of conditions, each of which may be in itself comparatively harmless, creates a power that becomes terribly destructive and beyond human control.

The people of Nanaimo did not know what the Board of Directors in London thought. Modern readers have been given the benefit of John Galsworthy's fictionalized description based on an intimate knowledge of that very board room.

... the six directors, all men of common sense and certainly humane, seated behind large turret-shaped inkpots; the concern and irritation in their voices asking how it could have happened ... He had a strong conviction that nothing of all this would disturb the common sense with which they would go home and eat their mutton.

On May 3rd, every year since the big explosion, the flag that flies from the Bastion is lowered to half-mast to remind people of the terrible loss the town suffered. People remember and miners shudder, but human beings never seem to really learn. From then on, miners on the Island were supposed to use clay or sand for tamping their powder charges, but they did so only when the inspector was around. The rest of the time "we all used coal dust dry with electric caps."

It took a year and a half for William McGregor to return the mine to normal. At first the ventilation had to be run by the old furnace-steam jet combination, which was very inefficient. New pumps and winches took much longer to install than anticipated, and until they were installed, McGregor needed Chinese in even larger numbers than before. When he finally agreed to pay them an increased wage of $1.50 a day they came to work until late August, when one of their number was jammed against the wall by a runaway car, and they all left the mine until McGregor negotiated their return.

By October the mine was firing shots with steam or electric batteries; the new fan machinery had arrived but had not been installed. Work went very slowly because there were so many new, inexperienced men and because the quality of the air was so poor.

Whether from fear or from a growing awareness of the power of labour when it withheld its services, the men working in the mine, white and Chinese alike, continued to be difficult. In February of 1888 the Chinese runners demanded $2.50 per day. There was such a shortage of runners that men were taken from their stalls to push boxes. When the Chinese did not come to work due to wet weather, there was no work done.

The problem with the whites was similar. McGregor summed it up when he said:

Output will be light as there is a scarcity of men to work due to the day being Payday. This idle time occurs every payday and the men seem to be getting worse every month. They know we can hardly get along without them due to the scarcity of men.

By December of 1888, twenty months since the coal dust exploded, Number One Mine was declared free of dust by its manager. Dross was now removed to the surface with the coal to be used as fuel for the steam engines. A regular system of pipes had been installed to take water to wherever it was dry in the slopes and levels of Number One Mine.

The most knowledgeable man at the inquest had been John Bryden, and he lost no time making the mines under his charge as safe as they could possibly be. Number Five Pit, the newest mine in the Wellington Colliery, was the best ventilated mine in the district.

There was no dry dust anywhere in the mine, water pipes having been laid along all the levels with smaller pipes to each of the stalls. In addition sprayed water was carried with the air.

Coal had only been reached three years before, but within a year the second shaft was completed, and there were steam jets to take over the ventilation should the fan or engines break down. That fan was also a large one; it, too, often blew out the miners' lights. With so much air, it was necessary to keep the mine wet, and the pipe system did just that. "Everywhere it is not only damp but wet in top, bottom and sides." Water came in unlimited supplies from the lake just outside, which acted as a huge reservoir, the depth of the shaft providing good water pressure.

But on January 25, 1888 at 8:15 a.m. all those precautions were in vain when another blowing out shot caused an explosion which rocked the big mine on the shores of Diver Lake. The force of the explosion stopped the working of the hoisting cage, broke the covering of the fan shaft eighty yards to the south, and destroyed the chimney. But Bryden acted quickly to order canvas to cover the fan house and fashion a temporary chimney, and so the fan kept working.

Dad was caught in that big explosion they had in Wellington. I don't know how many was with him. And he says "come on boys, I'll get you out." They were above the gas. And he went out, and he got kinda frightened before he did get out, because the explosion had brought the roof down a bit. They had to crawl on their bellies.

A crowd gathered quickly at the pithead. The cage could not be lowered due to derangement of the conductors. While a crew laboured to repair the damage, the watchers waited and listened, but nothing was heard from below. After what seemed like hours, Amos Godfrey emerged from the wreckage around the shaft. He had climbed up the hoisting cage rope. His brother was in that mine somewhere, and he wanted action taken fast. Then J. Jones appeared, having shinnied up the shaft's 234 foot partition.

Almost one hundred men waited below at the base of the shaft. They had struggled to get there through the wreckage and the darkness, ever fearful of the afterdamp they knew was lurking somewhere. When they finally reached shaft bottom, wet and almost perished with cold, they found that the cage could not be lowered all the way due to thirty feet of debris piled up in the shaft. When a ladder was finally obtained and lowered to the waiting men, they were gradually raised to the light and the fresh air of that winter morning.

They knew little more than the people on the surface. No one knew where the explosion had occurred, but since no one had been seen from the east level, it looked as though that might be the location. The afterdamp was so strong, it was impossible to get far into the workings. As the rehabilitated ventilation system gradually reestablished itself, rescuers were able to push their way through the debris and get to where the victims lay.

The news reached Victoria fast, and Robert Dunsmuir ordered a special train to take doctors and medical supplies to Wellington. Accounts vary with regard to that trip, but it is generally agreed that E and N Number One Locomotive with engineer Aaron Garland in command did seventy-seven miles in one and three quarter hours. That was too fast for Dunsmuir. Near the Alexandra Mine south of Nanaimo he asked Garland to slow down. The engine had just been fitted with new pony trucks the day before. When they reached Wellington they discovered a fourteen-inch-long section of the flange on the right leading wheel was missing.

By noon two days later all the victims except nine Chinese had been found. Nearly all the bodies were severely mutilated. Elisha Davis' head lay separate from his body which was cut almost all the way through the middle. His left leg was found six feet away. Someone said he must have had giant powder in his pocket. His father had also been in the mine but had survived. William Wilks, forty-nine and the father of five, was found sitting in his stall as if sharpening his drill, badly burned but only slightly mutilated. One Belgian had all his clothing burned off.

As each body was found it was wrapped in canvas and brought to the pit mouth, where a large carpenter shop and store room had been converted to a morgue. There, under the personal supervision of Robert Dunsmuir, the sad process of identification began. Dunsmuir was helped by Sam Robins and the oversmen from the VCML, who had shut that company down as soon as they heard word of the accident. The bodies were washed and dressed and placed in coffins. Those who had friends or families were taken to their homes, the rest to the Wellington Hall.

Forty-six Chinese men died in Number Five Mine that day, and the mine had no record of their names. Of the thirty-one whites who died, twenty were single. Ezra Godfrey was only nineteen and a half and lived with his brothers Amos and Seth. William Horn and John Ness had just arrived from Scotland to live with their relative J. Haggart, a long-time Wellington resident. John Stewart was sup-

277

porting his mother and sister in Manchester. The victims came from Piacenza and Venicia in Italy and Warma and Marchienne in Belgium, from Staffordshire, Lancashire, Bedfordshire, and Durham in England, from Cape Breton and Springhill in Nova Scotia, from St. Thomas in the West Indies and Fifeshire in Scotland. Robert Greenwell had been in Wellington three months. He left a young wife and two brothers: J. S. Greenwell in Nanaimo and J. B. Greenwell in Wellington.

Three years later, John Greenwell would tell a Select Committee of the Legislature that the two explosions were the reason why he joined the Knights of Labour. In 1886 he had been one of the men to sign a requisition asking Robert Dunsmuir to stand for reelection, but the death of his brother seemed to be a turning point for him. It made him realize that labour must look to itself to provide its own salvation. Workers could no longer rely on powerful men who did not have their interests at heart.

Tully Boyce called what happened after the Wellington explosion, "a small strike led by a partial organization." Boyce had come from Pennsylvania by way of Wyoming, and he had not been in Wellington very long. Pretty soon everyone would know who Tully Boyce was.

The Knights of Labour was the only labour organization in the mines at that time, but it did not represent a majority of the miners. Between May of 1887 and January of 1888, however, membership had increased, largely because of the anti-Chinese agitation carried on by the Knights of Labour members. "Men were excited at the time and the Knights of Labour took advantage of this to dress their point."

Following the Wellington explosion, miners from all over the district began to attend meetings and to delay returning to work. They let it be known that if one colliery agreed to exclude the Chinese, the men in that colliery would return to work and support the ones still off.

On February 1st a mass meeting was called for Wellington and Nanaimo miners *and* managers. The E and N provided a special train free of charge to transport the Nanaimo men. At the meeting Sam Robins and William McGregor read a list of recommendations, an inventory that condemned both management and miner.

Shotlighters, already required by the Coal Mines Regulations Act, should be appointed. Miners must refrain from firing shots from the solid. All coal, including dust, must be sent to the surface. Gas committees, another provision of the Act which had been ignored, must be appointed. Inexperienced people must work only with experienced miners. No shots were to be fired twice. All mines must be watered.

From the floor came other suggestions. Someone demanded the exclusive use of safety lamps. Someone else said you could not see the roof with a safety lamp. Someone else demanded total "abolishment" of Chinese and all those who could not speak English. Someone else said, "There are just as good German, French, and Belgian miners as English miners. If you chalk 'gas' on a shovel, not a Chinaman could be got to go past it."

After several meetings, Sam Robins for the VCML and John Bryden for the Wellington Collieries agreed to exclude Chinese from the mines. In the euphoria of the moment someone said that the date February 6, 1888, should be declared the anniversary of the abolishment of Chinese, and a statue should be erected on Mount Benson. A cynic in the crowd said they should wait a year and see if Bryden would put his verbal promise in writing. Nevertheless, a call for three cheers for Robins, Dunsmuir, and Bryden brought the meeting to a euphoric conclusion.

Work resumed after two weeks. Robert Chandler reluctantly agreed to go along with exclusion when his miners in East Wellington refused to work unless he fired his Chinese. Robert Dunsmuir had predicted that without Chinese in the mines, production would drop off and he was soon proven correct.

The trauma of two explosions within nine months had started debate in the legislature to amend the Coal Mines Regulations Act. The first of several attempts to legislate Oriental exclusion from the mines was underway. The member for Nanaimo, Robert Dunsmuir, rose to speak. He seemed already to have forgotten his pledge to remove Chinese from his mines.

The Knights of Labour only started anti-Chinese agitation because they were seeking members. The agitation was embarrassing to most miners and in fact genuine miners did not attend the meetings and took no part in the agitation.

In March the revitalized Knights of Labour called an idle day in order to ensure a good turnout at its meeting. Bryden let it be known that if the men did not come to work he would shut down the mine or put Chinese to work. His decision was confirmed in a telegram from Dunsmuir, which said that if the Nanaimo men caused trouble with the Wellington men he would close down the mines.

Once again, Dunsmuir firmness made the men back down, but some good had come of the heated meetings. By March every mine except East Wellington had a gas committee, appointed and paid for by the miners; shotlighters were being used in all the mines. Meetings of the Board of Examiners increased dramatically as credentials of miners and managers were tested and upgraded. A demand that firebosses be made to pass exams and be elected by the miners received serious consideration.

While East Wellington miners were active in the meetings that seemed to proliferate all that spring, the mines they worked in were in a chronic state of penury, and the man they worked for tried over and over to ignore the agreements made after the two explosions.

Robert Chandler was attempting to build an empire in the Millstone Valley on the former Westwood Estate. Since the San Francisco businessman was essentially a promoter, he employed a resident manager to make the actual mining decisions. On a narrow strip of land, bordered on one side by the Millstone River and on the other by the Bluffs, the East Wellington Coal Company searched with admirable perserverance for good coal.

The enormous expense of employing almost two hundred men, month after month, year after year, had been rewarded in 1886 when good coal was discovered, but the coal was a long way from the shaft. The mines' ventilation system was overtaxed and drew notice from the inspector. When the manager tried to wriggle out by saying that he knew he had too many men for the amount of air, but it was all right because two-thirds of them were Chinese, Inspector Dick said, "Those Chinese are men as well as the others."

By 1888 Number One and Number Two shafts were connected by winding and extensive works, a previous mine to the south having been abandoned. Two large bunkers sat astride the railway track, allowing cars to run underneath to be filled with coal.

The East Wellington mines were the only ones on the Island by then without a gas committee, the men saying they were quite happy without one. But in the matter of Chinese exclusion they were not so tractable. Chandler tried again and again to continue to use the Chinese underground. Each time they were brought down the mine the white miners would leave, causing Chandler to back down.

Having expended an enormous sum of money to find the coal he was sure was there, Chandler cut corners with safety measures. The mines were ventilated with a furnace, by then considered old-fashioned. In 1889, when the furnace shaft fire ignited the Number One shaft timbers, flames leaped out of the pit mouth and destroyed the head gear and one of the coal bunkers. Only by threading their way through the labyrinth of tunnels to Number Two shaft did the miners escape. As soon as all the men emerged, the shaft was covered and water from the Millstone River was pumped into the mine to extinguish the fire.

By 1891 the fortunes of the mines seemed to improve under the new superintendent, Chandler's eldest son. Four years of education in Germany studying geology and engineering, prospecting through Mexico, Oregon, Washington, Arizona, and Vancouver Island, and a two-year stint in the Cascades with Wellington Carbonate probably made W. S. Chandler the best educated manager on the Island. He replaced the renegade ventilation furnace with a fan and instituted the longwall method of mining. Longwall made thinner seams profitable where before they had been dismissed as worthless.

Two years later depressed markets rendered the thin coal too expensive to mine. When a suggested wage reduction was rejected by the miners, the machinery and rails were removed from the mines, and water was allowed to fill them. In 1895 the Company was purchased by Robert Dunsmuir and Sons, and the machinery and boiler sent to Alexandra Mine. When an 1896 fire burned the pithead, engine, and boiler house and eight uninhabited cabins nearby, no one seemed very concerned.[1]

Nothing was left in the Millstone Valley but a few farms. What had been a lively community a decade before was virtually nonexistent. Most of the three dozen company houses had been moved to Wellington by the energetic Robert Kilpatrick, and those that were left had been vandalized. But in the 1880's, East Wellington had been a good place to live.

The community was scattered along the river starting at Drew's sawmill at the northwest end. There was a meat market and the Leiser and Hamburger General Store. Dominion Day 1889 was celebrated in fine style at the circular track carved out of the newly cleared ground just that year for foot and horse races. Folks started dancing in the early afternoon on the "monster" platform and kept it up until late at night.

---

[1] "Fortuitous" fires often occurred in abandoned mines and mining towns.

The people there included Russian Finns, one of the first non-British group of immigrants to work the coal mines since the Italians arrived in the 1870's. You could tell who their kids were by their pale blonde hair. The British people called them "cotton-tops."

And there were lots of British people there, too. There were Muirs and Ramsays and Griffiths. The lively and militant Bowaters had come to East Wellington in 1885 or 1886 from West Bromich and Tipton. The father, William, had started working in the mines in England when he was seven, and would finally leave them in Extension when he was seventy. His grandson William McLellan said he could neither read nor write but

by Jesus I'll tell ya he really had a hold of things though. And once he had a hold of it, it was there to stay, because he couldn't look back on notes. He had to rely on his memory.

William Bowater had a great deal to remember. His long and eventful life would parallel the coming-of-age of unions in Britain and the early frustrating days of the battle for union recognition on the Island. He bred into his children a loyalty and commitment to unions that lasted through several generations to the present. Three of his daughters married Greenwells, thus joining two strong union families, and one of his sons, William Jr., child of his late middle age, became a legend when he was jailed after the Extension riot in 1913 at the age of sixteen.

At the southern end of East Wellington, a road led off over the Bluffs to join up with the main road to Nanaimo and Wellington. The East Wellington road had been built by the Company, and travellers were jokingly advised to take out life and accident insurance before travelling it. Even a light buggy sank up to the axles in the mud of that road. It was a relief to reach the junction with the main highway where the first Half-Way House Hotel had been serving customers and hosting union meetings since the late 1860's. The small shack on a dirt track was known at various times as Akenhead's, Peck's, and Craven's Half-Way Hotel. But now the action was shifting further up the road to the north, and the Half-Way Hotel was rebuilt on a site past Welshman's hill and closer to the new mining camp of Northfield.

East Wellington might have had the best educated manager on the Island, but Northfield had one of the most popular. And Robert Scott was not just well-liked, his credentials were impressive too. With experience working for both major coal companies, he was awarded the contract by the VCML to develop a new mine, which would, it was hoped, avoid all the mistakes of the past. Northfield Mine would tap the coal body lying along the VCML border with Wellington, its three narrow plies of coal only viable now that improved longwall methods made mining it feasible.

In those days of limited transportation facilities, when a man's surest form of locomotion was his own two legs, a new mine meant a new mining town. The site for the town of Northfield, on the opposite side of the Bluffs from East Wellington, was close to the new VCML operation and it was also convenient for people working at Dunsmuir's Number Four and Six mines on the Bluffs above. In the townsite below was a collection of new buildings of all imaginable shapes and sizes, from a ten by twelve foot "batch" cabin to a "comfortable and commodious" two story cottage.

In contrast to the random manner in which many of the buildings were situated, the Company cottages were set in regular rows, an equal distance apart, painted and fenced all around, "cosy, prim and somewhat saucy in appearance as if holding up their noses in proud disdain at the disorder all around." In addition to the usual complement of saloons and stores common to any mining camp, Northfield possessed two establishments quite unlike any seen before on the Island.

The City of Paris Parisian Store was owned by Count Leo Lilbard L'Euram, a French royalist who, it was said, had lost his large inheritance in a banking scandal and had been travelling the world ever since trying to build up a new fortune. That he felt the reclamation could be accomplished in a coal camp may have been some indication of the likelihood of his ever becoming wealthy again. Certainly the citizens were skeptical, insisting that the Post Office be moved out of the City of Paris to a more financially stable fruit store owned by a miner.

Exactly opposite the Count's store was the French Syndicate building, the second establishment unique to Northfield. The Syndicate was a group of Belgian miners — led by Arthur Bertreaux — who owned shares in the store. Such cooperative ventures were not unfamiliar to Island miners, but this one had grander pretensions. The shareholders were determined to quit mining and run the store as a committee. With a complete lack of business experience and as many formulas for success as there were members, the committee soon decided to return to mining and leave the running of the business to retail entrepeneur Simon Leiser.

The camp at Northfield Mine had more than one name. It was called Northfield for the mine, New Wellington for the coal seam it tapped, Belgian Town for the large numbers of immigrants from that country, and Rosstown for the man who owned most of the land.

Five hundred people lived in the new town in 1890. The population had a continental character previously unknown to coal camps on the Island whose white occupants had been almost exclusively British with a few Italians added to provide some flavour. The *Free Press* reporter outdid himself when he described the people of Northfield.

[They] are well versed in the rule of multiplication judging from the number of children to be seen running around. There are hundreds of them... pugnacious Irish, the stunted Welsh, the canny Scotch, and the prosy English. There is Swedes, Norwegians and Danes there. The volatile Frenchman and the phlegmatic Germans are there, Austrians and Italians. Huns, Finns and Belgians, moon-eyed Celestials, tobacco-chewing Yankees, and a few Nova Scotians.

Such a vibrant mix of people seemed to bode well for the purveyors of strong drink. The town was home to a number of prodigious tipplers who patronized Spisak's or Horth's Saloon, or the Northfield Hotel, or one belonging to the ubiquitous Mr. Peck, who seemed to own hotels everywhere. Despite the increased competition, the Half-Way Hotel in its new location continued to be a natural meeting place for union men from all the coal towns.

Determined to reap the recruitment benefits of the increasing number of miners' grievances, the Knights of Labour flexed its muscles once more in January of 1889. A telegram sent to Robert Dunsmuir in Victoria on January 2nd asked for more pay for men mining pillars and threatened a strike if the demands were not met by January 7th.

True to form, Robert Dunsmuir went on the offensive. When the men came to work on January 3rd the pits had been shut down. In a statement to the press he said:

I believe that it is the not unusual result of a large body of well-intentioned men being misled by the influence of a handful of professional agitators, who want to take the management of the mines out of my hands, and who have been assisted by a small portion of the local press.

Some men immediately went back to work, but most stood firm. Twelve private watchmen arrived in Wellington. A committee which included John Greenwell was appointed to go with John Bryden to Victoria to see Robert Dunsmuir. The deputation was treated to a long speech in which Mr. Dunsmuir assumed the role of a beleaguered father, loving but a little tired of his children's constant misbehavior.

Some of the miners at the meeting have used bad language about me, and I can not promise to forgive them all. I want them to understand that I have shut down the mines so that you could not strike, as I do not want to cast you out these cold days...

I have said this to scores of men before, and I now say it again, and I say also I will never change my policy, and if you do not like that policy you can go elsewhere to find work, though most of you I shall wish to employ again, because most of you are good men when the agitators are not working upon you...

I do not want one of you who is a practical miner to be working and not making a fair day's wages, and always remember, that the more you make, the more I like to pay you...

After offering a special train for them to return to Wellington, he sent the deputation away with this admonition:

...when you arrive home tell those men who would strike that I am a stubborn Scotsman, and that a multitude can not stop me from going to work if I wanted to.

When the special train returned to Wellington, the deputation met with the miners at the Old Chute to hear what Dunsmuir had said. They voted to stick to their guns and decided to add that they wanted the check weighman's fees automatically taken off their pay in the same way the doctor's fee was already.

They were no match for the stubborn old Scotsman. He told Bryden to evict the occupants of Company houses and hold any back pay until all the tools were returned to the store. On January 15th, just twelve days after sending their brave telegram, a large meeting in the Presbyterian Hall voted to go back to work. Bryden admitted quite freely that there would be a blacklist, but stated that he would not make it public. He claimed that by keeping their names out of print he was doing them a favour so they could get jobs in other mines.

While Dunsmuir contended with his recalcitrant underlings, Sam Robins had been dealing with problems of a different sort. The VCML had decided that in light of certain liabilities unintentionally incurred on behalf of the shareholders, the Company would be disbanded and its assets sold to a new company, which would be called the New Vancouver Coal Mining and Land Company (NVCML). The new company had the same board of directors and the same management staff and sent forth its management decisions from the same address: Number Twelve, Old Jewry Chambers, London.[2] It also had the same problems: the coalfield was badly faulted, local markets were small and had to be shared with Dunsmuir, the Canadian Pacific Railroad had begun to buy coal from Canmore in Alberta and the Crowsnest mines on the border between Alberta and British Columbia, the California market was unstable, and the quality of coal was questionable. It seemed the only bright spot was the person of Sam Robins.

Sam Robins was fifty-five years old in 1889 and he had already endeared himself to the community.

Oh, everybody liked Mr. Robins. He was a fine, old man. He had a big dog, and he had a walking stick, and he used to walk out, and he came to our place and they were building a little cottage so we rented one of those and he came then and he said to my mother, "Mrs. Storey," he said, "we are going to build a porch on your house. You have to have somewhere to put the little children to play." So he had these porches built on the company houses. He was such a good old fellow.

The Company was by now the owner of the Harewood lease, which adjoined company property to the south and west. In an effort to lessen the possibility of bush fires threatening the town, Robins had set scores of Chinese, recently removed from the mines, to clearing this land. The white men who replaced the Chinese in the mines had increased the need for housing in the already overcrowded town. For some reason no one could explain, there seemed to be an increased number of marriages as well.

Robins was as paternalistic as Robert Dunsmuir, but his fatherly concern tended more towards making it possible for the people to help themselves. He reasoned that if a man had enough property on which to grow all his food, he would be less at the mercy of the vagaries of the markets and the resulting layoffs in the mine. Robins therefore made five-acre plots of land available to miners on very reasonable terms.

The first lease was issued in 1888. For a twenty-one year lease, the miner agreed to pay $2.50 rent per year for the first two years and then $12.50 for the next three. After that he agreed to pay between five and ten dollars per acre per year. There were provisions for buying the land outright and there were conditions to be met. The land must be cleared, made fit for cultivation, and fenced with post

---

[2] The address was the law office of John Galsworthy II, Chairman of the Board. His son John III used him as a prototype for old Jolyon Forsyte in his *Forsyte Saga*.

and rail fencing. No trade or business of a publican, hotel keeper, inn keeper, saloon keeper, butcher, tanner, fishmonger or "any other noisome or offensive trade" was permitted.

Clearing of the Harewood lease continued well into the next decade, seven thousand trees being felled in 1894 alone. A gang of men built roads. They improved the old Harewood Mine Road, which for years had been just a trail crowded with salal and black-berry and shaded by evergreens. From the new homesteads it climbed the crest of the hill and plunged down the other side toward the water, joining Fitzwilliam Street, passing Cornishtown and Lubbock Square and the E and N station and the Occidental Hotel and finally meeting with the ravine bridge.

Robins himself lived on the Esplanade not far from Number One Mine. Like many Englishmen of the Imperial Age, he had a self-appointed mission to amass an impressive collection of trees from all over the globe. Ship captains brought him exotic specimens to add to his collection, but he was particularly fond of holly trees and had them planted all over Harewood as well as on his own property.

Robin's Esplanade home welcomed two young guests in the summer of 1891. John Galsworthy III was in his twenty-fourth year, and he had been called to the bar and had fallen in love with a penniless young woman almost simultaneously. Wishing to save him from an unsuitable marriage, his family sent him off to travel with his brother Hubert.

The two young swells arrived in Nanaimo in time to observe Sam Robins as he dealt with the dilemma of increasingly difficult markets versus his reluctance to lay off men whom he knew desperately needed regular wages. With a novelist's eye, Galsworthy stored up his impressions of Robins and transformed him into Pippin in his story "The Silence."

... at his age, [he] should cut himself adrift from the associations and security of London life to begin a new career in a new country with dubious prospects of success

When Pippin refers to the Board of Directors it could be Robins saying,

Let them try the life here! ... it's like sitting on a live volcano — what with our friends, "the enemy" over there; the men; the American competition. I keep it going ... but at what a cost — at what a cost!

The characteristic of Robins' personality that made him so effective in dealing with his employees was his genuine interest in their welfare and his preference for dealing with his men through unions. Testifying to a Royal Commission in 1902 he said, "Yes, most emphatically I prefer to deal with organized labour."

And labour continued to fight valiantly to be organized. The Settlement Act which awarded Robert Dunsmuir the vast E and N land grant became a grievance to be used by union organizers. The Knights of Labour in particular used resentment caused by the huge tract of land Dunsmuir had received for building the railway as a focus for miners' grievances even at the time the Settlement Act was signed. In its submission to the Royal Commission Investigating Oriental Immigration, the Knights of Labour delegation declared:

... by the terms of the infamous Settlement Act all the immensely valuable coal lands contained within the vast railway reserve has been handed over to one company, the principal shareholder in which but a few years ago, without a dollar, to develop a few acres of coal land, which the then favorable laws of the province allowed him to acquire. At that time the price of producing coal was much higher than now, while the price obtained was if anything lower. Yet so huge have been the profits that he has accumulated a princely fortune, and has become all powerful in the province, his influence pervading every part of our provincial government, and threatening its very existence.

The Knights of Labour delegation then combined their anti-monopolist argument with some racism.

It is unjust to place a few individuals already too wealthy, in possession of nearly all the natural resources of the country, and thus beyond the reach of all competition, and at the same time expose those who are the producers of wealth and the source of all prosperity to the competition of a degraded race who are practically slaves!

The miner who had come so far and had made himself so rich had become the focus of union grievances, his paternalistic approach to labour relations being resented as much as his boundless wealth. The more wealthy he grew, the more he was resented. At a miners' meeting in 1888, one man said:

He has nearly as much power in Victoria as the Czar in Russia. While he is erecting buildings, bridges and railways in Victoria, he is making widows and orphans in Wellington.

In 1889 Dunsmuir was putting the finishing touches on a castle. Legend has it that he promised his wife Joan that if she accompanied him to the New World he would one day build her a castle, and so he did. Craigdarroch was designed by a San Francisco architect who was given no limit to the money he could spend and no instructions other than it must look like a castle in Scotland.

Before Robert Dunsmuir could move in to the grand new edifice sitting in spendid isolation on a hill overlooking the city of Victoria, he died from "an accumulation of uric acid which resulted in blood poisoning." Victoria was plunged into mourning, and suddenly the man who had many bitter opponents and whose rise in the legislature had been the "theme of numerous diatribes in the House, in the Press, and on the Hustings," had "scarcely an enemy in the world," if the *Colonist* is to be believed. Flags flew at half-mast, all business houses left their shutters up, and trains were heavily draped in black.

In Wellington the mines were closed until after the funeral. Nanaimo stores were closed as well, and some were draped in black. It was announced that all Dunsmuir's employees could come to the funeral, three special trains being laid on from Wellington and Nanaimo, passes obtainable on application.

On April 16, 1889, thousands of people watched as the twelve hundred man funeral procession made its way through the major streets of Victoria. Attached to the hearse was rope of sufficient length for all his employees to pull the coach to the cemetery. That so many of his employees came on the special trains to Victoria could be due at least in part to the opportunity it afforded for a free excursion. That so many of his employees submitted to the degrading if popular tradition of the time, of acting as beasts of burden before the hearse of the man who had made so much money from their sweat, is very hard to explain.

One of the last things that Robert Dunsmuir did before his death was to agree to his son James' entreaties that he develop the Comox coalfield, which he had purchased a decade before and had allowed to lie fallow. Shortly after the Wellington men went on strike in January of 1889, the men in the Comox mines followed suit.

As Dunsmuir wrote to Sir Joseph Trutch in February of that year:

... it seems I have not quite got quit of one strike, but another one takes place at the Comox mines as last Tuesday because the Superintendent sent six Chinamen down one of the mines to run out some boxes every man quit work, and at present everything is at a stand up there and will be until I get other men as not one of the old hands will earn another dollar at any of my works, I would not have been shipping coal from that mine before the end of April anyway and this will put the shipping back some weeks, however it don't matter much as the bottom has dropped out of the coal market in San Francisco and prices are back to what they were a year ago.

289

The sentiments expressed applied to a new setting, but they were very familiar. Though the old man was dead three months after writing those words, the Dunsmuir credo lived on in the new mines of the Comox Valley.

CHAPTER VIII

"John" and Mr. James

Comox, we are told, has been a by-word on the Pacific Coast, and has sustained the reputation of being a tremendously godless place.

Methodist Missionary Society Report, 1889

Let anyone who is not, take a trip through Chinatown, and he will think Union's population is largely celestial.

Cumberland News

It seems dull because there are no workers roaming about, filling the hotel verandas, filing into the saloons, driving lively teams fiercely through the streets, filling the air with their boisterous laughter. The rough class have largely gone to the gold fields where it is to be hoped they will remain.

Cumberland News

At a political meeting in Comox, a powerful looking middle-aged man stood up in the audience. A big, black beard covered the lower half of his face and lay over the collar of a green blanket overcoat which encased the rest of his body. Taking a large-bowled pipe from his mouth, he addressed one of the politicians who was reported to have "prohibition leanings." Instead of questioning the candidate, he proceeded to make a speech which dwelt on the respective achievements of England and Turkey in world's history. Having effectively compared the lopsided accomplishments of the two countries, he ended his impromptu address with "Look at the beer-drinking Englishman! Look at the tee total Turk!"

The man was Samuel Jackson Cliffe, farmer and proprietor of the Lorne Hotel, which commanded Comox Harbour from the hill that sloped down to the wharf. It was said that no one had ever been refused bed and board there even when he could not pay. Cliffe had bought the hotel in 1883, not long after the coal company of which he was a part sold its claim to Robert Dunsmuir.

In some ways the Union Coal Company was typical of the many partnerships that were formed after 1864 to find and develop the many coal deposits on Vancouver Island. In these companies, there were at least ten partners and their numbers contained at least one promoter, often a man like David Leneveu or J. Ash, each of whom promoted more than one coal mining venture. In most cases their dreams of becoming wealthy entrepreneurs died when their capital ran out.

In one very important way though, the Union Coal Company was different from most of the other ventures, for although associated with the powerful Union Pacific Railway in the United States, it included amongst its members at least seven Island coal miners, each of whom had been able to contribute a minimum of two hundred dollars toward the total of twenty-two thousand dollars declared when the company was registered in 1872. David and William Hoggan, the brothers of Alex and later nemeses of Robert Dunsmuir during the 1877 Wellington strike, were two of the members. Adam Grant Horne, former Hudson's Bay Company (HBC) storekeeper in both Nanaimo and Comox and brother-in-law to Mark Bate, was a partner as well. His efforts to achieve wealth in the coal mining business would run up against Robert Dunsmuir again in 1879 when the latter purchased the Sabiston and Horne Estate in the Millstone Valley. [1]

By far the most colourful participant of a colourful lot was the aforesaid Sam Cliffe. Like so many other Island coal miners he was from Staffordshire, but he had not begun life in as humble circumstances as most miners had. He and his brother Robert had been medical student orderlies during the Crimean War when Sam was barely in his teens. They returned home to find their father had married his housekeeper and wanted his sons to call her "Mother." Having had a taste of independence, the boys were not likely to tolerate that situation for long. They left England in 1862 aboard the *Silistria*, bound for the Cariboo gold rush.

Also aboard that ship were William and Sophia Harmiston and their daughter Florence. The Harmistons' destination was the Comox Valley, a hitherto unsettled area north of Nanaimo. The six year old girl and the twenty year old world traveller had little in common, but

[1] The lists of shareholders vary with the source. James and John Blyth Allan, James Gillespie, Sylie or Stylie B. Hamilton, William and David Hoggan, all miners, and William Raymond Clarke, auctioneer and commission merchant, David Leneveu corn merchant, and Archibald and James Hamilton all appear on both lists. Adam Grant Horne and Sam Cliffe only appear on one each. Two prospectors associated with the group, S. C. Davis and Samuel Harrison, appear on neither list although Harrison is credited with the actual find.

when they met again at a picnic ten years later they fell in love and married. After a fortune in gold had eluded him, Sam had become a Nanaimo coal miner.

And Sam had left his mark on Nanaimo. He had been on the Committee of Management for the Literary Institute, had won notice when he risked a possible gunpowder explosion to help extinguish a fire in Platt and John's Store, and had led an unsuccessful expedition to prospect for precious metals on the Nanaimo River.

Having been a coal miner, Sam was very interested when he heard about the new government regulations regarding prospecting rights. If a partnership could invest ten thousand dollars, the members were granted access to twenty-five hundred acres of land for two years. How much better life would be if he could be the boss instead of the worker. For Sam and the Hoggans and the others, it was a dream worth pursuing.

The Comox area looked promising. As early as 1853, James Douglas had observed many pieces of waterworn coal at the mouth of the Puntledge River where it emptied into the harbour at Port Augusta (Comox). The source of the coal was determined when the Vancouver Island Exploration Committee under Dr. Robert Brown explored the Puntledge River basin in 1864 and found some fine coal seams.

From then on, several groups tried to make their fortunes in the area south of Comox, but each group was determined to find coal close to tidewater, that being crucial to successful exploitation of the resource. No one ventured as far inland as Puntledge Lake until the Union Coal Company did.

The first coal nearer tidewater was discovered by a group of local people who filed their claim in July 1866 to the lands bordering Baynes Sound, that narrow stretch of water separating Denman Island from Vancouver Island. Just two months after, an American group which styled itself the Black Diamond Coal Company sent four "practical miners" under the supervision of one C. E. Lansdale of San Francisco to claim the same seam. By allowing two groups access to the same claim, the colonial government seemed to be pitting one group against the other. When the original claimants threatened to take the battle to court, the American group withdrew from the fray, protesting that they had left only because of the snow.

The victors formed the Baynes Sound Coal Company and proceeded with their plans despite a lack of success in attracting a large source of capital. Joseph Trutch, the Surveyor General of the Prov-

293

ince, personally surveyed the line for the tramway. The possibility of a new mine delighted the farmers of Comox, a small collection of former gold seekers, sailors from Australia, and emigrants from Britain who had settled the rich open prairie land since 1862. Finally there would be an accessible market for their produce.

The news of a possible market for produce attracted eastern Canadian farmers to Denman Island as well, but little produce was sold. Instead, all but two of the miners from Baynes Sound were sent back to Comox in December 1867. Two men had stayed behind to build houses for the spring start-up but no one was very optimistic. By 1869, having acquired no outside capital, the Baynes Sound Coal Company was unable to proceed, and in 1871 it was sold to an English firm.

Two familiar names were associated with the new owners. One was the perennial promoter, David Leneveu, and the other was the new manager, Archibald Dick. Dick had come to Nanaimo six years before from Kilmarnock to work for the Vancouver Coal Mining and Land Company (VCML). He was injured in an accidental explosion of powder in 1867 and later left for the safer pursuit of prospecting for gold. He was almost thirty years old when he returned, the gold fever cured, to settle down to the business of mining coal.

The claim lay two miles inland near a deep gorge through which a small stream flowed to Fanny Bay. The stream had the rather grand name of Riviere aux Sables, river of sand, which gradually became bastardized into Tsable River. It would give its name to a far more successful mine in the twentieth century, but in the 1870's — although a road, a sawmill, a hotel, and a store were built and fifty-five employees sent six hundred tons of coal down the narrow gauge railway to the company wharf — it foundered on a lack of capital. The company was sold to Robert Dunsmuir, and Archibald Dick returned to Nanaimo to succeed Edward Prior as Inspector of Mines and become a chronic irritant to the Dunsmuir mining empire in his demands that they comply with the Coal Mines Regulations Act.

Among the many other companies that attempted to find and exploit the five major seams of the Comox coal basin, were the Perseverance Coal Company north of Baynes Sound on Union Bay, and the Beaufort, north of that again. Both these claims suffered the same fate as the Union Coal Company when the newly rich and doggedly acquisitive Robert Dunsmuir purchased them and let them lie fallow.

But the Union Coal Company came closer to success than the

others. Its saga began in 1869 with an adventurous expedition of eleven men leaving Port Augusta with packs on their backs. They suffered the necessary amount of hardship to create a legend, and then five miles from shore on the southwest side of Comox harbour they found four seams of coal. The mine inspector years later described it in lyric phrases.

Here is an almost perpendicular cliff, which rises on the north side of a small brook, tributary to the Puntledge River... The brook is about 500 feet above the sea and the road will have a pretty even fall the whole of the way to it.

By September of 1872 they had finished three miles of the seven mile road from the claim to a location at tidewater that soon came to be called Royston, for its owner William Roy. The road continued on to Port Augusta. Two months later workers at the site, under the supervision of manager Mr. R. George, had exposed two seams.

Soon after, the *Colonist* indulged in the sort of boosterism it reserved for projects which caught its fancy when it called the three miles of completed road "the finest road in the province." Considering the condition of the few other roads, this was faint praise indeed and considering that the cost of that road would tax the resources of the company to the limit, it would have been better if it had not been said at all. A specimen of Union coal won first prize at the American Centennial Exhibition in Philadelphia in 1876, but the mine it came from was by then shut down. It was too expensive to get coal from the mine to the water. It would need someone with a great deal of capital or a great deal of borrowing power.

In 1880 the four partners from Victoria sold their shares to a lawyer, who in turn sold them to Dunsmuir, Diggle and Company. One year later, Dunsmuir Diggle acquired the interest of one of the miners, James Gillespie. By 1883 the wildly successful Wellington company owned all the shares of the unsuccessful Union Coal Company.

For the farmers of the valley and the tiny community of Comox, which had grown up along the shores of the shallow harbour, the failure of the new mine was another bitter disappointment. The rich soil of the river valley hardly compensated for the isolation, the irregular mail service, the paucity of merchandise at the HBC store, the lack of doctors, and the absence of a market for their vegetables, meat, and dairy products. Export of their wares could occur only when the steamer from Nanaimo made its bi-weekly visit. So lacking in excitement were their lives that the entire population had the "steamer-day habit." Every other Wednesday they congregated at Comox Landing on the wharf in front of James Robb's barn to greet the side-wheeler, *Cariboo Fly*.

The antics of the Indians provided the only other diversion. When James Douglas first came in contact with the "Comux" tribes, he described them as wild and barbarous, at a time when the Kwakiutls of Fort Rupert and the Snenymous of Nanaimo were digging coal in peaceful cooperation with the whites. The Island's first bonafide settler, William Colquhoun Grant, visited the Comox area and observed,

... the Comux and Yukletah fellows, being savage uncivilized dogs, are the only tribes on the north and east coast, amongst whom a boat's crew of half a dozen white men, if well armed, might not trust themselves alone.

A decade later their disposition had not improved and their numbers had increased. In their multi-family longhouses of split cedar, where the smoke from the fires in the middle of the dirt floor found its way through the roof or the walls as best it could, they lived a seemingly carefree life with plenty of driftwood for fires, salmon and deer for meat, and potatoes bought from the white farmers to round out their diet. But the addition of whiskey-trader alcohol to their already fearsome temperament threatened to destroy their idyllic existence.

The *Nanaimo Gazette* reported that a large canoe loaded with a quantity of liquor in bottles and tins had been observed heading north from Nanaimo.

Last week the usual saturnalia consequent on a fresh importation of whiskey, was kept up by the Indians at Comox. It was attended by its indispensible accessory — a general scrimmage — in which two Siwashes were badly wounded with the knife.

Six Indian police had been appointed to deal with the illegal whiskey trade, but the murders and other depredations continued. When Royal Navy gunboats moved into the area, the Indians moved two miles inland out of reach. "They are very insolent to the settlers, defying authority and threatening to use their arms if interfered with," reported the *Gazette*. Magistrate William Franklyn was dispatched from Nanaimo to Comox harbour where he held court on the quarter-deck of the *Sir James Douglas*.

For the white farming community, false hope had been raised by the early success of the Union Coal Company. A coal company would mean a coal town, and that would surely bring proper roads, proper markets, proper medicine, and proper policing. No longer would they have to import their flour and feed from Oregon, there being no flour mill in the province; no longer need they fear the unruly Indians' nightly ructions, there being no constable to keep the peace; no longer need they search for home remedies to keep themselves healthy. "Green's August Flower" might well cure dyspepsia, but how much better a doctor would be than Ayers' or Jaynes' or Bristol's Almanacs.

Robert Dunsmuir put an end to those hopes for the time being. He was not interested in spreading himself too thin by investing in more mine works than he could manage. He was also not interested in seeing anyone else exploit a coal resource that in time he might wish to exploit himself, and so he bought struggling coal companies and stopped all development.

The Union Coal assets held much more promise than the others had, however. Dunsmuir kept himself informed by sending Frank Little to test the deposit. Frances Deans Little had been Dunsmuir's "right-hand man" even before 1877 when he testified on his employer's behalf at the Assizes following the Wellington strike. Someone even called him "Dunsmuir's handyman," but that failed to recognize the man's knowledge of mining. That knowledge, combined with an unswerving loyalty to the Dunsmuir family, pushed Little up the management ladder to eventually become manager of the Union Colliery and later General Manager of the entire Wellington colliery, which by then included the Alexandra, Extension, and Union mines.

In keeping with his desire to inform himself thoroughly, Dunsmuir had a team of surveyors plot out a possible route for a mine railway in 1884. One of the assets he had acquired when he purchased the Perseverance Coal Company was access to a deep water harbour at Union Bay, and it was there that he intended to build coal loading wharfs someday in the future.

Dunsmuir's reluctance to develop the Union mines bothered his son James. He felt the Company should expand its activities. But Robert's mind was on other things. He had become a member of the legislature with power out of proportion to his position as a mere member of the caucus. He was building the E and N Railway. The miners at Wellington were restless and looking to become troublesome again. There would be no mine at Comox until he was ready.

In those last years, Robert Dunsmuir's life had become increasingly complicated. He assumed the governmental position of President of the Council in 1887. Litigation occupied an increasing amount of his

CUMBERLAND AND SURROUNDINGS

Gary L. Crocker

0   5 mi.

N

Comox Lake

Puntledge River

CUMBERLAND

No.s 1,2 and 3

No. 4

No. 5

Trent River

No. 6

BEAUFORT
COAL CLAIM

trestle

COURTENAY

Comox Harbour

COMOX

ROYSTON

PERSEVERANCE
CLAIM

Tsable River

Union Bay

BAYNES SOUND MINE

Denman Island

Strait of Georgia

Hornby
Island

time as he sued the sender of a series of "Black Hand" letters and took the *Victoria Times* to court for having said "Mr. Dunsmuir carries the Government in his breeches pocket." In addition, he was building a castle and dealing with the furor created in Nanaimo and Wellington over the two explosions in 1887 and 1888.

Finally, early in 1888, Robert Dunsmuir gave in to the wishes of his eldest son, James, and agreed to develop the Comox coalfields. In fact work had already begun in March when four feet of snow halted it completely. By spring however, railway construction was well underway, the navvies none other than the Chinese miners from Wellington whom Dunsmuir had reluctantly agreed to remove from those mines just weeks before.

Miners and labourers began to arrive, carpenters to build houses, sinkers to start slopes and shafts, loggers to fell trees, sawyers to work the steam sawmill, miners to dig coal, hundreds of men to work at a frantic pace as if to make up for the years when nothing had been done. Late in that year Robert Dunsmuir presided over the official opening of the Union Colliery Company's mines at Union Camp.

Not three months later, the colliery was hit by its first strike. Robert Dunsmuir had just settled a three week work stoppage in Wellington when trouble erupted at Union, trouble caused by Superintendent Little sending six Chinese down one of the mines to run out some boxes. Every white miner quit work. But as Dunsmuir wrote to his long-time friend Sir Joseph Trutch, he had not changed his attitude toward strikers, and he was quite capable of waiting the men out, markets not being what they should be anyway.

Within two months of his writing that letter, the most successful coal miner in British Columbia was dead. But a beginning had been made in the Comox Valley. A series of tunnels, slopes, and shafts with various number designations had been begun and abandoned and modified as the managers searched for the best place to dig the coal that they knew was there. An eleven mile standard gauge railroad was completed with a very large bridge crossing the Trent River gorge, its Howe Truss and trestle a wonder to behold. Large wharves at Union Bay, deemed a much more suitable site for loading than the Union Coal Company's choice at Royston, were ready to load as many as four long ships at a time. A second wharf waited for the discharge of freight. All railroad, bridge, and wharf construction had been completed between March and December of 1888.

The farmers of the Comox Valley were ready. The hundreds of men at the camp had ravenous appetites. Soon there would be women and children too, and they all would be customers. The only trick was to get the produce from the Comox farms up the road to the hungry workers at Union camp.

A rough road led from Comox to Royston, followed by the three mile long railroad bed that had been constructed by the Union Coal Company. It ran "straight as a rule through the tall timber and was graded flat as a board." Its only disadvantage was its narrowness; it was only fifteen feet wide, which made "neat work for wagons passing each other."

At the end of the three mile stretch, the road abruptly became as rough as before. Eric Duncan, who had settled down to farm after his early career in the sawmill at Nanaimo, described the trail this way:

[It] was the roughest imaginable, and for long stretches the wagon-wheels rarely touched earth, but hopped from stone to root and from root to stone, and woe to any spring vehicle! Many a day I walked ahead of the wagon, throwing out stones; and eggs had to be solidly packed in straw to stand the racket... Few made the trip without an axe in the outfit.

There was a hill on that trail so steep that farmers with large loads had difficulty reaching the top. A certain Mr. Pottinger was jerked out of his wagon by the roughness of the road and fell in front of the wheels, which ran over his legs. He fortunately suffered no permanent damage.

The only consolation for the farmers on the return trip was that their wagons were empty and their pockets full. They still had to endure the rigours of rough road followed by narrow railroad bed followed again by the rough stretch from Royston to Comox.

That last section was part of the trail built from Nanaimo in the 1870's. To call it a road was an exaggeration for it was virtually unuseable. The bridges had washed out in the spring floods the first year after they were built. By the time there were people at Union, the Nanaimo-Comox road was overgrown with brush and trees. It was only after the *Cumberland News* and the *Wellington Enterprise* joined their voices to that of John Bryden that money was voted to repair the road and link up the communities in the Comox area. It was not until bridges were built over the Tsable and Trent Rivers in 1897, that it was finally possible to make one's way unimpeded by road from Nanaimo or Comox to the new coal mines.

There was a certain irony to the impact the new mines made on the isolated farming community of Comox. Where before the farmers had little outlet for their produce and had to contend with drunken, rowdy Indians, now they had markets aplenty and drunken miners to go with them.

The drunkenness of the Union Camp was all the more outrageous for its illegality. James Dunsmuir had decreed right from the beginning that intoxicating liquors were prohibited within the limits of the camp. He was backed up by the Presbyterian minister and the Temperance Lodge, whose austere presence belied the tolerance implied in its name, for what was required in the Union Camp was not temperance at all but abstinence.

But human beings do not react well to being told they cannot do something. It tends to make them want to do it all the more, and nowhere is that more true than in the consumption of alcohol. Just outside the borders of the camp, Mr. S. C. Davis, who had been in the area for over twenty years and had prospected with the Union Coal Company, enlisted the help of some other miners. They applied for a liquor license, "knocked together three old cabins," and called it the Union Hotel.

The Fourth of July 1890 was celebrated at the new hotel, nick-named "Castle Dangerous" by some wit. The men were occupied by games and sports all day and dancing all night, although the acute shortage of women must have made for some unorthodox couples on the dance floor. One drunken man grabbed an axe and smashed the large mirror over the bar, five windows, the bar itself, several doors, and a lot of bottled liquor. Mr. Davis ran away down the hill amid a shower of flying bottles, to lay low until the drunk got tired, surrendered, and was locked up.

The Queen's Birthday celebration one year later was much more sedate because there were women and children present. Picnic grounds had been cleared beside the lake not far from town and a dancing platform erected. The coal train took the ladies and children to the site where athletic events, quoits, and a lady's boat race ushered in a new era of gentility to the fledgling community. To the skirl of the pipes, a contingent of Comox people in Highland costume arrived on the scene in an expression of goodwill. Music for dancing was provided by the Roy Brothers and the Italian Band.

To have rejoiced over the apparent gentility would have been premature. The 1892 Queen's Birthday picnic was interrupted when someone saw a capsized boat floating on the lake. When a fifteen gallon beer keg bobbed gently to shore someone remarked that it gave "satisfactory evidence that the Queen's health was well drunk."

The cause of temperance, so nobly begun, was already fighting a rearguard action at Union Camp. "The prohibition mandate is strictly carried out, but for all that, there is more than one person gets 'a wee drop on the sly'." A Company built hotel inside the camp borders firmly refused to rent to anyone who sold liquor on Sunday, but by then any other day was all right. By 1895, four hotels in town had liquor licenses — the Half Way House, the Comox Hotel, the Waverly, and the Hotel de Vendome.

Some hotels would endure; others were as transitory as the one whose owner left on a business trip to Vancouver and did not bother to return, much to the chagrin of his wife and children. It seemed the more exotic the name the less likely the hotel was to survive. The Hotel de Caens made a brief attempt in 1889 to give the camp a taste of New Orleans. It was kept by a

coloured gentleman, the chef de cuisine is a dark complexioned Frenchman from Louisiana, and his assistant is also dark complexioned and hails from Mobile. The proprietor of this hotel is expecting by return of the steamship *San Mateo*, 500 watermelons so that you can come and enjoy a real plantation dinner.

The "coloured gentleman" and his expectations seemed terribly out of place in the rough mining camp. His presence so far from civilization may have had less to do with his desire to provide his clients with a "real plantation dinner" and more to do with his past business practices, but he soon disappeared from the Union camp scene.

This was a town for rough men unafraid of hard work and uncomfortable living conditions. They lived in Company houses built of split logs, fifty of which were erected by 1889. It was not possible to own land within the townsite, a fact that presented a golden opportunity to one Reginald Pidcock, who owned land a few miles away on the banks of the Courtenay River. He hired a surveyor, laid out a townsite, and managed to sell a few parcels of land to coal miners. The settlement even had a newspaper and a hotel when James Dunsmuir ruined everything for Mr. Pidcock by making building lots available for sale in a new townsite beside the Union camp. Courtenay's development came to a shuddering halt until the E and N Railway reached the area in 1912.

The distance between Courtenay and the camp was a long one if a man was on foot. It was better to get a room in one of the Company houses if possible. They were rough and crowded, but they were close to the mines. Someone was always trying to make things sound better

302

than they were, however. One such person compared the three rows of houses perched on a slope surrounded by stumps and slash with a Mediterranean scene such as one might witness when viewing Constantinople! The trying conditions or the recent addition of whitewash to the outside walls must have evoked the sunny Middle East to his backwoods vision.

In the summer of 1889 the climate could easily have been described as Mediterranean. The weather was warm and dry, and blue sky reminded one nostalgic Italian of the sky at home. That is, until the bush fires in the surrounding sun-dried forests clouded over the blue with an acrid haze. Mediterranean climate or not, the camp certainly attracted a large number of Italians, some of whom had arrived as early as 1886 and must have found work helping with the railroad survey. They came to Union the way they came to most other places in North America, as bachelors who sent their money back to elderly parents and spinster sisters in Italy. The Marocchi brothers worked in the mine until one of them was injured in a fall of rock in 1892; then they opened a bakery. It was said that their whole wheat bread was unbeatable. It was also said that you could buy pretty good bootleg liquor at Marocchi's, and on your bill it would be listed as bread.

Soon after the arrival of the first workmen, the small camp divided itself into racial groups. The Company encouraged segregation by setting aside a "Chinatown," "Japtown," and "Coontown." Although the terms jar the modern ear, most of the inhabitants preferred to live in the separate communities. That was especially true of the Italians.

You could tell where the Italians lived. They had painted the houses in their end of the camp with dark red paint. That was where the Bonos, the Crosattis, the Simondis, the Tobacco brothers, and of course the Marocchis lived. A lot of them sent for their wives and children, and they built a big hall where the growing community could gather. They were sufficient unto themselves and that seemed to satisfy everyone.

We didn't go into their houses. If you know what I mean. The Italians lived further down camp. But my goodness, we all went to school together and all, you know attended the same things and everything like that.

You didn't marry an Italian; people settled in ethnic communities and stayed there; religion was a factor too.

Catholic Italians married Catholic Italians. Italian women did not speak to the English women down at the other end of camp because few of the Italians could speak English. Italian miners kept to themselves, too, because they were still regarded as strikebreakers. That may have been why there were so many of them at the beginning at Union: the Dunsmuirs did not like troublemakers and the Italians had a reputation for keeping out of that kind of trouble.

There seemed to be a deliberate attempt to avoid potential union men or "troublemakers" in the hiring practices of the Dunsmuirs. Not that it ever worked very well. Even the men who appeared reliable could be swayed by union rhetoric as the deaths mounted in the mines in a direct relationship to the speed of mining development. After a long depression, markets began to pick up in 1893, and the pressure was on to produce and be damned.

In the Scotland that Robert Dunsmuir had left forty years before, many miners regarded unions with reservation. The tradition of the "independent collier" favoured reliance on hard won skills rather than on group action. To tap that same independent spirit, the management of Dunsmuir's Union mines now recruited several groups of miners from Scotland. As Frank Little saw it, most of the men who arrived were a major disappointment.

We brought out 200 Scotch miners and they were no good. We have twenty left. I do not think one third of them ever dug coal in their life. Very few paid their passage. They were supposed to pay $70 each for the passage, but never did. Many of them went to Seattle at once. They never came here at all. Mr. Dunsmuir paid $15,000 on them. I do not think he got $3000 back. I paid $3 a day for $1 day's work to some of them. I was longing for the Chinamen.

I had two spells of assisted immigration. I do not know which was worst, the niggers or the Scotch miners. We brought sixty-five niggers from Pittsburgh and Ohio and they were as bad as the others.

The arrival of black workers in 1889 took all the other working men in Union Camp by surprise. A new group of miners from Nanaimo refused even to apply for work when they realized the blacks were there. But the *Free Press* said that most people in Comox thought the blacks were preferable to Mongolians or other foreigners. This backhanded acceptance mattered little to the many of the blacks who were unimpressed by the living conditions and quit, walking all the way to Nanaimo in search of better accommodation. Ironically, most of the blacks ended up working for Dunsmuir anyway, in Wellington and later Extension.

Whites said they would not work with blacks. Blacks said they would not live in the camp. Frank Little said the Scots were inexperienced and unreliable. The Scots said they would not work with the Chinese. The Chinese would work anywhere.

Mr. Little liked Chinese miners, and his employers happened to have several hundred on the payroll, having promised to remove them from the mines after the 1888 Wellington explosion. When all those Chinese were added to the ones who had just completed building the Union Colliery railroad, it was inevitable that the Union mines would employ a large number of Chinese miners.

Employers liked Chinese workers. There was a group discipline that worked to the employer's benefit. They produced well, had fewer accidents, and worked for less than half the wages a white would demand. Being short of labour and having made no promise to keep Chinese out of his Union mines, Dunsmuir hired them to work at Union. In fact he hired more Chinese than white miners.

By the 1890's, the politicians and many of the citizens of British Columbia were on the side of the white miners when they demanded that the Chinese be excluded not only from the coal mines but from the province as well. While politicians used anti-Oriental sentiment to fire up the crowds at election rallies and tried over and over again to pass Oriental-exclusion laws in the legislature, fledgling unions had fastened on to the same issue in their efforts to sway more and more miners to the union cause.

The Ministry of Mines in the person of Inspector Archibald Dick was at the forefront of the battle between the Dunsmuirs and most of the rest of British Columbia society, represented most vociferously by the coal miners and their desire to be unionized. Dick was well-qualified in managing coal mines and he was nobody's fool, but the eight year battle he waged against the Dunsmuirs was fought without a great deal of support from the Ministry of Mines and mostly in courts of law. Out of his element and standing virtually alone, Archibald Dick fought a battle weighted heavily against him.

The new Oriental-exclusion amendment to the Coal Mines Regulations Act forbade Chinese to work underground. That the legislation itself flew in the face of common sense and the collected wisdom of many of the witnesses to two Royal Commissions made Dick's job of enforcing the legislation even more difficult.

And Dick was an unlikely champion. His obvious admiration for the Dunsmuirs' boldness and success was at war with his desire to do his job properly. Since his appointment as inspector in 1880, he had had the unenviable job of enforcing the Coal Mines Regulations Act against the recalcitrant mine owners, who had fought the Act as an infringement on their right to run their businesses as they saw fit. The Dunsmuirs had presented an especially obstinate front, refusing at times to file colliery returns and having to be prodded repeatedly to post special rules that informed the miners of the safety problems unique to each mine.

Stepping carefully through the battle zone, cajoling, encouraging, resorting to a toughly worded letter here, a congratulatory pat on the back there, Dick had laboured to increase the safety of Vancouver Island mines. He was equally vigilant when it came to miners' lapses and shortcuts. His reports exult over accident free periods and show genuine pain when the death toll mounts.

Against this background, the latest battle between Archibald Dick and the Dunsmuirs was joined in March 1890 when an anti-Chinese petition was signed by fifteen hundred miners. In response to the concerns of the men who had elected him, Nanaimo's Member of the Provincial Parliament (MPP), Andrew Haslam, proposed an amendment that would exclude Chinese from underground. Although a similar proviso had been included in the original bill in 1877, it had been meaningless as long as miners continued to hire Chinese helpers. In 1890, having discontinued this practice, the miners wanted an amendment with teeth.

At a meeting of the new and aggressive Miners and Mine Labourers Protective Association (MMLPA), Wellington branch, Inspector Dick was the guest speaker. He announced to the assembled group that "if the Chinese are not out of the Union Mines the next time I go there I'm taking steps to make sure they are." That his task would not be easy could be seen in the response of Alexander Dunsmuir, on one of his frequent visits to Wellington from his home in San Francisco, who said:

We will show you that the law you got passed prohibiting Chinese from working underground is not worth the paper it is written on — we will burst it in the courts and still work our Chinese!

In June of 1890, Inspector Dick notified Union Colliery Superintendent Frank Little that he had seen

a number of men at work who are known as Chinamen which is a contravention or non-compliance of the Coal Mines Regulations Act and the Amendment to the Act of 1890 both which you possess and are well acquainted with.

The Inspector brought three cases before Magistrate J. P. Planta. The first two cases were dismissed and the last withdrawn. Little continued to employ Chinese miners.

Six months later the branch of the MMLPA at Union Camp, which then counted a majority of the white miners among its membership, requested Dick to enforce the anti-Chinese amendment. Dick informed his boss, Minister of Mines John Robson, that he would bring another case to court. He asked the Minister for a "legal gentleman" to help him, as both the miners and the Company would be sure to have such assistance. Union Camp constable Elijah Smithurst, a former Nanaimo miner, was asked to serve four summonses, two on Mr. Little and one each on Mah Wing and Sam Sing, both of Number Two shaft. Little was to bring the two Chinese with him to the court of Judge Harrison in Nanaimo.

Despite Little's argument that it was necessary to use Chinese underground in Comox because they could not get white men to work the thin seams of coal at a price that made the coal worth mining, he was ordered to obey the law and remove the Chinese from the mines. Despite the Judge's order, however, Little merely paid the fine levied against him and went back to Union to continue as before. The law made no provision for enforcement.

The frustration of trying to administer an unenforceable law defeated Dick for the time being. The battle was taken up by Nanaimo's new MPP, Thomas Keith. A miner himself, Keith made persistent but unsuccessful attempts to amend the act further to allow for better enforcement.

That the amendment was having no effect on Dunsmuir hiring practices was graphically illustrated in 1892 when a second petition demanding Oriental exclusion was forwarded to the legislature. The printed version of the petition included so many names that it took ten pages in small print to list them, but the petition had no effect.

Japanese had joined the Chinese as targets for the ire of British Columbians. They had first appeared on the provincial scene in 1884 when five hundred were imported, presumably for work on the railroad. When the Union Colliery began to hire them in 1891, observers speculated that they would provide the same cheap labour as the Chinese did but would be exempt from the head tax, thus making them more attractive to their employer. Because the fifty dollar head tax was beyond the ability of a Chinese immigrant to pay by himself, it had become an added business expense borne by the employer.[2]

[2] By 1904, the head tax would have risen to five hundred dollars per Chinese, a sum paid by the employer and taken out of future wages. The repayment plan indentured the worker to the employer for many years.

Within a year, the jobs of both whites and Chinese had been usurped by the Japanese, and two hundred more immigrants were expected. In the townsite that was set aside near the Number One Mine, they paid ground rent to the Company but were allowed to build their own houses. Because they had every intention of making Canada their permanent home and because there were no immigration restrictions which applied to them, many of them had their families with them. This created a stability and a desire to assimilate that was lacking in the Chinese community of mostly bachelors.

The presence of family members, however, made living on the miniscule wage paid to Orientals extremely difficult. In 1893 Superintendent Little and local ladies' groups were required to provide them with food and clothing. By then the efforts of politicians and unions to exclude Chinese had expanded to include the Japanese as well.

The mines in Nanaimo were by this time entirely free of Oriental labour underground. The fact was celebrated in one of the entries in the 1895 Labour Day parade.[3] Included among the horsedrawn floats was one from the New Vancouver Coal Mining and Land Company (NVCML) that carried five loaded boxes of coal. Over the boxes floated a banner which read "Black Diamonds Mined by White Labour."

Stories about careless Chinese miners made the rounds and became true with constant telling. Many of these stories were told to members of two Royal Commissions which were appointed in 1885 and 1902 by the federal government to investigate British Columbia's Oriental "problem." On a visit to a Union Colliery mine one commissioner was said to have asked a Chinese miner carrying a safety lamp for a match and was given one.

However, even the most vociferous opponents to the Chinese appreciated the Chinese sense of humour, which bubbled to the surface even in testimony to commissions or in court, where some Chinese were finding themselves with increasing frequency. One such beleaguered Oriental gentleman was asked how long he had been a miner. "In good pigeon English" he replied that he had been a miner for sixteen years and was now a contractor supplying Chinese labour

[3] Although working class people on the Island had celebrated their cause on May Day for over a decade, the Dominion Parliament decreed in 1894 that Labour Day would be observed in September. Whether this declaration was a sincere recognition of the importance of labour or, more likely, the need for a holiday at the end of the summer, it was celebrated with great gusto in Nanaimo the following year.

to the mine company. He was asked to prove he could read all the rules in English, which he was unable to do. "If I could," he replied, "I would not work in mines, but would be lawyer, alla same attolney-genelal."

Wong Kee, a runner for five years, demonstrated his knowledge of mine rules. "Me savvey fire boss, chalkee markee me no go up, box full no takee up, no full me no takee up, no matchee, no smokee, man smoke no good, me savvey gassee."

Some Chinese chose to laugh at white people by parodying the practice in some mines of giving them numbers rather than referring to them by name. The Chinese miners in Number One Nanaimo had been designated Chinaman Number One, Two, Three, etc. In later years there seemed to be a preponderance of Chinese with the surname "Ah." It was the Chinese having the last laugh. Ah Yat, Ah Yee, and Ah Sam were merely Chinese for Number One, Number Two, and Number Three.

The 1885 Royal Commission on Chinese and Japanese Immigration numbered the Chinese population of British Columbia at nine thousand. By the time a similar commission had filed its report in 1902, there were sixteen thousand or one for every eleven whites. The Oriental "problem" was obviously growing rapidly, but just how rapidly depended on which white man was talking.

A major complaint against Chinese miners was that they agreed to work for low wages, thus competing unfairly with white miners and in particular boys and young men who wished to enter the mines for the first time. A Methodist missionary put a different light on the wage question when he said:

He does not willingly take smaller wages or sell at cheaper rates than others; but if he cannot obtain the price he wants, he wisely takes what he can get rather than waste his time in idleness; while his white competitor, if he cannot get all he demands, prefers to lounge about the saloons, grumbling at the country, cursing the unlucky Mongolian.

Both Sam Robins and Robert Dunsmuir had championed the Chinese cause, but for different reasons. Robins felt that anti-Chinese feeling was fostered by the trading classes, who knew that few Chinese spent money in their stores. He thought that both the Chinese and white race had "vicious and depraved people" in their ranks, but that one race was no worse than the other. His humanist sentiments had to come second, however, to his desire to satisfy his work force. And they had demanded that Chinese be excluded from the NVCML mines.

Dunsmuir was equally broad-minded in his assessment of the Chinese character and abilities, but his motivation lay firmly in the realm of getting the most for his money. When put to work they were suited for, Chinese were just as good as whites. He reckoned that if he gave them skilled work to do they would be ingenious and quick to imitate and could therefore learn successfully. Besides, "Chinese wages were the only thing that make mining pay...."

As the number of anti-Chinese incidents increased, the persecuted race took measures to protect itself. Wellington boys who attacked a lone Chinese with snowballs were surprised when he retaliated with his umbrella. When an onlooker intervened, the Chinese yelled, and a large number of his fellow countrymen appeared, carrying picks, pokers, and clubs. Reports increased of Nanaimo Chinese being abusive to merchants and going for a weapon if spoken to harshly at work. A white miner was immediately surrounded by ominous looking Chinese when he objected to the abusive language of one of their countrymen.

In the six years since the legislation was passed forbidding Chinese to be underground, the MMLPA had spent hundreds of dollars defending its constitutionality. James Dunsmuir was asked to comment on the effects of the anti-Oriental amendment to the Coal Mines Regulations Act on his collieries at Union. He replied, "...[it] troubles me about as much as water on a duck's back." Between 1890 and 1900, there were twelve attempts made by politicians to remove Chinese from the Union colliery by amending the Act. Only four bills were actually passed, and one of those was declared unconstitutional.

The amendments and constitutional challenges muddied the issue for many, not the least of whom was Archibald Dick, but in a letter to union agent Ralph Smith in 1897 he promised to enforce the most recent amendment. True to his word he instituted charges against the Union Colliery; true to what had become standard practice, the judge levied a statutory fine of one hundred dollars against the Company; and true to form the Company appealed.

Again and again, as the years went by, charges against Superintendent Little were proven and then rendered meaningless because the Act allowed for no penalty. The cost in fines, legal costs, and wasted time mounted. Then the Company played its trump card.

The courts were treated to the spectacle of John Bryden suing the Union Colliery Company. The announcement was greeted with incredulity. It must either be a joke or a fake. John Bryden was Vice-President of the very colliery he was suing! He was the son-in-law of the founder and brother-in-law of the President. The Attorney-General declared that his department would be watching the case closely. Archibald Dick, Ralph Smith, and union president Tully Boyce were subpoenaed to give evidence on behalf of the plaintiff.

Bryden was using this unusual ploy to test once and for all the constitutional right of the provincial legislature to pass the anti-Oriental amendment. But testimony covered more than just the constitutional issue. On cross-examination Dick was forced to admit that Number Two Mine of the Union Colliery, which employed Asiatics exclusively, had the lowest accident rate of any mine in his jurisdiction, and "that personally he would prefer to work with an ignorant Chinaman than an ignorant white man." Smith and Boyce held firm to their convictions that Chinese were dangerous.

The court declared it was within the jurisdiction of the legislature to pass the amendment. In the judge's view, no single case of Oriental carelessness had been brought forward but only "opinions formed on imperfect knowledge or vague generalities." In summary he said that the Chinese were more cautious and had fewer accidents, so the opposition to them was based on the fact that their employment tended to keep down the price of labour.

The bizarre case had yet to run its course. When the Company appealed to the Supreme Court, it confirmed the judge's opinion. When the Company appealed to the Judicial Committee of the Privy Council in London, it reversed the decision and found in favour of the Company and thus rendered the latest anti-Oriental amendment to the Coal Mines Regulations Act unconstitutional. No one was any further ahead, and there were no higher courts of appeal. Archibald Dick went back to chasing the Union colliery through the judicial system as he had before.

That year of 1898 saw the issue of Chinese labour dominate the provincial election campaign. By now all pretence of mine safety had been dropped and the real issue of wages hotly debated. Everyone could prove their point with sets of figures. That James Dunsmuir was elected as MPP for the Comox area and that his opponent was a miner was explained away. Dunsmuir had fooled the electorate, it was said, by implying that he would no longer employ Orientals underground.

Dick's battle had quixotic overtones. The list he sent to the Minister of Mines detailing his efforts to enforce the law in just one four month period read like an idealistic one-man crusade against impossible odds. Justices of the Peace refused to take his information;

judges refused to handle cases; defendants brought to court were fined and went back to business as usual; Dick swore out a complaint against his own brother, John, who ran Alexandra Mine for Mr. Dunsmuir; dates were set for trials and changed; funds became so limited Dick could not attend trials at the Union Camp any more.

Then Archibald Dick was fired as Inspector of Mines. The Cumberland News ruminated:

It was the unexpected that happened when Archibald Dick the inspector of mines was decapitated. However, we trust the place will be given to a practical man and not a politician; or will it be allowed to remain vacant, as unnecessary?

Dick was ever the obedient servant. He acknowledged the receipt of the letter giving him his notice and made note of "the complaint made therein." No one knew for sure what had happened, but it appeared that Dick had been removed because of his dogged persistence in bringing the Union Colliery to justice.

Almost one year later, Dick was hired by the very man he had been chasing for the past eight years. James Dunsmuir made him manager of the Alexandra Colliery, replacing his brother, John Dick, who was too sick to continue. His testimony at the Chinese arbitration hearings in 1899 contradicted everything he had stood for during the past decade. Chinese were as safe as whites. Literacy did not enhance safety. No whites ever complained to him about Chinese. "If a Chinaman and an Italian were both equally ignorant of English," he testified, "I would prefer a Chinaman because he would do exactly as he was told."

The whole affair had a comic opera atmosphere. The new Inspector, Thomas Morgan, took up where Dick had left off—laying charges, testifying in court, seeing fines paid, and changing nothing. For a time during the Bryden case Chinese were excluded from Dunsmuir mines, but as soon as the court of final appeal had declared in the Company's favour, the Orientals returned. By then they were employed in the new Dunsmuir mines at Extension, too.

Just when people thought they could no longer be surprised by this serio-comic scenario, the miners at Union reversed their anti-Oriental stand. At a well-attended meeting the white miners decided to let each man choose whether or not he would hire a Chinese helper. The resolution to exclude Chinese that was passed at a previous meeting was rescinded, and soon men would deny that it had ever been passed. The new measure was forced upon them, it seemed, by the fact that most white labour was uninterested in working for the low wages paid in the Union mines.

Although the Nanaimo press castigated the Cumberland miners for their new stand, their local newspaper editor, a former school-teacher and a woman, looked for scapegoats and took on the union and the NVCML on their behalf.

Liars, slaves, cowards, etc. are the choice epithets . . . use[d] to designate the men whose crime is that they wish to manage their own affairs as suits them, and decline to fight their employers at the biddings of the hirelings and other companies.

With whites and Orientals thus bound together in their need to survive, a relationship of sorts developed between the two communities in Union. The Chinese continued to live according to the customs of their homeland in their "rambling shacky extension of the town," and the whites looked on with wonder at their foreign customs and exotic food.

The queer nuts which are like dates when cracked, and contain a seed, are such misleading things; you eat one think how fine, another, and how sickening! To the children were passed a tray with funny looking little brown beans, and candy like vermacelli.

White people marvelled at the facility with which the Chinese used chopsticks and a china spoon.

I confess I have seen very many who call themselves refined, and are considered civilized who might with benefit to themselves and gratification to those who sit at table with them, gain from the derided Chinaman a few hints on decency in eating.

All was not sweetness and light, however. A visitor to Chinatown during its New Year celebration reported that the Chinese watched him "furtively and with distrust." The Chinese had suffered much indignity and abuse at the hands of whites, and that abuse continued. In addition, local citizens were only too eager to help when government agents raided Chinatown in an effort to clamp down on gambling.

Government agent Eugene Doyle had been lurking about town for several days, having gone "undercover" to reconnoiter. Then two provincial police constables arrived in town and organized a posse of specials. Nine local men were sworn in, and the posse rushed the Chinese town at 8:30 one night.

Doyle was inside. The Fan Tan was the game. The Johnnies were taken by surprise. They made for the back way; there stood Doyle who instantly presented arms. The Chinese to the number of thirty-three were captured and marched to jail.

The use of the term "Johnnies" reflects the continuing racism which prevailed. It was not vindictive or violent and sometimes it was even benevolent, but it was racism just the same. Even when the Methodist mission began to convert a few Chinese to Christianity, this bigotry continued. The newspaper reported:

...satisfactory results noted in the number of converts present, and the general look of intelligence visible in the countenances, a contrast to the dull, stolid and expressionless face of the average Chinaman.

Surely even the most fervent Christian would not claim that conversion bestowed increased intelligence.

A more balanced assessment of the Chinese came from the missionaries themselves, who found the Oriental miners generally quiet, peaceable, and industrious. That they loved to gamble and to smoke opium no one disputed, but few were interested in strong drink. Many came to the "Jesus men" not necessarily out of an interest in the white man's god, but out of a desire to learn English.

And gradually a measure of grudging admiration developed for the doughty Chinese.

You take all those Chinamen that worked down in those mines, you know, they really worked for what they got. They really did. And you know a Chinaman wasn't like a white man. A white man worked like hell for a while and then he'd take five, but not a Chinaman. He kept at it the same speed all day long. And when it come to the end of the day he was fresher than you or I.

The descendant of a Chinese immigrant explained their philosophy this way:

Our way of thinking is this. You rather drop your blood and save your tear. You make a man of yourself if you don't squawk, I mean, that's about the size of it.

The Japanese coal miners' story follows a much different path. While they had been included with the Chinese in the efforts of politicians and miners' unions to legislate their removal from mines and their exclusion from the country, all of that changed abruptly after March of 1899.

Japan had been a mysterious nation, whose borders were closed to trade with the outside world until 1897 when she allowed several countries to establish contact. Two years later the Canadian government joined the rush for spoils and let it be known that the Japanese must not be insulted. Overnight there was a complete reversal in the editorial content of the *Cumberland News*. Whereas before Japanese miners were deemed lazy and dangerous, now they were highly desirable. "I have met with miners in Union who would refuse to work in the mines if they were not allowed Japanese assistants," crooned the editor. The Japanese consul visited Cumberland and "found Canadians unanimous that Japanese labour was far ahead of Chinese."

But British Columbia's politicians defied the federal government and continued to press for anti-Japanese legislation. The Japanese government protested once, twice, three times to the government in Ottawa. By May, the *News* editorials were in full flight. The provincial government should not pass "class legislation." "Japan is a civilized nation comparing favourably with European nations." "China remains in the darkness of the old ages." "No one will say that a Jap is not in every way superior to a Chinaman." "It matters little what a man's nationality is if he possesses the qualities which make for good citizenship." But while all this opinion fulminated on the editorial page, the paper continued to list Chinese, Japanese, and Italian miners by their race only, never by their name. Apologies were later tendered to the Italians for the slight.

As the intricacies of racial politics raged on in Victoria, James Dunsmuir offered the Union Camp an opportunity for more permanent status as a town. At about the same time as he made building lots available in the new townsite of Wellington, he did the same in a newly surveyed townsite east of the Union camp. The pride engendered by home ownership in the newly christened town of Cumberland led the way to its incorporation in 1897.

The new city of Cumberland was well aware of its benefactor. The comings and goings of various of the Dunsmuir family were reported in detail in the newspaper. Dunsmuir daughters and sons-in-law arrived to a flurry of press reports and speculation. Even "Mrs. James," the doyenne of Victoria society, the chatelaine of "Burleith," the helpmate of her husband, and the mother of twelve children, graced the coal camp with her presence. Ten of Laura Dunsmuir's twelve offspring still lived, eight of whom were daughters who looked to their southern belle mother to guide them as they grew up in affluence and were groomed for suitable marriages.

The flamboyant and dissolute "Mr. Alex," who made frequent

315

trips to the Island on business and hunting trips, was a familiar figure in Wellington and Cumberland. It was said that he lived with a woman in San Francisco whom he was afraid to marry because his mother disapproved of her. It was said he was seldom sober in San Francisco but managed to refrain from alcohol when on the Island. It was said that he and his brother were locked in a battle with their mother over control of the Company. It was also said that he looked like a man not long for this world.

His mother Joan had become a lady of legend ensconced in her castle, alone except for visits from her children. The widow Dunsmuir's strength and devotion had been an important element in her husband's rise to wealth and power. Legend said that Robert always consulted her before making important decisions. After her husband's death, however, her indomitable spirit got in the way of her sons' plans for the family business.

In the first traumatic months after Robert's death, she had toyed with selling her interest in the firm. Experts visited and put the value of the mines at considerably lower than the price she had set. When she remained firm, potential buyers lost interest. Five years later she was still pursuing a sale. When an English firm agreed to the $2,600,000 asking price, Mrs. Dunsmuir raised it, thus discouraging the would-be buyer. The real estate firm handling the transaction sued for its commission.

Their mother's interference drove her two sons, James and Alexander, to reorganize the Company, changing it from a partnership to an incorporated company. They intended to consolidate all the holdings under their control and buy their mother's share from her for cash. In 1899 she finally agreed to an offer of $410,000.

Having secured his mother's capitulation, Alex no longer had to worry about her wrath if he married inappropriately. Accordingly, in December 1899 he wed Josephine Wallace, his companion of twenty years, and installed her in the mansion he had built in the east Oakland hills on Souther Farm.[4] One month later the man who had been born in a tiny frontier mining camp thousands of miles from anywhere died in New York on his honeymoon trip, rich, sophisticated, and in the grip of alcoholic dementia.

The diagnosis would have baffled the people of Cumberland, who had seen an able and sober Alex just two years before when a large

---

[4] Dunsmuir House on Souther Farm was designed by J. Eugene Freeman, son of Captain Joshua Freeman of *Glory of the Seas*.

party of Dunsmuir friends and relatives arrived in the area on board the family yacht *Thistle*. Hunting and fishing trips occupied the select group of what one miner characterized as "the cream of the crop." Alex excelled as a sportsman while his brother James basked in the glory of his recent election to represent the Comox district in the Legislature.

In that time of rising labour political consciousness, the choice of James Dunsmuir to represent a farming and coal mining constituency was not the foregone conclusion that his father's election had been over a decade before. Robert was elected at a time when working men still looked to community leaders as the logical people to state their case in Victoria, but the intervening years had wrought a change in that perception. The Knights of Labour and other union activists had shown that labour could and should be represented by people from its own ranks. And yet in the 1898 election, the archetypal business baron, James Dunsmuir, won the right to represent Cumberland.

Earlier that year Dr. Robert Lawrence, the colliery surgeon, had announced his intention to seek the government party nomination. Lawrence had experienced the usual tribulations of physicians employed by the miners' Sick and Accident Fund in that his skills were periodically called into question at miners' meetings, but he had weathered these meetings for four years and had achieved congratulations from the *News* for having kept the death rate low despite the growing number of people and the lack of sewerage.

One week after announcing his candidacy, however, Lawrence withdrew in favour of James Dunsmuir. Two hundred and fifty voters had signed a requisition requesting Dunsmuir to run, and Lawrence knew when he had been bested. He even seconded Dunsmuir's nomination.

The opposition candidate was William J. McAllan, a bachelor miner who had worked in Britain, Australia, and New Zealand before coming to Wellington and then Cumberland. Although he was known for his reasoned and well-presented arguments for exclusion of Chinese from the mines, his opponent refused to take him seriously.

James Dunsmuir said McAllan was "a nice young man" who had a "number of vagaries in his head." "What he needs just now more than any office is a good sensible wife," declared the man who by his own admission had done more for the district than any one else could possibly have done. "Everybody knows Dunsmuir and all of us know the condition we were in before Dunsmuir took hold of the Union mines," chided the *News*. It was hard to argue with Dunsmuir's contribution to a community that would have not even existed without him. It was hard to compete with a man who could promise daily mail delivery and good roads, and could really deliver on his promises. When in addition, James dangled the prospect of a creamery in front of the farmers of Comox, his election was assured.

Temperance was an issue, too, in that election. Agitation at the national level by a plethora of temperance groups had led Prime Minister Laurier to promise that a plebiscite would be held in late September. The opposition party in British Columbia, having allowed liquor advertisements in its paper and having attacked the Lieutenant-Governor for not serving wine at a public dinner, was identified with anti-prohibition sentiment. The government party was no paragon of abstinence virtue either; in fact, the Premier had been accused of being intoxicated. But the government candidate in Comox was a temperance man through and through.

Ever since his association with a temperance lodge in his early manhood, James had opposed the consumption of strong drink. As soon as he took over the Union Camp operation he insisted on a temperance lodge and prohibited all intoxicating liquor on his land. That the sale of alcohol had gradually become legitimized in the new town did not lessen his personal dislike of it. "He sees no pleasure or advantage in undue stimulation of the system," said a newspaper of the day.

But despite his election by a solid majority in the summer provincial election in 1898, and despite a growing number of temperance lodges in all the coal mining towns of the Island, and despite a slim majority of British Columbia voters being in favour, the national plebiscite result was inconclusive. Citing that ambiguity, Laurier refused to implement prohibition.

Having won the election, James Dunsmuir seemed true to his word. He personally put up one thousand dollars for a cooperative creamery and took his place in the legislature in Victoria, albeit on the opposition benches. Ralph Smith of the Nanaimo miner's union pointed this out when he attacked Dunsmuir in the succeeding months. He insisted that the people of Comox had made a mistake electing Dunsmuir, for he was powerless in opposition, and he had nothing to say in the House anyway.

With experience on the hustings, the son of the dynamic Robert Dunsmuir compared in accomplishment to his father in his knowledge of coal mining, in his loyalty to family, and in his objection to unions. "I object to all unions," he said to a Royal Commission hearing, "federated or local, or any other kind. I think I can treat with my own men without the interference of a union."

As a young man he had been given the same deferential treatment that his father had received in his early days in Nanaimo. When James and Laura left Wellington to reside only three miles away at Departure Bay, a dinner was given in their honour. During the dinner he was cited for his considerate manner, for making the safety of miners and mines his special care, for being courteous and gentlemanly, and for contributing to the harmony and security of the collieries. There are people today who remember a kindness he rendered to a crippled miner or his dislike of pomp or his honesty or his practice of talking to his men on a first name basis.

But James Dunsmuir lacked the human touch of his father. Although Robert Dunsmuir was immovable in his opposition to unions, he went out of his way to treat men fairly in other ways. As long as a miner agreed to place himself in the position of a beloved but somewhat misguided child, he could expect fair treatment from Robert. The son had not acquired that compassion.

In the turbulent days leading up to the strike in 1877, the young James had refused to accommodate the men's doubts about the accuracy of the Wellington scales. Whereas Robert wished to see the men's concerns addressed, James was stiff-necked and uncooperative. Robert refused to sell building lots to Wellington and Union Camp miners because he knew how transitory coal towns could be, and he did not wish to see them saddled with useless land should the mines close. James yielded easily to pressure for the sale of land, and, in Wellington at least, many families were forced to abandon property bought only four or five years before.

As his responsibilities grew, so did his stubbornness. By 1899 he was involved in at least five lawsuits ranging from a dispute with the NVCML over rights to Nanaimo harbour coal, to the bizarre Bryden vs Union Colliery, and to disputes with the settlers who had homestead rights in the new coal mining area south of Nanaimo at Extension. The most newsworthy disputes by far, however, were Walker vs Union Colliery, Grant vs Union Colliery, and Regina vs Union Colliery, which were all a direct result of the Trent River disaster.

The establishment of an export route to take the coal from the mines to tidewater had been crucial to the development of the Cumberland area. When Sam Cliffe and the Union Coal Company failed to finance the railroad, they had been left with no alternative but to sell to Dunsmuir, and once the Dunsmuirs were in control the railroad had been a top priority. The line followed the Trent River until it reached a point one mile from the sea, where it crossed a gorge over a very large bridge, truss, and trestle before dropping to Union Bay and the wharves.

The railroad made it easy to get coal to Union Bay and bring freight back to the coal camp, but it was still difficult for foot and buggy traffic to make the same journey. Because people bound to and from Union Bay on foot wished to avoid the notoriously bad road, it became common practice for them to ride the coal train, either in the locomotive or in one of the box cars.

Margaret Carthew was a case in point. When she arrived by ship at Union Bay in 1893 to join her husband at Union, she had a two year old toddler and a baby in her arms. She chose the preferred method of travel when she climbed aboard a boxcar and sat on a side of beef all the way to Union.

Company policy forbade passengers on the coal train. Superintendent Little caused notices to be circulated and had a special one posted right on the locomotive, prohibiting passengers and restricting them to the special car which ran twice a week. But no one paid any attention to those notices. In 1898, no one had even seen one for three or four years. Everyone rode the train, and the only time Little had anything to say was when a union organizer or other undesirable was seen trying to board. Little himself rode the locomotive often, and even James Dunsmuir had been known to do the same.

The locomotive was a ten wheeler Baldwin with a headlight, cap, and stack of polished brass. She had replaced a lighter engine in June of 1898 and weighed in at 116,000 pounds with her boiler full of water. She was the wonder of the district, was Number Four, and she could make the run from Cumberland to Union in twenty minutes on a good day, or "somebody is a liar."

Alfred Walker was no liar. He had been an engineer since before 1886 when he worked the locomotive that shunted cars onto the wharves at Departure Bay. Those wharves had been built by his father, Edward Walker, who had continued to follow his friend Robert Dunsmuir from Fort Rupert to Nanaimo and then to Wellington. When Robert died, Edward followed his son James to the Union camp. At least two of his own sons accompanied him: Enoch, who was a carpenter, and Alfred, the engineer.

Alfred was married and had five children. He had a beautiful voice, too, and often sang in public. During that summer of 1898, with the town in a jangle over the provincial election, he sang at a banquet honouring Thomas Russell, a mine manager who had resigned rather than work for James Dunsmuir, with whose labour policies he disagreed. Walker disagreed with his boss too, but he kept on working.

Every day, all day, Alfred Walker guided the coal train back and forth between the mine and the wharves, crossing the Trent River bridge many times. The bridge made him nervous. It was ten years old, and according to some people that was too old. The average life of a wooden bridge was between seven and eight years, but if they were kept repaired like the Canadian Pacific Railroad bridges were, they would last ten years. Some repair to the span had been done in 1896, but the bridge needed a new truss and a shorter span, and that would require new stone abutments, which were due to be started that very fall.

When the new, heavier engine arrived in June, Walker got really worried. He told Superintendent Little that Number Four was too heavy for the bridge. He took to clearing everyone out of the cab before he crossed the bridge, waiting for them on the other side while they walked across. Company carpenter George McLaughlin had inspected the posts in 1895 and 1896 and had found some rotten braces, which were replaced, but he and Mr. Little had not looked at the beams and chords when they decided the bridge would last one more year.

Two years later the old bridge still stood. McLaughlin and another carpenter named Walter Work examined it but did not bore into the wood to check for rot. They contented themselves with watching the span when the train moved across it, reasoning that if the chords were rotten they would squash.

John Harwood's job as the track foreman made him responsible for examining the track over the bridge every morning. He had been doing that for seven years and had never found anything wrong with the track. Harwood lived just one half mile away from the bridge, and he was on his way home at about 4:30 on the afternoon of August 16th when he slipped on the rails and broke four ribs. He hobbled home to bed.

Next morning Harwood was too disabled to check the tracks. He wrote a note to Walker and gave it to a little boy, telling him to wait at the bridge for the train and to give the note to the engineer before Walker took the engine across.

The first train of the day was ready to leave Cumberland with

321

twenty-one loaded cars. On board with Walker were Hugh Grant, fireman; Alex Mellado, head brakeman and grandson of *Princess Royal* miner John Thompson; carpenter Walter Work; two Japanese labourers named Nanka and Oshana, who sat on the coal cars; Richard Nightingale, that long time resident and pub owner of Nanaimo who had just returned from Wrangell, Alaska; and Frances Horn and Lavella Grieves, who were returning to Union Bay from a visit with friends. Matthew Piercy, rear brakeman, perched on the last coal car.

The train approached the bridge running smoothly and slowly, just a little faster than a man could walk, the engine backing up with the tender in the lead so it would be in position for the uphill grade on the return trip. The track foreman was nowhere to be seen nor had his young messenger arrived yet. The tender moved on to the bridge, followed by the heavy engine. Then the whole train disappeared.

William Bell was with fellow carpenter Enoch Walker, at work under the bridge preparing an area for one of the new stone abutments. Bell glanced up as the train started across.

The engine had got to the center of the span; it had a string of cars following after it, loaded. I can't tell how many cars were on the span. The cars were not uncoupled from the engine. I saw the thing when it commenced. It cracked and with a loud report the engine commenced to fall through.

It just seemed to come down all at once.

The giant locomotive turned a complete somersault and fell on its head beneath the trestle. Boiler telescoped into firebox; one loaded car after another fell on all sides. Matt Piercy at the rear of the train felt no break or jarring, but when he turned around and saw the engine gone he jumped from the plunging coal train and landed safely on the deck of the demolished trestle, which swayed dangerously. Scrambling down to where the train lay on its side like some wounded giant, he called to Bell and Enoch Walker to help him.

Matt Piercy gave a cry to come and give help. When I reached the spot where Piercy was he says, "Come on and give us help to get a girl out here." Reaching over to give my assistance, I found he had her out in his arms. Then seeing everything so quiet not calling for help, Matt Piercy said "My God! are they all dead?"

Everyone on board was dead except Hugh Grant and Lavella Grieves who were badly injured. Enoch Walker had seen it all and had watched as his brother plunged to his death. Someone said Enoch was nearsighted, but you did not have to have perfect vision to see what Enoch had seen that day. Afterwards he examined the bridge and found both sound and rotten timber, samples of which he brought with him to the inquest. McLaughlin had measured the shattered chords near the center of the span. The break was in sound wood.

The inquest jury heard conflicting testimony. Their subsequent inability to determine a cause satisfied no one and made them a target for criticism. Hugh Grant and Mrs. Walker both sued the Company and were awarded ninety-five hundred dollars and forty-five hundred dollars respectively. The Crown sued the Company for negligence, and the jury found that the Company had neglected its duty to take care of the bridge and trestle. In this first criminal case against the Union Colliery Company, a firm whose mines would kill hundreds of men, a mere five thousand dollar fine was imposed, but it opened the way for the survivors to seek more compensation.

Various legal proceedings dragged on until 1905. In 1902 Mrs. Nightingale was awarded seven thousand dollars; she appealed and a special jury in Vancouver awarded her ninety-five hundred dollars. A memo found in Mr. Little's papers advises him to settle with Mrs. Mellado for three thousand dollars and

When Mr. Dunsmuir returns see what he says about the same thing for Walker . . . use the fact she is saying her husband told her that the bridge was unsafe to persuade her.

It took no time at all for the Company to build a much lower alternate bridge on a new route. The passenger runs in the "Palace Car" were now available every day on the 3:00 p.m. "mixed daily" to the beach at Royston or on to Union Bay. Displayed prominently were Company placards prohibiting riding on the engine or coal trains.

When Edward Walker died at the age of seventy-seven in 1902, the town he had helped develop ten years before was unrecognizable. Not that it was beautiful or elegant or possessed any amenities beyond the bare essentials, but it had over one thousand people and a lot of them lived in houses they owned themselves. It had "The Big Store," as Simon Leiser's was called, with its five departments for dry goods, hardware and furniture, boots and shoes, groceries and liquor. C. J. Moore had offered similar wares since 1890, and T. H. Carey advertised fine tailoring in black worsteds, summer tweeds, or fine French trousering.

Cheap John bought for cash and sold strictly the same way. "We do not claim to give dollar per dollar, but as near as possible. Our SNAPS and big clearance sales are always on." Having followed his brother's example in leaving the mine, Daniel Kilpatrick ran the livery stable. With the Kilpatrick empire of stables, funeral parlours, and sawmills, they had no regrets about leaving the mines.

Some Cumberland businessmen had agreed to close their businesses at 7:00 p.m. except for Saturday and the week immediately following payday. In that week it was "no holds barred" as the private entrepreneur went after the miners' dollars. Sometimes the miner even benefitted in the rush to offer the most attractive deal, a decided change from conditions in the camp a few years before where miners had to buy their needs from a Company store. The prices then were almost twice as high as Nanaimo's, and each man had to sign a note empowering the Company to stop wages to pay store bills.

What with the extended store hours following payday, and the attractive deals offered by competing stores, and the lack of a bank in town to put any savings into, it was hard for a man to hold on to his wages. Anyone determined to save money had to deposit it with the post office. The money went to Ottawa, and it took three weeks' notice to make a withdrawal.

Mail delivery had improved somewhat. By 1899 the number of deliveries per week had risen from one to three, with the postage reduced from three cents to two to encourage use of Her Majesty's mails.

As progress caught up with Cumberland so did the law. Now able to boast its own police officer, the citizenry felt the restrictions of proper law enforcement. A curfew banned anyone under fourteen from being out after 8:00 p.m.; a new indecency bylaw imposed fines for any association with houses of ill-fame; swearing, drunkenness, vagrancy, gambling, and cruelty to animals all fell under the same edict. "Sporting woman" Minnie Clayton was fined fifty dollars for selling a bottle of beer to Mary Ella, who got six months hard labour for selling the same bottle of beer to an Indian. Cumberland had gone respectable.

There are more women in town than ever before; more families; more who keep their gains instead of squandering them.

Cumberland had also gone cultural. The Union Brass Band was now available for celebrations and concerts; the government provided a circulating library; the Bacher's Club provided refuge for unmarried men; debates were held to raise money for church organs; Presbyterians, Methodists, Roman Catholics, and Anglicans vied for the consumer's dollars and the consumer's soul. Greek Teas were an especially popular money raising event. In the church ladies' desire to raise money for good works, the incongruity of young girls serving supper in clinging gowns and Psyche knots was ignored.

By far the favorite cultural event in any isolated town was the "Entertainments," those amateur vaudeville extravaganzas that brought out the latent thespians and the closet musicians resident in the community. The Kumberland Koon Klub, unfortunately shortened to "K.K.K." to save time, provided Grand Minstrel Entertainment on a regular basis. "Doors open at 7:30, trouble commences at 8:00 sharp," read the ads. Mrs. Daniel Kilpatrick presided over the piano and accompanied the local celebrities, many of whom performed in black face.

The audience was not always as sedate as could be hoped. At one performance part of the crowd "behaved shamefully, knocking down benches and throwing articles and keeping up a general din."

There is an unruly element among the boys — and some boys not so young — in Union... It takes the form of whistling, throwing crumbs, nuts, etc. letting down benches, creating an uproar in some form, and disturbing those who take part, and of course those who come to enjoy themselves. This evil must be abolished. We trust no entertainment will be given in a public hall without the attendance of a police officer.

The call for "No entertainment without a police officer in attendance" was accompanied by a demand for no Sunday drinking at all. To assist in enforcement, the new constable published a notice warning all saloon keepers that the windows of their bar rooms must be kept free from shades so he could easily see the interior between 11:00 p.m. Saturday and 5:00 a.m. Monday.

Although there was still no sewerage system, there was a waterworks which drew out of Hamilton Creek, and while not perfect, it was hoped that it would prevent a repeat of the outbreak of typhoid which had been attributed directly to the water supply. It was fervently hoped, too, that the new system of pipes would eliminate one of the less attractive features of the original system, that of the occasional presence of black lizards in the water bucket.

"The town looks dull," moaned the *News*. The mines were busy; the miners were at work or quietly at home with their wives and families. The Sick and Accident Fund was solvent and had just purchased an "X-ray instrument," an incubator for bacteria, and a set of optical instruments.

For anyone trying to keep track of names and locations of mines, the early period of development in Cumberland had been a confusing one, but with the development of Number Four Slope about one mile from town, the Company had a sure winner. "Everything about the mine is got up on the best plan for labour saving," reported the Inspector. Electrical coal cutting machines "capable of doing the work of ten miners" and run by Chinese labour effectively reduced the number of skilled white miners required.

Number Two Slope excluded white men entirely, employing 150 Chinese miners for eight years and "never a man killed in it." The record at Number Five Single Shaft would not be so good. The mine was developed without a separate return airway, the plan being eventually to connect it with Number Six shaft in a tunnel running under the town. But the crucial connection was delayed year after year as the miners encountered faulting. As a result, the Company sought special permission to employ more men than could safely be accommodated by the inferior ventilation system. Each year — 1895, 1896, 1897 — the Inspector granted extensions to the rule.

In 1899 the Inspector recommended that the latest request be denied because there was not enough air to keep headings clear and there was no air at all at some of the faces. When the makeshift ventilation was improved, a further extension was granted in 1900. The connection between the two mines would not be made until 1908, and by then sixty-four miners would have died in a fire and sixteen in an explosion.

That terrible loss of life would rekindle the militancy of the Cumberland miners and lead to the Big Strike in 1912, but at the close of the nineteenth century, as the Boers fought for their rights in the Transvaal and Captain Alfred Dreyfus fought for his in France and Spaniards and Americans fought each other over who would have the right to Cuba and the Philippines, the miners of Cumberland had sacrificed their rights to the necessity of making a living wage.

What with explosions and fires and labour saving machinery and an all-Chinese mine, the white miner in Cumberland was beginning to look like an endangered species. When it became impossible for them to earn a living at the low wages Dunsmuir paid, they opted for a complete repudiation of all they had fought for and voted to commence employing Chinese helpers themselves. By 1902 there were 450 Oriental miners in the Cumberland mines and only 165 were employed by the Company. The remaining 285 worked for the very men who had said they were unsafe to have below ground.

326

The submissive state of the miners contrasted sharply with their militancy in 1895. Then 125 white miners, nearly every one in the camp, had requested MMLPA secretary Ralph Smith to come up from Nanaimo to help them organize their own local. Several days later the five men who were elected as officers of the union, all married men with families, had been discharged from the mines. Mr. Little told Mr. Smith, "My company has instructed me to prevent union by the men at any time." He said there were plenty of men who would work for him who wanted to have nothing to do with the union. The union broke up, but the miners continued to meet several times a year and demand exclusion of Orientals.

The premature collapse of the Cumberland union did not deter Ralph Smith and Tully Boyce. They had to protect the NVCML, with whom they had an agreement, from the cheaper coal that the Union Colliery could produce given the lower wages they paid. It was imperative for the health of the entire Island coal industry that the Cumberland union spirit not be allowed to wither.

By 1898 it was already too late. So broken was the spirit in Cumberland that when a controversy over the screening of coal and the payment of proper wages became the top priority of both the Inspector and union organizer Ralph Smith, the Union Colliery miners reacted against their would-be benefactors with hostility.

For some time it had been known that coal dust, which had formerly been left inside the mine as refuse, and which had caused the terrible explosions in 1887 and 1888, and which now had to be removed from the mines at considerable expense, could be used to make coke. Manager Thomas Russell had explored its possibilities before he left for Nanaimo to become manager there. Accordingly, in 1895 the foundations were laid at Union Bay to convert the formerly useless coal dust into the highly marketable coke.

In two years one hundred coke ovens were finished and turning out a "superior article." Construction on a second set of ovens was begun, so popular was the product. Close to the ovens, large bunkers received the fine coal as it came from the washers and breakers. There "nut" coal was ground fine to augment the dust from the miners' cars, which had been dumped and screened before weighing. Thus did the Company deprive miners of the income entitled to them for the dust they had laboriously loaded, dust with which the Company made a lucrative product.

It did not take long for the MMLPA in Nanaimo to catch wind of the practice. They asked Inspector Dick to investigate. Archibald

Dick was already deeply embroiled in trying to force the Union Colliery to comply with the Oriental-exclusion amendment but he took on this issue as well.

As he made his rounds from colliery to colliery he asked the management and the workers to describe how the coal was weighed and how the men were paid. In Nanaimo the coal was weighed before it came out of the mine. At Wellington the men were paid for all the coal in the car. But neither colliery used the dust. The story in Cumberland was different. Dick spoke to the men first.

I asked them if they were aware that the coal they sent out of the mine was not weighed before it was dumped and screened. All of them said "Yes we knew that was the system before we started to work." They also told me that they knew that they were not paid for what went through the screen, they only contracted to be paid for the coal that goes over the screen.

Mr. Russell confirmed this. Mr. Little gave more detail. The men were not asked to send out fine coal, so they were not paid for it. Twenty percent of what came out of the mine went through the screen. After clay and refuse were washed out, about eleven percent nut and fine coal, which was used to make coke, was left. The miners could not expect to be paid for that because it had cost seventy thousand dollars to buy the washer and machinery.

Little had a host of figures to justify the Company position. Miners were earning an average of fifty-six and one quarter cents per ton on coal actually dug. The Company had to pay pushers, tracklayers, water bailers, and shift Chinese. The miners could not expect to be paid for the refuse coal as well.

But the law required the coal to be weighed before it was screened. Smith checked this with the Inspector, who checked it with the Minister of Mines, and they all agreed. He told the Cumberland miners, and they said they were quite content with the big screen for that was the original agreement. When the Minister ordered the Company to cease violation of the Act, the Company replied that the Act did not apply to them, as they paid their men by the day not by the amount of coal. But the Inspector had been told the mines were working by the ton.

Ralph Smith appealed by letter to John Comb, the checkweigher at Cumberland, who was judged to be the most independent of the miners.

328

I am just afraid as time goes on, that the men at Union are having the fetters bound tighter every day, independent men are being discharged and allowed to leave your place, and not a thing is being done to resist the oppression...

The Inspector, by now Thomas Morgan, also contacted John Comb to clarify how the miners understood the method of payment. Were they paid by the day or by weight? At the miners' quarterly meeting they appointed Comb and two others to inform the Inspector that there had been no agreement with the Company regarding wages, and some miners did not even know how they were being paid. A second meeting was planned.

In the meantime, Morgan attempted unsuccessfully to get production figures from the Union Bay Customs Office and was finally reduced to travelling to the coal camp and making estimates based on conversations with outsiders. Ralph Smith visited Cumberland as well, where he was accused of being an agitator by James Dunsmuir. In reality he had only been able to communicate with one person, and that was John Comb, but Dunsmuir had somehow come into possession of copies of the letters Smith had written to Comb.

By now the most independent miner in Cumberland was being viewed as a traitor by some of his fellow workers. He welcomed any miner to call at his house and ask any questions he wished. The pressure was telling on the checkweighman as he lashed out at his opponents, calling them "hucksters, slaberdashers and remittance men."

John Comb redeemed himself in the eyes of his fellow miners and was reelected to his position, which he characterized as "the only place of trust in your gift." Discussion at the next meeting centered solely around the mode of paying Comb. No one wished to pursue the screening issue any further, despite the support of the Inspector, the Minister, and the Nanaimo union. In fact they doubted Smith's motivations, suspecting that he was urging them to organize so that the Union Colliery Company would be destroyed, to the benefit of the NVCML.

Unions had been declared legal in Great Britain fifty years before. They had been declared legal in Canada twenty years before. A union was functioning well in Nanaimo to the benefit of both the men and the Company. But in Cumberland, they had been declared illegal in all the mines owned by James Dunsmuir, and in Cumberland his word was law.

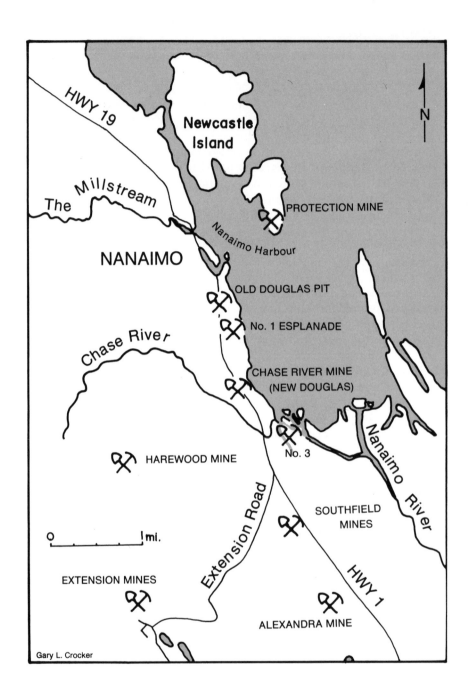

NANAIMO AREA MINES — 1870-1900

CHAPTER IX

THREE DOLLAR DREAMS

The Vancouver Coal Mining and Land Company has an agreement with the men. No man works for less than three dollars. If he is not able to earn it they don't employ him.

Samuel K. Mottishaw, Sr., miner

If I made three dollars I was satisfied. I had many conversations with Mr. Sharpe, and on one particular day I told him that the very moment labour got thoroughly organized man and master would shake hands and pull together; and I believe it is coming to that at the present day.

John Greenwell, miner

I object to all unions, federated or local, or any other kind. I think I can treat with my own men without the interference of a union.

James Dunsmuir, mine owner

James Dunsmuir's word was law in Wellington, too. From the day his father died in April of 1889, he had consolidated his power. In partnership with his brother Alexander, who ran the San Francisco office, and their mother, whom the two brothers gradually eased out of her position of influence within the Company, James controlled the present and future of thousands of mining families in Cumberland, Wellington, Alexandra, and eventually Extension and Ladysmith. As the decade wore on, he achieved political power as well, which culminated in his becoming Premier of British Columbia in 1900.

But even before he achieved political power, and even before his brother died and his mother had abdicated her official role in Robert Dunsmuir and Sons, James Dunsmuir's will was firm. There were some, however, who were determined to oppose this will. Samuel Robins refused to be bullied; Archibald Dick tried valiantly to enforce coal mining laws; and there were miners who were determined to change the way things were done in his mines.

Tully Boyce was such a man. The *San Francisco Star* described the expatriate Yankee as "a pleasing man, of good common sense, well informed and knows a 'hawk from a handsaw'." Joseph Hunter,

Member of the Provincial Parliament (MPP), and Superintendent of the Esquimalt and Nanaimo Railway (E and N) said, "Tully Boyce was a name which inspired a good deal of dread and far too much respect."

In February of 1890, Boyce had just begun to garner that respect Hunter found so threatening. He called a mass meeting of all miners to consider a rumoured wage reduction at the Wellington Colliery and the possibility of forming a Union for all district miners.

Mahrer's Opera House in downtown Nanaimo was packed with people from Nanaimo, East Wellington, Northfield and Wellington. They had come on foot, on the train, and on sleighs. One of the Wellington bosses said someone had spread a rumour that wages would be reduced just so they could declare an idle day and thereby ensure good attendance at the meeting.

In the past few years the British born population of the mine camps had been joined by hundreds of Finns, Belgians, Frenchmen, and Germans, who poured in to fill the jobs made available since the Chinese were excluded from the mines. An increased demand for coal by Her Majesty's Navy, by American war vessels and revenue cutters, and by ocean mail steamers had caused large production increases, and the mines would hire anyone who came along. There were so many new men at the Opera House meeting that Boyce had to ask for interpreters before he could proceed.

There was an air of caution in the hall. The chairman asked the newspaper reporter not to publish the names of the speakers. Someone said they should not be meeting in such a large group. But Boyce explained, "The men on this Island are scared to enter into any secret society and the only step I can see is to form an open meeting."

Discussion centered around conditions at the Wellington mines, conditions which had been deteriorating ever since the arrival of a new Superintendent eighteen months before. Old hands were gradually being replaced by new men who would work for two dollars a day. All the men at Number Five, the biggest mine, had been notified that they would be paid $2.25 instead of $2.50. A miner who had been working for three months said he could not make more than $1.50 and would have to leave. "It is the first place I have been where a miner could not earn more than he could barely live on," he said. If Wellington got away with paying two dollars then other collieries would soon pay that too.

The grievances began to pour out. There were too many men in the mines, so the Company could pick the men who would work for the lowest wages. Only Nanaimo had gas and pit committees, Wellington men having given up on a six month experiment with committees when they found them to be ignored by management.

A motion proposed "that we organize and let it be no secret meeting, for I don't believe in any secret meeting," and it was carried with only two opposed. A committee was appointed to draw up the rules for the Miners' and Mine Labourers' Protective Association (MMLPA), and the men left the hall with the slogans ringing in their ears.

Organize and keep it up. I have been here twenty years but the Wellington boys have let all their organizations go and then they come to the Nanaimo boys to help them. There are plenty of boys in Nanaimo to help you and damned good ones too.

We have been considering for a life time, especially the last twelve months and now we are brought to a starving point we shall have to do something.

The years of gradual buildup in union activity, of idealistic pronouncements and dismal failures, of Knights of Labour and political action, of depressed markets and stunning disasters, of looking for scapegoats and seeing gains stripped away had forged the militancy of the miners in the Opera Hall. They were beginning to feel their power; they had the strength of the internationally successful and affluent Knights of Labour on their side; and this time they would bring Dunsmuir to heel.

"Join the Ranks," cried a union paper which made the round of the mining camps, and the miners joined. Four independent branches were incorporated, with a district organization to coordinate activity. By May there were nine hundred members. On being informed of the new union, Samuel Robins, Superintendent of the New Vancouver Coal Mining and Land Company (NVCML), sent the following communication:

I am obliged by your letter of the 15th inst., giving me officially the names of the members of your Association forming the committees for the several mines of this company, whom I shall be pleased to confer with whenever any question arises upon which it is thought desirable to confer.

East Wellington miners soon had a similar agreement. The committee system handled grievances so well that most problems were dealt with before they ever reached upper management. But one company refused to cooperate.

Outside John Bryden's house, the Wellington MMLPA committee waited to meet with him. When he joined them in the yard, they asked if he would recognize their union and pit committees. He refused. He reminded them that he had already refused before, and so had James Dunsmuir. "Those pit committees are committees for manufacturing grievances," he later told a Select Committee of the Legislature.

The large hump of conglomerate rock called "the Bluffs" lay between the road to Wellington and the East Wellington mines of the Millstone Valley. It was big enough to accommodate two Dunsmuir mines, Number Four and Number Six; the Wellington Colliery Railroad, which collected coal at Number Six, Number Four, and at the top of the trestle from Number Three; a collection of tiny Company houses called the "white cabins"; and a large amount of open space. It was on the Bluffs twenty-one years before that Robert Dunsmuir had discovered his coal seam, and now it was on the Bluffs that the union leaders chose to hold a mass meeting.

A man could see for miles up there. On that 17th day of May, 1890, men from Wellington, more than four hundred strong, watched as Nanaimo miners arrived in procession with flags waving. As the visitors moved closer, the Wellington men formed into two rows for them to pass through, one man saying, "Gentlemen you have come out here to the 'lion's den'."

Surveying the hundreds of miners in their drab clothing — lounging, sitting, leaning, standing on the open rock-covered plateau — Tully Boyce called the assembly of over nine hundred men to order. He shouted out his message that Bryden was a tyrant and uneducated in comparison to the enlightened Sam Robins. "The day is passed [sic] when we must go to the rich man's door and beg. We shall not see our little children going about next winter without shoes on their feet. If they don't get shoes this winter they will the next." Having captured his audience, Boyce proceeded to compare them to the serfs of Russia. Island miners were well aware of the plight of Russian working men, and the rhetoric was compelling. He closed his introductory remarks by cautioning the men from Wellington that "unless we lift you up to our level, you will drag us down to yours." Then a stranger spoke.

Here we are about 1000 men strong, and each one a man. You have the will and the power to carry you through. When we send a committee to Mr. Bryden, from this mass meeting he will recognize then that we are not sending only three men along, but they will be backed by the forces that are present here, and he will be bound to recognize them.

Only a stranger would have misread Bryden so badly. The manager of the Wellington mines had always been true to his own principles even before he became associated with the Dunsmuirs through marriage and partnership in business. When he was confronted with the committee of three sent from the gathering on the Bluffs, Bryden agreed to nothing but a future meeting with Wellington men only, to be held as soon as Alexander Dunsmuir returned from Europe on May 26th. He would discuss nothing with the committee because none of them were Wellington men.

True to his word, Bryden convened a meeting at his home with James and Alexander Dunsmuir and the Wellington Miners' Committee, which consisted of six men, each representing one of the nationalities working in Wellington. There was a Canadian, a British citizen, a Belgian, an Italian, a Russian Finn, and a German.

The debate centered around the eight hour day. Well in advance of most other working people in Canada, the Island miners worked eight hour shifts, but whereas the rest of the district worked eight hours pithead to pithead, Wellington miners worked eight hours bank to bank. In other words, a Wellington miner's shift did not start until he was at the working face, and it ended when he left the face. Other miners were paid for the time it took them to descend into the mine and return to the top at the end of the day.

James Dunsmuir was firm. They must be at the face at 7:00 a.m. on day shift, and since they must take one half hour for lunch so the mules could be fed, they could not leave the face until 3:30 p.m. The miners said it was their business whether they wanted to stop for lunch or eat it as they worked. As things stood now they had to be at the mine at 6:20 a.m., and some men were not back up until four in the afternoon.

It was clearly not a battle about working a few extra minutes. Later, during the strike, James said the men who wanted to skip lunch could come up at 3:00 p.m. if they wished. He and the men knew that they would still dig enough coal to earn wages, so his production figures would not suffer. The eight hour issue was merely camouflage that scarcely obscured the real matter of contention. What management was opposing and the miners were promoting was union recognition. After eight hours of rancorous discussion, the meeting adjourned without agreement. The next morning, May 27, 1890, James Dunsmuir locked out his work force of over six hundred because the majority of them wanted a union.

Just outside the embattled Dunsmuir lands to the north, sat Somerset House. Because the pub was outside the coal lease and beyond Dunsmuir control, the Somerset was popular with the miners. It was there, on the grass outside, that Branch Two MMLPA met to discuss the lockout. Their reasonable request for a union had been rejected; a miner had been fired for singing at a union concert; discussion centered around a strike vote.

Included in the large group were twenty businessmen who had just as much at stake as the miners. Strikes took away their livelihood as well but they promised their support. So too did the longshoremen in San Francisco, who sent word that they would not unload Wellington coal.

"Think before you vote for a strike," the miners were cautioned, "it will be a long one." The vote taken and passed, a provisions committee was selected.

We will not be in want for something to eat. The eyes of the whole of the Pacific Coast are upon you now. There are men all over the coast who have been blackballed by this company.

Although they could select a provisions committee and deal quite effectively with food supply, housing was another thing entirely. On June 1st, Dunsmuir followed a family tradition and sent out written notices to the occupants of Company houses that they must vacate before June 30th.

All the people who had company houses, them white cabins on the bluff and all that, they had to get out and leave the scabs in. Robeson had property and a house on this place. So my dad went and stayed in a tent on this property until they got the house finished. Then my mother's brother built a house on the same street. Their name was Clark. One of their daughters named it Rock City.

Cutting timber and selling it to other mines, the four families got by in their camp in the bush between Wellington and Departure Bay. Some other mining families left almost immediately to get work in Puget Sound or back east. But most people stayed, waiting out the month of June lounging on the grass and fishing. A few recently arrived families required relief, which the MMLPA provided. All was well in hand and the miners were confident. Perfect order prevailed.

The loungers and the fishermen were aware of the five special constables who patrolled the lease, however. They saw the mules being taken out of Number Five and the carpenters, blacksmiths, and engineers discharged, a sure sign that the Company expected a lengthy battle. A Company steamship was said to have been tied up at Esquimalt and its crew let go.

Tully Boyce understood lengthy battles, too. He travelled to San Francisco to make sure the longshoremen were true to their word. He found Wellington coal well and truly boycotted. Non-union ships were met by hostile shoregangs; coal yards refused to take delivery for fear of a customer boycott. Some ships arriving at Departure Bay could only sail away empty when their crews refused to handle Wellington coal. Even the S.S. *Wellington*, a Company ship, found the bunkers empty and returned to San Francisco with a partial load of potatoes from the Dunsmuir farm.

With the union so new and untested, small cracks appeared early in the united front. Non-union men who had attended the meeting on the Bluffs told Bryden that union leaders were telling them who to vote for and pushing through motions to which not everyone agreed. One man said he wished to preserve his individuality and did not wish to be told what to do by union leaders.

Alexander Sharpe was the assistant manager of the colliery and he seemed to be everywhere, listening to complaints, ferreting out the dissatisfied, looking for chinks in the union armour. He noted that some miners joined the union after the strike started, just to get the strike pay, and others had gone to work in Nanaimo. A meeting of non-union men thrown out of work by the strike, but not eligible for strike pay, was broken up by union men from Northfield. There were charges that non-English-speaking miners were being misled, but one Belgian pointed out that he needed the union to fight for him because he was unable to argue for himself with the boss.

The deadline for vacating 130 Company houses passed peacefully, and the mining families docilely moved out. In the hot weather of July, it was easy to be philosophical about living in a tent. The furniture could be stacked up outside, and the children were happy to be in the open air. The miners who owned their own houses moved them off Company land to the road allowance between Northfield and the Half-Way Hotel, where some of the tents had already been pitched. Somerset House owner Dixon placed land at the disposal of displaced mining families, and soon houses and tents surrounded the hotel as well. A group of charitable Vancouver people sent tent canvas to be used by families if necessary or by single men if there were any left.

The citizenry of Nanaimo viewed the strike with alarm. Strikes were bad for business and Dunsmuir seemed determined to make it even worse. His resentment of Sam Robins for encouraging unions and paying higher wages had infected even the miners at Wellington and the Union camp up Island. They worried that Robins encouraged the union in order to prevent the Dunsmuir interests from paying even lower wages and thus rendering the NVCML unable to compete for markets.

Nanaimo city was synonymous with the NVCML and was therefore in the enemy camp. The *Free Press* no longer received ads from the E and N Railroad or steamers.[1] Later in the strike, when strikebreakers began to work the Wellington mines again, Dunsmuir offered a free train ride to Victoria after each payday so Wellington dollars would bypass Nanaimo.

In retaliation, a meeting called by Nanaimo's citizenry passed a resolution, which began:

> The late Hon. R. Dunsmuir and the present widow and orphans has been most liberally dealt with by the people of this fair Province, having been in the short space of fifteen years lifted from their almost chronic state of starvation to their present affluent position, when their wealth can only be estimated by millions if it can be estimated at all...

To characterize the Dunsmuir family's former economic situation as a "chronic state of starvation" stretched the truth mightily and weakened the moral indignation expressed in the resolution. The businessmen of Nanaimo were hurting and would continue to hurt for many months to come.

Wellington Colliery Company did not seem to be hurting much at all. Despite the closure of the mines, the Company was in a strong position. It could afford to wait the situation out because markets had gone into a slump. No one was selling much coal. The condition of the mines, however, was a cause for some concern.

A skeleton staff of foremen had been keeping the mines pumped out to prevent the damage that flooding could do to the tunnels and levels. But when the gob in Number Three Mine began to heat, and steam and smoke could be seen issuing from the return airway, water from the Millstone River was allowed to flow in. The union had offered to fight the fire, no pay desired or accepted, but the offer was declined with gratitude. This was only the first of several times that this mine or its twin, Number Four, with whom it shared a ventilation system, would have to be flooded in the next ten years.

By August, the Company had induced a few men to return to work. The MMLPA asked these men to join them in the strike, and they agreed to this request if the union would give them three dollars a day.

---

[1] James Dunsmuir tried to prohibit reporters from the *Free Press* from riding the trains but quickly realized the folly in that and rescinded the order.

Italian miners in particular had been offered that sum by the Company to return to work.

August also brought rain, and an end to the summer vacation atmosphere of the tent colony strung along Wellington Road.

> Between Half-Way House and the Northfield Mines the spectacle of these dwellings present a very dismal appearance ... so small that families must huddle up inside them, furniture left out in open air, new houses without roofs yet have furniture and bedding exposed to the rain, wretched tents of all sizes.

> In Wellington one can hardly see any tents but walk over the Bluff and the scene would only be worthy of a second Gettysburg, the tents there dot the grounds in all directions and the visitor would be impressed with the idea that he was in the midst of a military camp.

And the general atmosphere was still one of a successful military operation. The troops were well disciplined, strike pay was paid promptly to all who attended meetings regularly, the support staff was inventive and steadfast, and the mood was optimistic. In keeping with the soldierly air, daily processions of marching miners paraded through Wellington behind Knights of Labour and union banners. Bringing up the rear were four men carrying a scaffold from which an effigy of a "blackleg" hung by the neck, one black leg and one white leg dangling and swinging to the rhythm of the marchers' feet.

Special constables, somehow conspicuous despite their plain clothes, invariably followed the processions, which took great care never to trespass on Company property and were quiet and orderly. But the very orderliness of the marches seemed to threaten management.

One day not long after the daily processions began, the miners were just about to disperse when a special train pulling two passenger coaches arrived in Wellington. At the railway crossing in front of the Wellington Hotel on the shores of Diver Lake, the train stopped, and approximately fifty "red coats," militiamen of "C" Battery, disembarked and formed into a line.

As though not wishing to appear any less disciplined, the miners quickly re-formed their ranks. The impromptu honour guard sang and raised their hats to the soldiers as the militia marched past to the depot where Alexander Dunsmuir waited to greet them. To a suggestion by "Mr. Alex" that their first task was to disperse the miners' procession, the militia commander, Lieutenant-Colonel Holmes, replied that he could do nothing as long as they were peaceful. Holmes warned his soldiers that they must take orders only from him; they must not use ammunition unless ordered — and he doubted they would be — and anyone disobeying orders would be locked in the boxcar.

The presence of militia gladdened the hearts of Nanaimo merchants at first — a large order for blankets placed with a Nanaimo firm sweetened the pot. Wellington now had two military style camps and that was bound to be good for business.

The sound of a soldier's bugle morning and night shared the air with mine whistles as preparations were made to resume work at the pits. The deserted Company houses, so forlorn with their boarded up windows and doors, were made ready again for non-union men who had agreed to work as soon as their safety could be assured.

They did not go to work unaccompanied. Each day two hundred union men escorted the strikebreakers to the pithead, union flag at the head of the column, Belgian colours in the rear, the Belgian national anthem sung to mark the cadence. As each day passed, the processions became more lively. Two Nanaimo barkeepers provided refreshments on occasion. More and more banners appeared. There was one in red and white which said: "We want 8 hours a day and the recognition of our union"; another large one was made out of an Italian flag. On dispersal, the miners would give three cheers for the Queen, three for the soldiers, and three for the American flag. Excursionists from steamboats took pictures. Mingling with the tourists were many men with notebooks — journalists looking for a big story and policemen looking for incriminating behavior.

In contrast to the carnival atmosphere, the soldiers' lot was far less exciting. When not on duty they had to stay in the boxcars, which sat on a siding baking in the sun. But they were generally well fed and well treated. Although they had not left the depot since their arrival and their only diversion was a walk to the nearby Wellington Hotel, they could be seen there often, usually in friendly conversation with the miners. It had not proven necessary for them to guard the mine, and many of them felt their presence in the town was absurd. Fresh volunteers had to be brought in every day from Victoria to replace the members bored by the monotony of their routine.

Nanaimo was having second thoughts about the presence of this military unit in the district. An "Indignation Meeting" was called for August 11th in the Opera House. The three MPP's for the area, a miner, a former miner, and a farmer, sent a letter to Premier John Robson, who was also Minister of Mines. Thomas Keith, Thomas Forester, and C. C. McKenzie protested the presence of "C" Battery and requested its withdrawal, arguing that the militia would tend to

340

provoke the very disorders they were sent to prevent. Robson responded immediately. The government, he said, has no control over the militia.

Encouraged by the support they were now getting from Nanaimo, the strikers arranged a special procession on August 15th. Men, women, and children marched the five miles to Nanaimo, gave the *Free Press* three cheers, and paraded around the streets before dispersing to attend the trial of some of their own.

Summonses had been issued to Joseph Carter, a recent British immigrant and lifelong union man; John B. Greenwell, a former Dunsmuir supporter and now committed opponent; John Suggett, a recent immigrant; Arthur Bertreaux, the Belgian head of the French Syndicate in Northfield; Stephen Melzer; and Basil von Hugo. They were charged with "persistently following J. B. Hugo in and through the streets of Wellington."

The Dunsmuir counterattack swung into place. Employment agents in San Francisco advertised for men to go to Wellington. At the Dunsmuir coal depot in that city, men were told they could earn five to six dollars a day and that there had been some trouble but it was over. The S.S. *Wellington* had left Departure Bay with potatoes; it returned in mid-August with thirty men of all nationalities on board. Alex and James Dunsmuir waited on the wharf to greet the new workers just as their father had thirteen years before. They were determined to insulate the newcomers from contact with the strikers, but a fisherman had already crept on board and said there was still a strike and that the miners wished to meet with the new men at one o'clock that afternoon.

As the colliery locomotive pulled coal cars full of strikebreakers up the steep hill from Departure Bay, small slips of paper landed in the cars. Written in French, because all the newcomers were believed to be Belgian, the notes told them about the strike.

When the train arrived in Wellington, twenty of its passengers slipped away and blended into the union procession. The rest adjourned to the Company warehouse, where they were given dinner and were addressed by a Welshman named Jones. Jones had been languishing in jail on a drinking charge when he was recruited by the Dunsmuirs, who paid his fine and gave him ten dollars to support his wife. He became their spokesman. He announced to the newcomers that they would be familiarized with the mine that very evening by the Superintendent. Tour completed, the strikebreakers were treated to a round at the Wellington Hotel by a very jovial Alex Dunsmuir.

As August drew to a close, it looked like some progress had been made by the union. Financial support was strong, the *Victoria Times* had started a subscription list, NVCML employees were giving ten percent of their wages, Nanaimo people offered accommodation, and "Cheap John's" was generous with donations. Now the union could pay twice as much strike pay as it could at the beginning. Neither the provincial nor federal governments would grant Dunsmuir's request that they pay for the militia, which was shrinking each day as the soldiers were sent home one by one.

This made the non-union miners nervous. A trickle of men continued to return to work, but they were frightened by the processions and wanted the militia to stay. A petition "much soiled by being carried through the mines" was forwarded to Attorney General Theodore Davie asking that the militia be kept.

As a young lawyer in 1877, Davie had been serenaded by Wellington strikers banging kerosene cans as he conferred in his office with the Sheriff and Robert Dunsmuir. He was not swayed by the demands for a continued militia presence. Since the government had not put the militia there in the first place, he had no intention of removing it. If, however, the owners sent the militia away, he promised that the government would adopt extra precautions for the maintenance of order.

September 18, 1890 in Nanaimo saw the first Labour Day demonstration ever held on the Island. Each MMLPA lodge had a float with the members parading behind, under banners which read "WE CAN STAND COLD AND HUNGER BUT NOT INJUSTICE" and "EIGHT HOURS WE HAVE AND OUR UNION RECOGNIZED." The Nanaimo Brass Band, the Fire Engine and Hose and Reel, and the boys of the public schools were followed by Knights of Labour and MMLPA banners and then carriages for such dignitaries as Sam Robins.

The euphoria of a well-disciplined summer and a successful Labour Day was heightened when the Northfield and East Wellington union men entertained their striking brothers on the grounds of Somerset House with a picnic, concert, and dancing. But the days were growing shorter and the nights colder, and the inhabitants of the tent and shack encampments braced themselves for a long winter.

In the last week of September, the latest San Francisco recruits arrived to work the mines. None of them were miners. Tully Boyce wrote to the San Francisco-based Council of Federated Trades, urging them to keep it hot for Robert Dunsmuir and Sons in California. As the fall deepened, the Company began to create dissent among local Belgian and Italian union members by offering them as much as four dollars per day. The union members in East Wellington were cautioned to watch Chandler closely as it was suspected that he was supplying Dunsmuir with coal.

Strikebreakers continued to arrive. Thirty blacks from Comox were brought to Wellington on October 31st but refused to work. Fifty newcomers arriving on November 4th included in their ranks fifteen "practical miners" who refused to work as well. The union tried to help those jobless who agreed to respect the strike.

November brought some good news for the strikers. The four soldiers who constituted the rump of the militia force were replaced by one sergeant. An official from the national executive of the Knights of Labour visited and marched in one of the regular processions. The six miners who had been charged with intimidation were released on bail from a Victoria lockup to be met on their return to Wellington by two hundred people, who presented them with bouquets and escorted them to their makeshift homes.

But almost three hundred men were now working the mines. Many of them were inexperienced, and there had been an explosion in which seven were severely burned. Nevertheless the strikers' jobs were being done by someone else, and that made a lot of them very uneasy.

It rankled the Wellington men as well to know that union brothers in the other locals were unhappy about the ten percent of their wages being paid into the strike fund. A mass rally attempted to reinforce solidarity. Wellington, East Wellington, and Northfield men marched into Nanaimo behind the Northfield Brass Band to the Opera House, where they mingled on the main floor with Nanaimo men as their wives and children watched from the upper gallery.

When the president of the East Wellington local said he was discouraged by all the coal that was coming out of Wellington, he was shouted down. But Boyce said it was better to express doubts in the meetings than on the street corners. The citizens of Nanaimo must understand that the union was united, especially now that the strike was affecting the businesses of more and more people, and the incidence of violent crime was rising due to the presence of so many transient men.

The New Year began on a positive note when someone noticed that the solitary sergeant who had been patrolling Wellington was no longer there. However, he was soon replaced by provincial policemen, whose plain clothes failed to disguise them as they wandered about town, ostentatious in their make-believe indifference to the activities of the citizenry. About that time, Tully Boyce sent George Edwards to San Francisco to watch coal shipments carefully and to follow every delivery to dealers and customers. Edwards had already made a fund raising trip to the California city and knew the territory.

As strikebreakers continued to work the mines in increasing numbers, accidents continued to occur. "The rapidity with which one accident follows another is frightening many of the miners who are mostly green hands," reported the *Free Press*. Stableman Ellis Roberts was caught by the cage at the bottom of Number Five Mine and died seven days later on March 3rd. Fifty mourners escorted his body from Wellington to the cemetery in Nanaimo, through foot deep snow, in a procession of covered sleighs. During the burial service they all heard someone singing an "unearthly song" from just outside the graveyard.

Having consigned the deceased to the frozen earth, the mourners climbed into their sleighs for the return journey. As the procession reached Welshman's hill by the Half-Way House, they heard horrible noises and shouts of "bury them up," and suddenly the muffled quiet of the snow-laden day was broken by shouts of "why don't you drive white men not blacklegs?" and the clatter of tin pans beaten with fists and spoons.

The scene erupted in a flurry of snowballs hurled by people who appeared to be women and young boys, but the women had deep voices and flashed muscular legs below their skirts. Not that the Northfield women were above such behavior. Earlier that same day someone had been pelted with rotten eggs by women of that community, but the snowballers had a deadlier aim.

Thirty or forty icy missiles were directed at one sleigh in particular. It belonged to Assistant Manager Alexander Sharpe, a determined foe of the union. John Greenwell was sure the attackers were not strikers. From his tent in Wellington where the miners formed up three times a week for their regular processions, he had given orders to make room for the funeral procession as it passed. A passage through the strikers had opened, and the sleighs had proceeded through unmolested by either missiles or insults.

The general public refused to take the snowballing incident seriously even when the Select Committee on the Wellington Strike travelled to Nanaimo to hear testimony. This letter to the editor reflects the irreverence of the town's attitude.

Dere Mister Editer:

I red your report of the speshul committe to see why those little children snowballed those big miners on March 4 and I think they must have wanted a chepe holiday. Three small girls and a boy threw snowballs at my cat and broke my window do you think Mr. Editer that Mr. Davie would let the committe come up again and investigate the matter?

Anxious Mother

The presence of the special committee in Nanaimo signalled a change in the attitude of the government, and the union sensed this change. When the regular procession of strikers formed up on November 9th, discipline was tighter than before. Although the banners flew as usual, there was no singing, indeed no noise at all, as they made their way toward the Company houses in orderly formation, led by miner Robert Jervis on horseback.

At the corner of the road near the old colliery office, abandoned now for more sumptuous quarters in Victoria, several constables waited, some in uniform, some in plain clothes. As the procession approached, the officers divided into two columns, enclosing Jervis and his mount and the strikers at the head of the pack. Robert Jervis was arrested and charged with intimidation, as were fifteen of the strikers who were chosen at random and marched directly to the station. John Cottle was one of the arrested. He later told his son Bill what happened.

... old Chief of Police, old Stephenson, he said "grab that man, grab him." Old Charlie McGarrigle, old George Taylor, old Harry Ross. There were sixteen of them they grabbed. Put them on the train and took them back to Victoria. They kept them in the jail for three weeks before the trial.

Tongue-in-cheek, the Free Press reported,

... the Englishmen sang "We'll Soon Come Home Again" and Belgians sang "The Marseillaise." Informed they were going to Victoria at their country's expense they professed to be devoutly thankful for the cheapness of the ride.

In the name of peace and security, the judicial system of the province had been enlisted on the side of management. Justice of the Peace Planta read the Riot Act in Wellington to union members as they formed up for the next procession. The six men out on bail who had been charged with intimidation in August were called back to court. The arrested processionists were charged with conspiracy.

With the reading of the Riot Act, the orderly union processions had become illegal, but there were other willing people ready to take over from the arrested men. The commitment to the cause made by the wives and daughters of union men had been tempered in the weeks and months of living in tents, feeding families on reduced incomes, and cheering on the sidelines as their men stood fast.

On March 13th, eighteen women, sixteen of them Belgian, walked through Wellington on what they called a "March for Female Suffrage." The ranks were not so orderly as the men's had been, however. When Robert Bagster hollered at Naomi Poulet that Belgian women were no good for work, only for processions, and then struck her in the mouth with the back of his hand, he unwittingly unleashed a fury. Goaded by months of frustration and hardship, Naomi took after the loudmouthed seventeen year old, calling him a "blackleg son of a bitch" and threatening him with a rock. Naomi, not Bagster, was charged with assault.

Sir Matthew Baillie Begbie, for twenty years Chief Justice of British Columbia, belied his image as a friend of the little man when he sentenced Carter, Greenwell, Suggett, Bertreaux, Melzer, and von Hugo to six weeks in prison for "besetting one Joseph B. Hugo." As the small group prepared to leave Wellington to serve their terms, they wore masks of bravado and had themselves weighed on the E and N scales, offering bets on how much they would lose or gain on prison food.

Instead of marching in processions, the strikers now walked through Wellington in well-spaced knots of threes, fours, and fives, quiet and subdued, watched closely by policemen and special constables. There were still enough union funds to pay strike pay, and as one man said, "I am keeping the marrow on my bones, and not letting it go out." When the Grand Jury found "No Bill" against the miners charged with conspiracy, it gave the union men hope that perhaps the law was not always on the other side.

That spring of 1891 brought confirmation of what everyone had suspected anyway. The militia had been sent in at the request of three Victoria magistrates who had been approached by a member of the Dunsmuir family with a requisition which said "a riot or disturbance is anticipated at the mines of Robert Dunsmuir and Sons. . . ." The Honourable Theodore Davie, who would soon be Premier of the Province, had signed the order. But when Lieutenant-Colonel Holmes, the militia commanding officer, testified that there was no need to have sent the militia to Wellington, the Dunsmuirs were required to pay the entire cost of the unnecessary exercise in "aid to the civil power."

At a Miners' Mass Meeting on the Foresters' Picnic Ground in August, discussion was heated in anticipation of a vote on whether to continue the strike. Some said the Dunsmuirs were on their last legs, others said the Company could sell all the coal it wanted because there was a strike on in Washington too. There were rumours that the Wellington Collieries had been sold by Mrs. Dunsmuir. The Federated Trades Council in San Francisco wanted the boycott to continue. When the discussion ended, eighty-two voted against continuation and 342 in favour.

The overwhelming vote was not an optimistic sign, however. Most men recognized the fact that the men working in the mines during the strike were there to stay. Knowing they would not be hired back again anyway, the majority had voted to continue the strike out of a lack of alternatives.

By now many were in desperate need. Non-striking union members in the other coal camps were asked to "dig down in your jeans, boys." In his letter to the *Free Press*, one Nanaimo miner called the strike a laughable farce.

The issue of strike pay was causing cracks in the formerly united stand taken by the miners. When a meeting not sanctioned by the union was called for the Green, three hundred attended and sent a delegation to Sam Robins asking him not to fire men who had refused to give their ten percent assessment to the strike fund. They knew of miners who had found other work and were still drawing strike pay. Robins said he must stick to his agreement with the union.

Whereas in the first heady days of the strike one thousand dollars had been collected each payday, the totals now only reached four hundred dollars or less every two weeks. The names of delinquents were posted. The MMLPA pleaded with these men to attend union meetings and make their feelings felt there. The dissidents' committee met with a committee of the union.

In those meetings between the two parts of the union, the issue quickly became whether or not to call off the strike. Letters came in from outsiders begging the union men to settle their differences, noting that any gains could be lost in internal dissension. A rumour spread that the dissident miners would be discharged, which Robins denied, saying "they are restless spirits who constitute an element in all progressive organizations."

The strike dragged on into a second fall. At a November meeting in the Opera House in Nanaimo, attended by one thousand miners, George Edwards rose to report on the boycott of Wellington coal in San Francisco. It looked strong and good. The Dunsmuirs had had to rent a yard to have a place to unload coal, and they were offering the

347

coal at reduced rates. Even if the MMLPA decided to remove the boycott, they could not, so committed was the Council in San Francisco to continuing it. Despite his earnest entreaties to the contrary, the meeting decided to conduct a secret ballot on the continuation of the strike. The vote would be held in the lodge rooms of each local.

One week later the results were known. The union men had voted to end the eighteen month long strike. Boyce offered his resignation. A total of $84,033.91 had been paid out in strike pay, but Dunsmuir had won.

The Dunsmuirs, father and sons, always said that they would not rehire men who had walked out on strike. In the past, the shortage of labour had always made the threat somewhat hollow, but this time James Dunsmuir seemed to mean it. John Cottle was blacklisted in all Dunsmuir mines on the Island. His wife finally had to sell some furniture to keep the family in food. When Tom Mills' wife heard that Mrs. Cottle had sold her sideboard, she was shocked. A woman's sideboard was her most prized piece of furniture. Mrs. Mills spoke to her husband, who was an oversman for the NVCML, and he hired Cottle to work in Number One.

John Greenwell did work for James Dunsmuir again. He moved to Extension when it opened up, but things were much worse in Extension than in Wellington. The Greenwell family became leaders in the fight against the Company, a fight which lasted into the 1930's, many years after the Dunsmuirs had lost all interest in mining coal.

Coal was still of great interest to James Dunsmuir in 1891, however, and there were hundreds of men waiting around for the chance to dig it. The Wellington mines were reaching the outer limits of the coal body, but since two-thirds of the coal was contained in the pillars left standing to hold up the roof, it looked like the Wellington mines would go on for a long time yet. Inspector Dick, who was very impressed with how well the mines were run, wrote, "There is a large extent of coal in sight, which will last a long time."

The surfeit of manpower troubled at least one of the bosses at Wellington. James Sharp, a Lancashireman who had come to Wellington in 1879 via Pennsylvania, had been oversman in both Numbers Three and Four mines. Because the two were connected, both had to be flooded when one or the other of them caught fire, as they did on several occasions. Each time this occurred, the men had been unable to dig coal. Even when the mines were working there were too many men. Sharp testified:

There were two or three months there when there were more men working than we could take coal from. I was to blame for it, and I did it for pity. There was men lying around there week after week, and month after month begging for work, and I let them [go] down, and the consequence was that we couldn't take coal from them.

Some days the extra men, and there were about fifty of them, worked all day on contract and got no pay. The roof was low, the coal soft, and the shots kept knocking out the timbers, which then had to be reinstalled. Miner David Jones found it very frustrating, saying, "I don't go down the pit to lie down, I go down to work."

The extra men in Wellington made many people uneasy. Post-strike discontent seethed just beneath the surface, and the Wellington union seemed as dead as if it had never existed. In the minds of many, there were still old scores to be settled.

George Graham was a drifter. When he drifted down from Cumberland to Wellington in March of 1894, he needed a job. But so did a lot of other men. As he wandered the roads around the old mining camp one afternoon, Graham got lost west of town. It was getting dark when he finally figured out where he was and headed back towards Wellington.

George did not trust anyone. When he saw four men away in the distance walking toward him, he hid behind a tree to wait for them to pass, but instead they stopped in front of one of the larger Company houses by the Old Slope, close to where Graham was hidden.

By then it was too dark to see their faces, but he thought he recognized one of the voices. He had worked with him at the Union mines up Island. As he watched, the four stepped off the road into a secluded spot and lit a small lantern. From out of sacks and pockets came powder and dynamite, coal dust, wooden plugs, and a fuse, which they used to fashion a bomb inside a seven foot long pipe.

As the hours crept by, Graham was cramped and cold, but he remained hidden because he had seen too much. In the dark of the early morning of March 13th, the four men suddenly rushed up to the nearby house, laid the bomb on the verandah, lit the fuse, and ran.

The early-morning silence was shattered by the explosion. Graham used the confusion to run away as fast as he could go until he reckoned he had run far enough. Then he doubled back and melted into the crowd already gathering in front of the home of Alexander Sharpe, Assistant Manager of the Colliery.

Alex Sharpe had made some enemies among the miners since his arrival in 1889, fresh from Scotland. During the strike he had kept his eyes and ears open for information that would assist his employer. Some of the animosity felt towards Sharpe had been expressed during the snowball barrage in Northfield. Snowballs were one thing, but it was hard to justify what had been done to Sharpe's house with that bomb. George Graham and the other onlookers saw that every window was broken, the walls were torn, and the surrounding trees were cut to pieces. In some places bits of metal had pierced through two inch boards. Fortunately no one was hurt, due at least in part to the fact that Sharpe was not sleeping in his usual room at the front of the house.

Provincial police and colliery officials investigated. The bomb had been made by inexperienced hands and had spent most of its energy on the lawn, where it left a large hole. A fifteen hundred dollar reward was offered, and the police set out to scour the province for persons with knowledge of explosives, an impossible task in those under-regulated days of extensive mining.

It was almost two years before the police got the information they needed. Graham had left Wellington the day after the bombing and had been hiding from the four men ever since. Going from job to job, drinking too much, losing work because of the drink, he was a miserable figure when he returned to the Union mines in late 1895.

When he moved into a boarding house in Cumberland, Graham was appalled to find that he was sharing living space with one of the men he had been trying to avoid. Within a week the other three showed up. The strain and the alcohol turned Graham into a blabbermouth, and he was heard in a bar one night talking about a bomb.

The two police constables who overheard his conversation knew what bomb he was talking about. While one arrested Graham, the other notified Superintendent Hussey of the provincial police, who slipped quietly out of Nanaimo on the boat bound for Union Bay. When he reached Cumberland, Graham had already told his story.

Although he arrived in Nanaimo in January of 1896 in handcuffs, George Graham left one month later a free man. The four bombers were arrested and Graham collected the reward. He was never seen again in any Vancouver Island coal mine.

By this time, Alex Sharpe had been promoted to General Superintendent of the Wellington Colliery and the rumour mill had long since tried to hang the blame for the bombing on organized labour. The particular target was the Reform Club, a political action group with branches in each of the coal camps. In cooperation with the

Nanaimo MMLPA, the Reform Club worked for more political involvement by working men. A letter to the editor speculated,

It seems a coincidence that the recent dynamite outrage occurred but a few hours after the formation in Wellington of a branch of a certain political organization with well known feelings to anarchy and Sunday meetings.

The platform of the Reform Clubs was decidedly less sinister than the above writer implied. Women's suffrage, the settlement of E and N lands, extension of the E and N to Comox, the eight hour day for governments and municipalities, no Chinese or Japanese employed by governments, and temperance — all were current issues that appealed to the working class.

Temperance was particularly topical. At a time when local breweries made daily wagon deliveries to pubs around the mine sites, there was a growing awareness that liquor would be the undoing of the working class. Because drunkenness was a particularly acute problem among Russian Finns, they were especially active in the founding of temperance lodges.

Finnish lodges were founded in each of the mining camps and followed the miners from camp to camp as old mines closed and new ones opened. The *Lannen Rusko* moved from North Wellington to East Wellington and finally to Nanaimo, where the *Aallotar* lodge already flourished, having been founded in North Wellington several years before. The *Lannen Side* from Cumberland later moved its library first to Wellington, then to Extension, and finally to Ladysmith. In each place, the "Finn Hall" provided a focal point for the whole community.[2]

As a reflection of the increasing number of people right across the country who were concerned about the problem of alcohol consumption, every mining community had several temperance lodges. Authorities disagreed on the source and extent of the problem. The Sheriff in Nanaimo said the problem lay mostly with transients, and William McGregor, NVCML manager, said the Company dismissed habitual drinkers after a second chance was granted them. McGregor also told a liquor commission hearing that the Company forbade licensed premises on or close to Company property, but his testimony seemed to ignore the cluster of hotels within a few steps of Number One Mine.

---

[2] Entertainment consisted of lectures, recitals, singing, and reading from the Finnish library and from handwritten newspapers. Card playing and billiards were prohibited inside or outside Finnish Halls; smoking was prohibited inside.

The Methodists had great success with the Indians, sixty of whom took a pledge of total abstinence and adhered to it. The Good Templars, Sons of Temperance, Gospel Temperance Union, and the Women's Christian Temperance Union, their efforts coordinated by the Central Temperance Executive, campaigned vigorously though-out the decade for the prohibition plebiscite they knew would save the country from itself.

Not all the population was as concerned as the reformers were, however. A "No Drinking on Sunday" bylaw was passed in Nanaimo in 1896 but was not even enforced for two years. When it was finally implemented journalists commented:

The early closing by-law gave the general mixologists at the various hotels and saloons a much needed rest; but the citizens went dry all day Sunday.

Some of the water works officials who were not apprised of the license inspector's move and consequently had not prepared for the unusual drain on the reservoir, are, it is understood, making a robust kick over the matter.

The bylaw applied to everyone except *bona fide* travellers and restaurants that supplied alcohol with meals. The definition of a traveller as someone who had gone three miles made one wag wonder if people would drink to travel or travel to drink.

The national prohibition plebiscite of 1898 resolved nothing; in the coal camps, the consumption and abuse of alcohol continued. There were twenty-one licensed premises within the Nanaimo city limits, and the majority of arrests made by police were for drunkenness and assault. When the Sunday closing bylaw was finally enforced, the Nanaimo Silver Cornet Band organized Sunday excursions aboard a steamer, where people could listen to band music as they floated leisurely off shore enjoying the drink they were denied on shore.

The band was the pride of Nanaimo. Wearing "gorgeous uni-forms," their performances lit by three large torches held by boys hired for the occasion, the band, nearly all of whom were miners, entertained all comers at the bandstands on Dallas Square or Victoria Crescent. Their renditions of the "Burnt Cork Caprice" and "The Black Shoemaker" were particular favorites.

The band was not the only cultural institution in Nanaimo. The Nanaimo Literary and Athletic Association showed understanding of its audience and a certain pragmatism by offering a program which consisted of readings and songs alternated with wrestling matches.

And Nanaimo had its heroes to lift its everyday world out of the ordinary. "Our Invincible Dan" McLeod won the world's wrestling championship in 1897, and the Nanaimo Hornets Rugby Football Team in their black jerseys, white knickers, and black stockings won the British Columbia championship in 1894, only one year after the team was founded. The popularity of rugby football was reflected in the plethora of teams in the area. The Northfield Violets, Nanaimo Swifts, Nanaimo Athletics, Wellington Rovers, Tar Flats, Squaw Hills, and Thistles took on each other and teams from the rest of the province.

The enthusiasm of the spectators may have been reflected in the founding in 1899 of the Nanaimo Anti-Swearing Club, which was "gotten up to discourage profanity." The small fines that were imposed every time the first commandment was broken went to finance a banquet. "Judging from the menu provided Saturday night, some of the members are afflicted with lapus linguae in quite an aggravated form," wrote one satisfied participant.

Nanaimo was beginning to look prosperous. More houses were painted, the roads were straighter, electricity illuminated some buildings and gas others, and a huge park lay on Company land between Wellington Road and the Millstone River.[3]

But the town was still a mining camp and the population was still fluid and the single men still drifted in and out looking for jobs and the seamier side of life developed apace. In an effort to control prostitution, the city fathers had concentrated the brothels on the three blocks of Fraser Street, which ran along the lower part of the ravine. Starting at the north end with the "Red Light," which adjoined the Newcastle Hotel and Bell Johnson's and Star House and Clem Davis', the establishments flourished under madams like Jenny King, Ruby Howard, and Red River Annie Brown.

Fraser Street came alive after midnight. In an effort to control the worst abuses of the brothels, which also sold liquor and turned a blind eye to gambling, the small police force often found itself the subject of criticism when it was perceived as being too easy on the brothels or too eager to frequent them in search of "evidence." Saturday night after payday was especially hard on the law enforcement officers. That was the night Jenny Brown brought her "Saturday Night Specials" from Vancouver, meeting the girls at the dock with her bodyguard, loading them into a cab, and taking them to Fraser Street to handle the weekend crowd.

---

[3] The Company soon donated the park to the city, which named it after a Company official named Bowen.

Fraser Street was always busy and noisy after dark. Then in 1895, it became busy and noisy during the day too as the city in cooperation with the NVCML began to fill the ravine with waste rock from the mines. Eventually the fill reached the gap between Commercial Street and Victoria Crescent, eliminating the need for the bridge and putting an end to the abominable stench that rose from the tidal inlet on a hot day.

A nuisance of a different sort was handled with Company assistance as well. Before 1884, Chinese homes and businesses had suffered constant harassment from their white neighbours. Shortly after his arrival in that year, Sam Robins had set aside eight acres of land on the waterfront south of the Douglas Pit as a Chinese quarter, in an effort to remedy the situation. Robins had decreed that all Chinese residing on Company owned land must move there. As he told a Royal Commission:

We own the land on which Chinatown is built; the Chinese erected the buildings, such as they are, themselves. It was considered temporary. I wanted them outside of town. I removed them. We get fifty or sixty dollars a month rent for the whole of Chinatown. It is unsatisfactory to me. They tried to buy lots in the city. They offered very good prices on it. I refused. I refused to sell to them anywhere.

To other white eyes as well, the miserable collection of over-crowded shacks, each housing several men living as frugally as possible, was repugnant.

They live, generally, in wretched hovels, dark, ill-ventilated, filthy and unwholesome, and crowded together in such numbers as must utterly preclude all ideas of comfort, morality or even decency, while from the total absence of all sanitary arrangements their quarters are an abomination to the eyes and nostrils and a constant source of danger to the health and life of the community.

A mission built on land donated by the Company and financed by a Chinese merchant offered Christianity and succor to these outcasts from white society. The Methodist missionaries knew them well and put their knowledge to practical use. At concerts to which both whites and Chinese were invited, it was found that it was better to allow the Chinese in free because when they were not charged admission, they gave more money than when they had to pay.

The missionaries observed that their Oriental brothers were by nature gregarious and used to living in close quarters with family and relatives. Conditions which seemed intolerably crowded and unsanitary to whites were normal and comfortable to the Chinese, the

354

majority of whom were quiet, peaceable, and industrious, their main vices being confined to gambling and opium.[4]

Chinese working at the mines outside the city continued to live in smaller enclaves like the one near the Southfield Mine. Wellington Chinatown had shrunk after 1890, when Chinese miners were excluded from working underground. All that was left of the population of two hundred, who had lived near Dunsmuir's Old Slope, was a small collection of old characters who did washing for the whites. Sleepy Bob, Sam Pat, Long Tom, My You, and Ah Lee grew in legend as children passed the stories from one generation to the next.

Not many years after Robert Dunsmuir's death, the old Wellington townsite around the Old Slope was supplanted by a brand new one closer to Diver Lake. Robert's refusal to sell building lots had angered many, and during the 1890 strike, the *Free Press* criticized the family for its continued obstinacy. In anger James Dunsmuir had a survey done and sold lots to all comers.

At first it seemed to be a wonderful idea. Now the town could incorporate. Now hotels could be built and outsiders could be encouraged to settle. The Ancient Order of Foresters began a building which would house two stores and an Opera House besides the meeting rooms for the lodge. More substantial houses appeared, boarding houses like Noah's Ark, known for the range of nationalities living beneath its roof, and Rebecca Sanders', whose eleven children left a lot of empty spaces in her house when they grew up.

There were even a few sidewalks. The Kilpatricks opened a funeral parlour, and someone built a store to sell furniture. A person could buy shoes and groceries and dry goods and bread, and Simon Leiser opened a store near the old Wellington Hotel — a sure sign the town had arrived. When a new Wellington Hotel and the Abbotsford Hotel and the Delmonico Boarding House and Restaurant sprung up, people started to feel as though they were living in a proper town. When a bicycle track with a ball ground in the centre and a six hundred seat grandstand attracted large crowds on special days, and when the E and N built a car repair shop and roundhouse between the

---

[4] In the twentieth century, Nanaimo's Chinese organized the Rising Sun Holding Company by selling shares and bought eight acres on a hill near Pine Street just outside the city limits as a site for a new Chinatown. As their association with the mines ended, the former miners grew old living in the same crowded conditions in which they had always lived. They could sometimes by seen in the stream nearby picking watercress, which they carried in brown sacks to sell at the restaurants downtown, still harassed by young boys who would scare them badly by sneaking up and jumping out at them.

station and Diver Lake, people started predicting that the town would last forever.

There were still some drawbacks to living in Wellington. The postmaster was a retired clergyman who kept people waiting twenty-four hours for their mail, and the schools left something to be desired. There was no hospital or fire department, which was pretty nerve wracking during bush fire season, when there was sometimes a continuous fire from the Somerset Hotel to the new townsite, when burning trees fell over telephone lines, and when mine powder sheds were threatened.

But the town had a pretty good bucket brigade, and all the men at the E and N repair shop would come on the double if they were needed, and the folks in Nanaimo had offered their fire engine in an emergency. That engine could make the run in no time at all, belching black smoke behind its four galloping horses and looking like something on fire itself.

But a fire engine borrowed from a town six miles away did not satisfy A. J. McMurtrie, proprietor of the Abbotsford Hotel. He bought a Waterous steam engine and presented it to the town — and not a moment too soon. Even before the engine was officially christened, it saved most of the town from burning to the ground.

At 1:30 a.m. on a March night in 1899 during a St. Patrick's Day dance, a kerosene lamp was kicked to the floor of David Hunden's candy and fruit store, which shared the Opera House building. Without the McMurtrie Waterous, the whole south end of town would have been destroyed. As it was, the Opera House, the candy store, Grant Jessop's Drug Store, the library, John Evans' Bakery, and Thomas Bickle's house went up in flames.

The fire left a gaping hole in the brand new downtown and set people to thinking about the rumours that James Dunsmuir was planning to shut the mines down. Coal towns lived with that threat all the time, but this time the threats seemed real enough. And there seemed to be a lot of funny things happening that would make a superstitious person very uneasy.

Just a few months before, in September of 1898, oversman Tom Haggart's house had sunk without a trace into the ground. It was on a Sunday night that it started. Haggart had just come off evening shift and was sitting in the kitchen with his wife in their home in the old townsite when they heard a "rumbling noise like distant thunder" coming from their front room.

They rushed to open the door between the kitchen and the front room and it was jammed and they couldn't get it open. It was a good job they couldn't because the floor had gone down the mine. So they rushed out and got the kiddies out the window. Half the house went.

Just then a man arrived to say that water had broken in to Number Five Mine. A large part of the works were flooded, men were deep in water and mud, and two of them had had a very narrow escape. Leaving his wife and children in the care of neighbours, Haggart returned to the mine to see where the roof of the northwest level had caved.

The incident had not been entirely unexpected. The roof of that level was in a bed of gravel, and the superintendent had expected that it might flow like sand in an hourglass, especially if there was water to accelerate the flow. What no one expected was that it would affect anyone's house, least of all Haggart's, which was not even over any mine workings.

Theories have been expounded from that day to the present. The most likely one is that Haggart's house was atop the same extensive bed of gravel, and when it started to flow into the mine like some granular river, it took the house with it. Whatever the cause, Haggart returned from the mine in the early morning to find his neighbours, friends, fellow workers, and strangers watching the remains of his home. Among the hundreds of watchers was a reporter from the *Wellington Enterprise*, who described what Haggart saw.

... a cave thirty feet at the top and double that forty feet down and "shelved off" at sixty feet; masses of earth and boulders were continually detaching themselves from the sides and falling in, and there was a perpetual noise of running water. A maple tree that had been growing alongside the house had fallen in and its top could be seen a foot below the level of the ground. The bottom had dropped out of the well, and through it one could look at the shifting bottom of the cavity. Several loads of fir boughs were thrown in to check the opening of the mine.

Everyone knew that the Number Five workings did not extend as far as Haggart's house. The seeming mystery fueled some imaginative speculation and a few more coal town legends.

So the people who lived all around, you know, they said that the other half would go at twelve o'clock the next night. You know that's when a cave takes place. Something in the earth rolling over about that time. So there was a bunch of fellows there and the doctor lived in the house where Dunsmuir had been living and he was going to be braver than the rest. He had a bicycle, he took it over there, there were hundreds of people there watching at twelve o'clock. Sure enough, but when the house started to go he forgot about his bike. He ran with the rest of the crowd.

The player piano was heard playing for several days after the house disappeared.

Robert Kilpatrick, whose many sidelines included supplying timbers for the Wellington mines, provided a team of horses to haul trees to be dumped in the hole. Finally the Company laid a spur line of railroad track to the edge to faciliate the dumping of mine rock from Number Five into the chasm that had swallowed Haggart's home.

One month later the hole began to widen again. When it looked like it would threaten the mine storerooms, the contents of the buildings were removed. Then in March of 1899, hard on the heels of the Opera House fire, Number Five had another cave-in at the same location. This time fifty men barely escaped.

What was happening to the Wellington mines? Number Four had closed in 1897, its demise cutting the ventilation of its twin mine. The disabled partner, Number Three, limped on until 1899 on special dispensation from the Inspector. Number Six closed when its workings reached the boundary between Wellington and East Wellington. Number Two had been only an adit for the Old Slope for most of its life, and the original Dunsmuir mine had ceased production in 1888.

All that was left was Number Five, the biggest producer in the field, whose extensive workings stretched as far as the Number One shaft at the edge of the lease. Although Number One was almost as old as the Company itself, it had never been more than a small hole until permanent head gear was erected in 1892 to facilitate removal of the two bands of fire clay lying on either side of the coal seam. In 1895 the workings had been connected with Number Five, and longwall coal had been removed until 1899, after which the shaft served as an escape route from the larger mine two miles away.

But surely the larger mine on the shores of Diver Lake was inviolate. It supplied coal for the entire E and N from a branch line which ran right under its bunkers. Old hands said the mine was full of coal so good that it sold well even when markets were depressed, and they certainly were anything but depressed in 1899. Then there was the tunnel under Diver Lake. The Company had gone to a great deal of trouble and expense to construct that tunnel — five feet square and fifteen hundred feet in length — to lower the level of the water in the lake.

It was a funny thing about that tunnel. Everyone knew it existed.

Thomas Bickle had got the contract to construct it. It drained out into the Tunnel stream which flowed inland to meet the Millstone in the valley beyond the Bluffs. But the Inspector did not mention it in his reports, and so the tunnel from Diver Lake became another Wellington legend.

Dunsmuir drained the lake. What they call the Tunnel stream. The trout from the Millstream goes up into Diver Lake. I caught one one day that was all bruised up from making the climb.

They tell me that Dunsmuir was always scared of them lakes. He wouldn't venture too close to them.

In the summer of 1899, a *Free Press* reporter stood on Vittoria Avenue in Wellington.[5] The site of the Opera House fire lay empty except for a few pieces of charred wood. Wagonloads of furniture passed through town on their way south to the new Dunsmuir mines at Extension. Flat cars of the E and N carried houses and pieces of houses to be rebuilt in the raw bush of the new lease.[6]

...now only Number Five slowly struggles along; property on the new townsite was at a premium, now at a discount; every second man you see is either a Mongolian or a foreigner; houses and cabins unlet; merchants grumble; miners hang around the corner discussing the blueness of the outlook.

Number Five produced for another year. By then James Dunsmuir had moved the site of the new Extension Mine from the original 1895 slope to the new Main Tunnel. He had flirted with the people of Nanaimo, holding out the possibility that the shipping wharf for his new coalfields would be first at Newcastle Townsite, then at the Northfield wharf, and then back at Departure Bay. He had even started building a railroad from Extension in that direction when he ran afoul of Sam Robins.

Though Robins admired the skill and audacity of the Dunsmuirs, father and son, he considered them his enemies. Philosophically so different in their labour relations, Robins and first Robert and then James had developed over the years a rivalry that threatened to exceed mere business competition.

The problems began shortly after Robins arrived on the Island in 1883, when he reneged on an agreement with Robert to sell their coal

---

[5] Two avenues in the new townsite had been given the Italian sounding names of Vittoria and Corunna. The English were represented with Wellesley Avenue and Apsley Street.

[6] When the townsite of Ladysmith was established in 1900, A. J. McMurtrie had the Abbotsford Hotel moved in two sections on flat cars.

at an agreed fixed price.[7] In the 1890's legal proceedings had embroiled both companies for several years as they fought for the rights to the coal in Nanaimo harbour opposite the Newcastle Townsite.

Then James told the citizens of Nanaimo that he would be glad to keep his wharves in the city and thus enhance Nanaimo's business opportunities, if he could purchase the Northfield wharves from the NVCML at a reasonable price. A committee of citizens presented the proposition to Robins. Robins said he would be glad to sell the wharf and the ten to fifteen acres of land adjoining it provided James Dunsmuir agreed that no Chinese should be employed underground in Alexandra and Extension!

No one, least of all Sam Robins, told James Dunsmuir how to run his mines. The building of the railroad from Extension toward Nanaimo was discontinued, and the line went instead in the opposite direction to property around Oyster Harbour, property Dunsmuir had purchased in 1896. Not only would the wharves be at the new town of Ladysmith, as Dunsmuir christened it, but the beleaguered miners who had moved their homes from Wellington to the Number One Extension Slope, then three miles down the mountain to the new tunnel, would eventually be required to move them yet again to Ladysmith or lose their jobs.[8]

Extension coal lay under the enormous E and N land grant. And Dunsmuir controlled the surface and underground rights of all that land except for the parcels alienated before December 19, 1883, either by Crown grant, pre-emption, lease, agreement for sale, or as Indian or military reserves.

Jonathon Bramley had pre-empted a homestead in 1883 on the southern shoulder of Mount Benson. The acquisition of land, however, had not made him wealthy, and at least some of Bramley's sons had become coal miners. The eldest, and his father's namesake, was one of the victims in the Number One Mine explosion, which also

---

[7] In the 1890's the Dunsmuirs were involved in another case of price manipulation when James and Alexander and five hundred other coal merchants and suppliers were indicted in California under a new law against the restraining of interstate commerce. "[T]he barons and their vassals out-Peter Peter in their denials" said the *Free Press*. James and Alex first responded by saying that their mother, not they, owned the colliery. The charges were later dropped on the technicality that Robert Dunsmuir and Sons partnership had been involved and not the present organization of Robert Dunsmuir and Sons Company.

[8] For more details on the rivalry between Dunsmuir and Robins and the beginning of Extension and Ladysmith see the author's book *Boss Whistle*.

took one of Bramley's sons-in-law. Another son, Ezra, had been injured in Southfield Mine in 1890. But the family luck seemed to change when Mary Jane Bramley married Ephraim Edward Hodgson, for it was he who discovered Extension coal clinging to the branches of an upturned tree on E and N land south and west of Nanaimo in the summer of 1895.

Hodgson has been variously described as a rancher and a butcher, but as soon as he reported his find to James Dunsmuir, he was rewarded handsomely and became a Dunsmuir man. In the next few years, as Dunsmuir went about consolidating his find, it was often Hodgson who was sent to deal with recalcitrant homesteaders whose land lay in Dunsmuir's way or whose pre-emption entitled them to a part of the coal Dunsmuir regarded as his sole preserve.

One man who was an obstacle to Dunsmuir's plan was Hodgson's own father-in-law, Jonathon Bramley, who owned land right around the new Extension Mine tunnel and rented house lots to the miners. Many feel that it was Bramley's refusal to sell to Dunsmuir, and not the bad drinking water which was given as the official reason, that prompted Dunsmuir to found Ladysmith. Obedient miners moved to the new town and disobedient ones remained in Extension, resorting to subterfuge to make it look as though they had moved. Many settlers ran afoul of Dunsmuir and his man Hodgson, too. One was Louis Stark. His murder is one of the unsolved mysteries of Vancouver Island.

The mulatto son of a black American slave and her white owner, Louis Stark emigrated to Saltspring Island in 1860. He was forty-nine years old and married with a large family. Thirteen years later he left his wife behind in Saltspring and boarded the steamer *Maude* to take up residence in Nanaimo for two years until he pre-empted land in the Cranberry district south of the town. He was joined by some of his children.

The Starks fit in well. There was seldom mention of their skin colour, and Louis' daughter Emma soon became the teacher in Cedar, also providing meals for students who had a long way to come to school. Louis' son John went prospecting and then settled down to farm in Cedar as well.

In 1896, Louis Stark was in his eighty-fifth year and still lived on his 160 acre farm, where his nearest neighbour was none other than Ephraim Hodgson. Stark was financially secure and had no interest when Hodgson offered to buy his land and mineral rights. On February 26th, as Hodgson later told it, he went to Louis' cabin to tell

361

him that some dogs were at his sheep. The old man went to investigate and then had supper with his neighbour, who insisted that he take a lighted pit lamp with him when he left for home in the dark winter evening.

The next day when Hodgson went to check on the old man he found his door ajar; no fire had been lit and neither Stark nor his Chinese helper was anywhere to be seen. Then Hodgson heard a dog howling. Following the sound, he found Stark lying dead in the bush at the foot of a steep cliff. A cut over one eye had bled a considerable amount, and his leg was broken just above the ankle. His little dog barked nervously at his side.

The death of Louis Stark unleashed a bizarre series of charges and countercharges, of policemen refusing to act and of coroners finding contradictory inquest evidence. When the crown refused to pursue the case, John Stark hired a private detective.

The detective was a mystery all by himself. He seemed to be privy to a lot of interesting information and would eventually confess to being offered bribes by almost everyone involved in the case, including Hodgson's father-in-law Jonathon Bramley, John Stark, and Hodgson himself.

People started to point a finger at Hodgson. He seemed to know a lot more about Stark's private papers than he should. People said Stark had been dead for three days and not one when he had been found. People said his body was not bruised enough to have fallen from the cliff. John Stark said that Hodgson had made several attempts to kill him, too, and he had to spend his nights away from home, sometimes as far away as Wellington, in order to sleep safely. The detective hired by John Stark said he was asked by Hodgson to invest some anonymous money in Tom Peck's latest hotel, the Pink 'Un, on Departure Bay Road. Hodgson said he had been paid fifty thousand dollars by the owner of the new mine for some technical advantage Hodgson had shown him, and that was where the money had come from.

It did not surprise Ephraim Hodgson when he was arrested in August of 1896. At his preliminary hearing the prosecution outlined the many inconsistencies in both the evidence and in Hodgson's story, but admitted that the Crown had little direct evidence to link him to Stark's murder. Magistrate Mark Bate had no alternative but to release him.

Lewis Thatcher was the miner son of another family with settler's rights in the disputed area. His brief summation tells as much as anyone knows for sure.

Well, old Stark was murdered up there, and this here fellow by name of Hodgson stood trial for it and he got off. And then they turned around and made him a provincial policeman.

Once the Extension coal resource was consolidated under one owner, the town of Wellington was left to the railroad workers who manned the roundhouse and repair shops for the E and N Railroad. Extension became the new source of Wellington coal, for the new mines tapped an extension of the same Wellington seam originally discovered by Robert Dunsmuir.

On a January day in 1900, a notice appeared on the huge loading wharves at Departure Bay.

Masters of Vessels and Others

On and after this date you will be unable to load Wellington coal at Departure Bay, the shipping point for this coal being removed to Oyster Harbour, a point about twenty-five miles nearer Victoria.

The population of Wellington and Departure Bay had been five thousand in 1898. By 1901 it was one hundred. The town was a shell and the wharves were abandoned. Among the dislocated families at Departure Bay was one that had kept goats on Jesse Island. When the family left, the goats stayed behind and became a source of amusement and a target for torment by children who were brought there by their parents to picnic. One goat, having taken all the teasing he could tolerate, jumped in the water and swam until he reached Newcastle Island on the other side of the harbour.

The NVCML had a fan shaft on the northern end of the island to provide ventilation to the new mine recently opened on Protection Island. In order to ensure that the steam boilers continued to provide the energy to drive the fan, an engineer was stationed inside a small cabin. A very young Bill Cottle heard the story of the goat's visit.

He was in the fan room when he saw the goat coming, so he locked the door but the goat jumped through the window, busted the window and got in. He got up high where the goat couldn't reach him and the goat held him there for quite a while. The steam was going down and the fan was slowing. Finally he maneuvred to the phone—they had phones in them days—and he phoned Nanaimo and told them of his predicament. Two men had to go over in a boat with a gun and they shot the goat.

The thin seam discovered by the Hudson's Bay Company in 1855 on Protection (then Douglas) Island had been worked by Edward Walker for one month in 1856 and then given up as unprofitable. In the forty years since then, new longwall methods and mining machinery had made thin seams viable, and work was started on a new shaft that would tap both the Douglas and Newcastle seams and would eventually join with the huge operations at Number One Pit across the harbour.

It was the deepest shaft in the district, and it tapped coal under the harbour, under Newcastle and Protection Islands, and beyond into the rock under Northumberland Channel. When Protection Mine was in full production, its loading system was a wonder to behold.

Filled with coal from both the large mines on the harbour, six ton cars ran by gravity from either the cage or the bunker to a loading staith at the front of the wharf. One hundred cars per hour were lifted by hydraulics to thirty-eight feet above the highest tide and discharged into chutes adjustable to suit the height of any vessel. Empties returned by gravity along a high track which gradually graded down to return the cars for reloading. Invented by NVCML engineer W. H. Wall, this system made it possible for the Company steamer *Titania* to take on a full cargo in twelve hours. Forty years before, a similar one thousand ton cargo took a month to load.

The speed of loading had been a matter of fierce competition for years as had the speed of shipping. Collier captains vied with each other to see how quickly they could transport their cargos from Nanaimo to San Francisco. When a vessel entered either harbour with a broom at the mast, it was to announce that the ship had broken its own record. If that new time also bested the record of a rival ship, the ship's owners gave the captain a new suit of clothes. The winning captain was also allowed to go ashore wearing a stovepipe hat, to show all who knew the code that he and his ship were the fastest on the coast.

It was a decade to break records and forge ahead with new scientific developments. In 1892 Number One Mine became the first in the province to use electricity. An Edison General Electric engine and electric plant, housed in an imposing building close to the pit mouth, provided energy to light the shaft bottom and drive a small underground locomotive which could haul sixty tons of coal per trip at a speed of six miles per hour.

Better illumination made mines seem less intimidating to the

364

general public and it became chic to visit Number One. "Betsey Gadabout" of the *Canadian Home Journal* described her visit in 1897.

[The descent of the cage] gave me an almost overpowering sense of suffocation, and made me feel as though the top of my head was sliding off. The motorman was a cheerful, kindly soul, and beguiled the time in narrating blood-curdling stories of accidents which had occurred in days gone by and which he assured me were likely to repeat themselves at any moment.

The motorman was not merely acting for the journalist's benefit. Not long before, the area where the 1887 explosion occurred had been reopened, and mining had resumed there. Great care was now taken to prevent the accumulation of coal dust. It was swept from the roofs and sides and "other places of lodgment in the level" and carefully removed.

To the south of town lay several mines which had produced most of the coal dug by the Company in the early years of the decade. Number Three Chase River and Southfield Numbers One, Two, and Four were gradually scaled down until by 1893 the last one closed. Number Five Southfield disappointed many when it failed to take over from its predecessors, but it pointed the way to the future Black Track mines of South Wellington, which would produce a significant amount of coal in the first decades of the twentieth century.

The old Vancouver Coal Mining and Land Company in its new guise was at the forefront of labour management as well as scientific innovation. At a time in industrial history when paternalism was at its apex, when the "boss" knew what was best for the worker and was able to inflict his views on him, the NVCML under Sam Robins was experimenting with a new kind of labour management. It could be argued that Sam Robins was just as paternalistic as Robert Dunsmuir was, but the style of the man made his attempt at democratic labour practices more agreeable to his men and therefore more acceptable.

The early days of Robins' experiment with unions was a time of labour surplus and poor markets, a time when every mine in the district had twenty-five or thirty men waiting at the pithead for the chance to work, and a time when a nine year depression had cut profits to a minimum. Just as markets started to improve in 1897, a new area opened up in the Kootenay mountains of British Columbia to compete for the coal buying dollar, and a new influx of miners from the depressed Cape Breton fields arrived on the Island to compete for the available jobs.

It was against this background that Sam Robins attempted to deal fairly with the union. The MMLPA had been born in the heady days just before the 1890 Wellington strike when there were locals in Nanaimo, Wellington, Northfield, and East Wellington, and Tully Boyce was a force to be reckoned with. Then the new union collided with James Dunsmuir's rock hard anti-union stand. One year later, only the Nanaimo and Northfield locals had survived, but their status was secure by virtue of an agreement signed with the NCVML in August of 1891, an agreement which seemed to provide everything the union desired.

When Tully Boyce, John Humphries, Robert E. Lamb, John Horribin, and Peter Baine signed the agreement with Sam Robins in the presence of Mark Bate, Jr., the Company agreed to employ only MMLPA members and to dismiss no one without reasonable cause. The union promised to refrain from interfering with Company hiring and firing and to exhaust all other means of conciliation before calling a strike. All men under and above ground would be union members except officials, engine drivers, and mechanics. On the giving of thirty days' notice by either side, the agreement could be terminated.

In the years that followed, the road was not always smooth, but a remarkable number of compromises were made by both parties to the agreement. The pit committee system, where a miner and his foreman were required to try first to settle a problem before it could be brought before a grievance committee, worked splendidly. "I can remember . . . that we went without cases so long that we forgot who were the pit committee. That will give an idea of how the thing worked out," a miner told a Royal Commission.

When miners wished to attend funerals and mass meetings, NVCML mines closed for the day. Robins was always available to meet with union committees. When the Company proposed a wage reduction in 1893, the union agreed to comply. When a further reduction or three months' idleness was put to the men, they met on the Green to discuss the alternatives.

Sam Robins was asked to explain the situation. As he stood on the dilapidated platform of the old picnic grounds on the Green, with the huge trestle of the coal wharves looming behind him and the waters of Commercial Inlet lapping at the rocks and grass behind the men assembled before him, he bore a heavy burden. The Company had been losing money for eighteen months, and several of its customers owed it a great deal of money. A three month shut down would lose them customers, and many of the miners could not live without pay for that long. He promised that all Company employees in San Francisco and London would be subject to the wage reduction as well. Robins was not a dynamic speaker and his message was ominous, but when he had finished speaking forty minutes later he was loudly applauded. In a secret ballot, 380 men voted in favour of a twenty percent reduction in wages over three dollars and a ten percent reduction in wages under three dollars for at least three months.

Despite the majority giving Robins what he requested, ninety-six men had voted against the proposal. All through the period of union and management cooperation at the NVCML there was a strong undercurrent of opposition. At the regular Sunday morning meetings, attendance was often poor. "To hear around the stores or under the shade trees the grievances that these miners have, you would think that our meetings would last all day and all night when Sunday did come, but this is not the case, not one of those men attend the meetings," moaned a writer to the journal of the United Mine Workers.

Tully Boyce became a target for abuse. Someone said he had been bought by management. Boyce's chief crime seems to have been predicting the crisis twelve months before it occurred, but he sensed his effectiveness was so compromised that he stepped down. At a mass meeting in late 1893, Arthur Wilson was elected president to succeed him, and the miners agreed to an extension in the period when their wages would be reduced.[9]

The 1894 closure of Northfield and Southfield mines was explained to the employees by Robins at another meeting on the Green when he said that the San Francisco market was the deadest he had ever experienced. A committee demanded a meeting with their employer to even out the wage differences between the men from different mines. While complaining about the peremptory tone in the miners' demands, Robins agreed to the meeting, and when the next mass meeting was called, the employees voted to share the work still available in Number One Mine.

In this volatile climate of discontent, falling markets, and constant union-management meetings, the union executive asked the members

[9] Tully Boyce became an important member of the Liberal Party in 1895. He was still the object of criticism, however. In Wellington they continued to regard him as a dictator from the days of the 1890-1891 strike. When he became a bookkeeper for the NVCML's successor, The Western Fuel Company, certain militant miners regarded him as having been bought by the Company.

to agree to the hiring of a paid agent who would attempt to spread the organization to Wellington and Cumberland. Someone in the audience saw the position as a "soft snap," to which Boyce replied:

I would [rather] pack rock on my back for ten hours a day than fill this billet. Whoever gets the place will be placed in a very awkward, I might say, miserable position.

The man elected to that miserable position by a two-thirds majority was Ralph Smith, a former student minister from Newcastle-on-Tyne who had come to Canada in 1883 in search of a change of climate and to Nanaimo in 1892 with his young wife, Mary Ellen. Having become a miner, he soon rose in the ranks of the union due in large part to his persuasive oratorical powers.

Charged with bringing Dunsmuir employees back into the union, Smith travelled between Cumberland and Nanaimo, and later to Alexandra and Extension, in a fruitless and frustrating battle both with the Company and with the majority of Dunsmuir miners whose need for work overrode any desire for a union to fight for them. The experience convinced him that the only course for the working man was to become involved in politics.

Building on the successes of the previous decade, the working class had achieved remarkable results in the election in 1890. The MMLPA supported two candidates financially and endorsed a third. The issues that miner Thomas Keith and former miner turned farmer Thomas Foster centered their campaign upon were general miner unhappiness, the large land grants given to coal companies, class conflict, the single tax, and arbitration of labour disputes with enforceable awards. They were elected with a strong majority and allied themselves with the opposition in the next legislature.

In the subsequent election campaign in 1894, the Nanaimo Reform Club was formed, comprised of delegates from local temperance societies and city trade unions but dominated by the MMLPA. All three Reform Club candidates nominated for the legislature were miners. Thomas Keith, who had maintained a high profile since his first election by championing the cause of Oriental exclusion, Tully Boyce, and Ralph Smith looked like an unbeatable team.

None of them were elected. Some blamed over-confidence; others said there was too much dependence on labour. The temperance stand of the Reform Club was ridiculed. Keith felt that businessmen, saloon keepers, and church people had pulled together to oppose labour votes. A swing towards the Liberals was in evidence.

It had happened before. Just when labour appeared to be gaining solid political power and influence, it pulled back and cast its votes for the established parties and candidates. In the course of the next five years, Nanaimo would be represented federally and provincially by, among others, miner Ralph Smith, colliery surgeons William Walkem and R. McKechnie, businessmen James McGregor and Andrew Haslam, and mine owners John Bryden and James Dunsmuir. The choices followed no trend and seemed totally unpredictable. The day was not far off, however, when Nanaimo and district would elect solidly labour-oriented representatives and would influence at least the provincial legislature to an extent beyond all proportion to their numbers.[10]

In the closing years of the decade, as the NVCML fought an uphill battle against the new market obstacle that fuel oil represented, as Sam Robins presided over the decline of the Company he had worked for so ably for thirty years, as miners continued to take wage cuts and see mines closed, the MMLPA continued to thrive despite constant if minor opposition from some of its members.

A January 1898 meeting was packed to the doors of the hall, and another meeting the next month expressed a strong feeling of loyalty to the Company for its opposition to Robert Dunsmuir and Sons and resolved:

That as employees of the New Vancouver Coal Company, we have the utmost confidence in our employers, and pledge ourselves to stand by the management at this or any time of trial.

Such a remarkable statement was testimony to one man. All the years of tolerance by Sam Robins and loyalty by the majority of the miners paid off in March of 1898 when a notice from the union appeared in the *Free Press*.

NOTICE

I have received information from Mr. Robins to the effect that an advance of 10 per cent will be placed upon the current wages from February 1, 1898.

But there was a flaw in the arrangement. That flaw only became apparent when the NVCML was sold to the Western Fuel Company of San Francisco in 1903, and Sam Robins left amid banquets and

---

[10] Labour became influential federally as well when Ralph Smith became the first socialist M.P. in Ottawa. However, Smith's allegiance fluctuated between the Socialists and the Liberals during his tenure in both federal and provincial politics.

gift-giving to retire to England. The MMLPA was only a local union. Without affiliation to a strong international body, there was no strike fund to sustain the membership when they had to deal with a less enlightened employer. Sam Mottishaw, Sr. saw it this way when he testified to the Royal Commission on Industrial Disputes.

[The local union in Nanaimo] was a figurehead. It was no good. They could approach the management — it was good for that — but financially it was no good... Supposing there was a strike, there would be no backing.

Affiliation with a strong international union occurred when the MMLPA joined the Western Federation of Miners over the opposition of Ralph Smith. By agreeing to that affiliation, the MMLPA signed its own death warrant. Government opposition to the militant American union led to its being outlawed in 1903, and Nanaimo miners were without a union again.

Henry Carroll was another former NVCML miner who, like Mottishaw, was working for James Dunsmuir by the time he spoke to the Commissioners in 1903.

Our local union here kept conditions pretty good. We always have had nice pay, and the conditions no worse than anywhere else. They have not improved since the Western Federation took hold of it. There seems to have been strike after strike wherever they have got a foothold.

In the Nanaimo of 1898, however, the union was strong. And Sam Mottishaw was more interested in the Klondike gold rush than the Western Federation of Miners. His son, Sam Jr., had yielded to the call that had lured miners away from the coalfields so many times before.

The editor of the *Cumberland News* described the atmosphere in Nanaimo engendered by yet another gold rush.

Everything wears an aspect of hopefulness and expectation here. The waves of prosperity are rising so high at Victoria and Vancouver that a good deal of the spray falls in Nanaimo to the delight of its traders.

When I arrived in Nanaimo I followed the crowd on to Commercial Street and was first attracted by the large show windows and the handsome goods I saw through them in Good's auction rooms. There was everything from a baby carriage to a piano, and so cheap! I next noticed five Klondikers headed by Mr. John Fraser making their way to A. R. Johnson and Co.'s who with Stevenson and Co. do the outfitting here.

Boats loaded with men left Nanaimo and Union Bay every day for the Alaska Panhandle, where the intrepid gold seekers disembarked to begin the arduous overland trek to the gold fields of the Klondike. Ever since the outside world had heard of the gold strike in the Yukon in July of 1897, Vancouver Island miners had joined the hordes seeking instant wealth.

A man needed five hundred dollars for passage money and an outfit. Cumberland miners decided to pool their resources and "grub-stake" a few of their number. The first Nanaimo contingent was given a royal sendoff when the Silver Cornet Band serenaded two of its members who left with Sam Mottishaw and sons of other mining families like the Muirs, Meakins, McGarrigles, Hyghs, and Randles. Most of the new gold miners were young men, but not all of them. Sam Fiddick was sixty-five years old when he had a recurrence of the fever that lured him to British Columbia in 1858. Leaving behind his hotel and his homestead, he joined the swarms of fortune seekers heading north.

The Hoggan brothers headed for the Klondike too, in the company of ex-MPP Thomas Keith and Jack McGregor, son of Number One Mine manager William McGregor. Like his fiery grandfather John, Jack dreamed that gold would make him rich.

Jack's father William had devoted his life to coal mining, and the mines had done him proud. Number One Mine and her manager had grown up together, the man learning bitter lessons from the mine as the tunnels ate further and further into the coal under the harbour. As if to make up for the carnage of the first four years of operation, the mine had an enviable record for safety.

At the end of the afternoon shift about three months after Jack McGregor left for the Klondike, a feeder, that nemesis of the miners on the diagonal slope in 1887, was discovered in Lamb's Incline. The powerful spurt of gas was ignited by the open flame lamp on Benjamin Browitt's cap as he and his partner were leaving at shift end. A second explosion followed thirty seconds later; it ignited the main level and could not be extinguished.

The two men reported the explosions. While a crew returned to investigate and wait for William McGregor to join them, there were two more explosions. All the stalls were checked for gas. There was none in any of them.

At 1:00 a.m. that November night, McGregor ordered a stopping to be built to seal off the explosive incline. Working as quickly as possible and mindful of the previous unexplained explosions, the crew had almost completed the stopping when the gas burst again, striking the eight men present, including McGregor. Their faces and hands

371

were burned, and George Lee's leg was broken when he was thrown against the coal.

Despite their burns, the crew took turns carrying Lee towards safety until afterdamp overtook them and they had to leave him behind. A fireboss and a miner later returned for him and were able to save his life. Three of the burned miners were taken to hospital; the rest, including Lee and McGregor, were taken home to be nursed by their families.

At seven the next morning several men tried again to insert a stopping. They were struck by a blast and hurled against the rib. The smoke was so thick that the fireboss ordered the men out of the mine. The same fireboss was finally successful eight hours later when with the help of Joseph Randle, no stranger to explosion burns himself, they finally built the stopping — but not before Lamb's incline had burst one final time.

Two days later George Lee died, followed the next day by the manager of the mine, William McGregor. The forty-three year old man was survived by his mother Mary, two sisters, two brothers, two sons, three daughters, and his wife Amanda Meakin McGregor. She had lost her father in the big explosion eleven years before. Now her husband was dead.

When John McGregor — who had come to Vancouver Island with such dreams — had died thirty-two years before, his eleven year old son William had entered the service of the VCML as a door boy. Now, on November 19th, the former door boy was buried following the longest funeral procession Nanaimo had ever seen. The entourage of dignitaries, school children, football clubs, MMLPA, friends, politicians, and family took forty-five minutes to pass a given point. Memorial services were held simultaneously in several churches. Three thousand people, including enough people from Wellington to fill four railroad coaches, attended the burial.

The list of donors of the sixty-four floral pieces that adorned the solemnities read like a history of Nanaimo coal mines. Wall, Randle, Bray, Meakin, Dick, Westwood, Dunsmuir, Muir, Greenwell, Sabiston, Gough, Malpass, Norris, Prior, Bate, Bryden, Hunter, Bryant, Helmcken. Miners and sons of miners, managers, inspectors, engineers, union men — they had all lost someone to the mines. They or someone bearing their name had come to the Island with a dream. The dreams of some of them had come true. The dreams of most had died in the roar of an explosion or in other less spectacular ways.

A man can only dream for so long, and one day he realizes that from then on he will be content to survive. And if three dollars a day is enough to survive on, then he will work for three dollars a day. And his dream becomes modified, and instead of riches or power or fame, he will settle for a small concession from life so that his sons will work in a safer mine with a say in their own future, and his daughters will not become widows before their time, and he can say with John Greenwell:

If I made three dollars I was satisfied ... The very moment labour got thoroughly organized man and master would shake hands and pull together; and I believe it is coming to that at the present day.

SOURCES CONSULTED BY CHAPTER

CHAPTER I — Certain Rebellious Persons

G. P. V. and Helen B. Akrigg, James Audain, Hubert Bancroft, Alexander Begg, Hartwell Bowsfield, *British Colonist*, Alan B. Campbell, Eden Colvile, Elizabeth Forbes, Daniel Gallacher, Barrie Gault, Barry Gough, W. Colquhoun Grant, John Sebastian Helmcken, Pauline Hemmings, Heritage Conservation Branch, Hudson's Bay Company Correspondence, Patricia Johnson, John Haskell Kemble, W. Kaye Lamb, J. Anthony Lavin, David Lewis, B. A. McKelvie, Richard Somerset Mackie, James Morris, A. N. Mouat, Andrew Muir, Michael Muir, *Nanaimo Daily Free Press*, James Nesbitt, Margaret Ormsby, Brian J. Porter, Probate Files, H. Keith Ralston, E. O. S. Scholefield, Patricia Elizabeth Vaughan.

CHAPTER II — Stout, Hearty, and Able Young Men

G. P. V. and Helen B. Akrigg, James Audain, Hubert Bancroft, George J. Barnsby, Mark Bate, *Black Country Bugle*, *British Columbia Genealogist*, British Columbia Parks Branch, Rhoda Beck, Alexander Begg, James Borserio, Brechin Superior School, Cornelius Bryant, John Cass, *British Colonist*, Eden Colvile, A. W. Currie, *Daily Herald*, Donald C. Davidson, Elizabeth Forbes, Daniel Gallacher, Barrie Gault, Dorothy Maxwell Graham, W. Colquhoun Grant, Beth Greenwood, A. R. Griffen, Hal Griffen, John Sebastian Helmcken, Michael Hiley, Hudson's Bay Company Account Book of 1854, Hudson's Bay Company Correspondence, Pauline Hemmings, Adam Grant Horne, Patricia Johnson, M. A. Kenny, W. Kaye Lamb, David Lewis, Logbook of the *Princess Royal*, Joseph William McKay. B. A. McKelvie, Richard Mackie, Richard Charles Mayne, *The Methodist Missionary Society Reports*, *Ministry of Mines Annual Reports*, Nanaimo and District Centennial Museum Vertical File, *Nanaimo Daily Free Press*, *Nanaimo Gazette*, Nanaimo Letterbook, J. U. Nef, James Nesbitt, Elizabeth Norcross, Margaret Ormsby, Brian J. Porter, Probate Files, Caroline Ralston, H. Keith Ralston, Alexander Rattray, E. O. S. Scholefield, Barbara Sheppard, Anne Simeon, Charles E. Stuart, Arthur J. Taylor, F. W. Tickner, Patricia Elizabeth Vaughan, Randolph Sidney Vickers.

CHAPTER III — Drunkards and Skedaddlers

G. P. V. and Helen B. Akrigg, James Audain, Jon Bartlett, Bastion Archives, Mark Bate, Alexander Begg, James Boutelier, British Columbia Parks Branch, Cornelius Bryant, A. F. Buckham Collection, *British Colonist*, Thomas Crosby, A. W. Currie, George Edwards, Charlotte Erickson, Elizabeth Forbes, Daniel Gallacher, Beth Greenwood, John Sebastian

Helmcken, Michael Hiley, J. S. Hurt, Patricia Johnson, M. A. Kenny, Matthew Macfie, Richard Charles Mayne, *Methodist Missionary Society Reports*, *Ministry of Mines Annual Reports*, James Morris, *Nanaimo Free Press*, *Nanaimo Gazette*, Margaret Ormsby, Bryan Palmer, B. W. Pearce, Alexander Rattray, William Raybould, W. George Shelton, Dorothy Blakey Smith, Sisters of St. Ann, Charles Tate, F. W. Tickner, Vertical File Nanaimo Museum, Vertical File PABC.

CHAPTER IV — The Managing Partner

G. P. V. and Helen B. Akrigg, James Audain, Hubert Bancroft, Jon Bartlett, Mark Bate, Rhoda Beck, Alexander Begg, A. F. Buckham, John Bryden, Colonial Correspondence, *Daily British Colonist*, William Cottle, Marnie Crowe, George Edwards, *Nanaimo Free Press*, Daniel Gallacher, Beth Greenwood, Charles Frederick Houghton, Inspector of Mines Correspondence, M. A. Kenny, William Lewis, *Ministry of Mines Annual Reports*, B. W. Pearce, Brian J. Porter, R. H. Roy, Sessional Papers, Robert D. Turner, *Methodist Missionary Society Reports*, Vertical File PABC.

CHAPTER V — Celestial Colliers and Bunster Beer

G. P. V. and Helen B. Akrigg, James Audain, Hubert Bancroft, Jon Bartlett, Mark Bate, Rhoda Beck, Myrtle Bergren notes, E. E. Brown, John Bryden, *Daily British Colonist*, A. W. Currie, Eric Duncan, *Nanaimo Free Press*, Daniel Gallacher, Beth Greenwood, Patricia Johnson, M. A. Kenny, J. B. Kerr, William Lewis, *Methodist Missionary Society Reports*, *Ministry of Mines Annual Reports*, E. Blanche Norcross, Margaret Ormsby, Probate Files, Dorothy Blakey Smith, Barbara Stannard, Charles Montgomery Tate, VCML Director's Diary, Vertical File PABC.

CHAPTER VI — A Few Mostly Mischievous Fellows

James Audain, Rhonda Bailey, Hubert Bancroft, W. Henry Barneby, Jon Bartlett, Bastion Archives, Mark Bate, *BC Directory*, Rhoda Beck, Alexander Begg, E. E. Brown, Cornelius Bryant, John Bryden, A. F. Buckham, Canadian Centennial Committee, *Daily British Colonist*, William Cottle, Michael S. Cross, A. W. Currie, Nelson Dean, Eric Duncan, George Edwards, Daniel Gallacher, John Galsworthy, F. W. Gray, Archie Greenwell, Donald Greenwell, Beth Greenwood, *Illustrated British Columbia*, Inquisitions, Inspector of Mines Correspondence, Patricia Johnson, M. A. Kenny, J. B. Kerr, William Lewis, T. R. Loosemore, William McLellan, Donald Macleod, Marion Matheson, *Methodist Missionary Society Reports*, *Ministry of Mines Annual Reports*, Ben Moffat, *Nanaimo Free Press*, Bryan Palmer, Probate Files, Martin Robin, Patricia Roy, John Saywell, Select Committee, Sessional Papers, Sister Mary Theodore, Barbara Stannard, Arthur J. Taylor, Robert D. Turner, Mark Tweedy, VCML Director's Diary, Vertical File PABC, Joseph White, A. J. Woodman, Louis Zaccarelli.

CHAPTER VII — Shot off the Solid

James Audain, Rhoda Beck, *Daily British Colonist*, William Cottle, A. W. Currie, Nelson Dean, Eric Duncan, Harry Ellis, Elizabeth Freeman, John Galsworthy, Hal Griffen, Inquisitions, Inspector of Mines Correspondence,

William Johnstone, Donald Macleod, William McGregor Journal, *Ministry of Mines Annual Reports*, James Morris, *Nanaimo Free Press*, James Nesbitt, Brian J. Porter, Select Committee, Olive Spencer, Sister Mary Theodore, Royal Commission on Chinese and Japanese Immigration, Royal Commission on Chinese Immigration, *Nanaimo Times*, Robert D. Turner, Vertical File PABC, Mrs. Frank Wall, Seiriol Williams.

CHAPTER VIII — "John" and Mr. James

G. P. V. and Helen B. Akrigg, James Audain, Wallace Baikie, *British Colonist*, *British Columbia Genealogist*, Canadian Centennial Committee, Marie Bono Conti, Gordon A. Craig, Cumberland's Diamond Jubilee, Cumberland Museum Vertical File, *Cumberland News*, Eric Duncan, Elizabeth Forbes, Daniel Gallacher, Genesis Project, Christine Godfrey, John Gourlay, Dorothy Graham, W. Colquhoun Grant, Rene Harding, Hudson's Bay Company Correspondence, Inspector of Mines Correspondence, Ed Lee, Effie McIntosh, William McLellan, John Marochhi, Archer Martin, *Methodist Missionary Society Reports*, Mining and Engineering Record, *Ministry of Mines Annual Reports*, *Nanaimo Daily Free Press*, *Nanaimo Gazette*, Probate Files, Royal Commission on Chinese Immigration, Royal Commission on Chinese and Japanese Immigration, Royal Commission on Industrial Disputes, Select Committee, Sessional Papers, Robert D. Turner, *Weekly News*.

CHAPTER IX — Three Dollar Dreams

Rhonda Bailey, Alexander Begg, Edward Bell, David Bercuson, John Bryden Diary, William Cottle, Marnie Crowe, *Cumberland News*, A. W. Currie, Nelson Dean, George Edwards, Mary Edwards, Elizabeth Forbes, John Galsworthy, Inspector of Mines Correspondence, J. B. Kerr, *Lantzville Log*, Bradley Lockner, T. R. Loosemore, A. R. McCormack, Archer Martin, Marion Matheson, *Methodist Missionary Society Reports*, *Ministry of Mines Annual Reports*, Ben Moffat, *Nanaimo Daily Free Press*, NDCM Vertical File, PABC Vertical File, Brian J. Porter, Vera Riddell, Royal Commission on Chinese Immigration, Royal Commission on Industrial Disputes, John Saywell, Select Committee, Sessional Papers, Sisters of St. Ann, Barbara Stannard, Lewis Thatcher, *Wellington Enterprise*, Joe White, J. Donald Wilson, Zaccarelli Diary.

COAL TYEE BOARD OF DIRECTORS

GLOSSARY

adit: entry to a mine that slopes slightly upward thus allowing for natural drainage of water.

afterdamp: mine air with a high concentration of carbon monoxide; present following a mine fire or methane explosion.

blacklist: list of miners who will no longer be employed by a particular company; disciplinary measure following a strike; miners who were especially troublesome could be blacklisted from all the companies in an area.

bottom man: employee of a mine who tends the bottom of the shaft.

brattice: curtains made of sacking or canvas which direct the flow of air from the mine ventilation system into places where gas can collect such as at the face or in potholes in the roof.

brushing out gas: the practice of using a piece of cloth such as a man's shirt to sweep gas out of places where it has collected; usually only necessary in poorly ventilated mines.

check weighman: miner who checks that the men are credited with the proper weight when their cars are weighed and unloaded; his wages are usually paid by the miners.

chokedamp: also called blackdamp; mixture of carbon-dioxide with either air or nitrogen; heavier than air; can kill by explosion or asphyxiation.

clinker: a hard mass of fused stony matter formed in a furnace or boiler from impurities in the coal.

cog: four-sided structure built of timbers and filled with waste rock used to hold up a dangerous roof.

crosscut: tunnel joining two parallel levels; a pillar of coal is left when two levels are joined by two crosscuts.

darg: concept of a "day's work" used in Scotland and Northern England based on how much the average man could dig per day in a given location.

door boy: boy employed to sit by a light stopping, open it when necessary, and make sure it closed again; see also trapper.

drawing gas: indication that a safety lamp is not airtight and it is possible for explosive gas to reach the flame inside.

drift: a horizontal passageway driven into or along the path of a coal seam.

dross: coal dust; regarded as harmless until its explosive characteristics were discovered, and useless until it was used for making coke.

face: leading surface of the mine workings; the wall of coal which the miner is working to advance his stall or the tunnel.

firedamp: mixture of mine air and methane released when the coal is loosened; lighter than air; cause of many mine explosions.

fireman: the "corporal" or lowest echelon "boss" who is in charge of several miners and carries a safety lamp to check for firedamp; also called a fireboss.

gob: area of mine where coal has been removed and where waste rock is dumped.

horse roads: the tunnels and levels of a mine that are large enough to accommodate horses and mules.

Kanaka: native of Hawaii.

Klootchman: slang word for an Indian woman, particularly one living with or married to a white man.

lagging: rough lumber or slabs laid on stringers and fastened to timber to line roof and sides of tunnels.

level: horizontal passageway in a mine.

level free: a mine with an adit entrance which drains itself of water.

lighter: large open barge which can be brought alongside a ship.

longwall: method of mining narrow seams of coal; long stretch of coal is undercut either by hand or machine and loosened by firing shots; loose coal is shovelled on to a conveyor belt and dumped in cars at end of wall; can be done with much less skilled labour.

midden: archaeological term meaning a heap; on the Pacific coast the term applies to a site where Indians have habitually camped.

outcrop: the place at the earth's surface where a seam of coal breaks through.

overcast: an arch in a mine supporting an overhead passage.

oversman: a foreman; also overman.

pillar and stall: method of mining in thicker seams; levels and crosscuts form a grid which conducts the air of the ventilation system; the grid leaves behind pillars of coal which support the roof.

pothole: irregularity in the roof where methane gas can be trapped.

potlatch: an Pacific coast Indian feast where gifts are distributed by the host to display wealth and hospitality.

rancharee: coastal Indian encampment consisting of several longhouses.

refuse coal: coal too fine to be useable; see also dross.

rib: side of the mine tunnel.

runners: employees of mine who bring empty cars to the miners at the face; Chinese were particularly good at being runners; runners are able to make their influence felt by the number of cars they deliver to an individual miner.

second firing: a dangerous practice where a miner reuses a drill hole when the initial shot fails to loosen any coal.

shaft: perpendicular entrance to a mine.

short weight: occurs when the weight of a car is estimated instead of actually weighed and the miner is cheated by too low an estimate.

shotlighters: mine employees who check to see if miners' shots are properly set and then light the shots; a job often performed by a fireboss.

slope: an inclined entrance to a mine.

squibs: method of lighting a shot.

staith: stage or wharf with equipment for loading and unloading

stall: "room" off a slope or tunnel where one or two miners dig coal.

steam jets: primitive method of ventilating a mine; steam is used to heat air and thus cause movement.

stoppings: barriers used to block off openings in tunnels; "heavy" stoppings are permanent barriers constructed of two-inch timber, rock, or brick; "light" stoppings are wooden doors or curtains that can be opened briefly by trappers or door boys to allow for passage of coal or personnel.

stringer: timber that forms the top of the three-sided arch used to support mine tunnels.

tamper: stick or metal rod used to pack clay, sand, dust, etc. around the charge in a drill hole; must not be made of iron or steel because those metals can cause a spark.

"to the dip": following the angle of the seam.

touch paper: similar to a "punk"; used for lighting a shot.

trapper: boy employed to sit by a light stopping, open it when necessary and make sure it closed again; see also door boy.

tunnel: horizontal entrance to a mine.

tyee: Indian word meaning "chief."

upcast: ventilating shaft of a mine where the air is drawn up to the surface.

whin: hard rock, inferior kind of jade associated with drilling boreholes; also called greenstone, whinstone, or whinsay.

SOURCES CONSULTED

Abbreviations
Bastion Archival Collection - BAC
British Columbia Genealogist - BCG
British Columbia Historical Quarterly - BCHQ
Canadian Historical Review - CHR
Hudson's Bay Company Archives - Provincial Archives of Manitoba
  - HBCA - PAM
Nanaimo and District Centennial Museum - NDCM
Nanaimo Daily Free Press - NDFP
Provincial Archives of British Columbia - PABC
Vancouver City Archives - VCA

Articles

Bate, Mark. "Early Settlers Offered Protection from Indians," *NDFP*, May 13, 1953.

———. "Reminiscences of Early Days in Nanaimo," *NDFP*, February 16 to April 13, 1907.

———. "A Story of Olden Days Graphically Told by One Who Knows," *Daily Herald*.

Beck, Rhoda. "When Miners Landed in the Nanaimo Area," *NDFP*, November 26, 1954.

Bercuson, David Jay. "Labour Radicalism and the Western Industrial Frontier: 1897-1919," *CHR*, Vol. LVIII, NO. 2, June 1977.

Berton, Pierre. "Klondike Gold Rush," *Canadian Encyclopedia*. Edmonton; Hurtig PUblishers, 1985.

Borserio, James. "Pioneers From Local Mines Built Nanaimo Out of Wilderness," *NDFP*, November 26, 1954.

Brown, Cuthbert. "Horse, Whistles and Bells," *Daily Colonist*, May 15, 1977.

Buckham, A. F. "The Nanaimo Coal Field," *The Transactions of the Canadian Institute of Mining and Metallurgy*, Vol. L, 1947.

"Buckpole Pub Where the Brierly Hill Pioneers 'Struck Gold' in 1854!", *Black Country Bugle*, Stourbridge, England, September 1984.

Currie, A. W. "The Vancouver Coal Mining Company, A Source for Galsworthy's *Strife*," *Queen's Quarterly*, Vol. 70, No. 1, Spring 1963.

Davidson, Donald C. "The War Scare of 1854. The Pacific Coast and the Crimean War," *BCHQ*, Vol.V, No.4 (1941).

Douglass, Dave. "Pit Talk in County Durham," *Miners, Quarrymen and Saltworkers*, Raphael Samuel, ed. London: Routledge and Kegan Paul, 1977.

Erickson, Charlotte. "The Encouragement of Emigration by British Trade Unions, 1850-1900," *Population Studies*, Vol. III, no. 3, 1949.

Gallacher, Daniel T. "Dunsmuir, Robert," *Dictionary of Canadian Biography*, Vol.XI, 1881 to 1890. Toronto: University of Toronto Press.

Galsworthy, John. "The Silence," *Villa Rubein and Other Stories*. New York: Charles Scribner's Sons, 1926.

Gault, Barrie H. E. "First and Last Days of the *Princess Royal*," *BCHQ*, Vol. III (1939).

Gough, Barry M. "Fort Rupert, Its Coal and Its Spar Trades," *The Company on the Coast*. E. Blanche Norcross, ed. Nanaimo: Nanaimo Historical Society, 1983.

Grant, W. Colquhoun. "Description of Vancouver Island," *Journal of the Royal Geographical Society* 27, 1857.

Gray. F. W. "Coal Mining and Geology in Canada," *The Transactions of the Canadian Institute of Mining and Metallurgy*, Vol. LI, 1948.

Griffen, Hal. "A Century of The Nanaimo Tradition," *Pacific Tribune*, November 26, 1954.

Harding, Rene. "Thomas Russell, M.E., of Union Mines," *Comox Free Press*, 1977.

Holmes, H. Cuthbert. "Some Notes on the Economic Past, Present and Future of Vancouver Island," *BCHQ*, Vol.XVI (1952), No. 1,2.

Howay, F. W. "The Negro Immigration into Vancouver Island in 1858," *BCHQ*, Vol. III (1939).

Illerbrun, W. J. "Kanaka Pete," *The Hawaiian Journal of History*, Vol. 6, 1972. Hawaiian Historical Society.

Johnson, Patricia M. "Fort Rupert," *The Beaver*, Vol. 302: 4, 1972.

———. "Teacher and Preacher: Cornelius Bryant," *The Beaver*, (Winter 1961).

Johnstone, William. "Galsworthys and Nanaimo," *Daily Colonist*, January 7, 1979.

Kealey, Greg and H. Keith Ralston. "Myers, Samuel H.," *Dictionary of Canadian Biography*, Vol. XI. Toronto: University of Toronto Press, 1982.

Kemble, John Haskell. "Coal from the Northwest Coast 1848-50," *BCHQ*, Vol. II (1938).

Kenny, M. A. "Some of Nanaimo's Early Buildings," 1955. VCA.

Lai Chuen-Yan. "Chinese Attempts to Discourage Emigration to Canada: Some Findings from the Chinese Archives in Victoria," *BC Studies*, no. 18, summer 1973.

Lamb, W. Kaye. "The Census of Vancouver Island, 1855," *BCHQ*, Vol. IX, No.1 (1940).

———. "The Governorship of Richard Blanshard," *BCHQ*, Vol. XIV, No. 1, 2 (1950).

Lavin, J. Anthony. "The Date and Place of Robert Dunsmuir's Birth," *BCG*, Vol. 10, No. 4, Winter 1981.

Macleod, Donald. "Colliers, Collier Safety and Workplace Control: The Nova Scotia Experience, 1873-1910," *Historical Papers*. Dana Johnson and Claudette Lacelle, ed. Ottawa: Canadian Historical Association, 1983.

McCormack, A. R. "The Emergence of the Socialist Movement in British Columbia," *BC Studies*, Spring 1974.

McKelvie, B. A. "The Founding of Nanaimo," *BCHQ*, Vol. VIII, No. 3 (1944).

———. "Nanaimo's Day of Death — The Blast That Killed 150," *B.C. Magazine*, December, 8, 1956.

———. "Nanaimo Pioneer Looks Back Down the Years," Clipping from Laura Meakin Scrapbook, NDCM.

Morton, Desmond. "Aid to the Civil Power: The Canadian Militia in Support of Social Order, 1867-1914," *CHR* 51 (1970).

Mouat, A. N. "Notes on the *Norman Morison*," *BCHQ*, Vol. III (1939).

"Nanaimo Pioneer Cemetery," *BCG*, Vol. 12, No. 2, June 1983.

Nef, J. U. "Coal Mining and Utilization," *A History of Technology*, Vol. III. Charles Singer, E. J. Holmyard, A. R. Hall, Trevor I. Williams, ed. Oxford: Clarendon Press.

Nesbitt, James. "The Diary of Martha Cheney Ella 1853-1856," *BCHQ*, Vol. 13, 1949.

———. "Dunsmuir: the Strike Breaker," *Daily Colonist*, March 4, 1979.

Porter, Brian J. "British Columbia Mining Casualties," *BCG*, Part One-Vol. 9 (Spring 1980), No. 1; Part Two-Vol. 9 (Summer 1980), No. 2; Part Three (with Alice Marwood) Vol. 9 (Fall 1980), No. 3; Part Four and Five Vol. 9 (Winter 1980), No. 4; Part Six-Vol. 10 (Spring 1981), No. 1.

———. "Robert Dunsmuir — An Exercise in Genealogical Reconstruction," *BCG*, Vol. 10, No. 2, Summer 1981.

Ralston, H. Keith. "Miners and Managers: The Organization of Coal Production on Vancouver Island by the Hudson's Bay Company, 1848-1862," *The Company on the Coast*. Nanaimo: Nanaimo Historical Society, 1983.

Roy, Patricia E. "The *West Shore*'s View of British Columbia," *Journal of the West*, Oct. 1984, Vol. XXIII, No. 4.

Roy, R. H. "In Aid of a Civil Power, 1877," *Canadian Army Journal*, 7:3, 1953.

Saywell, John Tupper. "Labour and Socialism in British Columbia: A Survey of Historical Development Before 1903," *BCHQ*, Vol. XV, 1951.

Sheppard, Barbara. "Some Notes on Gabriola Island - Its Early History and the Edgar Family," *BCG*, Vol. 9, No. 2, Summer 1980.

Simeon, Anne. "Nanaimo Flashback," *B.C. Motorist*, NDCM.

Smith, Allan. "The Myth of the Self-Made Man in English Canada, 1850-1914," *CHR* 59 (1978).

Stark-Wallace, Marie. "The Murder of Louis Stark," *Gulf Islands Driftwood*, February 6, 1980.

Tate, Charles Montgomery. "Autosketch," *The Western Recorder*, 1929.

Taylor, Arthur J. "Labour Productivity and Technological Innovation in the British Coal Industry, 1850-1914," *Economic History Review*, Vol. XIV, No. 1, 1961.

"The Late Thomas Russell," *Mining and Engineering Record*, Vol. XXII, No. 17, October 30, 1917.

"Union City and Colliery, Vancouver Island, 1889," *BCG*, Vol. 7, No. 3/4, 1978.

Vickers, Randolph Sydney. "George Robinson: Nanaimo Mine Agent," *The Beaver*, Autumn 1984.

Warburton, R. "Race and Class in British Columbia: A Comment," *BC Studies* 49 (1981).

Ward, Peter W. "Class and Race in the Social Structure of British Columbia, 1870-1939," *BC Studies* no.45 (1980).

White, Elwood. "Death Plunge at Trent River," *Daily Colonist*, January 15, 1961.

Willmott, W. E. "Some Aspects of Chinese Communities in British Columbia Towns," *BC Studies*, no. 1, Winter 1968-69.

Wilson, J. Donald. "Culture and Politics in Finnish Canada," *Polyphone*, Vol. 3, No. 2, 1981.

Books

Akrigg, G. P. V. and Helen B. Akrigg. *British Columbia Chronicle 1778-1846. Adventurers by Sea and Land.* Vancouver: Discovery Press, 1975.

———. *British Columbia Chronicle. Gold and Colonists.* Vancouver: Discovery Press, 1977.

Audain, James. *Alex Dunsmuir's Dilemma.* Victoria: Sunnyland Publishing Co., 1964.

———. *From Coalmine to Castle.* New York: Pageant Press, 1955.

Bancroft, Hubert Howe. *History of British Columbia, 1792-1887.* San Francisco: The History Co., Publishers, 1887.

Barneby, W. Henry. *Life and Labour in the Far, Far West.* London: Cassell and Co. Ltd., 1884.

Barnsby, George J. *Social Conditions in the Black Country, 1800-1900.* Wolverhampton: Integrated Publishing Services, 1980.

Begg, Alexander. *History of British Columbia From Its Earliest Discovery to the Present Time.* Toronto: McGraw-Hill Ryerson Ltd., 1894.

Bowsfield, Hartwell, ed. *Fort Victoria Letters 1846-1851.* Winnipeg: Hudson's Bay Record Society, 1979.

British Columbia Parks Branch. *A History of Newcastle Island Provincial Park.*

Campbell, Alan B. *The Lanarkshire Miners: A Social History of Their Trade Unions, 1775-1974.* Edinburgh: John McDonald, 1979.

Carroll, H. *History of Nanaimo Pioneers.* Nanaimo: Herald Presses, 1935.

Colvile, Eden. *Letters 1849-1852.* London: Hudson's Bay Record Society.

Craig, Gordon A. *Europe 1815-1914.* New York: Holt, Rinehart, Winston, 1966.

Crosby, Thomas. *Among the An-ko-me-nums of the Pacific Coast.* Toronto: William Briggs, 1907.

Cross, Michael S., ed. *The Workingman in the Nineteenth Century.* Toronto: Oxford University Press, 1974.

deVolpi, Charles P. *British Columbia A Pictorial Record 1778-1891.* Longman Canada Ltd., 1973.

Duncan, Eric. *Fifty-seven Years in Comox Valley.* Comox: J. Barrett Gilmer, 1967.

———. *From Shetland to Vancouver Island. Recollections of Seventy-Five Years.* Edinburgh: Oliver and Boyd Ltd., 1937.

Finlay, J. L. and D. N. Sprague. *The Structure of Canadian History*, second edition. Scarborough: Prentice-Hall Canada Inc., 1984.

Foerster, Robert F. *The Italian Emigration of Our Times.* New York: Russell & Russell, 1919

Forbes, Elizabeth. "Wild Roses at Their Feet." *Pioneer Women of Vancouver Island.* Vancouver: Evergreen Press Ltd, 1971.

Graham, Donald. *Keepers of the Light: A History of British Columbia's Lighthouses and Their Keepers.* Madeira Park: Harbour Publishing Co. Ltd., 1985.

Griffin, A. R. *The Collier.* Shire Publications Ltd., 1982.

Griffin, Harold. *British Columbia: The Peoples' Early Story.* Vancouver: Tribune Publishing Ltd., 1958.

Helmcken, John Sebastian. *The Reminiscences of Doctor John Sebastian Helmcken.* Edited by Dorothy Blakey Smith. Vancouver: University of British Columbia Press, 1975.

Hiley, Michael. *Victorian Working Women: Portraits from Life.* Boston: David R. Godine, 1980.

Hughes, Herbert W. *A Text-Book of Coal-Mining.* London: Charles Griffin and Co. Ltd., 1904.

Hurt, J. S. *Elementary Schooling and the Working Classes 1860-1918.* Toronto: University of Toronto Press, 1979.

Johnson, Patricia M. *Nanaimo, A Short History.* North Vancouver: Trendex Publications, 1974.

————, John G. Parker and Gino A. Sedola. *Nanaimo. Scenes From the Past.* Nanaimo: Nanaimo and District Museum Society, 1966.

Johnson-Cull, Viola, compiler. *Chronicle of Ladysmith and District.* Victoria: Ladysmith New Horizons Historical Society, 1980.

Kerr, J. B. *Biographical Dictionary of Well-Known British Columbians.* Vancouver: Kerr and Begg, 1890.

Kilian, Crawford. *Go Do Some Great Thing. The Black Pioneers of British Columbia.* Vancouver: Douglas and McIntyre, 1978.

Lewis, David. *Yesterday's Promises. A History of the District of Port Hardy.* Victoria: Robinson Press, 1978.

Macfie, Matthew. *Vancouver Island and British Columbia. Their History Resources and Prospect.* London: Longman, Green, Longman, Roberts and Green, 1865.

Martin, The Honourable Archer. *Reports of Mining Cases Decided by the Courts of British Columbia and the Courts of Appeal Therefrom to the 1st of October 1902.* Toronto: The Carswell Company, Ltd., 1903.

Mayne, Richard Charles. *Four Years in British Columbia and Vancouver Island.* New York: Johnson Reprint Corporation, 1969.

Methodist Missionary Society Reports. Toronto: The Methodist Mission Rooms, 1858-1900.

Morris, James. *Heaven's Command.* Penguin Books, 1973.

Morton, Desmond. *Working People.* Ottawa: Deneau and Greenberg Publishers Ltd. 1980.

Norcross, E. Blanche. *Nanaimo Retrospective.* Nanaimo: Nanaimo Historical Society, 1979.

Ormsby, Margaret A. *British Columbia: A History.* Vancouver: Macmillan of Canada, 1958.

Palmer, Bryan D. *Working-Class Experience. The Rise and Reconstitution of Canadian Labour 1880-1980.* Toronto: Butterworth and Co. (Canada) Ltd., 1983.

Ralston, Caroline. *Grasshuts and Warehouses - Pacific Communities of the Nineteenth Century.* Canberra: Australian National University Press, 1977.

Rattray, Alexander. *Vancouver Island and British Columbia. Where They Are; What They Are; and What They May Become.* London: Smith, Elder, and Co., 1862.

Robin, Martin. *Radical Politics and Canadian Labour 1880-1930.* Kingston: Queen's University Centre for Industrial Relations, 1968.

Scholefield, E. O. S. *British Columbia From the Earliest Times to the Present.* 4 vols. Vancouver: The S. J. Clarke Publishing Co., 1914.

Shelton, W. George. *British Columbia and Confederation.* Victoria: Morriss Printing Co. Ltd., 1967.

Smith, Dorothy Blakey, ed. *Lady Franklin Visits the Pacific Northwest: Being Extracts from the Letters of Miss Sophia Cracoft, Sir John Franklin's Niece, February to April 1861 and April to July 1870.* Victoria: Provincial Archives of British Columbia Memoir No. XI, 1874.

Sutherland, A., ed. *The Missionary Outlook.* Toronto: The Methodist Mission Rooms, 1882-1900.

Tickner, F. W. *A Social and Industrial History of England.* London: Edward Arnold and Co., 1915.

Turner, Robert D. *Vancouver Island Railroads.* San Marino: Golden West Books, 1973.

Winks, Robin W. *The Blacks in Canada: A History.* New Haven and Montreal, 1971.

Correspondence

Beaven, Robert. Letter to Surveyor, Dec. 15, 1873. Cumberland Museum Archives.

British Columbia. Correspondence Outward, Inspector of Mines 1877-1900.

Houghton, Charles Frederick. Letterbook. No. 1 from December 1, 1873 to May 30, 1877.

Hudson's Bay Company. Fort Victoria Correspondence to Hudson's Bay Company on Affairs of Vancouver Island Colony May 16, 1850-November 6, 1855. HBCA-PAM.

———. London correspondence inward, general, July-December 1848. HBCA-PAM.

———. London correspondence inward, general, Landale to Barclay and London correspondence outward, general, Barclay to Landale, June-December 1850. HBCA-PAM.

———. London correspondence inward, general, Robinson to Barclay and London correspondence outward Barclay to Robinson, March-May 1854. HBCA-PAM.

———. "Nanaimo Letterbook." Copy in NDCM.

Lowe, Elizabeth. Letter to Mrs. Agnes Childers. PABC.

Pearce, B. W. Correspondence with Robert Dunsmuir, 1871. Vertical File PABC.

Robson, Ebenezer. Correspondence with Robert Dunsmuir. PABC.

Diaries and Journals

Bate, Mark. "Directors Diary July 1, 1880 to September 30, 1881." Vancouver Coal Mining and Land Company Nanaimo, B.C. PABC.

Bryant, Cornelius. Diaries - 1855-56 and 1878-82. VCA.

Bryden, John. Diary and Letterbook. 1878-1880. PABC.

Gale, Charles. *Princess Royal* Log of Years 1854-55. Copy in NDCM.

Horne, Adam Grant. Diary from July 1854 to March 1855 and 1856. Copy in NDCM.

Hudson's Bay Company. Account Book of 1854. Copy in NDCM.

Greenwell, Ellen. Written reminiscences in author's collection.

Kenny, M. A. "Extracts From My Little Red Notebook." VCA.

McGregor, William. Journal May 1887-June 1888. PABC.

McKay, Joseph William. "Recollections of a Chief Trader in the Hudson's Bay Company, Fort Simpson 1878." PABC MS photostat in NDCM.

Muir, Andrew. Private Diary Commencing 9th November 1848. PABC.

Muir, Michael. "Reminiscences." Recorded for H. H. Bancroft in *B.C. Sketches*, 1878. PABC.

Raybould, William. Diary, 1863-1864. VCA.

Stuart, Captain Charles E. "Nanaimo Journal: August 1855-March 1857." PABC.

Woodman, A. J. Diary. NDCM.

Zaccarelli, Louis. Diary. Mrs. Louis Zaccarelli Collection.

Government Records

British Columbia. Canadian Centennial Committee of British Columbia Pioneer Medallion Application Forms. PABC.

———. Inquisitions from April 1879 to July 1891. PABC.

———. Inquisition on Explosion of May 3, 1877, Nanaimo. PABC.

———. *Ministry of Mines Annual Reports*. Victoria: Richard Wolfenden, Government Printer, 1874-1900.

———. Probate Files. PABC.

———. Report for the Heritage Conservation Branch compiled by G. Howe. "The Suquash Colliery." 1980.

———. Report of the Royal Commission on Indian Affairs for the Province of British Columbia, 1913.

———. *Report of the Select Committee on the Wellington Strike*. Victoria: Queen's Printer, 1891.

———. Sessional Papers 1877-1901.

Canada. Report of the Deputy Adjutant-General Military District No. 11, 1877. PABC.

———. *Report of the Royal Commission on Chinese and Japanese Immigration*. Ottawa: Queen's Printer, 1885.

———. *Report of the Royal Commission on Chinese Immigration*. Ottawa: King's Printer, 1902.

———. *Report of the Royal Commission on Industrial Disputes in the Province of British Columbia*. Ottawa: King's Printer, 1904.

Great Britain. Parliament, House of Commons. Colonial Correspondence, 1865.

Newspapers

British Colonist

Comox Free Press

Craigdarroch Castle Historical Museum Society Newsletter

Cumberland News

Daily British Colonist and Victoria Chronicle

Daily Colonist

Lantzville Log

Nanaimo Daily Free Press

Nanaimo Gazette (Tribune)

Nanaimo Herald

Nanaimo Morning Courier

Nanaimo Times

Pacific Tribune

Vancouver Province

Victoria Daily Times

Weekly News

Wellington Enterprise

Pamphlets

"The Comox Valley and Its Pioneers Part I," Genesis Project.

"Cumberland's Diamond Jubilee," Courtenay: The North Island Advertiser, 1975.

"History of Nanaimo 1852-1939," Division I, Brechin Superior School.

Ministry of Agriculture. *Illustrated British Columbia*. Victoria: J. B. Ferguson and Co., 1884.

———. *Province of British Columbia. Its Climate and Resources with Information for Emigrants*. Victoria: Richard Wolfenden, Government Printer, 1883.

Special Catalogue of Mine Safety Lamps, Zwickau, Saxony, Germany: Frieman and Wolf Safety Lamp Co. Ltd. William Lowther Archival Collection.

Step into History. The Downtown Nanaimo Heritage Walk, Nanaimo: Heritage Advisory Committee of the City of Nanaimo, 1984.

Theses and Manuscripts

Bailey, Rhonda Sahlstrom. High School Social Studies paper based on interview with John Loudon.

Bartlett, Jon Norman Griffith. "The 1877 Wellington Miners' Strike." Unpublished UBC Honours BA Essay, 1975.

Beck, Rhoda May. "Nanaimo's Bastion." Bastion Archival Collection, Nanaimo.

———. Written reminiscences. In author's collection.

Brown, E. E. Essay. NDCM.

Buckham, A. F. Canadian Collieries Papers. PABC.

———. "History of Coal Mining Companies, Vancouver Island." PABC.

Cass, John. "The History of Nanaimo's City Parks." NDCM.

———. "The Wellington Story 1869-1900." NDCM.

Crowe, Marnie and Mable Saunders. "North Wellington." BAC.

Gallacher, Daniel T. "Coal Management in British Columbia, 1864-89." Paper presented to the BC Studies Conference, University of Victoria, 1979.

———. "Men, Money, Machines. Studies Comparing Colliery Operations and Factors of Production in British Columbia's Coal Industry to 1891." UBC, PhD Dissertation, 1979.

Godfrey, Christine. "An Analysis of the Members of the British Columbia Legislative Assembly between 1890 and 1900 and Their Voting Patterns on Bills to Amend the 'Coal Mines Regulation Act, 1877' and 'Amendment Act, 1890'." Unpublished History paper, University of Victoria, 1982.

Greenwood, Beth. Collection of articles by M. A. Kenny under pen name. VCA.

Harding, Rene. "Seven Killed, Two Hurt in Trestle Collapse." Cumberland and District Historical Society. PABC.

Mackie, Richard Somerset. "Colonial Land, Indian Labour and Company Capital: The Economy of Vancouver Island, 1849-1858." Unpublished MA Thesis. University of Victoria, 1984.

Mary Theodore, Sister. "St. Ann's Convent, Nanaimo, B.C." Unpublished manuscript. Archives of Sister of St. Ann, Victoria, B.C.

Matheson, Marion Henderson. "Some Effects of Coal Mining Upon the Development of the Nanaimo Area." Unpublished MA Thesis, UBC, 1950.

Meyer Zu Erpen, Walter. "Towards an Understanding of the Municipal Archives of Nineteenth Century British Columbia: A Case Study of the Archives of the Corporation of the City of Nanaimo 1875-1904." Unpublished UBC MA Thesis, 1985.

Moffat, Ben. "The Residential Environment of Nanaimo, B.C.: 1874-1891," Paper presented to Canadian Association of Geographers, Malaspina College, 1984.

Lockner, Bradley. "Miners in Nanaimo from 1880-1930." Simon Fraser University student paper, 1980.

Loosemore, T. R. "The BC Labour Movement and Political Action, 1879-1906." Unpublished UBC MA Thesis, 1954.

Orr, Allan Donald. "The Western Federation of Miners and the Royal Commission on Industrial Disputes in 1903 with Specific Reference to the Vancouver Island Coal Miners' Strike." Unpublished UBC MA Thesis, 1968.

Ralston, H. Keith. "Coal Miners' Contracts with the Hudson's Bay Company, 1848-1854." Paper presented to BC Studies Conference, Simon Fraser University, 1981.

Silverman, Peter Guy. "A History of the Militia and Defense of British Columbia 1871-1914." Unpublished UBC MA Thesis.

Tweedy, Mark Lee. "The 1880 and 1881 Strikes by the Miners of the Vancouver Coal Company." Unpublished UBC BA Honours Essay, 1978.

Vaughan, Patricia Elizabeth. "Cooperation and Resistance: Indian-European Relations on the Mining Frontier of British Columbia 1835-1858." Unpublished UBC MA Thesis, 1976.

Interviews

Jack Atkinson
Wallace Baikie
Victor Ballatti
Rhoda Beck
Tom Bentley

Herschel Biggs
Elmer Blackstaff
Ann Bryant
Marie Bono Conti
William Cottle
Nelson Dean
Lillian Maki Dixon
George Edwards
Mary Robeson Edwards
Harry Ellis
Richard Fiddick
Elizabeth Inez Freeman
Jock Gilmour
Dorothy Maxwell Graham
John Gourlay
Archie Greenwell
Donald Greenwell
Ed Lee
William Lewis - Nanaimo Historical Society Interview
Effie McIntosh
William McLellan
John Marochhi
Vera Cornish Riddell
Janet Robertson
Olive Storey Spencer
Barbara Freeman Stannard
Lewis Thatcher
Mrs. Frank Wall nee Roberts
Joseph White
Seiriol Llewelyn Williams

Index

395

in races, 197

Hoskin family, 180

Hoskin, Joseph, 154, 159, 171, 180

Hospitals, 200-1, 232-33

Hotels, 116, 119, 141, 142, 147, 214-15, 218, 241, 242-43, 248, 252, 253-54, 267, 282, 284, 301, 302, 335, 337, 340, 351, 352, 355, 356, 359, 362, 371

Houghton, Lieutenant-Colonel C. F., 167, 168, 180

Housing, 20, 28-29, 60, 77, 91-92, 99, 102, 142-44, 194, 212-13, 231, 241-42, 252, 283, 286, 302-3, 308
  See also Eviction

Hudson's Bay Company. *See* HBC

Hughes, Thomas, 270

Hunter family, 53, 88

Hunter, Andrew (engineer), 50, 55, 56, 63-64, 86, 105, 108, 183, 184

Incher, Sarah, 69, 73, 82

Incher, William, 69, 82, 83

"Independent collier." *See* Scottish miners

Independent Order of Oddfellows. *See* Lodges

Indian, 78, 127
  and alcohol. *See* Alcohol
  appearance, 27, 74, 114
  attitude toward murder, 44, 51, 75, 76
  attitude toward war, 27, 42
  attitude toward whites, 31, 35, 37, 41, 53, 76, 115, 248
  clothing, 27, 74
  coal rights. *See* Coal, rights
  customs, 26, 27, 80
  decapitation, 26, 53, 74
  and disease, 90, 113, 201
  fishing, 57-58, 148
  housing, 114-18
  and justice, 44, 87, 115-17
  labourers. *See* Labourers, Indian
  language, 73-74, 187, 212
  marriage to whites, 53, 74-75, 117
  miners, 20, 27, 52, 54, 113, 183, 191, 296
  potlatch, 18, 115, 118
  reports of coal, 18, 18
  slavery, 75, 113
  trade, 18, 26, 27, 33, 35, 36, 44, 52, 59-60
  treaties. *See* Coal, rights
  villages, 27, 74, 113-14
  women, 53, 64, 74-75, 113, 115, 117

Indian tribes
  Coast Salish, 57, 73-75

Comox (Comux), 296, 297

Cowichans, 61, 75, 191

Haidas, 75

Kwakiutl, 26, 45-42, 57, 59, 75, 76, 296

Newittee, 42-44, 51

Qualicums, 75

Snenymos, 57-58, 59, 73-75, 296

Industrial Revolution, 64-66

Inquests, 113, 229, 230-32, 237, 259, 264, 272, 274, 323

Inspector of Mines, 145, 146, 217, 218, 227, 256-58, 280, 295, 305, 312, 326, 327, 328, 329, 358
  See also Dick, Archibald; Prior, Edward; Morgan, Thomas

Irishmen, 25, 153, 178, 189, 235

Isbister, William, 63, 94, 135, 208

Italian, 239, 243, 278, 282, 284, 335, 340, 343
  miners, 178, 312, 339
  origins, 222-23
  strikebreakers, 153, 155, 222-23, 304
  in Union Camp, 301, 303-4

Italian Boarding House, 252

Jail, 87, 111, 202, 241

Japanese, 303, 307, 308, 309, 314-15, 322

Jenkins, John, 155, 156

Jingle Pot Mine. *See* Sabiston-Horne Estate

Jones, Captain Jemmy, 195, 196

Jones, Dr. William McNaughton, 200, 232

July 1st. *See* Holidays

July 4th. *See* Holidays

Justice, 34, 37-38, 42, 86-87, 97, 109-10, 111, 112-13, 118, 166, 190, 202, 311-12, 345
  See also Indian, and justice

Justices of the Peace. *See* Justice

Kanakas, 26, 32, 35, 38, 53, 60, 72, 78

Keith, Thomas, 307, 340, 368, 371

Kilpatrick, Effie Galena (nee Lowe), 238

Kilpatrick family, 243, 324, 325, 355

Kilpatrick, Robert, 238, 281, 358

Klootchman. *See* Indian, women

Knight, James, 155, 156, 180, 274

Knights of Labour, 230, 235-36, 250, 269, 278, 279, 284, 333, 339, 342, 343
  and Chinese, 236
  and Dunsmuir, 236, 288
  and politics, 235-36, 249, 317, 333
  and temperance, 236, 249

Kwakiutl. *See* Indian tribes

403

(Union); Number Six Shaft (Union)
map, 298
railroad. *See* Railroads, Union Colliery
use of Orientals, 307, 311, 326
Unions, 221, 233, 234-35, 278, 365-66
British. *See* British, unions
Coalminers' Mutual Protective Society, 152, 156, 157-58, 160, 163
Miners' Mutual Protective Association, 223-35
MMLPA, 306-7, 310, 327, 332-33, 334, 335-36, 338, 339, 340, 341, 342, 343, 346-47, 351, 366-68, 369-70, 372
and Orientals, 234, 257, 273-74, 278, 306, 307, 310, 314
and temperance. *See* Temperance
at Union Colliery, 307, 312-13, 326, 327, 328-29
Western Federation of Miners, 370
Workingman's Protective Association, 221
See also Knights of Labour; Reform Clubs

Vaccinations. *See* Smallpox
Vancouver, 252, 323, 337, 370
Vancouver Coal Mining and Land Company. *See* VCML
VCML, 140, 146, 160, 175, 194, 200, 216, 218, 247, 256, 283, 294, 331, 365, 372
management, 97, 98-99, 142, 181, 182-84, 191-92, 205, 217, 219, 220-21, 224, 226, 253-55, 274
mines, 251, 255
See also Douglas Pit; Fitzwilliam Mine; Harewood Mine; Newcastle Mine; New Douglas Mine (Chase River); Northfield Mine; Number One Esplanade Mine; Number Three Pit (Chase River); Number Four Southfield; Protection Mine; Southfield Mines
map, 107, 330
purchase from HBC, 97, 98, 99
Vegetation, 78
Ventilation, 146, 179, 192, 194, 217, 227, 228, 260-61, 263, 264, 266, 273, 276, 277, 280, 326, 358, 363
fans, 227, 229, 257, 260-61, 264, 265, 266, 275, 276, 281

furnaces, 64, 66, 94, 145, 146, 260, 275, 280, 281
steam jets, 64, 66, 260, 275, 276
See also Brattice
Victoria, 102, 105, 190, 191, 205, 232-54 *passim*, 289, 338-46, 363, 370
during 1877 strike, 162, 173-74
as seat of government, 101, 108-9, 112, 133, 184, 202, 315
See also HBC forts
Vipont, George, 153, 157, 160, 161, 180
Von Hugo, B., 341, 346
Voting qualifications. *See* Politics
Voyages
City of Panama, 213
Freeman family, 207
Harpooner, 21-23
Manitoban, 213
Norman Morison, 29-30
Pekin, 49, 50-51
Princess Royal, 71-73

Wages. *See* Coal miners
Walkem, Dr. William Wymond, 230, 231-32, 369
Walkem, George, 146, 161-62, 164, 173, 199, 211, 245
Walker, Alfred, 80, 320-23
Walker, Edward, 50, 52, 69, 76, 78, 80, 92-93, 126, 180, 320, 323, 364
Walker family, 69, 80, 320, 322, 323
Wall, Tom, 141, 242
Wall, W. H., 148, 364
Water,
household, 91, 134, 214, 252, 325
in mines, 28, 64, 65, 94-95, 192, 193, 225, 255
Watering, 263, 272, 275-76, 279
Webb family, 69, 82, 83, 119
Wellington, 141, 179, 221, 230, 235, 241-43, 248, 277, 281, 285, 289, 328, 331, 332, 337-50 *passim*, 351, 355, 356, 358, 359, 362, 363, 368
bomb, 349-51
businesses, 238, 355, 356
liquor outlets, 141, 215, 242-43
new townsite, 355
population, 144, 242-43
sinking house, 356-58
Wellington Brass Band. *See* Entertainment, bands
Wellington Colliery, 338, 347
early loading methods, 137, 140
management, 148, 149, 193